God's Praise
and
God's Presence

God's Praise and God's Presence

A Biblical-Theological Study

Gabriele G. Braun

Foreword by Bruce Waltke

WIPF & STOCK · Eugene, Oregon

GOD'S PRAISE AND GOD'S PRESENCE
A Biblical-Theological Study

Copyright © 2020 Gabriele G. Braun. All rights reserved. Except for brief quotations in critical publications or reviews, no part of this book may be reproduced in any manner without prior written permission from the publisher. Write: Permissions, Wipf and Stock Publishers, 199 W. 8th Ave., Suite 3, Eugene, OR 97401.

Wipf & Stock
An Imprint of Wipf and Stock Publishers
199 W. 8th Ave., Suite 3
Eugene, OR 97401

www.wipfandstock.com

PAPERBACK ISBN: 978-1-5326-5506-7
HARDCOVER ISBN: 978-1-5326-5507-4
EBOOK ISBN: 978-1-5326-5508-1

Manufactured in the U.S.A. 07/30/20

Scripture quotations, unless otherwise noted, are based on or taken from The ESV® Bible (The Holy Bible, English Standard Version®), copyright © 2001 by Crossway, a publishing ministry of Good News Publishers. Used by permission. All rights reserved.

In memory of my parents,
Matthäus O. Braun († 1972) and Ruth G. Braun († 1999)

*For the earth will be filled with the knowledge
of the glory of the Lord as the waters cover the sea.*

—HABAKKUK 2:14

Contents

List of Charts and Tables — xi

Foreword by Bruce Waltke — xiii

Preface — xvii

Acknowledgements — xix

Abbreviations — xx

1.0 Introduction — 1

2.0 God's People's Praise—Approaches Towards a Theology of Worship — 8
  2.1 Neil Hudson: Worship: Singing a New Song in a Strange Land — 10
  2.2 James Steven: Worship in the Spirit: Charismatic Worship in the Church of England — 12
  2.3 Philip Greenslade: Worship in the Best of Both Worlds: Theological Explorations between Two Extremes — 15
  2.4 Howard Marshall: "How Far Did the Early Christians Worship God?" and "Worshipping Biblically" — 19
  2.5 David G. Peterson: Engaging with God: A Biblical Theology of Worship — 25
  2.6 Peter Wick: Die Urchristlichen Gottesdienste [Worship Services of the Early Church] — 28
  2.7 Daniel Block: For the Glory of God: Recovering a Biblical Theology of Worship — 37
  2.8 John J. Davis: Worship and the Reality of God: An Evangelical Theology of Real Presence — 42

2.9 Tobias Faix and Tobias Künkler: Generation Lobpreis
und die Zukunft der Kirche [Generation Praise
and the Future of the Church] 47
2.10 Summary and Conclusion 48

3.0 Biblical Theology—a Distinct Discipline and Its Methods **51**
3.1 Biblical Theology: Development and Debate 52
3.2 Brevard Childs: A Canonical Approach 57
3.3 James Barr: Biblical Theology and Canonical Criticism 63
3.4 Critique of the Canonical Approach 67
3.5 Narrative and Intertextual Models 71
3.6 Some Contemporary Hermeneutical Models 74
3.7 Summary 79

**4.0 God's Glory-Presence in the Praises of His People
in the Old Testament** **81**
4.1 Divine Presence and Human Praise in
1 Kings 8: Temple Inauguration 82
4.2 Divine Presence and Human Praise in
2 Chronicles 5–7: Temple Inauguration 91
4.3 Similarities and Differences between 1 Kings 8
and 2 Chronicles 5–7 105
4.4 Human Praise and Divine Presence without
Temple Context 107
4.5 Human Praise and/or Divine Presence? 117
4.6 Summary 120

**5.0 God's Spirit-Presence and God's People's Praise
in the New Testament** **122**
5.1 General Remarks on Luke-Acts 123
5.2 The Initial Spirit-Infilling and Praise
of God's New People: Acts 2 124
5.3 The Initial Spirit-Infilling and Praise
of God's New People: Acts 10 and 11 138
5.4 Human Praise and Spirit-Refilling in Acts 4 147
5.5 Human Praise and Divine Presence in Acts 16 153
5.6 Human Praise and Spirit-Refilling in Ephesians 5 158
5.7 Summary and Conclusion 168

**6.0 Results from a Biblical Theology Perspective:
Three Intertextual Themes and Related Issues** **171**
6.1 The Connection between Divine Presence
and Human Praise 172

    6.2 The Divine Indwelling: The Infilling of God's House
        with his Presence   177
    6.3 The Divine Human Covenant Relationship   195
    6.4 Contraindications and Queries about Worship   213
    6.5 Interdisciplinary Transitions to Systematic Theology   218
    6.6 Summary   234

7.0 Conclusion and Outlook   **236**

Bibliography   *245*

Author Index   *263*

General Index   *267*

Scripture Index   *270*

List of Charts and Tables

Chart 1:   Triangle of service and praise (chapter 2)
Chart 2:   Glorious circle (chapter 6)
Chart 3:   Table on intertextual links with a connection between presence and praise (chapter 6)
Chart 4:   Table on house of God metaphors in the OT (chapter 6)
Chart 5:   Table on temple metaphors in the NT (chapter 6)
Chart 6:   Table on the divine indwelling (chapter 6)
Chart 7:   The divine indwelling in the OT (chapter 6)
Chart 8:   The divine indwelling in the NT (chapter 6)
Chart 9:   The divine indwelling in BT (chapter 6)
Chart 10: Table on the divine-human covenant-relationship (chapter 6)

Foreword

IN OUR WESTERN SOCIETY God is 'dying' because our institutions are stamping out his name as fast as they can. If they succeeded, the rock would cry out his name, as Jesus said. It occurred to me that ontologically God cannot die; but epistemologically—in human knowledge—he could if people stopped praising his name. As God 'dies' epistemologically, his beneficent presence and glory depart. But of course, God will always have his elect to praise him (cf. 1 Pet 2:9; Eph 1:11–12). In view of that, I have become more and more aware of the importance of praising God's name. The more we praise, the greater his glory and benediction. I now understand what the psalmist means that *I Am* inhabits the praises of Israel. David sings, albeit in a lament: "You are holy, enthroned on the praises of Israel" (Psa 22:3, ESV).

This connection between God's presence and God's people's praise is precisely what Dr. Gabriele G. Braun explored in her book *God's Praise and God's Presence*, which is based on her doctoral thesis with Northwest-University, Potchefstroom, RSA. Until now, as Gabriele G. Braun comments, interest has centered either on divine presence in its various expressions or on God's people's praise in its different forms. As far as I am aware, there exist very few biblical-theological studies on a potential connection between both. In her book, Gabriele Braun argues from the Old and New Testaments as well as from a biblical theology perspective that God's praise and God's presence enjoy a reciprocal correlation. In the Old Testament, she reflects upon the sequence of events in the inauguration of Solomon's temple. According to 1 Kings 8, before the Levites brought the ark of the covenant, the symbol of God's throne, into the inner sanctuary of the temple, King Solomon and the assembly sacrificed, presumably with praise and thanksgiving, so many sheep and cattle that they could not be counted (v. 5). After the Levites had positioned the ark beneath the wings of the cherubim in the inner sanctuary (vv. 6–7), the priest withdrew from the Holy Place, whereupon an escalating terminology of 'cloud,' 'glory of the Lord,' and 'thick darkness' emphasizes that "the Lord himself had entered with his presence the inner sanctuary of his new house."[1] Then Solomon blessed the assembly and said: "Praise be to *I AM*, the God of Abraham . . ." Braun rightly notes that the sequence of events does not provide evidence to draw the conclusion that prayer and praise are "the instrumental condition" for God's glory and presence to enter the temple.[2] What the text does show, however, is a relationship between Presence and praise.

The synoptic account in 2 Chronicles 5–7 establishes an even stronger correlation between God's people's praise and his presence by adding to the sequence—between the priests withdrawing from the sanctuary and the glory cloud filling the temple—that the Levites who were musicians played their instruments and the singers raised their voices in praise to *I AM* and sang: "He is good; his love endures forever" (2 Chr 5:13). In this context of praise, the glory of *I AM* filled the temple (2 Chr 5:11–14). Moreover, the Chronicler adds another perspective to Solomon's dedication of the temple and *I AM*'s consecration of it: "When Solomon finished praying, fire came down from heaven and consumed the burnt offering and the sacrifice, and the glory of *I AM* filled the temple. . . . When all the Israelites saw the fire coming down and the glory of *I AM* above the temple, they . . . worshiped *I AM* and gave thanks to *I AM,* saying, "He is good, his love endures forever" (2 Chr 7:1–3). Braun summarizes the Chronicler's account: "the sequence of events suggests that 2 Chronicles 5–7 depicts human praise in temporal correlation with divine presence, once before and once after the infilling of the Lord's house with his glory."[3]

Braun finds the same correlation of Presence and praise when the Spirit inaugurated the Church, a spiritual temple. In Acts 1–2, the Holy Spirit filled, as God's glory had Solomon's temple, the initial, prayerful Jewish believers in Jesus as Messiah, and they manifested his presence by glossalalia[4] (ἑτέραις γλώσσαις "speaking in another language/tongue," Acts 2:4), presumably with praise. In Acts 10, the Holy Spirit filled the initial, prayerful Gentiles, and, as they heard about Jesus Christ, they

---

1. Braun, *Praise and Presence*, 88.
2. Braun, *Praise and Presence*, 86.
3. Braun, *Praise and Presence*, 98.
4. Braun refers to this instance as "xenolalia", *Praise and Presence*, 135.

also manifested his presence in glossalalia (γλώσσαις) and praise (Acts 10:44–46).

Braun establishes her argument citing other texts in both Testaments. She emphasizes that a connection between Presence and praise does not depend on temple context, but on a holy covenant relationship between God and his people, as is evidenced in some of the Holy War narratives, e.g. in 2 Chronicles 20. These narratives witness a reverse connection in that God's people's praise is narrated to have instigated manifestations of divine presence in action. Braun points out the same reverse connection in Acts 4 and Acts 16 where God's people's praise is related to have prompted manifestations of divine presence in terms of a repeated infilling of the young Christian community with Holy Spirit and/or other supernatural manifestations. She rightly concludes that Scripture witnesses to a reciprocal correlation between Presence and praise.

Dr. Braun offers not only a substantial study, but also a valuable contribution to how biblical theology can be done as a discipline with the help of both a canonical and intertextual method. Her approach is synchronic serving the reader to identify the message of the text rather than its historical development although she does not ignore the existence of a diachronic approach. I have known Gabriele for more than twenty-five years when she first helped me with some translation work. During that time I have come to appreciate the way she developed scholarly and spiritual qualities at high level. Therefore, I sincerely recommend this book on *God's Praise and God's Presence*; it will benefit scholars and students alike—whether from Old or New Testament or biblical theology or any other discipline—to explore a discipline and its methods, which may seem exotic to some. Not too many scholars, still some coming particularly from the Old Testament, have in the past ventured to tread upon this rather unknown and yet promising territory. The above study represents an example which will benefit anyone who takes an interest in God inhabiting the praises of his people, including those of scholarship.

Reverend Dr. Bruce K. Waltke
Professor Emeritus of Old Testament
and Biblical Theology

Preface

The title "God's Praise and God's Presence" conceals a question: Is there a connection between both? This question has arisen in the light of contemporary Christian worship culture and its need for further biblical studies, which represents the background for the present project. Hence, the main aim of this book is to provide an answer to the question: Do the Scriptures actually confirm a connection between God's people's praise and God's presence? The answer is that Scripture in both Testaments does testify to a correlation between human praise and divine presence, yet, in the context of a human-divine covenant relationship.

For that purpose, biblical theology has been applied as a distinct discipline, and canonical and intertextual models as a method. This has been done in the hope to infuse life to a discipline somehow long lost and rarely rediscovered. This discipline is full of potential to facilitate drawing treasures from the Scriptures with the purpose to recover their meaning and message for present-day readers.

Thus, this project represents a modest biblical-theological study based on the writer's doctoral dissertation with North-West University, RSA, and no liturgical investigation, yet, with the hope to provide some results which may be applicable to pastoral theology, and especially in liturgical studies, in order to serve contemporary Christian worship and its needs.

Acknowledgements

SINCERE THANKS AND ACKNOWLEDGEMENT are due to quite a few international scholars including professors emeriti, colleagues, and friends from Canada, the UK, the RSA, and Australia, who have encouraged me to believe in the potential of this project and provided support in various ways along the way. Among them are particularly mentioned Professor Dr. Bruce Waltke, Professor Dr. Max Turner, and Professor Dr. Francois Viljoen, as well as Dr. Stuart Rochester. Thanks is due to Tyndale House, Cambridge, UK, and their staff for providing an atmosphere stimulating fruitful research, as well as to the colleagues from AfeT, FEET, and SBL for their encouragement. I am indebted to unnamed friends for their unswerving support throughout the entire process. Finally, I think with heartfelt gratitude of my late parents, Matthäus Braun and Ruth Braun, for having invested into my life in many different ways, which enabled me to walk this path. And ultimately: Soli Deo gloria!

Abbreviations

AB	Anchor Bible
aci	*accusativus cum infinitivo*
AfeT	Arbeitskreis für evangelikale Theologie [Workshop for evangelical theology, German branch of FEET]
ANET	Ancient Near Eastern Texts
ASOR	American Schools of Oriental Research
AsTJ	*Asbury Theological Journal*
Bell.	*Bellum Judaicum* (Josephus)
BECNT	Baker Exegetical Commentary on the New Testament
BHGNT	Baylor Handbook on the Greek New Testament
BibInt	Biblical Interpretation Series
BJS	Brown Judaic Studies
BSac	*Bibliotheca Sacra*
BT	biblical theology
BT	*The Bible Translator*
CBQ	*Catholic Biblical Quarterly*
CCCM	Corpus Christianorum: Continuatio Medievalis
CCOT	The Communicator's Commentary Series Old Testament
corr.	corrected
CTQ	*Concordia Theological Quarterly*
De Ebr	*De Ebrietate, de Sobrietate* (Philo)

diss.	dissertation
ed.	editor, edition
eds	editors
EDNT	Exegetical Dictionary of the New Testament
EJT	*European Journal of Theology*
enl.	enlarged
equiv.	equivalent
ESV	English Standard Version
EvQ	*The Evangelical Quarterly*
FAT	Forschungen zum Alten Testament
FB	Forschung zur Bibel
FEET	Fellowship of European Evangelical Theologians
Gk.	Greek
HBS	Herders biblische Studien
SHBC	Smith & Helwys Bible Commentary
HBT	*Horizons in Biblical Theology*
HvTSt	*Hervormde teologiese Studies*
ICC	International Critical Commentary on the Holy Scriptures of the Old and New Testaments
JSOT	*Journal for the Study of the Old Testament*
JSOTSup	Journal for the Study of the Old Testament Supplement Series
IJST	*International Journal of Systematic Theology*
IJT	*Indian Journal of Theology*
ICC	International Critical Commentary
JBL	*Journal of Biblical Literature*
JETS	*Journal of the Evangelical Theological Society*
JPT	*Journal of Pentecostal Theology*
JSNT	*Journal for the Study of the New Testament*
JSNTSup	Journal for the Study of the New Testament Supplement Series

JSOT	*Journal for the Study of the Old Testament*
JSOTSup	Journal for the Study of the Old Testament Supplement Series
JTS	*Journal of Theological Studies*
JTSA	*Journal of Theology for Southern Africa*
KD	Kirchliche Dogmatik (Karl Barth)
LCL	Loeb Classical Library
LD	Lectio Divina
LHBOTS	The Library of Hebrew Bible/Old Testament Studies
LNTS	The Library of New Testament Studies
LXX	Septuagint
Macc.	Maccabees
MDiv	Master of Divinity
MS	manuscript
MT	Masoretic Text
MTh	Master of Theology
NAC	New American Commentary
NASB	New American Standard Bible
NICOT	New International Commentary on the Old Testament
NIV	New International Version
NSBT	New Studies in Biblical Theology
NT	New Testament (in terms of Greek Bible)
NTL	The New Testament Library
OBT	Overtures to Biblical Theology
OT	Old Testament (in terms of Hebrew Bible)
OTL	The Old Testament Library
OTS	Old Testament Studies
PBM	Paternoster Biblical Monographs
prelim.	preliminary (title of edition)

PTMS	Princeton Theological Monograph Series
PTR	*The Princeton Theological Review*
1 QH	Hodayot or Thanksgiving Hymns
1 QM	War Scroll
1 QS	Community Code
RBL	*Review of Biblical Literature*
repr.	reprinted
rev.	revised
RTR	*Reformed Theological Review*
SBAB	Stuttgarter Biblische Aufsatzbände
SBET	*Scottish Bulletin of Evangelical Theology*
SBJT	*The Southern Baptist Journal of Theology*
SBL	Society of Biblical Literature
SBLDS	Society of Biblical Literature Dissertation Series
SBLG	Society of Biblical Literature and Logos Greek New Testament Bible Software
SBLHS	*Society of Biblical Literature Handbook of Style*
SBLMS	Society of Biblical Literature Monograph Series
SBLStBL	Society of Biblical Literature Studies in Biblical Literature
SBS	Stuttgarter Bibelstudien
sic	thus
SHS	The Scripture and Hermeneutics Series
SJT	*Scottish Journal of Theology*
SSN	Studia Semitica Neerlandica
ST	systematic theology
StBibLit	Studies in Biblical Literature
SVTQ	*St. Vladimir's Theological Quarterly*
TANZ	Texte und Arbeiten zum Neutestamentlichen Zeitalter
TF	Tyndale Fellowship

TJ	*Trinity Journal*
Them	*Themelios*
trans.	translated, translation
TRu	*Theologische Rundschau*
TVG	Theologische Verlagsgemeinschaft
TWNT	Theologisches Wörterbuch zum Neuen Testament
TynBul	*Tyndale Bulletin*
VE	*Vox Evangelica*
VT	*Vetus Testamentum*
VTSup	Supplements to Vetus Testamentum
WAWSup	Writings from the Ancient World Supplement Series
WBC	Word Biblical Commentary
WCC	World Council of Churches
WTJ	*The Westminster Theological Journal*
WUNT	Wissenschaftliche Untersuchungen zum Neuen Testament
ZECNT	Zondervan Exegetical Commentary on the New Testament

1.0

Introduction

STUDIES IN THE ANGLOPHONE world in the past few decades have explored the impact of contemporary pop culture and charismatic culture on Christian mainstream worship. Contemporary Christian praise seems to imply a correlation between human praise and divine presence. In view of these influences, the need for further biblical studies in that domain becomes evident. This worship scene and its needs represent the real-world setting for our question: God's praise and God's presence—is there a connection?

And so, the main aim of this book is to attempt to provide an answer to the question whether the Scriptures intimate such a connection between God's people's praise and God's presence. The central hypothesis is that Scripture in both Testaments testifies to a correlation between human praise and divine presence which can be reciprocal at times. This argument has been tested in the light of contemporary Christian worship culture and its need for further biblical studies as background for our project. We will achieve the above aim by employing biblical theology as a distinct discipline and a canonical-intertextual model as a method to meet five specific objectives.

First, the need for further biblical studies will be demonstrated by testing existing approaches to a biblical theology of worship with regard to an interaction between human praise and divine presence.

Second, it will be established that biblical theology as a a distinct discipline and a canonical approach combined with an intertextual model as a method serve our purpose to explore texts from both Testaments regarding a bond between human praise and divine presence.

Third, the above argument will be corroborated in narratives from the Hebrew Bible, i.e., the First or Old Testament: God's glory filling his new temple prompts his people's praise and vice versa (1 Kgs 8 and 2 Chr 5–7); additionally, God's people's praise instigates manifestations of divine presence (Josh 6 and 2 Chr 20; 1 Sam 16 and 2 Kgs 3).

Fourth, the argument will be verified in texts from the Greek Bible, i.e., the Second or New Testament: God's Holy Spirit filling his new people prompts their praise (Acts 2 and 10/11); additionally, God's people's praise instigates their refilling with Holy Spirit and/or other manifestations of divine presence (Acts 4 and 16; Eph 5).

Fifth, support will be offered for these results from a biblical theology perspective which reveals three intertextual themes: the connection between divine presence and human praise, the divine indwelling, and the divine-human covenant relationship.

In sum, the central argument of this investigation is that Scripture in both Testaments testifies to a connection between God's people's praise and God's presence. It is suggested that at times, there is even a reciprocal correlation between these two elements which can be regarded as a dynamic process of divine-human interaction within a holy covenant relationship. In connection with that, the fundamental line of reasoning sustains that the praise of God's people as an expression of their worship extends beyond their doxological activity in a worship service and involves a corresponding life of worship.

Therefore, the above issue will be raised from different angles of view, whether from an Old Testament or a New Testament perspective, a biblical theology perspective or a systematic theology point of view, to finish with a philosophical excursus. The main aim is to attempt to provide an answer to this overarching question whether, in general, there is a connection between God's people's praise and God's presence and whether, in particular, there is a reciprocal correlation between both.

Accordingly, in the second chapter, we will test to what extent the two elements of human praise and divine presence play a part in approaches to a theology of worship. Some of the representative ones will be reviewed, which come mostly from the UK and the USA, but also from the German scene. The question asked of them is: To what extent do these approaches to a theology of worship contribute to an answer to the question about a potential link between human praise and divine presence?

To begin with the above-mentioned influences of charismatic culture and contemporary pop culture on Christian praise and worship, the reviews by Neil Hudson and James Steven, as well as Philip Greenslade will be introduced.[1] These scholars have tasted and tested "doxological spices growing in Pentecostal and charismatic lands." The need for going back to the biblical roots of worship was taken up early by scholars such as I. Howard Marshall who in his exegetical treatises tackles the issue of worship and worship service in the context of their terminology.[2] Then, David Peterson and Peter Wick apply biblical theology as a discipline, each resulting in a comprehensive monograph on biblical worship:[3] Peterson is one of the first scholars to offer an approach to a biblical theology of worship. Wick investigates the origins and development of temple, synagogue, and house worship of the early church and early Judaism including their terminology; his understanding of worship is mainly seen against the background of worship services, but is not limited to that. The approach by Daniel Block of recovering a biblical theology of worship concentrates on the ethical aspect of a corresponding life-setting and involves a pastoral-liturgical view.[4] Fairly close to the theme of this project comes the illuminating analysis of evangelical worship by John Jefferson Davis who keeps in view both the role of human praise and divine presence or rather absence in worship and praise.[5] Last but not least features a more recent study on youth culture in the church in Germany focusing on the so-called "generation praise" by Tobias Faix and Tobias Künkler.[6]

These critiques of contemporary Christian worship culture expose similar characteristics which can be perceived at international and interdenominational levels. Furthermore, the above studies reveal an important phenomenon in our contemporary world, namely the merging of cultural and Christian categories, which requires a clear distinction between cultural and biblical aspects. A careful exegesis of both lay a sound foundation towards that goal. Therefore, the exegesis of Scripture and of Christian worship culture has been the concern of a biblical theology of worship and its contributions.

---

1. Hudson, "Worship"; Steven, *Worship in the Spirit*; Greenslade, *Worship in the Best of Both Worlds*.

2. Marshall, "How Far Did the Early Christians Worship God?"; "Worshipping Biblically."

3. Peterson, *Engaging with God*; Wick, *Urchristliche Gottesdienste*.

4. Block, *For the Glory of God*.

5. Davis, *Worship and the Reality of God*.

6. Faix and Künkler, *Generation Lobpreis*.

Nonetheless, these few existing approaches towards a biblical theology of worship point to a twofold need: first, an increased demand for studies in the area of a biblical theology of worship; second, some of these studies refer to the two elements of God's presence and God's people's praise individually, but most of them do not explore a potential connection between them, which may not have been their purpose.

Hence, the above arguments make clear the essential need to explore in both Testaments a potential relationship between God's people's praise and God's presence. This need and challenge represent the main rationale for this book. The present investigation is naturally situated in the domain of biblical theology, which encompasses the First and the Second Testament. Still, biblical theology has not always and everywhere been recognized as an independent theological discipline, at least not at present in Germany. In contrast to that, in Anglophone countries, biblical theology saw a renaissance during the second part of the twentieth century up to now, which however, has triggered much debate.

Consequently, in the third chapter, the development and history of biblical theology as a discipline in its own right, including the main lines of the debate, will be briefly sketched. Representative methods in this domain will be introduced and evaluated like canonical and intertextual approaches. Accordingly, the question raised is: How can biblical theology as a discipline with canonical and intertextual models serve to interpret biblical texts from both Testaments with regard to a potential interaction between God's praise and God's presence? In this connection, the term "canonical" is used for the method which deals with the final form of the biblical texts and which interprets each one in the context of the biblical canon covering both Testaments. This method receives particular attention because it can be combined with other methods, like an intertextual model, and it works well with the final textual form.

At first, the canonical approach of Brevard Childs will be contrasted with the model of James Barr.[7] Their appraisal will be followed by a critical German response.[8] Then, recent intertextual approaches by Thomas Brodie and Kenneth Litwak will be briefly introduced, which also includes their application to Luke-Acts.[9] These models have been

---

7. E.g., Childs, *Biblical Theology*; Childs, *Biblical Theology of OT and NT*; Barr, *Concept of Biblical Theology*; Barr, *Holy Scripture*.

8. Ballhorn and Steins, *Bibelkanon in der Bibelauslegung*; Köhlmoos, "Kanon und Methode."

9. Brodie, *Birthing of the New Testament*; Litwak, *Echoes of Scripture in Luke-Acts*.

chosen also because the Book of Acts contributes significant texts in this study. Subsequently, a limited choice of contemporary hermeneutical paradigms will be put to the test which are relevant for the application of the results of this study: the "principlizing" model by Walter Kaiser, the "redemptive-historical" model by Daniel Doriani, the "drama-of-redemption" model by Kevin Vanhoozer, and the "redemptive-movement" model by William Webb.[10]

Thus, despite the above challenge regarding the discipline, biblical theology will be presented as a discipline in its own right which may well serve the purpose of this book: the investigation of passages in both Testaments and their intertextual links regarding a potential correlation between God's people's praise and God's presence.

On this basis, we have analyzed the hypothesis that Scripture in both Testaments testifies to a connection of God's people's praise and God's presence. This hypothesis has been explored in the context of the inauguration of God's new temple in the Old Testament and the beginning of God's new people in the New Testament. The passages, which mostly belong to the narrative genre, were chosen as representative because they depict the dynamics of divine-human communication at the beginning of a new period: divine glory-presence and human praise in God's new house on the one hand, and divine Spirit-presence and human praise in and among God's new people on the other. Accordingly, these texts are able to shed light on a potential link between those two elements. The structural analyses of the narratives take into account the sequence of events and the literary structure, while the exegetical analyses consider aspects of grammar and semantic structure.

Accordingly, chapter 4 on the Old Testament will deal in its first two sections with the narratives of the dedication of the first temple built by King Solomon and investigate whether a connection can be observed between God's people' praise and his presence in the passages of 1 Kings 8 and 2 Chronicles 5–7. The questions asked of these narratives is: Did God's glory filling his new temple prompt his people's praise, and did this praise also prompt the Lord to fill his house with his glorious presence in return?

The third section will investigate a potential connection between human praise and divine presence beyond the temple context in these narrative texts: Joshua 6:20 (Joshua and the battle at Jericho) and, similarly, 2 Chronicles 20:22 (Jehoshaphat leading Judah in battle), 1 Samuel

---

10. Gundry and Meadors, *Four Views on Moving beyond the Bible to Theology*.

16:23 (David playing the harp before Saul) and, similarly, 2 Kings 3:15 (Elisha and the minstrel). Psalm 22:3 (God inhabiting the praises of Israel) also features in this section. Again, the question raised is: What do these texts, which involve the two elements of God's people's praise and God's presence, but mostly no temple context, convey about a potential interaction between this praise and this presence?

The fourth section will only briefly touch on expressions of human praise, e.g., in Psalms 145 to 150 and Psalm 136, the latter of which is quoted in some of the above texts. Even though no explicit link between presence and praise is mentioned, these psalms display a covenant setting. Similarly, in Ezekiel, God's glory-presence and his absence in the temple in the context of judgment will be referred to only in brief, e.g, in Ezekiel 10, 11, and 43. No immediate praise is involved there, while covenant context is implied. Nevertheless, these texts may shed light on a potential link between presence and praise through their covenant context.

The last and fifth section summarizes the terminology of divine presence and human praise that occurs in the above texts and contexts.

Then, chapter 5 will explore texts from the New Testament about presence and praise with God dwelling in his new people through his Holy Spirit, individually and corporately.

After a general introduction in the first part of the chapter, narratives from Acts (2:1–4; 10:44–46; and 11:15–18) will be explored. They depict the praise of God's people in connection with their initial reception of the Holy Spirit. Similarly, the question asked is: Did God's Holy Spirit filling his new people for the first time instigate their praise?

The second half of the chapter will concentrate on texts which relate the new Christians' repeated infilling with the Holy Spirit and/or other divine manifestations in the context of their praise. Relevant narrative texts in Acts 4:24–31 and 16:25–26, and an exhortatory text in Ephesians 5:18–20 will be examined. There, the question posed is: Did God's people's praise in return instigate their refilling with Holy Spirit and/or other manifestations of divine presence?

In the attempt to answer these questions and verify the above hypothesis, the structural and exegetical analyses of texts from both Testaments display cases in which such correlation is validated: God's presence prompting his people's praise and human praise instigating manifestations of divine presence.

Chapter 6 will review these results from a biblical theology perspective identifying intertextual themes in the context of divine presence and human praise. This way, the witnesses of the Old Testament are heard and heeded together with those from the New and vice versa. As a consequence of this "biblical-theological concert," these intertextual echoes and themes will be identified: first, the connection between divine presence and human praise, second, the divine indwelling as the the infilling of God's dwelling with his presence and, third, the divine-human covenant relationship.

In connection with that, the following issues relating to a divine-human interaction will be raised: Does God's self-revelatory presence initiate divine-human communication? Is God's people's praise always the response to such divine self-revelation? Is there an analogy between God's presence filling his temple with his divine glory and God filling his people with his Holy Spirit? Is there an analogy between God's incarnation in the person of Jesus and Jesus' incarnation in the person of the Spirit? And do human-divine interaction and relationship always occur in a covenant context?

Furthermore, it will be demonstrated that the connection between divine presence and human praise basically encompasses literal and nonliteral dwellings filled with divine glory or divine Spirit and involves a divine-human covenant relationship. All the same, it will be made clear that there are contraindications, which exclude a connection between divine presence and human praise, such as human idolatry and rebellion. In addition, queries about worship, praise, and Trinitarian worship will be addressed because our worship depends on our perception of the triune God including the Holy Spirit. Scholarly debates will only be touched upon where pertinent to this study, but not handled exhaustively. These questions again lead to matters of divine and human personhood and relationality, such as the concepts of perichoresis and *imago Dei*, which will be considered in their systematic theology setting. We will conclude on a minor philosophical note.

This way, the present investigation endeavors to answer the question about a potential connection between God's people's praise and God's presence, and to verify the hypothesis that, indeed, there is such connection in the context of divine indwelling and a holy divine-human covenant relationship.

2.0

God's People's Praise—Approaches Towards a Theology of Worship

As long as we approach prayer and worship wondering what we are going to get out of it, we are likely to remain discontented and bored.

—CARLO CARETTO

BESIDES, WE COULD ADD, then we are likely to loose God's presence in our praise. Analyses of studies, especially in the Anglophone world in the past few decades, have explored the influence of both contemporary pop culture and Christian charismatic culture on Christian mainstream worship. When looking at these influences, the need for biblical studies in that area becomes obvious. Admittedly, a biblical theology of worship is still a young scholarly subdiscipline because until about twenty years ago studies had approached the topic from a rather liturgical and pastoral theology view. Only more recently approaches have aimed at a biblical theology perspective of worship covering pertinent studies from both Testaments. In that context, the term "praise" is used as an expression of worship.

The contemporary worship and praise of God's people embodies the real-world setting for our key question: Is there a connection between God's praise and God's presence? This question is repeatedly posed from different angles of view throughout the present inquiry. In this chapter, we will test to what extent the two elements, human praise and divine presence, play a part in contributions to a biblical theology of worship.

Necessary restrictions lead to a limited selection of examples, which range from articles to monographs and comprehensive biblical studies, as well as theological and inter-disciplinary assessments of worship. We did not focus on assessments of liturgical expressions conditioned by culture, denomination, age or music styles, although some illustrations may appear along the way. The worship scenery covered ranges from evangelical Protestant to Pentecostal or neo-Pentecostal and from denominational to nondenominational camps, mostly in the Anglophone world. Even so, their findings are applicable at international and interdenominational levels.

To begin with the above mentioned influences of contemporary pop culture and Christian charismatic culture on Christian worship, the reviews by Hudson and Steven are introduced.[1] The headings take up the titles of each survey. Then, Greenslade's investigation explains polarities in charismatic worship through sociological and philosophical categories.[2] The exegetical studies by Marshall tackle the issue of worship and worship service in the context of their terminology.[3] Peterson and Wick apply biblical theology as a discipline informing about biblical worship.[4] Block's approach of recovering a biblical theology of worship concentrates on the ethical aspect of a corresponding life-setting and involves a pastoral-liturgical view.[5] Davis' illuminating analysis keeps in view human praise and divine presence in worship.[6] Finally, Faix and Künkler analyse the Christian youth culture of the so-called "generation praise" and its consequences for the church in Germany.[7]

---

1. Hudson, "Worship"; Steven, *Worship in the Spirit*.
2. Greenslade, *Worship in the Best*.
3. Marshall, "How Far Did the Early Christians Worship God?"; "Worshipping Biblically."
4. Peterson, *Engaging with God*; Wick, *Urchristliche Gottesdienste*.
5. Block, *For the Glory of God*.
6. Davis, *Worship and the Reality of God*.
7. Faix and Künkler, *Generation Lobpreis*.

2.1 Neil Hudson: Worship: Singing a New Song in a Strange Land

The study by D. Neil Hudson under the above title is part of a volume which encompasses contributions to various theological topics by British Pentecostal authors.[8]

2.1.1 The Characteristics of Pentecostal Worship

Neil Hudson[9] pays tribute to the vibrant vitality of Pentecostal and charismatic praise which he believes facilitates the believers' encounter with God.[10] This vitality can be seen in physical expressions, like the raising of hands or dancing. Such vivacious times of praise are followed by more soothing times of adoration with the ministry of spiritual gifts, like prophecy or gift of tongues, and singing in tongues (1 Cor 14:15); the worship leader coordinates these times.[11] Preaching, prayer, and intercession have their place in traditional Pentecostal worship services as well.[12] Yet, as the author affirms,[13] the classical Pentecostal expectation of an "existential encounter with the risen Lord" in the act of communion is now concentrated on the worship time.

2.1.2 Strengths and Weaknesses of this Praise

Hudson states that among the strengths of their worship Pentecostals have "rediscovered a particular form of intimacy with God and stressed the immanence of God."[14] In connection with that, he appreciates the Pentecostal contribution to meeting the expectations of a postmodern generation: "This generation, which longs for authentic spiritual experiences, may be ready to respond to the Pentecostal message of a God who

---

8. Hudson, "Worship," 177–203.
9. Hudson, "Worship," 190–94.
10. Hudson comes from an Elim church which is the name of one of the Pentecostal denominations with over five hundred churches in the UK and about 9000 worldwide. The Elim Pentecostal Church was founded by George Jeffreys (1889–1962) from a Welsh Congregational church background.
11. Hudson, "Worship," 189.
12. Hudson, "Worship," 191–93.
13. Hudson, "Worship," 191.
14. Hudson, "Worship," 203.

wishes to communicate with people, before whom we can live our lives, and whose presence we can experience."[15]

Nevertheless, Hudson self-critically shares some of his theological concerns regarding the weaknesses of Pentecostal praise.[16] He refers to recurring issues, like the danger of individualism[17] and "the problems of excessive emotionalism, spiritual sensualism and the danger of becoming increasingly irrelevant to the wider world."[18] Hudson also points to the dangers of a theology shaped by experience, of triumphalism, and an inadequate view of spiritual warfare.[19] In connection with that, he also mentions an over-realized eschatology and positive confession, which involve the dichotomy of pressing faith and pressing problems. With regard to the issue of "experience theology," Hudson refers to the worship of the "Toronto Blessing" movement, which had started in a charismatic Vineyard church at Toronto, Canada, in 1994 and was reported to have experienced revival.[20]

According to Hudson, antidotes to the above Pentecostal fallacies, which are reflected in their worship, can be found in their own tradition, but also in the wider evangelical tradition where there is a "greater concentration on a theology of the cross in the context of the sovereignty of God."[21] To avoid such pitfalls he recommends that Pentecostals grow in theological maturity.

2.1.3 Summary

In total, Hudson evaluates in a balanced manner the impacts of the Pentecostal contribution to Christian worship while recognizing the expectations of the present generation for authentic spiritual intimacy. His contribution is significant with regard to discerning denominational influences on Christian worship. However, it was not Hudson's intention to research a connection between worship and divine presence.

15. Hudson, "Worship," 203.
16. Hudson, "Worship," 195–201.
17. Hudson, "Worship," 200.
18. Hudson, "Worship," 203.
19. Hudson, "Worship," 196–99.
20. Hudson, "Worship," 195–96. Since then we have seen two similar Pentecostal-charismatic "revival waves" which originated from the US cities of Pensacola and Lakeland.
21. Hudson, "Worship," 203.

The following author assesses the influence of contemporary pop culture on charismatic worship in Great Britain.

2.2 James Steven: Worship in the Spirit: Charismatic Worship in the Church of England

In his book with the above title, James Steven applies an interdisciplinary approach to his liturgical studies on charismatic worship.

2.2.1 Method

In six case studies,[22] Steven uses sociological analysis[23] besides theological appraisal.[24] He applies the approach of *Verstehen* [understanding][25] and the ethnographic methods of participant observation and interviews.[26] As the author explains, referring to the anthropologist Barth, "If a researcher is to understand a ritual fully, they must participate in its performance."[27] The research field he ploughed was mainly the Church of England. Steven examined the social reality of public worship which,[28] referring to the liturgical theologian Kelleher, he calls the "public horizon" of worship:[29] this public horizon is shaped by the common presupposition pool of the worshiping community and their surrounding culture and tradition. It can be analyzed according to categories, like ritual subjects, symbols, and process.[30] This aspect is relevant because sometimes cultural and denominational elements have been mistaken for biblical categories. False theological conclusions result when elements of contemporary pop

---

22. Steven, *Worship in the Spirit*, 55–90.
23. Steven, *Worship in the Spirit*, 37–54.
24. Steven, *Worship in the Spirit*, 167–208.
25. Steven, *Worship in the Spirit*, 37–41.
26. Steven, *Worship in the Spirit*, 42–47; in the meantime, similar approaches have been undertaken, such as an ethnographic participant study by the psychological anthropologist Luhrmann, or a different approach on the charismatic expression of American evangelicals in the Vineyard Church by McNamara, "Theology of Wisdom," 151–68.
27. Steven, *Worship in the Spirit*, 44.
28. Steven, *Worship in the Spirit*, 49–54.
29. Steven, *Worship in the Spirit*, 49.
30. Steven, *Worship in the Spirit*, 50–52.

2.2.2 Case Studies on Charismatic Worship

According to Steven, two charismatic elements of worship can be found in every case study: the distinctive style of sung worship characterized, first, by the "time of worship"[31] and, second, by forms of "prayer ministry."[32] Both elements reflect two influences: the impact of Pentecostal and charismatic traditions on worship in the Church of England and the stimuli of contemporary cultural norms on liturgical expression.

2.2.3 Influence of Modern Pop Culture on Charismatic Worship

By contemporary cultural norms Steven thinks of "romantic music styles" of a popular discotheque culture reflecting a contemporary understanding of social relationships.[33] He elucidates that "the live performance culture of popular music and rituals associated with discotheques and nightclubs,"[34] which implies the elements of presence, visibility, and spontaneity, has permeated the rituals of worship times and prayer ministry. As a result, these contemporary cultural norms foster expectations of God's authentic "live presence" and intimacy, which is what Stevens, referring to the liturgist Kavanagh, calls an unconscious process of "liturgical inculturation."[35]

He then poses the question: How was it possible that "the seemingly unbridgeable gulf between modern culture and Christian worship" has been overcome?[36] The author suggests the answer: first, because of the evangelical character of charismatic renewal and, second, because of its cultural adaptability. Steven explains, "Whilst holding to its core characteristics . . . evangelicalism's capacity to be moulded and remoulded by its

---

31. Steven, *Worship in the Spirit*, 91–134.
32. Steven, *Worship in the Spirit*, 135–66.
33. Steven, *Worship in the Spirit*, 211.
34. Steven, *Worship in the Spirit*, 54.
35. Steven, *Worship in the Spirit*, 211.
36. Steven, *Worship in the Spirit*, 212.

cultural environment has been the most significant factor in its continuing growth and development."[37]

Nevertheless, the author states that evangelical charismatics would not want their style of worship to be compared with pop culture; instead, they would like to reflect the theological conviction that their worship "gives expression to an authentic worshipful relationship to God 'in the Spirit.'"[38] By "in the Spirit" Steven means that the Holy Spirit inspires the time of worship of God's people, as they offer their praises to him. At this point, Steven associates God's people's prayer/praise with God's presence through the Holy Spirit being at work in both realms.

2.2.4 Theological Reflection

Steven welcomes an "instinctive" Trinitarian impact of worship in the Spirit that encourages the return to historical pneumatological biblical roots, thus, counterbalancing pneumatological deficiencies in worship traditions of the Western Church: "There were aspects of case study worship that affirmed an historic Trinitarian understanding of worship in the Spirit, particularly by providing a corrective to established Western liturgical patterns that have underplayed the role of the Spirit."[39]

Nevertheless, he does not ignore a charismatic problem, which he labels a "poverty of expression" given to worship that is in Christ; such "impoverished" worship discloses "a theology of the Spirit that had become dislocated from the economy of God's action in and through the Son."[40] As a remedy he suggests that charismatic worship should partake more fully in the new humanity revealed in Christ. Hence, Steven's critical reflection indirectly advocates a return to the Christological and pneumatological foundations of Scripture in Christian worship.

---

37. Steven, *Worship in the Spirit*, 212: these characteristics are: concentration on conversion, active evangelism, and the cross and Scripture.

38. Steven, *Worship in the Spirit*, 212.

39. Steven, *Worship in the Spirit*, 213.

40. Steven, *Worship in the Spirit*, 213; a similar argument was already expressed by Begbie, "Spirituality," 227–39, who critically examined the spirituality of renewal music in Britain through the doctrinal lenses of systematic theology.

2.2.5 Summary

Steven raises our awareness of contemporary pop culture and charismatic culture influencing Christian worship, thus, helping us to better differentiate between biblical and cultural issues. Furthermore, he links a charismatic understanding of God's Spirit presence in worship with a Trinitarian understanding inherent in Scripture, thus, providing a sound biblical counterbalance. Through his idea of "worship in the Spirit" Steven unintentionally alludes to a connection between God's presence and the praises of his people, which, however, was not the focus of his study.

2.3 Philip Greenslade: Worship in the Best of Both Worlds: Theological Explorations between Two Extremes

In this book, Philip Greenslade explains polarities in Christian worship by means of theological as well as sociological and philosophical categories.

2.3.1 Greenslade's Thesis of Integrated Worship

Greenslade's thesis can be best summarized in the statement that structured liturgical and free charismatic worship include the best of both worlds. He is convinced that biblical worship is paradoxical by nature because it embraces polarities of divinity and humanity which are basic and innate to worship.[41] Greenslade asserts that biblical worship is the place where the polarities of our human experience, such as praise and lament,[42] meet redemptively with the polarities of God that are expressed in his holy love.[43] Therefore, our antagonisms with regard to worship are inevitable and not simply to be explained away by cultural and personal preferences, but they can be understood, overcome, and integrated by way of theology. Consequently, he investigates bi-polar pairs in the context of worship, like heaven and earth, divine pleasure and human self-fulfilment, order and freedom, divine transcendence and immanence, praise and lament, old and new, memory and hope.[44]

---

41. Greenslade, *Worship in the Best*, xiv.
42. Greenslade, *Worship in the Best*, 72–92.
43. Greenslade, *Worship in the Best*, 50–71.
44. Greenslade, *Worship in the Best*, 139–49.

For him, such integrated worship is mutually fertile, and this "cross-fertilization" has the potential to overcome the weaknesses of each camp, such as stiff traditions on one side and immature eccentricities on the other.[45]

2.3.2 Polarities and Integrated Worship

Greenslade admits that his penchant for extreme polarities has been influenced by Brueggemann's concept of "pain embraced and hope released";[46] similarly, his inclination towards a comprehensive and integrative concept of worship was impacted by Dawn's "broad horizon of worship."[47]

Following Greenslade, integrated worship holds together the poles of order and freedom, with structure serving as stepping stones and charismatic freedom enabling spontaneous response:[48] stepping stones would help us to cross the thresholds of time and space, as we move from the world into the sanctuary, from the unholy and unclean into the holy and clean, from structure to anti-structure, from order to freedom. He calls the crossing of these thresholds "liminality,"[49] a term which he borrows from the social anthropologist Turner. Accordingly, worship is understood as a "liminal" event where there is a permanent transition from the prepared to the spontaneous, from Word to Spirit, from certainty to mystery. In connection with that, the author identifies structured order with Word and charismatic freedom with Spirit. As we step out into the realm of the Spirit, we would experience charismatic freedom. Following Greenslade, such freedom enables us to communicate creatively with God and offer our spontaneous responses. Still, after having moved freely in the realm of the Spirit, we need to return to some stepping stones and secure a safe footing. Given the biblical concepts of Exodus and Exile, such "liminal" worship experience would not be limited to a church service. Greenslade quotes the liturgical theologian Kavanagh with regard

---

45. Greenslade, *Worship in the Best*, 139.

46. Greenslade, *Worship in the Best*, 74–76.

47. Greenslade, *Worship in the Best*, xi–xii. Likewise, Greenslade, *Worship in the Best*, xvii–xix, acknowledges the impacts of the philosopher Ricoeur and the sociologist Berger.

48. Greenslade, *Worship in the Best*, 28–49.

49. Greenslade, *Worship in the Best*, 28–30. The Latin term *limen* means doorsill or border.

to the liturgical ritual that "increments meaning with style."[50] In other words, both structured order and charismatic freedom are necessary to bring together form and content in Christian worship.

Furthermore, Greenslade suggests that integrated worship also serves to overcome the polarity of heaven and earth: as these poles are bridged in worship, God's kingdom is extended and the world is reshaped as a result. Hence, for him, worship as a "world-making" and "empire-building" activity constitutes a political act.[51] This prophetic praise is holistic, it involves our lips and lives as partakers in God's creative activity. Greenslade develops his argument as follows: through original sin following God's Sabbath rest at the completion of Creation[52] original worship degenerated, which led to the destruction of the created world order.[53] New worship, however, would rebuild it. At this point, he links God's glory-presence with worship in tabernacle and temple,[54] which both represent the location of such prophetic praise through which God's Creation at Eden becomes "re-creation."[55]

Likewise, Greenslade urges that in worship we need to keep God's transcendence and his immanence together in balance, a balance which he defines in terms of a "creative tension": "Glory is a way of speaking about Yahweh's powerful, sovereign, transcendent presence without making a claim that is flat, one-dimensional or crassly material."[56] Thus, he perceives a continuity of this divine presence in the glory-cloud filling tabernacle and temple (see Exod 40 and 1 Kgs 8).

In connection with that, Greenslade distinguishes God's name as a link in worship which holds together divine transcendence and immanence: God resides in heaven and through his name his presence is represented on earth in his temple where he communicates with his people. It is significant that Greenslade expresses this tension in relational terms "God is transcendent in relationship" and describes the nature of this relationship in terms of God's "anthropomorphic condescension" and holy love.[57] This

50. Greenslade, *Worship in the Best*, 143.
51. Greenslade, *Worship in the Best*, 7, 16, 6–27.
52. Greenslade, *Worship in the Best*, 12.
53. Greenslade, *Worship in the Best*, 16.
54. Greenslade, *Worship in the Best*, 13–15, 54.
55. Greenslade, *Worship in the Best*, 13.
56. Greenslade, *Worship in the Best*, 54.
57. Greenslade, *Worship in the Best*, 61.

means that God's holy otherness would help us refrain from the attempt to domesticate him in our relationship.[58] Therefore, as he concludes, the above polarity is not meant to be dissolved. In sum, God's "transcendent immanence" would be viewed best in these relational terms.

Another argument of the author in favor of integrated worship deals with the polarity of God's glory on the one hand and our self-fulfilment on the other, and these are of mutual benefit.[59] Of course, God being the ultimate reason of our praise does not need any benefit coming from our side. Our edification comes as a positive side effect, which, however, is not the purpose of our worship. All the same, Greenslade identifies a "God-sponsored hedonism": "The human heart's passion for pleasure and God's passion for praise converge in a way that makes sense of human existence and brings Godly self-fulfilment."[60]

2.3.3 Summary

Greenslade's study is invaluable in that it welcomes polarities in worship as natural, for they correspond to the nature of God and humankind. We can only agree with the author that these polarities serve as theological aids, which can prevent "worship wars" and relieve from the pressure of harmonization.[61]

Greenslade's perception of God's passion for praise is helpful because if God is passionate about praise, human worship will not be left without divine response, which is God's presence revealed in his people's praise. Greenslade's relational understanding of God's transcendent presence revealed is relevant, since it alludes to divine-human communication and relationship, which implies divine presence in worship.

All the same, his concept of prophetic praise which amounts to a political world-reshaping pursuit does not differentiate between the worship of believers and the cultural mandate of all humankind. According to Genesis 1:28–29, this cultural mandate is part of God's covenant with humankind in Creation which is still valid after the Fall and involves every human being.[62] A concept of worship as "world-making" activity,

---

58. Greenslade, *Worship in the Best*, 50–71, esp. 70–71.
59. Greenslade, *Worship in the Best*, 1–5.
60. Greenslade, *Worship in the Best*, 2.
61. Greenslade, *Worship in the Best*, 148–49.
62. See ch. 6, section 6.5.2.

God's People's Praise—Approaches Towards a Theology of Worship 19

however, addresses believers and omits non-believers, although the believers' worship may have some implications on the world around them. As a consequence, issues of environmental care and political concern would then be placed in the responsibility of believers only. Presumably, the author would not be happy with that inference from his theory. In sum, Greenslade's anthropocentric, sociological critique of a certain status quo is not identical with a theocentric, prophetic critique.

Some smaller, but not minor treatises by the following author tackle the issue of worship and worship service in the context of their terminology.

2.4 Howard Marshall: "How Far Did the Early Christians Worship God?" and "Worshipping Biblically"

In his earlier article,[63] the New Testament scholar I. Howard Marshall already specified two distinctions established in Peterson's book:[64] worship as a service beyond a church service and worship as a human response to a divine initiative. Similarly, in his subsequent article,[65] Marshall differentiates between worship as an "individual or corporate activity of people acknowledging the greatness of God" and "whatever is done in a meeting of such group."[66]

According to Marshall, many Christians think that worship mainly consists of the service we offer to God in the context of a church meeting as the "outward expression of our homage and adoration."[67] He challenges such a reductionist understanding of worship which is limited to what we call "worship service." Marshall argues that, if we regard as normative the New Testament patterns for Christian meetings and the New Testament terminology for worship, then we have to reassess our understanding of Christian practice.[68]

Considering a biblical understanding, Marshall, at first, presents an overview of the terminology of worship in the New Testament.[69] Com-

---

63. Marshall, "How Far?" 216–29.
64. See section 2.5.
65. Marshall, "Worshipping Biblically," 146–61.
66. Marshall, "Worshipping Biblically," 146.
67. Marshall, "How Far?" 216.
68. Marshall, "How Far?" 217.
69. Marshall, "How Far?" 217–19.

menting on the concept of sacrifice[70] he expounds worship through Christian activities.[71] Then, he elucidates the nature of the church in the context of worship by using various metaphors, like spiritual house and body of Christ.[72]

2.4.1 What Do Christians Do When They Meet?

Marshall identifies patterns for Christian meetings particularly in Acts 2 (but also Acts 4 and 20) and 1 Corinthians 12–14.[73] He repeatedly emphasizes that God takes the initiative in worship, an idea which is relevant for the basic understanding of our inquiry. The divine action initiates the human response of worship,[74] which constitutes only one feature of service in a Christian meeting.[75] There are other features of service, such as God serving us in the first place by offering salvation through the means of teaching and we serving each other by administering spiritual gifts. This is what Marshall calls the "perlocutionary" function of worship.[76] The hoped-for effect of the teaching and serving on people may then be seen in their offering praise back to God by attributing greatness to him through attitudes and actions.[77] This is what Marshall calls the "illocutionary" function of worship.[78] Accordingly, he imagines a two-way movement at vertical and horizontal levels. As a matter of fact, it is a three-way movement in the shape of a triangle. This triangle involves a flow of divine grace from above, and a mutual exchange of grace gifts and worship going back to the divine source of that grace.[79]

---

70. Marshall, "How Far?" 219–20.
71. Marshall, "How Far?" 222–23.
72. Marshall, "How Far?" 224–26.
73. Marshall, "Worshipping Biblically," 150–53.
74. Marshall, "How Far?" 223–24; Marshall, "Worshipping Biblically," 155.
75. Marshall, "How Far?" 226, 228.
76. Marshall, "Worshipping Biblically," 153–55.
77. Marshall, "How Far?" 223–27.
78. Marshall, "Worshipping Biblically," 153–55.
79. After this table was drawn, the present writer came across a similar chart used by Peterson, *Engaging with God*, 221.

Chart 1: Triangle of service and praise

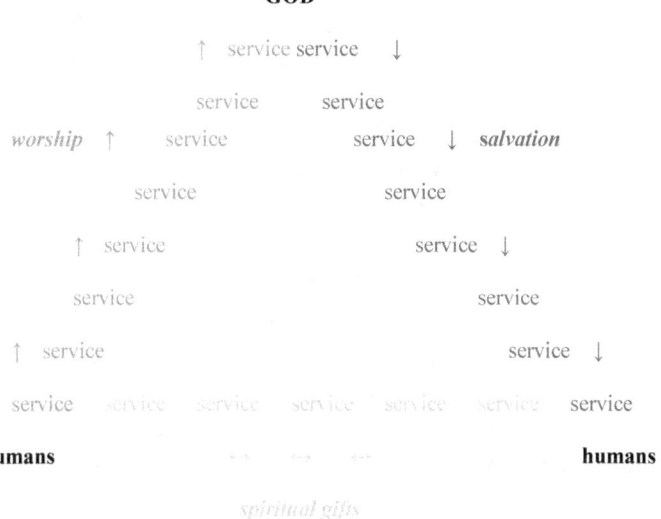

2.4.2 Terminology of Worship in the New Testament

Marshall explains that the verb λειτουργέω (15 times in the NT) is used of Jewish priestly duties performed towards God, but also of Christian activities.[80] In contrast to Wick,[81] Marshall affirms that the term is not limited to a cultic context and that it does not refer specifically to Christian meetings.

Marshall expounds that terms in connection with σέβομαι are used to express respect and reverence that his people show towards God as in Matthew 15:9 and Mark 7:7;[82] σέβομαι refers generally to Jewish, Christian, and pagan contexts, but also specifically to cultic meetings. However, it is used only once in connection with a Christian meeting (in Acts 18:13) by Jews when they reproach Paul for persuading people to worship God in what they consider an illegal manner.

---

80. Marshall, "How Far?" 217–19.
81. See section 2.6.
82. Marshall, "How Far?" 218.

Following Marshall, the term λατρεύω is referred to in the New Testament in connection with the Old Testament ritual expressing service to God (Rom 9:4, Heb 9:1);[83] it is also mentioned frequently in Hebrews in connection with Jewish ritual worship and in Revelation in connection with adoration offered to God (Rev 7:15 and 22:3). All the same, λατρεύω is not limited to cultic use, but also used of Christians to describe their service and obedience to God in their general way of life (2 Tim 1:3; Heb 3:3; 9:14; and 12:28). Marshall indicates that Paul avails himself of this term to portray his apostolic and missionary ministry as worship to God (Acts 24:14).

In contrast to that, as Marshall holds, προσκυνέω is used for specific forms of worship and cultic activity in connection with the physical act of prostration;[84] this act relates to people falling on their face before the king or God and also to the disciples' attitude towards Jesus (Matt 2:2; 28:9, 17; Luke 24:52). Marshall emphasizes that the term is also used of the new worship offered to the Father in Spirit and in truth in John 4:23–24[85] (also John 12:20; Acts 7:43; 8:27; 24:11; Rev 4:10; 19:10; and 22:8).

Concerning sacrifice in connection with Christian meetings, Marshall maintains that this sacrificial terminology is not related specifically to Christian meetings, but used in the context of the total dedication of believers to God, like that of Paul in Philippians 2:17 and 4:18;[86] he points out that sacrificial language is applied in connection with Christian meetings only twice (θυσία in Heb 13:15–16 and 1 Pet 2:5). Later, as Marshall resumes, in the New Testament, the concept of sacrifice is spiritualized in terms of offering praise to God and doing good to other people.[87]

Then, Marshall elucidates the activities in a Christian meeting in connection with the three-way movement mentioned above:[88] first, God ministers salvation to Christians through Word and sacraments; second, Christians edify each other through the gifts of the Spirit, and, third, they address God in praise. In connection with the activity for mutual

---

83. Marshall, "How Far?" 218–19.

84. Marshall, "How Far?" 219.

85. Marshall, "Worshipping Biblically," 147–49; see also Baigent, "Worship," 26.

86. Marshall, "How Far?" 219–20; meanwhile, more publications on worship language appeared, among them e.g., Costa, *Worship*, on worship in Paul.

87. Marshall, "Worshipping Biblically," 149.

88. Marshall, "How Far?" 220–23; Marshall, "Worshipping Biblically," 150–53; see the three sides of the triangle in the chart above.

God's People's Praise—Approaches Towards a Theology of Worship

edification, Marshall refers to the terms διάκονος/διακονία and οἰκοδομή.[89] In connection with the activity of praise, Marshall refers to the terms αἰνέω, εὐλογέω.

2.4.3 Christian Group Activities in the New Testament

Marshall elucidates what takes place in a Christian meeting:[90] first, God takes initiative in ministering salvation to Christians through their teaching the Word of God and administering the sacraments; second, Christians respond by edifying each other through exercising the gifts of the Spirit and, third, by addressing God in praise (αἰνέω, εὐλογέω). Regarding the activity for mutual edification, Marshall explains the terms διάκονος/διακονία and οἰκοδομή:[91] διακονία refers generally to all kinds of services in the church and also specifically to the ministry of a specific group of church functionaries; οἰκοδομή is used to describe the activity of edifying the church, which is the aim of all the spiritual gifts (1 Cor 14 and Eph 4).

2.4.4 The Nature of the Church and the Ministry

As for the church's ministry, Marshall emphasizes that God's revelatory activity precedes the doxological activity of God's people.[92] In other words, God initiates worship.

Regarding the terminology that describes the nature of the church, the author asserts that terms in connection with ἐκκλησία evoke an analogy with the synagogue rather than the temple (συνέρχομαι in 1 Cor 11:18 and ἐκκλησία in 1 Cor 14:19, 28, 35).[93]

According to Marshall, the temple metaphor is suggested when the church is depicted as a spiritual house (οἶκος πνευματικὸς in 1 Pet 2:4–5) or as the temple of God and the Holy Spirit (ναὸς in 1 Cor 3:16–17; 6:19).[94] This language purports to express that God himself is present as Father, Son, and Spirit and that the church is to praise him. Here, Marshall implies a connection between divine presence and human praise.

---

89. Marshall, "How Far?" 220–21.
90. Marshall, "How Far?" 220–23; Marshall, "Worshipping Biblically," 150–53.
91. Marshall, "How Far?" 220–21.
92. Marshall, "How Far?" 223–25.
93. Marshall, "How Far?" 222.
94. Marshall, "How Far?" 225.

Besides, he sustains that the metaphor οἶκος πνευματικός in 1 Peter 2:4–5 is used to picture the membership of God's household and the family of God—images which particularly depict the relational aspect of spiritual fellowship among the church. Similarly, he asserts that God's presence is known in the gathering of his people, which is conveyed through the term κοινωνία, a two-way relationship between God and humans (1 John 1:3) and also among humans; this fellowship is mediated by the Holy Spirit and experienced in the Lord's Supper as well.

As to the character of the church and her ministry, Marshall also refers to other metaphors like the body of Christ (Rom 12:5; 1 Cor 12:12–31). For the rest, he tends to be convinced that the nature of the church is expressed in terms of ministry and edification language rather than temple language, a conviction which is debatable.[95] Still, Marshall believes that the temple metaphor is used in particular to transport the relational aspect of spiritual fellowship between God and humans from the Old Testament into the New. This aspect is significant in view of our goal to explore God's presence in our worship and praise.

2.4.5 Summary

Marshall's main point is that worship is perceived in terms of service, but not exclusively of a worship service. He infers from his biblical studies that worship was only one feature of the Christian meeting and that the service which takes place there is seen in relational terms and is primarily a case of God serving us first: divine activity precedes human response with praise being a part of the whole process. Marshall's idea of God taking the initiative is relevant in that he connects God's revelatory presence with his people's worshipful response.

Hence, his understanding of God's presence in the context of a two-way human-divine relationship in worship implies a link between human praise and divine presence. The same is true with regard to Marshall's interpretation of the temple metaphor in the context of divine-human communication in worship.

The subsequent authors Peterson and Wick apply biblical theology in the true sense of the term having each produced a monograph on a biblical theology of worship.

---

95. Marshall, "How Far?" 225.

2.5 David G. Peterson: Engaging with God: A Biblical Theology of Worship

David G. Peterson's comprehensive biblical theology of worship under the above title likewise aspires to bring Christian worship back to biblical terms. And so, one of the aims of his book is to observe how key terminology on worship is used in the Old and New Testaments and what we can learn from that.[96] Worship that is acceptable to God means for the author "an engagement with him on the terms that he proposes and in the way that he alone makes possible."[97] By engaging with God Peterson refers to our honoring, serving, and respecting God and, thus, abandoning any attachment that gets in the way of an exclusive relationship with him.[98] Therefore, this engagement with God involves a person's entire life.[99]

The structure of Peterson's monograph is similar to the one by Wick.[100] Peterson sets out to trace the theme of worship chronologically throughout Scripture.[101] For him, this also involves evaluating the historical context of each biblical book. Concerning worship in the Book of Acts, for example, Peterson recommends keeping biblical principles without making a law out of them, but translating them into any given context where possible while not holding on to every detail.[102] This is a standard that he applies to other biblical books as well.

Like Marshall, Peterson maintains an understanding of Christian worship that goes beyond a worship service. Like Wick, he emphasizes a discontinuity in worship between the Old and New Testaments as far as cultic activities are concerned. Peterson's volume represents a significant contribution among the approaches towards a biblical theology of worship. A simulated interview with Peterson and his book raised questions which are of particular interest for our inquiry.

---

96. Peterson, *Engaging with God*, 17.
97. Peterson, *Engaging with God*, 20, 283.
98. Peterson, *Engaging with God*, 55–63, 283.
99. Peterson, *Engaging with God*, 73.
100. See section 2.6.
101. Peterson, *Engaging with God*, 20.
102. Peterson, *Engaging with God*, 160.

2.5.1 What are the Basis and Essence of Christian Worship?

For Israel, as Peterson asserts, "Revelation and redemption are the basis of acceptable worship in biblical thinking."[103] Similarly, Christian worship is based on God's self-manifestation in Christ and part of the service that God's people are offering to him in return.[104]

Essentially, Peterson maintains that worship is "faith expressing itself in obedience and adoration."[105] For him, this obedience towards God is also expressed in concrete relationships within this world.[106] As he resumes, "Fundamentally, then, worship in the New Testament means believing the gospel and responding with one's whole life and being to the person and work of God's Son, in the power of the Holy Spirit."[107] Following this line, worship implies that God's people present themselves to God as a living sacrifice based on Christ's sacrifice.[108] For him, Christian praise is service in more ways than one because "Even psalms and hymns and spiritual songs, which are expressions of faith and thankfulness to God, are to be considered simultaneously as the means of teaching and admonishing each other."[109] This evokes the triangle of worship in Marshall's model.

2.5.2 How Do Divine Presence, Spirit, and Worship Connect?

Peterson points out that God's self-revelation has always been mediated by his Spirit.[110] Similarly, after Jesus' incarnate presence on earth, God's revelation in Christ is mediated through the Holy Spirit poured out: "Through the ministry of the Son and the Spirit, the Father obtains true worshippers ... Each person of the Godhead plays a significant role in establishing the worship appropriate to the new covenant era."[111] Thus, Peterson perceives the role of the Holy Spirit with regard to God's

---

103. Peterson, *Engaging with God*, 284.
104. Peterson, *Engaging with God*, 284–85.
105. Peterson, *Engaging with God*, 283; also 16–20, 55–56, 269.
106. Peterson, *Engaging with God*, 177.
107. Peterson, *Engaging with God*, 286.
108. Peterson, *Engaging with God*, 177.
109. Peterson, *Engaging with God*, 221.
110. Peterson, *Engaging with God*, 97–99.
111. Peterson, *Engaging with God*, 285.

God's People's Praise—Approaches Towards a Theology of Worship

revelatory presence and the praises of his people as embedded in a Trinitarian ministry in worship. This pneumatological understanding implies a link between God's Spirit-presence and God's people's praise through the instrumental role of God's Spirit.

2.5.3 How do Temple and Covenant Relate to Christian Worship?

Peterson writes: "Salvation, temple, covenant and acceptable worship are intimately linked in biblical theology."[112] He develops his argument as follows: since the person and work of Jesus served to replace the temple as God's dwelling place including its sacrificial system, the covenant with Israel is reestablished on a new basis as well.[113] One can deduce from this that for Peterson the place of God's revelatory and abiding presence is also reestablished on that new basis. Still, in both Testaments, divine presence initiating human worship is primarily perceived in the context of covenant and temple as the place of divine revelation or the dwelling place of God's Spirit-presence, whether in a literal or metaphorical sense.[114] This line of argument reveals that Peterson perceives covenant relationship as the link which keeps God's presence and God's praise together.[115] Instances of pre-temple worship by Abraham and the other patriarchs would have to be perceived as anticipating "God's earthly dwelling place."[116]

As to the new covenant, Peterson elucidates that God is building a new spiritual house (cf. Eph 2:20–22), a temple of living stones: "God dwells in their midst through his Spirit . . . and he has chosen to manifest his glory to the world through them."[117] This interpretation of Pauline metaphors clearly shows that the author considers the church the place of God's abiding presence and glory. Therefore, no literal building or specific temple cult is required anymore for Christians to worship God and to cultivate spiritual fellowship with him. As Peterson emphasizes, there is a discontinuity between the old and new covenant era as far as cultic activities are concerned.[118] Again, his line of argument demonstrates that

---

112. Peterson, *Engaging with God*, 108.
113. Peterson, *Engaging with God*, 123.
114. Peterson, *Engaging with God*, 137, 200–205.
115. See ch. 6, section 6.3.
116. Peterson, *Engaging with God*, 43–45.
117. Peterson, *Engaging with God*, 285.
118. Peterson, *Engaging with God*, 187.

he perceives God's presence and God's praise to be linked through covenant relationship, whether in the Old or New Testament.

2.5.4 Summary

In sum, Peterson's idea of an "engagement with God" presents worship as responsive and relational in that it presupposes divine initiative and is perceived within the divine-human covenant relationship. Through this relationship divine presence and human praise are linked. This connection is again reinforced through the role Peterson attributes to God's Spirit and God's dwelling place in the context of worship. Although these aspects, which are basic to the premise of our study, do not represent the main line of argument of Peterson's book, they are present in the background.

It seems there has not been much interaction between German and Anglophone scholars in the domain of a biblical theology of worship. Therefore, more space will be dedicated to the following German contribution.

2.6 Peter Wick: Die Urchristlichen Gottesdienste [Worship Services of the Early Church]

This comprehensive volume in German on the worship services of the early church by Peter Wick expounds in detail the origins and development of early Judeo-Christian spirituality in the context of temple, synagogue, and house worship in order to provide a context for a biblical understanding.[119] Likewise, his conception of worship aims at the setting of a worship service, but is not limited to that.

Some time later, N. T. Wright proposed a similar, and yet slightly different approach to early Christian worship: similarly, he examined early Christian worship in the setting of first-century Judaism, but he is convinced that the roots of a new Spirit-led worship are to be found there where Spirit-infilling takes the place of temple worship.[120] Basically,

---

119. Full title: *Die Urchristlichen Gottesdienste: Entstehung und Entwicklung im Rahmen der frühjüdischen Tempel-, Synagogen- und Hausfrömmigkeit* [Worship Services of the Early Church: Origins and Development in the Context of Early Jewish Spirituality in Temple, Synagogue and House Worship].

120. Wright, "Worship and the Spirit," 3; Wright's contribution is based on a paper at a Yale Conference in February 2008.

Wright holds that this new Spirit-led worship needs to be discovered in Scripture and that present scholarship is not overly concerned about discovering a connection between Spirit-infilling and worship.

Wick elucidates the complex relationship between the cultic (temple), the less-cultic, and noncultic spheres (synagogue and house) in Judaism.[121] He is convinced that these relationships form the basis for the developing early Christian worship services. Wick clarifies that at the period relevant for his study the Hebrew canon was already complete.[122] This is probably why he chose a synchronic approach to Scripture.

At first, Wick presents detailed Hebrew and Greek terminology and their development.[123] Then, he analyzes the functions of ancient Israelite pre-temple worship,[124] of first temple,[125] second temple,[126] synagogue,[127] and house worship.[128] The author explores these functions each time in connection with sacrifice, teaching, and prayer.[129] He also looks at the social dynamics of institutions and groups in Judaism and early Christianity, and their influence on the development of early Christian worship.[130] The main part of Wick's research is dedicated to Pauline and non-Pauline letters[131] while not neglecting the gospels and other New Testament writings.[132] He includes noncanonical Jewish and also early Christian writings to draw a picture of the developing worship services in the first centuries CE.[133] Given the importance of biblical terminology and concepts for a theology of worship, this section will receive particular attention.

---

121. Wick, *Urchristliche Gottesdienste*, 18, 131–36.
122. Wick, *Urchristliche Gottesdienste*, 37.
123. Wick, *Urchristliche Gottesdienste*, 21–26.
124. Wick, *Urchristliche Gottesdienste*, 37–40.
125. Wick, *Urchristliche Gottesdienste*, 41–51.
126. Wick, *Urchristliche Gottesdienste*, 52–87.
127. Wick, *Urchristliche Gottesdienste*, 88–116.
128. Wick, *Urchristliche Gottesdienste*, 117–30.
129. Wick, *Urchristliche Gottesdienste*, 131–36.
130. Wick, *Urchristliche Gottesdienste*, 137–67.
131. Wick, *Urchristliche Gottesdienste*, 168–243.
132. Wick, *Urchristliche Gottesdienste*, 244–359.
133. Wick, *Urchristliche Gottesdienste*, 367–87.

2.6.1 The Terminology of Worship Services

Wick expounds that originally the relevant Greek terminology was based on sacrifice terminology.[134] However, the Greek terms in the LXX translation of a pre-Masoretic text changed in some cases their previous meaning, whether cultic or noncultic, and acquired the status of new technical terms. Thus, the biblical terms may denote both cultic and noncultic spheres: temple with sacrifices on the one hand and synagogue and house without sacrifices on the other.

Wick makes clear that the Hebrew key term for service and worship עבודה was translated into Greek on the one hand by ἐργασία and δουλεία as "service" and by λατρεία and λειτουργία as "worship" on the other.[135] And so, the Hebrew root עבד refers not only to the general meaning "to work" and "to serve as slave" (ἐργάζειν and δουλεύειν), but also denotes the more specific cultic meaning "to serve God" (λατρεύειν and λειτουργεῖν). In connection with the cultic duty of priests, λειτουργεῖν is used exclusively. In a similar way, the term λειτουργία, originally referring to political ministry, then to any kind of service, and finally to cultic relationships with the gods, became a technical term for priestly worship through sacrifice and prayer in Israel.[136] The term λατρεία, initially specifying any kind of service or work, was later used for the cultic worship of the Jewish people. Wick emphasizes the cultic meaning of λειτουργεῖν and λατρεύειν more than Marshall does. Yet, in accordance with Marshall and Peterson, Wick maintains that the originally cultic terms עבודה and λατρεία eventually assumed the noncultic, ethical meaning of serving and obeying God with one's entire life (see Rom 12:1–3).[137]

2.6.2 The Function of Ancient Israelite Worship Service

Wick expounds the role of sacrifice in the context of prayer and praise in ancient Israelite worship. He regards sacrifice as a reaction of humankind to their separation from God because sacrifice has been considered a

---

134. Wick, *Urchristliche Gottesdienste*, 21–26.
135. Wick, *Urchristliche Gottesdienste*, 21–24.
136. Wick, *Urchristliche Gottesdienste*, 23–24.
137. More recently, Heil in *Luke-Acts* on patterns for Christian worship points to concepts other than the terminology treated by Wick, e.g. the four Lukan canticles Mary's Magnificat, Zechariah's Benedictus, the angels' Gloria, and Simon's Nunc Dimittis (cf. Heil, Review of *Luke-Acts*).

God's People's Praise—Approaches Towards a Theology of Worship

"cultic guarantee for wellbeing" and peace with God as an ancient human reaction common to all religions.[138] Wick argues that prayer and praise were of secondary importance, only relevant in crisis situations,[139] which is a debatable argument.

The author supports his argument with the creation accounts. Because there was no prelapsarian sacrifice, he deduces that the accounts of the Fall and of Cain represent a pattern for sacrificial worship activities throughout the entire Bible.[140] Still, how does this argument work with regard to the Abraham narratives? Wick holds that Abraham's obedience is expressed in altar-building with sacrifice.[141] When his relationship with God extends beyond obedience and sacrifice, Abraham's prayers would emerge as intercessory crisis intervention. One wishes to argue against Wick that Abraham's prayers and praise go beyond this limited setting because whenever God revealed himself to Abraham, Abraham built an altar and called upon the name of the Lord (e.g., Gen 12:8).

Taking up the case of sacrifice again, Wick mentions two reasons for the Exodus:[142] first, the political reason for liberation and, second, the doxological reason for worship with sacrifices. Passover would occur in the context of sacrifice, whereas Moses' prayers would again be characterized by crisis intervention. Thus, for Wick, prayer and praise follow salvation from danger, which limits the scope and import of worship and praise.

The Sinai events in connection with the giving of the Ten Commandments and the instructions for Moses' altar-building activities were meant to introduce the central role of the sacrifice cult. Service is then identified as an expression of covenant loyalty of God's people. Consequently, the idolatry of the golden calf episode is considered covenant disloyalty, and, again, Moses' prayer would come in as a crisis intervention. Yet, as Wick concedes, the tent of the covenant introduces a new function of prayer as "dialogue between partners" with prostration as a physical expression of worship.[143] Still, for him, ethical obedience was still a necessary prerequisite for sacrifice.[144]

---

138. Wick, *Urchristliche Gottesdienste*, 37.
139. Wick, *Urchristliche Gottesdienste*, 47–48.
140. Wick, *Urchristliche Gottesdienste*, 38.
141. Wick, *Urchristliche Gottesdienste*, 39.
142. Wick, *Urchristliche Gottesdienste*, 40–41.
143. Wick, *Urchristliche Gottesdienste*, 41.
144. Wick, *Urchristliche Gottesdienste*, 43.

Accordingly, Wick explains that cultic holiness and separation from the pollutions of everyday life were emphasized in the temple era at Jerusalem:[145] to the priests belonged the sacrifices and to the Levites the prayer and praises. This cultic centralism brought about a reduced participation of the people simply for geographical reasons. Hence, synagogue services in the postexilic era were meant as compensation, a development which also strengthened the function of house and family in the context of religious education and obedient living.[146] As a result, prayer and praise, and Torah observance were increasingly "outsourced" to non-cultic spheres and considered elements of Israel's worship independently from the central sacrifice cult.

2.6.3 Temple, House, and Synagogue Worship Service in the First Century

As Wick grants, Solomon's prayer of dedication of the first temple already points to the tension between God's omnipresence and his presence in the temple (1 Kgs 8:27; cf. Isa 66:1–2).[147] He affirms that in the first century, the temple was still perceived as God's dwelling place, a holy place meant for sacrifices, prayer, worship, instruction, and for divine revelation and prophecy.[148] As Wick explicates, the Levites assumed doxological functions in instrumental and vocal praise (see 1 Chr 9 and 23) which, however, would remain in the background, given the importance of sacrifice.[149] Nevertheless, he admits that in the Psalms, sacrifice is considered less important than prayer, praise, and repentance (see Pss 69 and 51).[150] Then, the temple is regarded as the place of God's revelation and prophecy:[151] Scripture testifies to divine manifestations in the temple context, like theophany and angelophany. From this can be inferred that, for him, the temple implies a link keeping together God's presence and his people's praise, although he does not say so explicitly.

---

145. Wick, *Urchristliche Gottesdienste*, 47.
146. Wick, *Urchristliche Gottesdienste*, 49.
147. Wick, *Urchristliche Gottesdienste*, 56.
148. Wick, *Urchristliche Gottesdienste*, 58.
149. Wick, *Urchristliche Gottesdienste*, 61–62, 78.
150. Wick, *Urchristliche Gottesdienste*, 79–80.
151. Wick, *Urchristliche Gottesdienste*, 85.

God's People's Praise—Approaches Towards a Theology of Worship 33

As Wick repeatedly emphasizes, the synagogue never entered into competition with the central temple worship.[152] In the Diaspora, the synagogue functioned to compensate the lack of religious activity outside of Jerusalem, and by concentrating on Torah instruction there was no competition in worship. Similarly, as Wick clarifies, in the Diaspora, the house assumed an even stronger compensatory function in worship than the synagogue because representing the private sphere and family the house was the most important place for everyday life, meals, Torah instruction, and religious socialization.[153] This development increased the importance attributed to prayer and praise.[154]

And so, following Wick's line of argument, the originally important role of sacrifice in ancient Israelite worship service decreased with an increasing cultic discontinuity already coming up in pre-Christian worship. While refuting any idea of replacement of cult and sacrifice, Wick elucidates in the subsequent chapters of his book that this discontinuity came to be fully revealed in early Christian worship and praise. As a result, Wick's understanding of Christian worship is bare of any cultic and sacrificial ideas.

The interaction with Wick will concentrate on sections which may touch on God's presence in the context of his new people's praise.

2.6.4 Pauline Metaphors in Church Context

Wick interprets Paul's use of metaphors in connection with church worship as *"metaphorische Kultmoralisierung"* [metaphorical cultic moralization].[155] In other words, Christ's life and death, and the discipleship life correspond to the cultic burnt offerings which are a God-pleasing λατρεία (Rom 12:1–3). Therefore, Paul's cultic metaphors serve the purpose of ethical reinterpretation and not of cultic replacement. This ethical purpose aims at the everyday life service of the disciples in their bodies.[156] In connection with that, Wick points to Romans 12, 1 Corin-

---

152. Wick, *Urchristliche Gottesdienste*, 115–16.

153. Wick, *Urchristliche Gottesdienste*, 117–19, 130.

154. Wick, *Urchristliche Gottesdienste*, 135–36.

155. Wick, *Urchristliche Gottesdienste*, 171–83; this is what Gäckle later calls a *"Metaphorisierung kultischer Terminologie"* [metaphorization of cultic terminology] which encompasses the temple (cf. Gäckle, *Allgemeines Priestertum*, 183, esp. 277–381).

156. Wick, *Urchristliche Gottesdienste*, 182.

thians 6 and 3, 2 Corinthians 6, and Ephesians 2 talking about a *"metaphorische Kultsomatisierung"* [metaphorical cultic somatization] with the disciples' bodies as a holy and God-pleasing burnt offering.[157]

Accordingly, he links two Pauline metaphors which refer to the community of believers, the body metaphor and the temple metaphor.[158] The σῶμα, the "body," with believers representing the members of the body of Christ, is a ναὸς, a "temple" of the Holy Spirit (1Cor 6:19), hence, this congregational body is a dwelling place of divine Spirit-presence. For Wick, this temple metaphor serves as interpretation and not as replacement because here Paul uses "temple" without a definite article for the believers. Therefore, Wick clarifies that not the ἐκκλησία "church," but the believers are God's temple. In 1 Corinthians 3:16a and 17b, Paul applies a grammatical paradox to make this clear: "You are (a) ναὸς of God."[159] Similarly in 2 Corinthians 6:16b, the believers are identified as "temple of the living God." By quoting Leviticus 26:12 where the people of Israel are promised that God dwells in their midst, Paul would implicitly identify the new people of God with God's new dwelling place. Again, for Wick this metaphorical interpretation means identification, individually and corporately, and not a replacement of the Jerusalem temple and its cult.[160] In Ephesians 2:19–22, Paul identifies the church as a dynamic building in a growth process which is God's κατοικητήριον, his "dwelling place." Wick interprets this mixed metaphor of building and agriculture as a nonliteral place of God's abiding presence being in dynamic growth (cf. 2 Chr 30, Ps 32, and Ps 75). This dynamic aspect of God's dwelling place expressed through the image of a building in expansion touches a relevant aspect of this study, as we will demonstrate in chapters 5 and 6.[161]

As to the metaphor of Spirit-infilling in the context of praise in Ephesians 5:18–22, Wick perceives all five participles—four of them referring to praise and thanksgiving—as representing influential instruments for the infilling with the Holy Spirit.[162] By including the fifth participle about mutual submission, he connects the following *Haustafel* with the previous command not to get drunk with wine, but to be filled

---

157. Wick, *Urchristliche Gottesdienste*, 183–91.

158. Wick, *Urchristliche Gottesdienste*, 183–86.

159. No definite article with temple and verb in second person pl. or personal pronoun pl. for the believers.

160. Wick, *Urchristliche Gottesdienste*, 191–93.

161. See sections 5.3 and 6.2.

162. Wick, *Urchristliche Gottesdienste*, 215–17.

with the Holy Spirit. Thus, Wick implies that this passage encourages not only multi-facetted praise, but also an ethically impeccable Christian lifestyle as instruments for believers for a continuous infilling with God's Spirit, which certainly plays an important role in the process. Still, one could reason that vv.18–20 and vv.21–33 represent two independent paragraphs, given their different context.[163] In connection with praise, Wick explains that psalms, hymns, and spiritual songs, even in the form of glossolalia (Eph 5:19; Col 3:16; 1 Cor 14:26), may occur both at church meetings and in personal prayer.[164] Still, for him, this only underlines the importance of a conforming personal lifestyle. Differently, Wick favors an imperative interpretation of the participles in the corresponding passage in Colossians 3:16–17, as he considers the teaching of God's Word predominant compared with the infilling with God's Spirit.[165] Nevertheless, Wick's argument is coherent: a consistent ethical lifestyle is required for his people's praise to be acceptable to God and for them to be filled with his Spirit-presence. This also concurs with our line of argument.

2.6.5 Luke and other Biblical Material

As Wick accentuates, Luke depicts the same respectful continuity in Acts as in his Gospel regarding the temple as the disciples' meeting place (Acts 2), their place of public prayers and praise (Acts 3), as well as of preaching, teaching (Acts 2, 3, 5), and healing (Acts 3).[166] However, a separation from the temple was forced upon the disciples by the Jews themselves (Acts 3, 5) resulting in the spreading of the gospel outside the Jewish homeland (Acts 6–11). The Hellenistic Jew Steven would criticize the traditional function of the temple as God's dwelling place (Acts 7:48). According to Wick, the meaning of this critical distance demonstrates that for Luke the outpouring of the Holy Spirit and, thus, God's Spirit-presence, are not bound to the Jerusalem temple. And so, the respectful cultic temple observance would end in a compulsory separation.

---

163. See ch. 5, section 5.6.
164. Wick, *Urchristliche Gottesdienste*, 227.
165. Wick, *Urchristliche Gottesdienste*, 218–19.
166. Wick, *Urchristliche Gottesdienste*, 278–80.

For Wick, the situation with the synagogue is similar: Paul preached and taught in synagogues from the beginning until he was persecuted by his own compatriots (Acts 9, 13–14, 16–21).[167]

Wick describes that the meaning of the house environment for the young church increased in Acts:[168] the disciples met in a private home for prayer and praise (Acts 1). The birth of the church through the outpouring of the Spirit also occurred in a private home (Acts 2). As he argues, homes offered the appropriate frame for the activities of worship service, like teaching, fellowship, breaking of bread, and prayer (Acts 2) until persecution set in through the Pharisee Saul (Acts 8).[169] Therefore, prayer and praise in the home context were emphasized to show that no temple was necessary for the new people of God to be filled and refilled with Holy Spirit (Acts 4). For that reason, Luke would place Spirit-outpouring and Spirit-infilling in the setting of Jewish homes and not of the Jewish temple (Acts 2 and 10/11). Wick argues that the breach with the Jewish home, unlike the breach with the Jewish temple and synagogue, was caused directly by God himself, who opens up pagan homes for the *ecclēsia* in order to create a space for fellowship between Jews and Gentiles.[170] Again, Wick stresses that the house worship does not represent a substitution of the temple cult and, therefore, is not to be considered in terms of עבודה or λατρεία.[171] Still, through these breaches the house worship created identity for the *ecclēsia*.

Furthermore, Wick demonstrates that the Johannine writings and Hebrews go even further than Paul and the synoptic gospels:[172] there, Jesus Christ is depicted as a better temple and a better sacrifice, but not as a replacement for the temple cult, since no further sacrifice in terms of עבודה or λατρεία is required any more. Admittedly, this argument may represent a sophisticated differentiation of the author. All the same, for Wick, Christian faith and life are still considered a sacrifice, but in a metaphorical sense.[173] Along these lines, the author makes a case that only

---

167. Wick, *Urchristliche Gottesdienste*, 280–81.

168. Wick, *Urchristliche Gottesdienste*, 281–82.

169. Wick, *Urchristliche Gottesdienste*, 287–93; the same argument was held more recently by Heil, *Luke-Acts*, 8–30; similarly, Heil, *Luke-Acts*, 16, maintains the transition from temple worship to house worship via synagogue worship.

170. Wick, *Urchristliche Gottesdienste*, 283.

171. Wick, *Urchristliche Gottesdienste*, 295.

172. Wick, *Urchristliche Gottesdienste*, 313–20.

173. Wick, *Urchristliche Gottesdienste*, 321–22.

God's People's Praise—Approaches Towards a Theology of Worship   37

praise can be considered a sacrifice because of the allusions in Hebrews 13:15, e.g., to Leviticus 7:12[174] where the LXX translates תּוֹדָה "praise" as θυσία αἰνέσεος "sacrifice of praise" which takes the metaphorical place of animal sacrifice.

Wick draws the final picture in the Book of Revelation:[175] the New Jerusalem coming down from heaven upon earth (Rev 19–21), the dwelling place of God and his people filled with his glory (Rev 21:23). This represents an Eden-like precultic situation—a new worship in which God, the Lamb, and their kingly and priestly servants will be united. No temple, no human sacrifice on earth or in heaven will be required any more.

2.6.6 Summary

To summarize Wick's clear and uncompromising conclusion as to the consequences for a biblical understanding of Christian worship: as Christians we "embody" a new divine dwelling place and celebrate a new quality of worship which is a "cultless" worship, bare of any idea of sacrifice.

The inference which can be drawn from Wick's conclusion: this new worship does not allow any "worship sacrifice" as a means to make God's presence appear "on stage," but it represents the context for the reciprocal interaction between God's presence and his people's praise. Wick touched on this connection more or less implicitly several times. Nevertheless, one may not agree with Wick's understanding of prayer and praise originally being of secondary importance only, and with his limited idea of prayer as crisis intervention in the developing early Jewish, pre-Christian worship.

2.7 Daniel Block: For the Glory of God: Recovering a Biblical Theology of Worship

In his above book, Daniel Block deplores the lack of a scriptural theological basis in modern worship. With his attempt at "recovering a biblical theology of worship."[176] Block adds a considerable "block" of stone to this biblical foundation by extracting patterns of worship from both Testaments.

---

174. See also 2 Chr 29:31; Ps 49:14.
175. Wick, *Urchristliche Gottesdienste*, 348–50.
176. See also Block, Review of *Glory of God*, 97–99.

At first, he describes worship as a profoundly human need directed at "someone higher than ourselves," a need which is responsive in nature and which involves reactive communication.[177] Block objects to reducing worship to singing songs and differentiates between attitudes, acts, and rituals of worship.[178] In his own definition of worship, which he repeats at the beginning of each chapter of his book, Block declares: "True worship involves reverential acts of human submission and homage before the divine Sovereign in response to his gracious revelation of himself and in accord with his will."[179]

Focusing on a lifestyle of worship over against a liturgy of worship,[180] Block still gives ample attention to the terminology and phenomena involved and provides helpful graphical illustrations throughout the entire book.[181]

2.7.1 God as the Object of Worship and We as Subject

In order to detach true worship from idolatry, Block presents God and his covenant name YHWH (Exod 3 and 34) as the "true object" of Israel's worship.[182] Expounding on the titles and attributes of Israel's God and the covenants with his people Block gives ample attention to the Old Testament, which reveals his intention to verify continuity of the divine nature revealed in the New.[183] He refers to examples of worship in Old Testament texts like Exodus 19–24 and Psalm 95.[184] As for the New Testament, Block relates to texts which display God the Father and God the Son as "objects"[185] of our worship as in Ephesians 1:3 and Revelation 1:5–6.[186] By doing so, however, he limits the role of God the Spirit to mediating this worship.[187]

---

177. Block, *Glory of God*, 1.
178. Block, *Glory of God*, 8–23.
179. Block, *Glory of God*, 23.
180. Block, *Glory of God*, 24, refers to Webber, who, in contrast to him, concentrates on the active liturgical involvement of the congregation.
181. E.g., Block, *Glory of God*, 26.
182. Block, *Glory of God*, 35–38.
183. Block, *Glory of God*, 35–46.
184. Block, *Glory of God*, 41–46.
185. If it is possible at all to talk about God as the "object" of our worship.
186. Block, *Glory of God*, 46–49.
187. Block, *Glory of God*, 50–53.

Because of Block's effort to prevent the Holy Spirit from being the "object" of our worship, the Spirit risks to suffer from the author's own lack of attention rather than from the New Testament's "inattention given to the Holy Spirit."[188] As a result, Block endorses Christo-centric Trinitarian worship in theory, but tends to support binitarian worship in practice.

With regard to the "subject" of worship,[189] he confronts a "come-as-you-are attitude" common in contemporary worship with a biblical view of acceptable worship:[190] Scripture differentiates between a come-as-you-are attitude for salvation and a come-with-righteousness attitude for worship. He spells this out starting with Creation, moving through the postlapsarian period, and arriving at the new Creation.[191] This is what distinguishes Block from authors who focus on a cultic context in worship while not denying its ethical weight.

Block clarifies that, because of a God who is holy in his glory, the Old Testament distinguishes between ritual/ceremonial purity (Exod 19 and Lev 11) and moral/spiritual integrity (Pss 15, 24, 51).[192] Both were qualities required of worshipers.

He further argues that with the "arrival of YHWH incarnate in Christ" the ceremonial expressions of worship changed, as the temple and its sacrifices became irrelevant with Christ's sacrifice.[193] Nevertheless, in the New Testament, the requirements of holiness and integrity of the worshipers have not changed. Consequently, he emphasizes their validity and continuity throughout the gospels (e.g., in Matt 5 and John 3) and the epistles (e.g., in Rom 2:12–24; 12:1–2; 1 Cor 11:17–34; Heb 10:19–31; 12:14; and Rev 3:1–6).[194]

As a result, Block concludes that the conditional command addressed to worshipers from the old covenant "Be holy, for I, the Lord, am holy" resonates in the new (e.g., in Lev 19:2 and 1 Pet 1:16). According to him, this means primarily righteousness and integrity in the context of everyday life.

---

188. Block, *Glory of God*, 50.

189. If we can perceive ourselves as "subjects" of worship.

190. Block, *Glory of God*, 55–56.

191. Block, *Glory of God*, 65–80; like Wick (see previous section 2.6), Block, *Glory of God*, 60–62, understands acceptable worship in the postlapsarian period to start with sacrifices, but unlike Wick, he attributes a more significant role to prayer in worship.

192. Block, *Glory of God*, 63–64, 67–73.

193. Block, *Glory of God*, 73–76.

194. Block, *Glory of God*, 74–78.

2.7.2 Worship in Life and Liturgy

Like Peterson and Wick,[195] Block highlights that "all of life is to be viewed as worship."[196] Therefore, in chapters 4 and 5 of his book, the author elucidates the relevance of daily life,[197] family life, and work[198] as ethical expressions of relational covenant worship. He illustrates these expressions by turning to examples from the Pentateuch and their echoes in the gospels and epistles.

Block still addresses the specifics of worship in the cultic/liturgical sphere in chapters 6–10 of his book:[199] he refers to ordinances like the initiatory rite of baptism and the repetitive rite of the Lord's Supper,[200] both ordained by Jesus himself. Block also dwells on the ample use of Scripture in Old Testament worship, e.g., in Torah and Psalms, drawing out implications for the use of Scripture in modern-day worship.[201] Moreover, Block elucidates the role of prayer as a means of communication in worship between human subjects and their divine sovereign.[202]

Raising the issue of "worship wars" in music,[203] in particular in North American evangelicalism, which revolve around people and their various tastes, Block points to the role Scripture attributes to music in worship:[204] music is congregational and intended to express homage before God, to seek his glory, and to keep a Christocentric focus, but music is not to be equated with worship.[205] Block's effort to balance the overemphasis on the role of music in contemporary worship entails negative side-effects: he not only downplays the role of music as in tabernacle worship, but also underestimates the role of the Spirit in melodic worship by interpreting, e.g., Ephesians 5:18–20 entirely through the lens of Colossians 3:15–17.[206]

---

195. See sections 2.5 and 2.6 of this chapter.
196. Block, *Glory of God*, 82.
197. Block, *Glory of God*, 81–107.
198. Block, *Glory of God*, 109–39.
199. Block, *Glory of God*, 141–67.
200. As Block, *Glory of God*, 141, explains, in free churches sacraments are called "ordinances."
201. Block, *Glory of God*, 169–92.
202. Block, *Glory of God*, 193–220.
203. Block, *Glory of God*, 236.
204. Block, *Glory of God*, 221–45.
205. Block, *Glory of God*, 241.
206. Block, *Glory of God*, 232.

As a consequence, he virtually eclipses God's Spirit-presence and role in worship, which, of course, touches the core of our project.[207]

Then, Block refers to the function of sacrifice and offerings as worship.[208] Providing extensive terminological explanations from both Testaments he maintains that the original function of sacrifice was not to placate the deity (contra Wick), but to provide divine-human communion.[209] Still, Block agrees with most scholars in that the sacrifice of Christ rendered any other sacrifice unnecessary.[210]

In chapters 11–13, he deals with aspects of formal worship:[211] Block explains the "drama of worship," festivities, and heptadic cycles in Israel as having a memorial function, which may also motivate celebrating Christian festivities in the annual cycle. In connection with that, Block holds that the biblical witnesses portray the seventh-day Sabbath primarily as a day of rest and, therefore, he pleads for rediscovering the Sabbath as a gift from God and a day of repose intended for God-worship.[212] Besides, Block points to a "theology of sacred space," which may serve as a model to point worshipers to God.[213] Consequently, he develops the theme of temple in terms of a Christocentric replacement.[214] Finally, Block rightly criticizes the contemporary overemphasis on the role of worship leaders in the light of the biblical witnesses[215] and closes with a helpful graphic on doxologies in the New Testament.[216]

2.7.3 Summary

Together with other authors Block emphasizes that worship entails attitudes, acts, and rituals which find their expression above all in life, but

207. In contrast to Block and others, examples from worship in the early church testify to adoration addressed to the Holy Spirit; see ch. 6, section 6.5.1.

208. Block, *Glory of God*, 47–70.

209. Block, *Glory of God*, 247–49.

210. Block, *Glory of God*, 269; therefore, Block, *Glory of God*, 263, opposes modern tendencies to pressurize people to tithe "as prepayment for personal material gain" on the basis of Malachi 3.

211. Block, *Glory of God*, 271–96.

212. Block, *Glory of God*, 282–85.

213. Block, *Glory of God*, 297–332.

214. Block, *Glory of God*, 317–21.

215. Block, *Glory of God*, 333–60.

216. Block, *Glory of God*, 361–74.

also in liturgy. To Block's characteristic contribution belongs his criticism of some phenomena in modern-day worship. He challenges a come-as-you-are attitude which he confronts with the biblical view of a come-with-righteousness attitude. He also criticizes the prominence given to the role of music and music leaders.

Unfortunately, because of Block's effort to prevent the Holy Spirit from being the "object" of our worship, he practically eclipses God's Spirit-presence and function in God's people praise.

2.8 John J. Davis: Worship and the Reality of God: An Evangelical Theology of Real Presence

The above astute analysis of contemporary worship in North America by John Jefferson Davis tackles the nature of Christian worship and God's real presence—or rather the sense of his absence in it,[217] which touches the very heart of this study about a potential connection between God's people's praise and God's presence.

During a sabbatical as a seminary professor, Davis attended thirty-five churches from denominational to nondenominational settings, whether traditional-conservative, evangelical, or Pentecostal-charismatic. He sums up his critique of contemporary worship services with the slogan: "Sit back, relax and enjoy the show."[218] Davis observed that in most evangelical churches, the preaching was superb, and the praise bands were performing at professional level, whereas a vivid awareness of God's presence in worship was missing.[219] For him, such absence is attributed to a deficient understanding of reality.

Davis' diagnosis is that the trouble lies at a level deeper than theology: it is ontology and the way we perceive and approach reality.[220] He identifies a deficient understanding of the ontology of worship, its priority and elements, as well as of its participants. He also recognizes a deficient understanding of the ontologies of modernity (scientific materialism) and of postmodernity (digital virtualism), and how they undercut true worship.[221] Thus, Davis refers not only to a multitude of "religious ontolo-

---

217. Davis, *Worship*, 9, 78.
218. Davis, *Worship*, 8.
219. Davis, *Worship*, 9.
220. Davis, *Worship*, 13–15, 77–112.
221. Davis, *Worship*, 21–25, 80–84.

gies" in North America, but also to the influence of digital media with their potential to create virtual worlds: "My claim is that alien, nonbiblical ontologies are at work to wash out the churchgoers' consciousness of God even before the 'worship' service begins."[222] Or, what is worse, they would create a virtual world in worship that fakes the sense of God's presence. The author identifies a poor perception even of the need to acquire new doxological skills for the enjoyment of true worship. Consequently, he aims at uncovering these alien ontologies and confronting them with a biblical view of reality. As a result, the central concern of Davis book is "to recover a sense of the holiness and majesty of God, and of the real, personal presence of the risen Christ in the midst of his people in the power of the Spirit as the central realities of biblical worship."[223]

2.8.1 A Biblical Renewal of Evangelical Worship

With this renewal in view, Davis in his second chapter calls "for a fresh way of looking at the major participants in worship: God, the church, and the Christian (or the self)."[224] He argues in favor of a biblical understanding of the ontology of God and his divine attributes, among them the "weightiness" of God," the source of all existence and reality, over against the "lightness" of our degenerated worship.[225] As to the ontology of the church, the author evokes a "theantropic" reality which embraces the divine-human relationship of the triune God with his people.[226] As a consequence, the nature of the church is *Trinitarian* and *pneumatic*, and not *pragmatic*. His distinction, however, between the gathered church (at meetings) and the scattered church (individuals), with each having a different quality of authority, could be disputed. And so, Davis carries on, Christians understand their identity as Trinitarian, ecclesial, and doxological selves who exist in union with the triune God and for the sake of his glory, but not as "self-defining, self-constructing, autonomous individuals."[227] It is true that defining human identity as "Trinitarian" could be misread, but Davis' conclusion that human identity is relational may serve as a corrective.

222. Davis, *Worship*, 14.
223. Davis, *Worship*, 33.
224. Davis, *Worship*, 37–75, quote in 33.
225. Davis, *Worship*, 50; see, e.g., Exod 3:5, 14.
226. Davis, *Worship*, 65–66.
227. Davis, *Worship*, 71; see 2 Cor 5:17; Eph 4:1–6.

In his third chapter, the author looks into the "real presence" of God in Sunday morning worship.[228] At first, Davis explains ontology within a broad scheme of reality with five levels: the triune God, the domain of angels and spirits, humankind, the nonhuman creation, and the realm of the symbolic and cultural.[229] Correspondingly, the "ontology of the context of worship" is redeemed space and time of the kingdom of God where God meets with his people.[230] For this "kingdom time," the author spells out a fourfold pattern of biblical worship and the historic elements of Christian worship:[231] gathering, ministry of the Word, ministry of the Table, and dismissal. He explores and deplores how through the course of history some of these elements have come to be neglected, which contributed to a loss of divine presence. Davis elucidates that a God who is always metaphysically present makes his presence specifically known and felt in kingdom space and time.[232] By that he means "the real, personal presence of the risen Christ in the assembly in the power of the Spirit as the central and fundamental fact of true worship" as opposed to the primacy of worship leaders, preachers, teachers, and evangelists.[233] Thus, Davis emphasizes that worship is not man-made or controlled by humans, but created by God, who calls us to worship in order that he may commune with us.[234] Consequently, Davis asks for a paradigm shift in our attention and imagination, away from human control and action to the presence of God and his action.

In his fourth chapter,[235] Davis argues for a restoration of frequent Communion as one of the elements in worship in evangelical churches which had come to suffer from neglect. He explores church history diagnosing the causes for a decrease in celebration of the Lord's Supper.[236] Among these causes he identifies an unintended side effect of the

228. Davis, *Worship*, 77–111.

229. Davis, *Worship*, 87–91.

230. Davis, *Worship*, 92.

231. Davis, *Worship*, 97–104.

232. Davis, *Worship*, 103; as to the metaphysical presence of God, Davis, *Worship*, 154, 173, points to texts such as Ps 139:7–10 which balances the transcendence of God over creation (God above us) and the immanence of God within creation (God among/within us).

233. Davis, *Worship*, 34.

234. Davis, *Worship*, 102.

235. Davis, *Worship*, 113–70.

236. Davis, *Worship*, 114–37.

God's People's Praise—Approaches Towards a Theology of Worship 45

Reformation which apparently reduced the Eucharist to a "memory function" in reaction to the Catholic doctrine of transubstantiation.[237] Davis infers that such doctrinal tendencies together with a post-Enlightenment rationalism and pragmatism inadvertently contributed to a sense of real absence of Christ in the Holy Communion;[238] he pleads for a return to the biblical practice affirming that Jesus' phrase "Do this in remembrance of me" (εἰς τὴν ἐμὴν ἀνάμνησιν in Luke 22:19 and 1 Cor 11:24–25), does not mean to remember the past, but to actualize in the present.[239] He also sheds light on the κοινωνία, the "participation" of the believers as ἐν σῶμα "one body" with Christ (1Cor 10:16–17).[240] Such insights would facilitate a more frequent celebration of the Holy Communion with "the risen Christ, alive and present in the Spirit" who "continues to meet his people in joyful fellowship at the table."[241]

In the fifth chapter,[242] Davis moves from ontology to doxology with the aim of a renewal of worship. He suggests ways to implement a new understanding by teaching a biblical theology of worship and a biblical ontology of the church, and by giving practical recommendations for an order of service.[243] For examples of teaching a biblical theology of worship the author refers to Exodus 19–24 and Hebrews 12:18–29.[244] Regarding the ontology of the church, he alludes to biblical metaphors and images which illustrate the theantropic reality of the church: "The family of God the Father, the body and bride of Christ the Son, and the temple of God the Holy Spirit."[245] Davis quoting Zizioulas explicates that the Spirit relates not to "the well-being, but to the very being of the church," thus, concluding that "pneumatology is an ontological category

---

237. In the doctrine of transubstantiation, the Ambrosian "realistic," physical view of the elements with a repeated sacrificial enactment had prevailed over the Augustinian "spiritual," symbolic view (cf. Davis, *Worship*, 122–23).

238. Here Davis, *Worship*, 134–37, refers to a so-called North American pragmatism in evangelization from Finney to Willow Creek.

239. Davis, *Worship*, 138.

240. Davis, *Worship*, 148.

241. Davis, *Worship*, 35, 137–47; he also mentions a beautiful quote from J. F. White, who describes the Eucharist as an "act that conveys the very heart of the gospel in dramatic form Sunday after Sunday" (*Worship*, 116).

242. Davis, *Worship*, 171–206.

243. Davis, *Worship*, 171.

244. Davis, *Worship*, 174.

245. Davis, *Worship*, 175.

in ecclesiology."[246] Or, we may say, the Spirit is essential for God's presence in his people's praise.

Additionally, Davis suggests a return to a multigenerational, "mesochurch"[247] community which can be described as *deep, thick,* and *different*: *deep* quality worship, *thick* personal relationships, and *different* from the surrounding culture before trying to impact it. Likewise, he recommends an "ancient-modern" style of worship service which means considering elements together with their value and right use like "liturgy, tradition, and ritual, the celebration of the visual arts and the right use of electronic media"; Davis mentions further "the promotion of spiritual gifts, the use of an ancient-modern musical canon, and a weekly Eucharist as the climax of the church's worship."[248]

2.8.2 Summary

Davis analysis of evangelical worship services in contemporary North America tackles the very nature of God's people's praise and God's presence or rather his absence in it. The author identifies deficiencies at the level of ontology, that is, a perception of reality, in modernity and in postmodernity which evidently contributed to a loss of a sense of divine presence in worship. He contrasts these deficiencies with a biblical view of reality in worship: God, the nature of the church, and the Christian self. The characteristic contribution of Davis can be summarized: God's "heavy" glory counteracts the "light," degenerated modern worship. Christian identity is relational, doxological, and pneumatic at the vertical and horizontal levels. Worship is "kingdom space and time" in which God's metaphysical presence is made known in a special way. A return to the biblical pattern of worship service with ministry of the Word and ministry of the Table is meant to correct human control and action and to facilitate a return of God's presence.

As a result, Christian worship in general—and not only Pentecostal-charismatic praise in particular—is considered Trinitarian, Christocentric, and pneumatic in nature. This represents Davis' most important and beneficial input. A slightly different analysis of contemporary youth worship features last but not least.

---

246. Davis, *Worship*, 178.
247. A midsize community versus a megachurch, Davis, *Worship*, 181.
248. Davis, *Worship*, 185–86.

2.9 Tobias Faix and Tobias Künkler: Generation Lobpreis und die Zukunft der Kirche [Generation Praise and the Future of the Church]

2.9.1 Generals

Most recently, two German theologians, Tobias Faix and Tobias Künkler, presented an empirical youth study among more than three thousand young people from 16 to 29 years of age.[249] At least sixty percent of them are considered "highly religious" coming mainly from Protestant State Churches and Free Churches.[250] These are by no means religious "weirdos," but religiously highly motivated teens and twens who come mostly from a conservative background and hold at least a medium level of education.[251] They may vary in faith orientation and range of engagement, but they have in common a preference for worship, and through their contributions they are able to influence the future of the church.[252]

2.9.2 Empirical Method

Through a variety of specific questions the study investigated the priority these young people attribute to religion and faith, their experiences, and the consequences of their faith on their lives. The outcome: the "generation praise" does not only prefer a certain way of worship as some kind of "liturgy of post-modernity," but their praise also conveys a specific attitude towards life and faith beyond a religious intensity.[253] This attitude is marked by subjectivization and emotionalization combined with a comprehensive aestheticization of life and faith.[254] Focusing on experience and consumption, these young people express at the same time a profound sincerity in their relationship with God and a genuine desire to meet with him in worship.[255] For many of them, and this is significant, praise has become a more important resource for faith than Bible

---

249. Faix and Künkler, *Generation Lobpreis*, 17–29 (ch. 1).
250. Faix and Künkler, *Generation Lobpreis*, 13, 22–24.
251. Faix and Künkler, *Generation Lobpreis*, 31–45 (ch. 2).
252. Faix and Künkler, *Generation Lobpreis*, 47–81 (ch. 3).
253. Faix and Künkler, *Generation Lobpreis*, 221, 14.
254. Faix and Künkler, *Generation Lobpreis*, 84.
255. Faix and Künkler, *Generation Lobpreis*, 83–153.

reading.[256] Correspondingly, the traditional church and their religious language appears to be foreign to them.[257]

2.9.3 Summary

As a conclusion, the authors suggest that we draw on these young people's resources and preferences, like their passion for praise and for fellowship with God and their peers.[258] We should welcome their new competences as an enrichment for the church, like global consciousness, digital skills, ecumenical identity, relationality, and a lifestyle of worship.[259] Still, we would have to develop new concepts to enhance their biblical literacy and make Bible reading more palatable to them, not to speak of theological literacy. These goals require more full-time youth workers who are culturally multi-lingual interpreters and bridge-builders as much-desired examples to the youth. Additionally, new structures for voluntary work and new forms of faith life are essential.

2.10 Summary and Conclusion

At the beginning of this chapter, we asked to what extent specific approaches towards a theology of worship incorporate the two elements of God's praise and God's presence, and their connection.

Some of the studies approached the topic of worship from a biblical theology perspective covering material from both Testaments. Many of them were not concerned about a connection between God's presence and his people's praise, as this was not their primary goal. Therefore, it would be unfair to criticize the authors for that, in particular, since their studies represent a foundation, vital for the development of a biblical theology of worship.

Hudson's contribution is significant in that it represents a thoughtful and balanced evaluation of Pentecostal influence on Christian worship. Researching the connection between God's presence and his people's praise was not his intention.

---

256. Faix and Künkler, *Generation Lobpreis*, 22.
257. Faix and Künkler, *Generation Lobpreis*, 155–217.
258. Faix and Künkler, *Generation Lobpreis*, 219–31.
259. Faix and Künkler, *Generation Lobpreis*, 268–71 (conclusion).

Steven raises our awareness of how contemporary pop culture has influenced Christian worship and helps us to distinguish between biblical and cultural issues. He counterbalances a charismatic concentration on Spirit-presence by pointing to Trinitarian concepts inherent in Scripture. Similarly, Steven did not intend to investigate a relationship between divine presence and human praise.

Greenslade's study on polarities in worship provides insights regarding the nature of God and humankind. Unfortunately, his preference for polarities led him to anthropocentric sociological maxims and the ambiguous postulate of prophetic praise as a "world-making" activity. All the same, his idea of a "God-sponsored hedonism" is indirectly related to an interaction between divine presence and human praise: both of these elements converge in the double pleasure which God's people's praises bring to God and God's presence brings to his people.

Marshall's significant treatises, particularly with regard to terminology, perceive worship in the context of a service without being limited to that. He encourages a return to Scripture in order to remedy incorrect ideas of worship. His understanding of the temple metaphor as the place of God's presence in his people's praise implies a link between both, which is supported through the conclusion of Marshall's study: worship is relational and responsive in its nature.

Peterson's study represents one of the first examples of a biblical theology of worship. Like Marshall, he keeps emphasizing that worship is not limited to a worship service and that worship is responsive and relational: worship presupposes divine initiative and entails a divine-human relationship. Therefore, Peterson implicitly allows for a connection between God's presence and God's praise, while that was not the focus of his book.

Wick's oeuvre represents a comprehensive contribution to a biblical theology of worship. His thorough dealing with biblical terminology and concepts of worship also insinuates a connection between God's presence and God's people's praise, especially in his interpretation of Paul's and Luke's metaphors. One may infer from Wick's uncompromising result that a new and "cultless" Christian worship does not allow for sacrifices of praise to make God's presence "appear on stage."

Like Wick and Peterson, Block emphasizes that worship needs to be expressed both in life and liturgy. His criticism of certain phenomena in modern-day worship recalls Steven's critique and Marshall's call back to the biblical roots. Block challenges a come-as-you-are attitude to worship which he confronts with the biblical view of a come-with-righteousness attitude. Unfortunately, given his effort to prevent the Holy Spirit from being the object of our worship, Block practically eclipses God's Spirit-presence and its vital role in God's people's praise.

Davis' perceptive analysis of evangelical worship services in contemporary North America tackles the very topic of God's people's praise and God's presence or rather absence in it. He suggests a change of perspective for the recovery of God's real presence in church worship: God's "heavy" glory is seen to counteract the "lightness" of a degenerated modern-day worship. Christian identity is seen as pneumatic, doxological, and relational at vertical and horizontal levels. Worship is seen as "kingdom space and time" in which God's metaphysical presence is made known in a special way. A return to the biblical pattern of worship service with ministry of the Word and ministry of the Table is seen to correct human control and facilitate a return of divine presence. As a result, Christian worship in general is perceived as pneumatic, since it embraces God's Spirit-presence and his family's praise. This is Davis' important and beneficial input.

The empirical study by the scholars Faix and Künkler, which analyzes the situation of "highly religious" youth in Germany, may also apply to other countries, as the "generation praise" conveys a cross-cultural, contemporary attitude towards life and faith. This attitude is characterized by a focus on worship and relationship, and they expect God to be present in their praise. These are resources on common ground we may want to draw on.

In conclusion, we may wish to bear in mind that, while quite a few of the analyses treated in this chapter were critical of certain characteristics of contemporary Christian praise, this criticism never applies to heartfelt and sincere expressions of Christian worship. Actually, God delights in his people's praise backed up by a conforming life style, whether offered by a traditional organ or by a modern pop band.

The next chapter will deal with the question how biblical theology as a distinct discipline with a canonical and intertextual model as a method can help to interpret passages from both Testaments which deal with God's praise and God's presence, and a potential connection between both.

3.0

Biblical Theology—a Distinct Discipline and Its Methods

Revelation requires more than interpretation. It calls for obedience. Such obedience changes history.

—VISHAL MANGALVADI

THE LAST CHAPTER REVEALED that if cultural aspects in Christian worship are not identified as such, they might be mistaken for biblical ones, a peril which may easily lead to false theological conclusions. This risk can be avoided by going back to careful exegesis and hermeneutics as a basic necessity for the interpretation of biblical texts. Yet, frequently in the past and present, diverse hermeneutical perspectives have set off vibrant scholarly debates about biblical theology and its appropriate methods. After a historical introduction on the development of biblical theology, this chapter will sketch a summary of that debate.

As a matter of fact, biblical theology has not always and everywhere been considered a distinct discipline in its own right. This is why we will begin by exploring the development and history of biblical theology including some of its representative methods, i.e., canonical and intertextual approaches with their hermeneutical paradigms. In connection with that, the question is raised how biblical theology as a discipline can serve to interpret biblical texts from both Testaments concerning an interaction of God's praise and God's presence.

With Brevard Childs a leading representative of a canonical approach will be introduced. His model will be contrasted with the one by James Barr. Following their appraisal, which includes a critical German response, selected current approaches in the domains of narrative criticism and intertextuality will be presented. Some of the intertextual models pertain to the Book of Acts, which contributes texts to our study as well. Then, in a brief outlook, a choice of contemporary hermeneutical models will be put to the test regarding their practical application in connection with the results of our investigation.

3.1 Biblical Theology: Development and Debate

Given the variety of ideas as to what biblical theology is about, a comprehensive definition by Brian Rosner, scholar in this field, will help:

> Biblical theology may be defined as theological interpretation of Scripture in and for the church. It proceeds with historical and literary sensitivity and seeks to analyse and synthesize the Bible's teaching about God and his relations to the world on its own terms, maintaining sight of the Bible's overarching narrative and Christo-centric focus.[1]

Accordingly, biblical theology is spelled out, first, as encompassing a theological and church-relevant interpretation of the Bible in both Testaments, second, as involving historical-literary and synchronic theological methods,[2] and third, as sustaining a Christ-centered and humanity-relevant relational approach. This relational aspect also ties in with the question posed in this chapter as to how biblical theology as a distinct discipline may facilitate exploring texts on a potential connection between God's presence and God's people's praise.

The above definition may sound clear-cut. Still, questions rise about the "comprehensiveness" of biblical theology and what Scripture actually comprehends, whether its constitutive parts are labelled "Old Testament" and "New Testament," "First Testament" and "Second Testament," or "Hebrew Bible" and "Greek Bible" and how these parts relate to each other.[3] While Rosner emphasizes "the Bible's overarching

---

1. Rosner, "Biblical Theology," 10.
2. For a synchronic reading see, e.g., Wick and Egger, *Methodenlehre*, 105–14.
3. Mead, *Biblical Theology*, 4.

Biblical Theology—a Distinct Discipline and Its Methods

narrative,"[4] other scholars, especially in Germany, understand biblical theology primarily to be characterized by an apparent tension between the unity and diversity of the Old and New Testaments, and an internal tension within each Testament.[5]

In this connection, Andreas Köstenberger sketches the present state of biblical theology.[6] He summarizes and assesses contemporary positions, like those by Alexander and Rosner, Hafemann, Goldsworthy, as well as Beale. Köstenberger warns with regard to classical approaches to biblical theology against "positing a single center" and points to a scriptural metanarrative that "provides a promising avenue of exploring the biblical writers' message, which involves unity as well as diversity."[7]

Then, the question arises as to how biblical theology as a distinct discipline relates to other disciplines such as systematic theology and pastoral theology, which prompts further tensions. Unfortunately, biblical theology has not always and everywhere been acknowledged as a theological discipline in its own right, as will be elucidated.

3.1.1 Debate on Historical-Critical versus Theological Approaches

One glance at the history of biblical theology reveals how diverse the assessment of this discipline and its mission has always been among scholarship. The seventeenth and eighteenth centuries saw the development of biblical theology into a distinct discipline. In Germany, the naissance of a *gesamtbiblische Theologie*,[8] which comprises both Testaments, took place within the dogmatics of Lutheran orthodoxy, the pietism of Spener and Franke, and the new historical-critical approach of Semler and others.[9] However, in the long run, biblical theology has not been able to remain a distinct theological discipline.

The history of the developing discipline has been shaped by two main tendencies in Germany: in the eighteenth century, the post-Gabler separation drove a wedge between historical-biblical investigation and dogmatic assessment, which led to an "ugly ditch" separating biblical

---

4. Rosner, "Biblical Theology," 10.
5. Mead, *Biblical Theology*, 3–6.
6. Köstenberger, "Diversity and Unity," 445–64.
7. Köstenberger, "Diversity and Unity," 449, 144–58.
8. The German term for biblical theology.
9. Scobie, "History," 12–14.

theology from systematic theology.¹⁰ It was Johann Philipp Gabler who, in his inaugural speech at Altdorf University¹¹ of 1787, had used the attribute "*rein*" to identify "pure" theology in terms of a doctrinal interpretation of Scripture, thus, distinguishing between a dogmatic and a historical approach.¹² As a result of this distinction, Germany in the eighteenth and nineteenth centuries saw an increasing separation between a historical investigation in biblical theology ("what it meant") and a dogmatic assessment in systematic theology ("what it means").¹³ As a consequence, in Germany, biblical theology has increasingly been perceived as a purely historical-descriptive discipline.¹⁴

Subsequently, the renowned Old Testament scholars Walter Eichrodt and Gerhard von Rad with their schools sought to overcome this beginning division in both Testaments between a historical-critical and a revelatory-theological approach.¹⁵ Eichrodt established a synchronic scheme of organization by concentrating on a theme as centre—the covenant between God and humankind. In contrast to that, von Rad chose a diachronic approach by opting for Israel's faith statements and, thus, focusing on salvation history.

All the same, strong emphases on the aspect of discontinuity led to an increasing separation between Old and New Testament theology.¹⁶ Moreover, a certain "Christianizing" of the Old Testament could be observed even up to its complete neglect, especially by Rudolf Bultmann.¹⁷

10. The term *garstige Graben* [ugly ditch] used by German scholarship to describe this separation goes back to Lessing (1777).

11. A small town in the environs of Nuremberg, Germany, which once before held a renowned university.

12. Scobie, "History," 13; see also Scobie, *Ways*, 15–16; Childs, *Biblical Theology of OT and NT*, 11, evaluated Gabler rather favorably in terms of creating a methodological distinction and "of emancipating biblical studies from ecclesiastical restraints."

13. Childs, *Biblical Theology of OT and NT*, 4–11; Mead, *Biblical Theology*, 8–9, attributes this differentiation to Stendahl. The distinction caused an ongoing debate on the difference between the two German verbs *auslegen* and *erklären* with the former relating to a philological-historical interpretation of the text and the latter determining the reasons behind a particular reading.

14. In view of such division, Ebeling emphasized the need for inner unity of theology in general and of biblical theology in particular while keeping the diversity of the disciplines; this attempt of Ebeling Childs, *Biblical Theology of OT and NT*, 8–10, critically evaluated as a return to a pre-Gabler status quo.

15. Mead, *Biblical Theology*, 42–44; Scobie, "History," 15.

16. Mead, *Biblical Theology*, 77–80; Scobie, "History," 17.

17. Mead, *Biblical Theology*, 44–45, 64, 151–53; Bultmann even called the OT "a

Biblical Theology—a Distinct Discipline and Its Methods

This development led to a renaissance of the "Jewishness" of the Old Testament Scriptures through Jacob Neusner, which, again, resulted in a quest for unity in biblical theology.[18] The issue of discontinuity, however, was not solved. Perhaps this is one of the reasons why biblical theology has not been established as a theological discipline in its own right in Germany.

Meanwhile, scholars kept emphasizing that the historical-descriptive thrust of an approach should not be detached from its theological one, nor should the analytical focus be separated from the revelatory one. This issue is still subject of the more contemporary debate. In connection with that, some German scholars[19] have criticized the *historisch-kritische Methode*[20] because of its alleged lack of biblical substance.

To summarize the major tendencies: the critical source analysis of the nineteenth century with a history of religion approach was followed by a concern for theological synthesis in the twentieth century, which affected the quest for the unity of both Testaments.

3.1.2 Ongoing Debate

In addition, in the late twentieth century, new interests in various areas developed at international level: the linguistic-literary methods of

---

miscarriage of history" and a "history of failure" (cf. Mead, *Biblical Theology*, 64); Bultmann favored a historical-descriptive and existentialist approach to the NT, and his contribution to solving the above tension was by "demythologizing" away the revelatory aspect.

18. Scobie, "Structure," 163–94: this quest for unity was among others shared by Gese, Oeming, Schmid, and Stuhlmacher.

19. E.g., Maier, *Ende der Historisch-Kritischen Methode*, or Linnemann, *Synoptisches Problem*. Maier is a German scholar and former Lutheran bishop; the late Linnemann, a former Bultmann disciple and German NT professor, had revoked most of her writings prior to her conversion (according to Linnemann's personal testimony to the present writer dating from 1991).

20. In English, the term "criticism" mainly refers to analytical scientific methods, whether historical, literary, or other. In German, however, the term "*kritisch*" [critical] is inextricably linked with the *historisch-kritische Methode* [historical-critical method] and the ongoing controversy involved in Germany and beyond. Thus, the German term "*Kritik*" [criticism] does not always assume a neutral meaning, but has also been used to brand that method as disparaging of Scripture and holding a methodological monopoly.

narrative criticism,[21] sociological criticism,[22] and feminist criticism.[23] Consequently, the focus shifted from a historical-versus-theological to a critical-versus-theological debate. Some models sought to combine these different strands, like the so-called biblical theology movement in the Anglophone world in the middle of the twentieth century.[24] This movement came to an end due to increasing influences of source and redaction criticism, and a splitting-up of theology into diverse theologies.

In view of this development in biblical theology, the contemporary debate reveals a critical-versus-canonical penchant. Peter Balla, a biblical theology scholar, points to this tendency: "There are two main challenges to biblical theology: first, the argument against confining study to the Bible as defined in the canon; and secondly, the argument against the basic theological unity of the biblical authors and books."[25]

Having already touched on the second argument in the above debate we come across the first one in connection with James Sanders, an Old Testament scholar associated with canonical criticism.

James Sanders concentrates on the process of canon formation attempting to build a bridge between the historical and the canonical domains. He wishes to correct some of the negative side effects of historical criticism and to bring the Bible and canon back from the "scholar's lecture" to the "church's lectern."[26] For Sanders, canon is an ever-changing entity, which depends on its reception by the early believing community and by on-going communities.[27] Through rereadings in the liturgical and instructional life of the believing community, the relevant texts were repeated, selected, and adapted in form and content in the canonical process.[28] This may have occurred through a midrashic contemporizing of earlier value traditions of the community.[29] By and by, an increasing stabilization took place with several books being attributed sanctified

---

21. Frei, *Eclipse*, and Frye, *Great Code*, were considered pioneers of narrative criticism.

22. Gottwald is counted among the early representatives of liberation theology.

23. Trible and Schüssler-Fiorenza pioneered feminist theology.

24. Hafemann, "Biblical Theology," 15, is opposed to biblical theology being called a movement, for movements would only be temporary.

25. Balla, "Challenges", 20.

26. Sanders, *Canon and Community*, 21–45.

27. Sanders, *Canon and Community*, 29–30.

28. Sanders, *Canon and Community*, 33.

29. Sanders, *Canon and Community*, 26.

authoritative tradition.³⁰ This represents Sanders' view in a nutshell on the development of canon. As a result, Sanders does not see a clear cut between where the canonical texts stop and the interpretation starts because for him canon contains both tradition and interpretation and, therefore, is open-ended.³¹ So, he would not want to see canon being frozen into some final form.³² However, this relativizing of canonical boundaries leads to reducing the relevance of canon and, eventually, the authority of Scripture.

In view of the two above arguments directed, first, against confining the Bible to canon and, second, against the Bible's unity, one needs to acknowledge that tensions exist in both areas. For example, unresolved tensions based on the diversity of Scripture cannot be forcefully dissolved because they exist "as poles on a spectrum" or "mutually interpretive lenses in a prism," as biblical theology scholar Scott Hafemann declares.³³ Those tensions need to be respected and explored, concerns which will be addressed in the next sections on the canonical model of Brevard Childs and the contrasting view of one of his main opponents, James Barr, to be concluded by a critical evaluation.

3.2 Brevard Childs: A Canonical Approach

Brevard Childs, scholar in Old Testament and biblical theology, is inseparably connected with canonical methodology. It may not be exaggerated to call Childs the "father of the canonical approach."³⁴ He takes up both challenges to biblical theology of the above quote by Balla: Childs argues in favor of Scripture as defined by the received canon and as embodying a basic theological unity of biblical authors and books.³⁵ Of course, other scholars besides Childs such as Sanders and Barr have presented their canonical models as well.³⁶ Nevertheless, none of them took up these two main challenges against biblical theology as Childs

---

30. Sanders, *Canon and Community*, 24, 34.
31. Sanders, *Canon and Community*, 46–60.
32. Sanders, *Canon and Community*, 32.
33. Hafemann "Biblical Theology," 16.
34. A term originally shaped by Childs.
35. See, e.g., Childs, *Biblical Theology: A Proposal*; Childs, *Biblical Theology of the Old and New Testaments*.
36. For Barr see section 3.3 below.

did. Since then scholars like Seitz[37] have undertaken to evaluate Childs and his canonical approach.

3.2.1 Canon and Authority

As for the different meanings of canon—whether it is, first, a collection of texts, second, a collection of the final textual forms of both Testaments, or, third, the authoritative norm for both church and scholarship—Childs tends to concentrate on the third meaning of canon which for him also implies the second one.[38] It is appropriate to mention at this point that in our context the term "canon" is used to refer to the collection of biblical books as defined in the canon of the Hebrew Bible/Old Testament which differs from the Roman Catholic canon and, again, from the Greek and Russian Orthodox canon.[39]

With regard to discussions about different Christian canon traditions, Childs in his earlier years already states the problem: "The fundamental theological issue at stake is not the extent of the canon, which has remained in some flux within Christianity, but the claim for a normative body of tradition contained in a set of books."[40]

By focusing on an authoritative norm for church and scholarship Childs mediates between the critical stance of the academy and the confessional stance of the church.[41] Thus, he advocates the complete canon of the Christian church not only as the rule-of-faith for the community of faith, but also as "the object of critical theological scrutiny subordinate to its subject matter who is Jesus Christ."[42] Childs, pointing to Frei, elucidates this function of canon:

---

37. The volume *The Bible as Christian Scripture* was edited by Seitz and Richards as a tribute to Childs who died in 2007. In an earlier volume on canon and biblical interpretation, Seitz, "Canonical Approach," 61–63, even identifies the canonical approach as a vast discipline, comprehended and controlled only by such as Childs; see also Seitz, *Character of Christian Scripture*.

38. Beckwith, "Canon," 27–34.

39. The Roman Catholic and Orthodox canons contain different apocrypha in addition to the Hebrew Bible/OT; see also *SBLHS*, 261–63.

40. Childs, *Crisis*, 99; this "flux" refers not only to the extent of various canon corpora, but also to their Masoretic and LXX textual traditions (cf. Driver, "Childs," 243–78).

41. Childs, *Biblical Theology of OT and NT*, 70–78; Childs, *Biblical Theology*, 40.

42. Childs, *Biblical Theology of OT and NT*, 68, 71, 78.

> The role of the canon as scripture of the church and vehicle for its actualization through the Spirit is to provide an opening and a check to continually new figurative applications of its apostolic content as it extends the original meaning to the changing circumstances of the community of faith.[43]

Hence, for Childs, in contrast to Sanders, the Christian canon as Scripture is not open, but only its original meaning and application may extend to suit the church's new situations.

While Childs makes clear that only the final canonical form of texts from both Testaments is theologically reliable, he does not neglect the process which leads up to this form: "The authoritative norm lies in the literature itself, as it has been treasured, transmitted and transformed."[44] Basically, the question of the final canonical form comes down to the question of theological authority. Paul Noble suggests that Childs' canonical principle "is equivalent to the Bible being divinely inspired."[45] Yet, Childs himself prefers talking about the "special authority of sacred scripture" in its final canonical form.[46] "Canonical intentionality," a term coined by Childs,[47] can be understood as the scriptural witness in its final canonical form of the Holy Spirit to the Father and the Son.[48] Accordingly, Childs' understanding of biblical authority involves the relation between the witness of Scripture to the reality of the triune God and the community of faith. And so, for Childs, canonical authority is seen in relation with the "reception of this corpus [canon] by a community of faith and practice".[49] He believes human perception to be responsive to the nature and "coercion" of the text.[50]

---

43. Childs, *Biblical Theology of OT and NT*, 724.
44. Childs, *Biblical Theology of OT and NT*, 71.
45. Noble, *Canonical Approach*, 340.
46. Childs, *Biblical Theology of OT and NT*, 264.
47. Childs, *Introduction*, 79.
48. Seitz, "Canonical Approach," 100.
49. Childs, *Biblical Theology*, 11.
50. Seitz, "Canonical Approach," 87–88, identifies the term "coercion" used by Childs with the "pressure" of the literal sense of Scripture; similarly, Sumpter, "Brevard Childs," 11, argues: "Theologically, the creation of the canon of Scripture was never claimed by the church to be its own work, but was itself understood to be a response to the divine coercion of the living Word of God."

3.2.2 Witnesses versus Sources

For Childs, sources exist in any religion, whereas Israel's faith statements represent witnesses to the reality of Yahweh, as he revealed himself to his people. And only the final canonical form of texts is decisive for the community of faith as witness to its subject matter which is divine reality. For Childs, the distinction between witness and source is due to the nature of the text: "The whole point of the Christian canon is to maintain such a distinction and thereby to acknowledge the special authority of sacred scripture."[51] This, however, does not prevent Childs from affirming that both a theological-canonical reading and a historical-critical reconstruction of the biblical text may exist independently of each other.[52]

He illustrates that listening to the "discrete witnesses" of the Old and New Testaments is like listening to voices in a choir or instruments in an orchestra. Playing with this metaphor, he underscores how important it is to listen to each individual voice discretely before one is able to listen to the concert of all: "Both Testaments make a discrete witness to Jesus Christ which must be heard, both separately and in concert."[53] Listening to the "discrete witness" means, first, to identify the plain, literal sense of Scripture. Only then, second, one is able to listen to the witnesses in the "concert" of both Testaments without mingling them. And only after that, third, theological reflection can move "from the dual witness of scripture to the reality of God and Father of Jesus Christ to which the witnesses point."[54]

This way, Childs through his canonical approach seeks to restore a proper balance to biblical theology in that the discrete voice of the Old Testament would not suffer from being heard on its own,[55] nor would the witnesses of the New Testament suffer from being detached from the Old Testament.

---

51. Childs, *Biblical Theology of OT and NT*, 264.

52. Childs, "Canon," 52, does not hesitate to compare witness and source as the divine and human dimensions of the Bible with the incarnation of Jesus Christ being "truly man and truly God"; see also Childs, *Biblical Theology of OT and NT*, 38–55 (ch. 3), 56–74 (ch. 4); also his last work, Childs, *Struggle to Understand Isaiah*, 321.

53. Childs, *Biblical Theology of OT and NT*, 78.

54. Childs, *Biblical Theology of OT and NT*, 380.

55. Childs' earlier works, e.g., *Exodus*, established his reputation as an OT scholar.

3.2.3 Hermeneutical Implications for Biblical Theology

Listening to the text as a discrete witness does not call into question the diachronic dimension of God's history with his people in the old and new covenants. Using two examples Childs illustrates how this listening to the witnesses in their final textual form may function at the level of biblical theology: first, Abraham's testing of faith in Genesis 22 is a theme which also relates to the New Testament[56] and, second, the parable of the wicked tenants in Matthew 21 demonstrates the theme of rejection of the Messiah which also refers to the Old Testament.[57] This way, Childs attempts to discover layers of theological continuity and discontinuity of a theme or concept.

In connection with that, Childs elucidates historical trajectories in that they recover "depth dimensions of growth and change within the witness."[58] He also points out that the practice of recovering such historical trajectories is hermeneutically different from the historical-critical practice of reconstruction which does not distinguish between witness and source. Besides, he affirms the plain sense of the scriptural witness as the literal sense for the community of faith, while he allows for multiple senses of Scripture for their ongoing life.[59]

Accordingly, Childs uses the argument of the essential theological unity of both Testaments to adopt a holistic reading of the Bible: "What binds the Testaments indissolubly together is their witness to the selfsame divine reality, to the subject matter, which undergirds both collections."[60]

So, for Childs, biblical exegesis moves dialogically between the witness of the text and the reality of the subject matter the text refers to. He affirms that biblical theology knows a similar movement and that the hermeneutical circle also works vice versa from the reality of God back to the witness of the text. In other words, not only does the text testify to the reality of God, but also the reality of God relates to the text and its interpretation: "Through the Spirit the reality to which the text points, namely to Jesus Christ, is made active in constantly fresh forms

---

56. See Heb 11:17–19; Childs, *Biblical Theology of OT and NT*, 325–36.
57. See Isa 53:3–5; Childs, *Biblical Theology of OT and NT*, 337–47.
58. Childs, *Biblical Theology of OT and NT*, 264.
59. Childs, *Biblical Theology of OT and NT*, 725.
60. Childs, *Biblical Theology of OT and NT*, 721.

of application."[61] This implies that Childs attributes to the Holy Spirit a significant interpretive and hermeneutical role.

3.2.4 Summary and Outlook

At times, Childs felt misunderstood both by conservative proponents and liberal opponents.[62] This is what he expressed in his final book.[63] Yet, this only demonstrates that Childs does not fit into any Procrustean bed.

Some may think that Brevard Childs and his ideas have undergone a certain change throughout the decades of his scholarly life, as Daniel Driver pointed out.[64] Nevertheless, Childs' canonical commitment has undoubtedly remained unchanged from his early period on and can safely be considered the heart of his work. Still, it is true that Childs and his oeuvre disclose the influence that historical-critical scholarly training had on his theological career.[65] Therefore, contrary to the opinion of some of his opponents, Childs understood and knew how to use historical-critical tools. All the same, he summarizes critically the historical-critical approach to Scripture because it has failed to identify the reality to which the scriptural witnesses point.[66] And so, he laments that various twentieth century theologies at times have silenced this reality, and finds fault with attempts which interpret the Bible in purely functional terms.

Such disapproval can be understood on the basis that, despite modern historical-critical questions, Childs takes into account the doctrinal

---

61. Childs, *Biblical Theology of OT and NT*, 724.

62. OT scholar Schultz, one of the earlier PhD students of Childs, confirms in "Childs' Contribution," 75: "Overall, however, Childs' work has received the same mixed responses within evangelical circles as within the broader academic community, although for different reasons"; so, the attempt of R. Rendtorff to introduce Childs' canonical approach in Germany in 1993 was welcomed by only a few, like Lohfink and Zenger. Rendtorff's own canonical approach was considered to range in proximity to a history-of-religions approach (cf. Schultz, "Childs' Contribution," 73). For a German discussion of canon, see also Childs, "Canon," 43–53.

63. Childs, *Struggle*; Sumpter, "Brevard Childs," 103–5.

64. See Driver, "Childs," 245.

65. Childs had received theological training in a Swiss-German historical-critical context. In connection with that, Petersen, "Brevard Childs," 9–19, reckons Childs' adherence to form criticism in his earlier years at Basel under scholars such as Baumgartner, a former student of Gunkel, turned into a commitment to the "canonical form" of Scripture.

66. Childs, *Biblical Theology of OT and NT*, 719–27.

traditions of a premodern history of reading.[67] In view of that, Childs may appear to some scholars, whether modern or postmodern, like a theological alien or a "brontosaur who survived cataclysm only to plod through a smouldering landscape."[68] As a matter of fact, scholarship has not always given Childs the regard he deserves, at least not in Germany.[69] His merit, however, of having presented a biblical theology approach with a full-scale horizon is irrefutable.[70]

Furthermore, Childs' particular contribution lies in distinguishing between the process of canon formation and its final textual form. This way, his model permits to preserve canonical unity and scriptural authority and facilitate a holistic reading of both Testaments.

In sum, Childs' theory is relevant for our inquiry, since a method which is based on the final textual form of the canon allows the discovery of layers of theological continuity and discontinuity of a theme running through Scripture. Thus, the historical trajectory of the theme of God's praise and God's presence, and their potential connection can be followed through the Old and New Testaments.

One of the most trenchant critics of Childs is James Barr, who represents a different canonical understanding in terms of an open canon.

3.3 James Barr: Biblical Theology and Canonical Criticism

James Barr provides his own definition of biblical theology:

> "Biblical theology is an aspect of exegesis, directed towards individual texts, parts of texts and interrelations between texts . . . and with openness to questions of truth-values as represented within the Bible, within the environing world cultures and within the religious/theological traditions that existed before it and were developed afterwards."[71]

---

67. Seitz, "Canonical Approach," 72.
68. Driver, "Childs," 248.
69. See critical German response in section 3.4.1.
70. Seitz, *Bible,* 1–7, and Olson, "Seeking," 55, confirm Childs' broad-scale scholarly horizon encompassing the intersection points of ancient text/modern faith, Jews/Christians, OT/NT, and biblical theology/dogmatic theology which shaped the structure of Childs' work throughout his career.
71. Barr, *Concept,* 251.

Apparently, Barr favors an open-ended canon and, as a result, would consider biblical theology rather in terms of a "descriptive" discipline.

3.3.1 Biblical Theology: A "Descriptive" or "Prescriptive" Discipline?

Concerning the relationship between the Old and the New Testaments, Barr even asserts that the contrast between them is of a theological and not simply of a historical nature, since in the New Testament "a new substance of revelation" can be found which was not fully revealed before.[72] Accordingly, he emphasizes the discontinuity between both Testaments.[73] At this point Barr struggles with his own model of a "pan-biblical theology," as he labels it.[74] He complains that in the attempt to achieve such a pan-biblical theology often one of the Testaments suffered from a lack of due attention while an over-emphasis was laid on the other. As Barr spells out, scholarship has not answered in a satisfying way the question how the New Testament relates to the Old.[75] Yet, one gets the impression that he simply criticizes where other scholars have failed to meet his norm of a pan-biblical theology without giving enough evidence himself of how such theology might work at a practical level.[76]

Then, the present and yet ancient issue Barr sees himself confronted with is: Does biblical theology have only a "descriptive" or also a "prescriptive" value? Does it only explain "what it meant" or also "what it means"? As he cautiously articulates, biblical theology needs to be open towards "questions of truth-values as represented within the Bible."[77] In actual fact, Barr supports the descriptive "what-it-meant" option because defining what the Bible means is for him tantamount to a prescriptive verdict which he may identify, if at all, at the level of systematic theology. Of course, no theological discipline can hold the claim of normative authority, since none of them represents an absolute norm (*norma normans*). Each theological discipline has only as much influence as it reflects the "truth values" of Scripture (*norma normata*). Hence, the

---

72. Barr, *Concept*, 373.
73. Barr, *Concept*, 186.
74. Barr, *Concept*, 4.
75. Barr, *Concept*, 172–88.
76. Barr, *Concept*, 362–77.
77. Barr, *Concept*, 251.

real question Barr faces up to is whether the canon sustains this "norm-giving" authority and biblical theology this "norm-reflecting" authority. Barr answers this question in the negative.

Barr grapples with Childs. He suspects Childs of maintaining a "normative," i.e., an authoritative claim in his canonical approach.[78] Hence, Barr accuses him of adhering to "theological fundamentalism" and "theological inerrancy."[79] Perhaps the reason can be found in that Barr denies that biblical theology in particular and theology in general could hold any of this "norm-reflecting" influence. This can be seen from his idea of theology as a mere "collection of different disciplines," whether theological or nontheological.[80]

3.3.2 Barr on Scripture, Tradition, and Canon

The concept of theology as a multi-disciplinary, reflective activity subject to discussion is based on Barr's conviction that the biblical material in its nature is not "theology" because much of it would not have this character. As he clarifies, "If they [the biblical texts] were theology in the proper sense, there would be no need for a discipline such as biblical theology."[81]

Furthermore, Barr places religious traditions inside and outside of Scripture at the same level: "'Today it is almost universally agreed that the Bible itself is a product of tradition. This makes it difficult to suppose that theological tradition within the Bible is wholly different in nature from theological tradition after (and, indeed, before, and in the midst) of the Bible."[82] This again makes it hard for him to concede that Scripture could hold a more prominent position than pre- or postscriptural, or any other extrascriptural tradition. Then, the key questions become: First, which norm is used to weigh these various traditions and, second, where does this norm come from? Where, for Barr, would the issue of scriptural authority come in? He does not provide an answer to these questions.

Consequently, this decline of borderlines between scriptural and extrascriptural traditions affects his canonical position: "We see how unsatisfactory the idea of a 'canon' is, for it implies a clear distinction

78. Barr, *Concept*, 401–12.
79. Barr, *Concept*, 437.
80. Barr, *Concept*, 83.
81. Barr, *Concept*, 248.
82. Barr, *Concept*, 214.

between scripture and non-scripture, inspired and non-inspired, divine and human, authoritative and non-authoritative, which very probably was not there."[83] As a result, Barr perceives canon as an open-ended body of texts defined only in a vague sense.[84] His canonical position can be summarized with his own words: "Scripture is essential, but canon is not."[85] Then again, Barr would go so far as to claim the existence of a canon for biblical theology that includes the Dead Sea Scrolls because they elucidate the content of the biblical canon. Nonetheless, this does not imply for him that "canons can give hermeneutical guidance and are intended to do this."[86] This contradictory statement again reflects Barr's understanding of biblical theology as a "nonprescriptive" discipline. It seems that he is suspicious of canons exercising "scriptural control of the religion," a position he firmly repudiates for New Testament Christianity.[87] Evidently, fear of control has also led him to strongly object scholars like Childs. For those reasons, Barr may be not be able to accept either the man or his approach.

As a corollary of Barr's mingling of scriptural and extrascriptural traditions, he regards the hermeneutical task of biblical theology for people of today's world as not being limited to Scripture alone, but also to include the interpretation of this world. Interestingly enough, he concedes that "It is not we who interpret the Bible, but the Bible which interprets us and our world."[88] As Barr makes clear, the biblical message may change because of a changed context. This is why he declares that a hermeneutical model of interpretation based on past meanings is misguided because its interaction affects different worlds in past and present. For him, meaning and message are not transferable. Still, the question remains: How can this biblical message interpret us and our world, as Barr demands? It appears that he does not provide a satisfying answer to this question. Still, precisely this is relevant for the present inquiry which seeks to offer biblical guidance for our worship culture.

---

83. Barr, *Holy Scripture*, 57.

84. Barr, *Concept*, 579; Barr, *Holy Scripture*, 71; Barr's understanding evokes the approach by Sanders as in section 3.2.

85. Barr, *Holy Scripture*, 63.

86. Barr, *Holy Scripture*, 67.

87. Barr, *Holy Scripture*, 64.

88. Barr, *Concept*, 202–3.

Obviously, Barr's argument hints at an important debate in hermeneutics about the "transferability" of meaning and message, which will also be touched on later in this chapter.

3.3.3 Summary

By identifying Scripture with tradition, whether prebiblical, biblical, or postbiblical, Barr obviously places extrabiblical traditions at the same level as biblical ones. As a result, his theory not only brings along the decline of canonical boundaries, but also of scriptural authority. Furthermore, his conviction that canon is of no hermeneutical value practically rules out any final-form approach to biblical texts. In addition to that, Barr tends to criticize other scholarly approaches rather than to present his own model of a biblical theology.

In sum, Barr's idea of an open-ended canon and his idea of biblical theology may not serve as a suitable example of how biblical theology could work in the context of our project that seeks to trace the theme of God's praise and God's presence through canonical texts.

3.4 Critique of the Canonical Approach

A concluding evaluation of the canonical approach will start with a critical response from German scholarship to the canonical approach of the Anglophone world.

3.4.1 A Critical German Response

The purpose of including a response from the German scholarly world to Anglophone canonical approaches is to make evident that this canon debate does not seem to have brought about any lasting outcome in Germany. As Childs remarks, the Germans had joined the contemporary international canon debate quite late, and this mainly in the context of a biblical theology discussion and an ecumenical, church-related dialogue.[89] Likewise, other Anglophone scholars observed the meagre results of this debate.[90] One gets the impression that in the German-speaking world a reorientation towards

---

89. Childs, *Canon*, 44, points to Protestant scholars such as Rendtorff and Oeming or Catholic scholars such as Lohfink and Dohmen.

90. Driver, "Childs," 243–78, esp. 247.

canon appears to be negligible with some of the crucial implications of a canonical approach for biblical theology being ignored.

This tendency can also be observed in the contemporary critical canon discussion in Germany. The debate is reflected in a volume comprising a variety of interdenominational contributions coming mainly, but not exclusively from the German ecumenical world, which is based on an ecumenical conference on canonical Bible exegesis and edited by Egbert Ballhorn and Georg Steins.[91] Melanie Köhlmoos provides a review of this work and the debate.[92] She summarizes that canonical exegesis has particularly been shaped by a characteristic application of the intertextual paradigm and by its basic understanding as a distinct theological discipline. Köhlmoos claims that a canonical approach is generally characterized by a decided distance from historical and/or diachronic approaches,[93] which, however, is a controversial issue, particularly in view of the above discussion about Childs.[94] Besides, this method may well be characterized by an affinity to literary exegesis, but this does not necessarily entail reception-orientation, as Köhlmoos also admits herself. One may agree with her assessment that canon does not owe its existence to an authoritative decision coming from the outside. Still, the inherent authority of the canonical texts is *only recognized and not created by the community of reception*. For that reason, not everyone may concur with her opinion that the result of canonical reading is produced by the reader.[95] Besides, the canonical approach has been considered a methodological subdiscipline of biblical theology, at least to some extent in the English-speaking world, and not a theological discipline in its own right, as she suggests.

---

91. Ballhorn and Steins, *Bibelkanon in der Bibelauslegung*.
92. Köhlmoos, "Kanon und Methode," 135–46 [Canon and Method].
93. For a diachronic reading see Egger and Wick, *Methodenlehre*, 221–37.
94. Köhlmoos, "Kanon und Methode," 136, writes: "Kanonische Exegese ist demnach geprägt von a) einer dezidierten Distanz zu historischen und/oder diachronen Ansätzen, b) einer Affinität zu rezeptions-orientierten Methoden der Literaturwissenschaft, c) einer charakteristischen Umsetzung des Intertextualitätsparadigmas und d) einer Begründung kanonischer Exegese als genuin theologischer Disziplin."
95. Köhlmoos, "Kanon und Methode," 140–42, together with Müllner holds: "Der Kanon verdankt sich keiner von außen an die Schriftensammlung angelegten autoritativen Entscheidung, sondern wächst organisch aus der Rezeptionsgemeinschaft heraus." And Köhlmoos, "Kanon und Methode," 140–42, together with Pellegrini opines: "Das Ergebnis einer kanonischen Lektüre ist ein Produkt des Lesers."

Biblical Theology—a Distinct Discipline and Its Methods   69

Furthermore, Köhlmoos assumes a tension between the fixed boundaries of canonical exegesis and the open nature of intertextuality.[96] In order to solve that tension, canonical exegesis could only work with a restricted and limited understanding of intertextuality and would be characterized by the search for "privileged inter-texts."[97] Given such restriction, she wonders whether it is still justified to speak of intertextuality in connection with the canonical model. Yet, the actual issue lies in that canon is identified as an open process on the side of the community of reception allegedly producing canonical texts. Köhlmoos rightly acknowledges the difference between such understanding and Childs' approach. She even concedes that canonical exegesis according to Childs could be fertile when it comes to perceiving biblical texts comprehensively and in their respective contexts, a statement one can only support.[98]

3.4.2 Summary and Evaluation

As has been expounded, the canonical approach of Childs not only values the unity of Scripture without which the canon of both Testaments cannot serve as foundation for biblical theology, but also allows room for its diversity by listening separately to the voice of each biblical book. As a result, this method allows tracing the theme of God's praise and God's presence through individual biblical texts while permitting a synoptic perspective on the trajectories detected on this journey.

The main asset of that canonical approach undoubtedly lies in its high regard for the basic nature of the biblical texts which affects the choice of method.[99] Childs provokes divergent interpretive questions which arise when biblical texts are being read in their final canonical form, a clash which is adequately summarized in the statement by Mark Brett: "What we have here is foremost a conflict of interpretative interests and not a substantive conflict on method at all."[100] This clash of different interpretive interests can hardly be avoided if the nature of the text is

---

96. Köhlmoos, "Kanon und Methode," 140–42.
97. Köhlmoos, "Kanon und Methode," 136.
98. Köhlmoos, "Kanon und Methode," 145.
99. Similarly, the German scholars Stuhlmacher, *Biblical Theology*, 71–72, and Gese, *Alttestamentliche Studien*, 249, concur in that the nature and self-understanding of a text decide on the way to approach and comprehend it.
100. Brett, *Biblical Criticism*, 12.

regarded as impinging on the choice of the method. In sum, the hallmark of such canonical approach and its legacy for today is found in its "desire for comprehensiveness."[101] This challenge represents both its strengths and its weaknesses.

With regard to its weaknesses, Seitz points out that flaws were postulated by those who hold opposite views, which may rather enhance the appeal of the approach. Among such presumed faults Seitz cites dogmatic biases, a prejudiced preference of the final textual form, an insufficient attention to historical facts, and an overemphasis laid on the Old Testament at the expense of the New or vice versa. Others pronounced the canonical approach to be confusing and unworkable and, therefore, in need of "rehabilitation."[102] Similarly, Gerald Bray, biblical theology scholar, refers to critical remarks on the canonical approach to be self-contradictory and antihistorical: self-contradictory because it allows historical criticism at one level, while disallowing it at another, and antihistorical because it ignores the life-setting of the canonical redactors.[103] In spite of that, Childs discerns what the historical-critical method is able to do, namely to detect the origins and settings of the historical sources, but not to identify the message and meaning of the scriptural witnesses.

Moreover, some scholars, as could be seen with Barr, refer to a certain exclusiveness of Childs. Brett identifies a "totalitarian tendency," but at the same time he concedes that Childs pictures "a more pluralist situation" for biblical studies.[104] Nonetheless, if the method simply tries to do justice to the nature of the text, much of this criticism appears to be contradictory and not justified.

The contribution of German scholars allows insights into different canonical perspectives. Then again, identifying canon and authority in terms of an open process of reception on the side of the reading community is debatable, given that the intrinsic weight of the canonical texts can only be recognized and not created by this community. Besides, to speak of limited intertextuality in connection with a canonical approach seems bizarre in view of its undeniably comprehensive horizon.

In sum, the real issue at stake is whether in the near future biblical theology will be recognized as a distinct theological discipline in

---

101. Seitz, "Canonical Approach," 62–63.

102. Driver, "Childs," 244, points to scholars like Brett, *Biblical Criticism*, Noble, *Canonical Approach*, and Steins, *Bindung Isaaks* [Binding of Isaac].

103. Bray, *Biblical Interpretation*, 482.

104. Brett, *Biblical Criticism*, 11.

Germany and elsewhere. The canonical approach along with an intertextual model may well represent a good advertisement for biblical theology as a discipline in its own right. Still, this issue has not yet been solved in the present debate.

3.5 Narrative and Intertextual Models

Given the narrative genre of most of the texts analyzed in this study, in this section representative samples of narrative and intertextual models will be introduced. Particularly some intertextual models have been probed to what extent they may serve to explore a connection between human praise and divine presence in texts of both Testaments. Certain models, such as those by Brodie and Litwak,[105] have been applied to Luke-Acts which also contributes narrative texts to this study. At first, we will elucidate the difference between narrative, intertextual, and canonical models.

3.5.1 Narrative Criticism and Intertextuality

Intertextual models have often been applied in the narrative genre, although they function in other genres as well.

As to the difference between narrative and intertextual approaches, to put it simply: narrative approaches deal with the telling of stories examining the way in which a story is told and how this illuminates what the author is doing. Having originated in secular literary criticism, narratology has increasingly influenced biblical criticism in the last few decades. As a result, biblical texts are being perceived from the narrator's point of view as pieces of literature or discourse, skilfully planned, with plot, characterization, and dialogue. All the same, particularly narrative criticism, a subdiscipline of narratology, has been censured for not taking into account the historicity of the literature it deals with.[106] At the beginning of this millennium, narratology experienced a renaissance in the shape of cognitive narratology which came to inspire biblical hermeneutics, just as narrative criticism did in earlier decades.[107]

105. Brodie, *Birthing*, and Litwak, *Echoes*.
106. See Frei, *Eclipse*, and Frye, *Great Code*.
107. Sönke Finnern, *Narratologie* [Narratology], a German scholar and Lutheran pastor, claims that a "cognitive narratology" approach has the potential to mediate between historical-critical and evangelical camps. Narratology refers to a narratological

Intertextuality in the broadest sense of the term as used in literary sciences refers to structural, thematic, and terminological parallels between texts. It allows for repeated patterns opening up a wide horizon which extends beyond schemes of prophecy-fulfilment, quotations, allusions, and typology.[108] Scholars found it difficult to define the term "intertextual" given its polyvalence or multiple meanings, just as they found it problematic to identify the term "canonical."

At this point, Georg Steins attempts to close a methodological gap which he thinks Childs left.[109] Reading Steins one gets the impression that he wishes to advance Childs' canonical approach while holding on to historical-critical methodology.[110] In his own model, Steins blends canonical and intertextual readings in a "canonical-intertextual" reading of the Bible.[111] As a matter of fact, canonical and intertextual methods work at different levels. The canonical approach according to Childs considers the full perspective of both canons taking into account the salvation-historical progression from the old covenants to the new covenant. An intertextual model concentrates on trajectories between texts, even within one Testament only. Both methods may be combined, but such a combination requires clarifying the methodology because historical-critical premises would not work together with Childs' methodological principles. Still, combining an intertextual model with Childs' approach is possible, which offers a stimulus for our project.

Thomas Brodie, for example, uses an intertextual model to explain the development of the New Testament, which he applies in particular to Luke-Acts.[112] His literary study appears to represent a new version of source and redaction criticism under the label of intertextuality which he perceives as literary dependence. His central hypothesis is that "Proto-Luke," an assumed first version of Luke-Acts which replaces the Q hypothesis, had a major impact on the development of the gospels and other

---

approach in general, and narrative criticism to a specific approach within narratology coming particularly from the Anglophone scholarly world.

108. Litwak *Echoes*, 31–34.

109. Steins, *Bindung Isaaks*, 2.

110. On the methodological foundations of such a canonical-intertextual reading see Steins, *Bindung Isaaks*, 9–102, 103–224, which he exemplifies with Abraham in Gen 22; see also Steins, *Kanonisch-Intertextuelle Studien*, 169–82 [Canonical-Intertextual Studies].

111. Steins, *Bindung Isaaks*, 45–83.

112. Brodie, *Birthing*, 258–74.

New Testament writings. Brodie presumes this Proto-Luke to be fed by Deuteronomy and Chronicles and to feed again into New Testament texts starting with Matthew's logia and 1 Corinthians, to be followed by Mark and Matthew down to Luke-Acts.[113] Since Deuteronomy epitomizes the narrative tradition from Genesis to Kings, Brodie identifies intertextuality, for example, between the Elijah-Elisha narratives and Proto-Luke with Luke-Acts.[114]

Basically, Brodie's complex theory claims that existing texts, e.g., Deuteronomy and 1 Corinthians, were transformed when feeding into Proto-Luke and, thus, into Luke-Acts.[115] During the course of Brodie's comprehensive book, a difficulty becomes more and more obvious, i.e., a confusing hypothesis about a process of multiple and reciprocal "resourcing." All the same, Brodie's ideas may be stimulating in that they encourage the search for intertextual trajectories between narrative passages in 1 Kings 8, 2 Chronicles 5, and Acts 2, texts which feature in this study.

In a different way, Kenneth Litwak assesses intertextuality in Luke-Acts in terms of intertextual echoes and the frequency with which textual patterns are supposed to be repeated.[116] For Litwak, intertextual echoes are understood as "transumption" or "metalepsis," i.e., the way in which one text is transformed by the echo of a former; these echoes would pervade Luke's narrative and create "echo chambers," i.e., rooms which enable hearing intertextual messages.[117] Litwak, referring to Tannen, calls the structure of these echo chambers "framing-in discourse."[118] Accordingly, Luke 1–2 and Acts 28 would form the frame for the entire discourse in Luke-Acts. Consequently, Litwak asks how Luke creates frames and

---

113. Brodie, *Birthing*, 536–37, esp. 282–537 (part 3).

114. Brodie, *Birthing*, xxviii–xxx, 82–144.

115. Brodie, *Birthing*, xxx; Brodie's charts are helpful to understand his complex theory.

116. Litwak, *Echoes*, 35–65; Litwak has been influenced among others by Hays, *Echoes of Scripture*, who hears "intertextual echoes" in Paul; Litwak, *Echoes*, 62–63, develops two of Hays' criteria for discovering echoes: availability and volume.

117. Litwak, *Echoes*, 52.

118. Litwak, *Echoes*, 55–60; the concept of framing-in discourse is based on the contextual meaning of metanarrative in discourse analysis, see Runge and Levinsohn, "Discourse Studies"; in connection with Acts, see Levinsohn, *Textual Connections*; a similar model of narratological-literary discourse analysis has been applied to Luke-Acts by McCollough, *Ritual Water*, 43–80. On an intertextual reading of Acts see Mallen, *Reading and Transformation*, who explores how Luke uses and transforms material from Isaiah.

which interpretational function these frames serve. The purpose of Luke's framing would be to make his audience hear echoes, e.g., of the transfiguration of Moses (Exod 19), as they listen to the story of Jesus' transfiguration (Luke 9).[119] Such prominent themes serve as an interpretative frame for the whole discourse. For Litwak, the purpose of framing-in discourse is to show continuity between the people of Israel and the early Christian movement, a continuity which serves ecclesiological purposes, namely to legitimate the true people of God in the present. This idea may well apply not only to the true people of God, but also to their worship.

Litwak's main argument in sum: Luke's usage of Scripture in connection with intertextual echoes is much broader than the restricted space of direct quotations and obvious allusions would allow.[120] Moreover, this framing-in discourse extends beyond typology and promise-fulfilment schemes, which hold on tightly to comparative reference points (contra Marshall and others).[121] The advantage of Litwak's stimulating study is that no programmatic element puts the biblical message into a Procrustean bed. Canonical texts are allowed to speak and resonate for themselves. His line of reasoning in favor of framing-in discourse is persuasive in that it allows for a broad horizon, which coheres well with biblical theology and narrative texts.

3.6 Some Contemporary Hermeneutical Models

After having sampled narrative and intertextual paradigms, in this section, some hermeneutical models which are characteristic of the recent discussion will be introduced. They have been tested as to whether they are compatible with biblical theology and its methods and suitable to apply the results of this inquiry to the real-world setting of Christian worship.

Naturally, this study needs to be limited to a representative selection, which does not mean that scholars in biblical theology whose models have not been dealt with are considered negligible. This applies, for example, to Francis Watson and his so-called "evangelical" hermeneutics which limits Scripture to gospel.[122] Or to Walter Brueggemann, a repre-

---

119. Litwak, *Echoes*, 58–60.
120. Litwak, *Echoes*, 31.
121. Litwak, *Echoes*, 59–61.
122. Watson, "Gospel and Scripture," 371, esp. 161–82; the new "arithmetic" in Watson's biblical theology approach goes as follows: gospel equals God-speech, and

sentative of postmodern social-critical thinking, and his hermeneutics of "hurt and hope" which aims at a social-critical deconstruction and reconstruction of textual interpretation.[123]

At the occasion of the FEET conference at Berlin, Germany, in 2010, the late Howard Marshall presented an overview of the more recent hermeneutical debate.[124] Marshall criticized contemporary evangelicalism for restricting themselves mainly to identifying principles in the text and applying them. He observed that many scholars still limit themselves to this hermeneutical approach, although they admit that changes in social and cultural situations require an adaptation of the biblical principles. Whether one approves of such approach or not affects the practical application of the results of this study in the area of present-day Christian worship. Marshall illustrated his critique using four examples of hermeneutical methods in contemporary evangelicalism: Kaiser, Doriani, Vanhoozer, and Webb.[125]

3.6.1 Walter Kaiser Jr.: "A Principlizing Model"

Walter Kaiser advocates a "principlizing" hermeneutical model:[126] Starting with a specific biblical text the interpreter moves up a "ladder of abstraction" attempting to identify the "generalizing principle," which may lie behind the text, and then moves downward trying to apply this principle in a new cultural context.[127] The lower on the ladder, the more

---

God-speech equals Scripture; therefore, gospel equals Scripture, an equation which is based on Watson's understanding of promise overruling law.

123. Brueggemann and Miller, *Old Testament Theology*, 145–46; Brueggemann's hermeneutics aims at deconstructing contrary and controlling ideologies in the community of interpretation before reconstructing the "social dynamics" of the text; one wonders whether social-critical categories, like hurt and hope, construct a Procrustean bed into which "words from God" are pressed or stretched accordingly, which, again, would defeat the purpose of entering into the "dynamics of the text." For that reason, the social-critical hermeneutics of Brueggemann is not convincing.

124. Marshall's paper is reflected in his article "Evangelical NT Interpretation," 4–14.

125. The volume by Gundry and Meadors, *Four Views*, is based on a symposium with the title *Four Views on Moving beyond the Bible to Theology*; it compiles and compares four different and yet complementary methods of interpreting Scripture; see Marshall, "Evangelical NT Interpretation," 10–13.

126. Kaiser, "Principlizing Model," 19–50; see also Kaiser and Silva, *Introduction to Biblical Hermeneutics*;

127. Kaiser, "Principlizing Model," 24–27.

culturally-bound, the higher on the ladder, the more abstract and universal the principles are. Kaiser illustrates his theory through the examples of slavery, the role of women, homosexuality, embryonic stem cell research, abortion, and euthanasia.[128] This "process of principlizing," as Kaiser argues, is not going beyond Scripture, but applying its principles more widely.[129] He acknowledges progressive revelation in that there is "perfection of revealed truth at all stages along the process, albeit in "seminal form."[130] This view makes Kaiser infer that Paul avows the abolition of slavery, which is still a contested issue among scholars.[131]

Marshall argued that this "process of principlizing" represents a change of principle rather than a change of application, since we are not dealing with the relationship between slave-owner and slave any more, but between that of employer and employee.[132] These issues reveal that the boundaries between fresh applications and new principles are not easily to be defined. For example, if we discover a connection between God's praise and God's presence in texts of both Testaments, should we then apply this finding to charismatic worship as a biblical principle with a new application or as an altogether new principle? How do we decide which biblical principle or application is appropriate in the face of the challenges of today's charismatic worship?

3.6.2 Daniel Doriani: A "Redemptive-Historical Model"

Daniel Doriani presents a "redemptive-historical" hermeneutics which relates to a progressive revelation within the history of salvation.[133]

First, Doriani places narrative material alongside didactic, propositional material, thus, underlining the indirect impact of its instruction.[134] This also applies to our study, as most of the texts analyzed belong to the narrative genre. Then, Doriani presents an agenda of "right questions" which he addresses to a biblical passage asking what we can learn from

---

128. Kaiser, "Principlizing Model," 28–45.
129. Kaiser, "Principlizing Model," 26.
130. Kaiser, "Principlizing Model," 47.
131. Kaiser, "Principlizing Model," 73.
132. Marshall, "Evangelical Interpretation," 6.
133. Doriani, "Redemptive-Historical Model," 75–120; Marshall, "Evangelical Interpretation," 6.
134. Doriani, "Redemptive-Historical Model," 86–88.

it about duty, fine character, valuable goals, and biblical vision.[135] This way, he aims at "distilling" a principle from a biblical text and applying it to new situations.[136] This method is not so much different from Kaiser's principlizing approach.

Although practicing similar methods, Kaiser and Doriani arrive at different conclusions, e.g., regarding the place of women in the church. Doriani applies the principle he "distilled" from biblical texts on women with the result that women may not preach or teach authoritatively.[137] Yet, neither of the two, as Marshall complains, examines the modern Christian and non-Christian world to see which factors make people uneasy about the hierarchist position.[138] This point may encourage us to inquire into the factors that make people uneasy about some issues of charismatic worship which were brought up in the last chapter.

3.6.3 Kevin Vanhoozer: "A Drama-of-Redemption Model"

Kevin Vanhoozer identifies an on-going "drama of redemption" in which we take our place on the stage of life working out individually and corporately what the text is saying to us.[139] He is essentially concerned with our involvement as actors in this drama who show their understanding of Scripture by doing God's will and not just discussing it. This is what for him biblical interpretation is about. We would have to interpret Scripture by living and acting it out: "*Sacra pagina* is profitable for *sacra doctrina*, which again is profitable for *sacra vita*."[140]

Vanhoozer claims that as participants in this redemptive-historical "theodrama" we must find the big picture by cultivating some kind of canonical sense of its script.[141] Key questions to help us grasp the performance of this drama are: Who and where are we in this theodrama?[142] What is God doing and what is our role? In this connection, Vanhoozer

---

135. Doriani, "Redemptive-Historical Model," 99–103.

136. Doriani, "Redemptive-Historical Model," 105.

137. Doriani, "Redemptive-Historical Model," 117.

138. Marshall, "Evangelical Interpretation," 7.

139. Vanhoozer, "Drama-of-Redemption Model," 151–99; Marshall, "Evangelical Interpretation," 7.

140. Vanhoozer, "Drama-of-Redemption Model," 155.

141. Vanhoozer, "Drama-of-Redemption Model," 155–59.

142. Vanhoozer, "Drama-of-Redemption Model," 162–65; Marshall, "Evangelical Interpretation," 7.

insists that our "interpretive performance" is not about us extracting or applying a principle, but living our understanding of the drama of redemption.[143] This means that at times we perform the missing final act in this theodrama, which requires of the actors the skill of contextual judgment.[144] The author illustrates his approach through the example of transsexuality.[145]

One wishes to concur with Vanhoozer in that Scripture reading is not only meant to lead to intellectual understanding, but also to changed action and character. Still, how could this "theodramatic performance" be spelled out practically in the context of human praise and divine presence? The relevant questions would then be: Who and where are we in this worship relationship with God? What is God doing and what is our role in praise? Besides, would it be appropriate to label a life of worship "theodrama"?

3.6.4 William Webb: "A Redemptive-Movement Model"

William Webb advocates a dynamic hermeneutics in connection with cultural and transcultural analysis.[146] This hermeneutical model concentrates on trajectories in understanding and practice which exist in Scripture itself. According to him, these trajectories lead us to new patterns of living which are scripturally based and in continuity with Scripture, but take us beyond an "isolated or static understanding."[147] This is what Webb calls "movement meaning" inherent in Scripture, which can be seen from the "logical extensions of its redemptive spirit trajectories."[148] He illustrates these trajectories by the examples of slavery and corporal punishment.[149]

---

143. Vanhoozer, "Drama-of-Redemption Model," 170.

144. Vanhoozer, "Drama-of-Redemption Model," 174–86.

145. Vanhoozer, "Drama-of-Redemption Model," 186–97.

146. Webb, "Redemptive-Movement Model," 215–48; Marshall, "Evangelical Interpretation," 8–12; Webb also elucidates this cultural analysis in *Slaves,* 67–72.

147. Webb, "Redemptive-Movement Model," 215.

148. Webb, "Redemptive-Movement Model," 217.

149. Webb, "Redemptive-Movement Model," 219–28, 228–48; Webb, *Slaves,* 263–68, gives another example of a redemptive-movement model in connection with women in 1 Tim 2:13: he interprets the primogeniture argument as a cultural-component value and ends up with a "complementary egalitarianism" or an "ultra-soft patriarchy."

Webb asserts this dynamic movement cannot cease with canonization and, therefore, the tracks found in Scripture contain the momentum to take its application further. Such an approach is canonical in as far as it recognizes canon as the result of progressive revelation. Still, one may want to join Marshall who in his overall favorable critique asks how these trajectories are to be recognized and tested.[150]

As attractive as this dynamic hermeneutical model may appear, one needs to be aware that it could lead to an opening of canonical boundaries.

3.7 Summary

The question raised at the beginning of this chapter was: How can we benefit from biblical theology and its hermeneutical paradigms for the interpretation of texts from both Testaments which deal with a connection between divine presence and human praise?

To approach this question, the historical background of biblical theology as a distinct discipline was elucidated, which revealed the following major tendencies: the critical source analysis of the nineteenth century with a history of religion approach was followed by a concern for theological synthesis in the twentieth century, development which affected the issue of unity of both Testaments. Similarly, the contemporary debate dealing with the canonical issue revealed two main challenges for biblical theology: first, the argument against confining the Bible as defined in canon; and second, the argument against the theological unity of the biblical authors and books.

In view of that, representative methods in biblical theology were tested, the canonical approach by Brevard Childs along with the contrasting view of James Barr, to be followed by a German critique. Finally, an overview introduced samples of current intertextual models and hermeneutical paradigms which were put to the test regarding their relevance for this study.

As a result, the canonical approach of Childs offers a significant alternative to the historical-critical method in the discipline of biblical theology which allows preserving the unity of canon and the authority of Scripture while respecting their diversity.

By and large, the canonical debate revealed conflicting interpretative interests depending on how one perceives the nature of the text.

---

150. Marshall, "Evangelical Interpretation," 9–13.

This became clear in the work of antagonists of Childs such as James Barr or of German critics. The question whether in the near future biblical theology could be acknowledged as an independent theological discipline in Germany, or whether even a canonical approach could be accepted as a method among others in this setting still remained unanswered in the debate.

As far as intertextual models are concerned, Brodie's hypothesis of literary dependence with the example from Luke-Acts revealed a confusing speculation about a process of multiple "resourcing" and proved to be too complex and controversial to be suitable. Litwak's approach of intertextual echoes within a framing-in discourse is more beneficial in that it allows for a broad horizon which is coherent with biblical theology and consistent with narratives and their purposes.

The contemporary hermeneutical debate made clear that no method should be considered on its own, whether we deal with the principlizing method of Kaiser, the redemptive-historical approach of Doriani, the drama-of-redemption hypothesis of Vanhoozer, or, the most valuable of all, the redemptive-movement model of Webb.

In sum, it can be proposed that biblical theology as a theological discipline in its own right and a canonical-intertextual approach as method promote the purpose of our study, i.e., to explore the theme of a relationship between God's praise and God's presence in canonical texts of both Testaments. This is what the textual analyses in the two chapters to follow attempt to spell out.

4.0

God's Glory-Presence in the Praises of His People in the Old Testament

Sorry, Old Testament: most theologians don't use you.

—CALEB LINDGREN

THE CONCEPT OF DIVINE presence in our context is understood to relate to a specific divine presence among God's people which shows differing degrees of intensification in contrast to a general divine presence in the created order.[1]

The first two sections of this chapter will deal with the narratives of the dedication of the first temple built by King Solomon exploring a correlation between the praises of God's people and his presence in the passages of 1 Kings 8 and 2 Chronicles 5–7. These texts were chosen because they depict the initial infilling of the Lord's first temple with his glory in the context of his people's praise. The question raised here is whether God's glory in his temple, a specific form of his presence, prompted his people's praise and whether this praise persuaded God to fill his new temple with his glory-presence again. Hence, exegetical aspects which go beyond this issue will not be dealt with. Similarities and differences between the two passages will be highlighted. The structural analyses will take into account the sequence of events and literary structure. The exegetical analyses will consider aspects of grammar and semantic structure.

---

1. Fretheim, *Suffering*, 60–61; for different modes of divine presence see also ch. 6, section 6.2.4.

The third section of this chapter will look at a potential connection between human praise and divine presence beyond the temple context in some conflict narratives: Joshua 6:20 (Joshua and the battle at Jericho) and similarly 2 Chronicles 20:22 (Jehoshaphat leading God's people in battle), then 1 Samuel 16:23 (David playing the harp before Saul) and 2 Kings 3:15 (Elisha and the minstrel), as well as Psalm 22:3 (God inhabiting the praises of Israel). There, the question asked is whether God's people's praise instigated manifestations of divine presence.

The fourth section will touch briefly on some examples of praise psalms, Psalms 145–50, but only in as far as there might be a link with the above texts, even if there is no presence-praise connection. Likewise, the perspective of God's glory-presence in his temple in Ezekiel is only mentioned in brief, e.g., in Ezekiel 10, 11, and 43, even if there is no immediate context of praise.

The fifth section will summarize terminology and concepts of divine presence and human praise occurring together in the above settings.

4.1 Divine Presence and Human Praise in 1 Kings 8: Temple Inauguration

4.1.1 Introduction

The books of 1 and 2 Kings serve as a sequel to 1 and 2 Samuel and describe the history of Israel's monarchy from the end of King David's rule and the beginning of King Solomon's reign throughout the divided kingdoms of Israel and Judah until the Babylonian Exile. Israel's kingship is regulated by the covenant between God and his people. Accordingly, the general theme in 1 and 2 Kings, presumably written in exilic times, is that the welfare of God's people and their kings depended on their obedience to the Sinai covenant. Hence, both books intend to demonstrate to God's people the consequences of their disobedience through a retrospective analysis of the history which finally led to the Exile.[2] The purpose of this

---

2. The writer of 1 and 2 Kgs relied on sources previously written like those of the annals of Solomon (1 Kgs 11:41), the annals of the kings of Judah (1 Kgs 14:19 and 15:7, 23), or the annals of the kings of Israel (1 Kgs 16:20); these annals represent common sources which also might have been used by the writer of 1 and 2 Chronicles. The temporal indicator "to this day" in 1 Kgs 8:8b points to the time of such earlier sources. Former source-critical scholarship unanimously attributed 1 Kgs 8 to a "Deuteronomistic" writer who relied on earlier sources which he supposedly adapted and expanded (cf. de Vries, *1 Kings*, 121).

God's Glory-Presence in the Praises of His People in the Old Testament 83

demonstration may have been to restore the remnant of Judah and their people to their covenant with God. This purpose could be seen to be supported by the specific function of conditional prophecies and their fulfilment or non-fulfilment, which is stated time and again. For example, 1 Kings 6:12–13 affirm in the context of the temple building process God's conditional promise of his presence to King Solomon, and 1 Kings 9:1–9 refer to the fulfilment of this promise. So, if Solomon and his royal successors keep the commandments of the covenant, God would keep "residing" in his temple. This aspect of God's abiding covenant presence in connection with the covenant fidelity of his people touches the core of our inquiry.³

4.1.2 Sequence of Events and Structure in 1 Kings 8

The sequence of events represents one of the main criteria which determine narrative and literary structure.⁴ Textual markers in Hebrew indicate that the flow of the narrative may go beyond the actual dedication ceremony. These narrative markers occur at the beginning of almost every other verse, e.g., in v.1 (then), v.5 (*waw-narrativum/consecutivum*), v.10 (copulative *waw* in the *wayehi* construction), v.12 (then), v.14 (consecutive *waw* plus imperf.), v.15 (consecutive *waw* plus imperf.), vv.17–18 (*wayehi*), vv.20–21 (consecutive *waw* plus imperf.), vv.22–23 (consecutive *waw* plus imperf.) etc. Although the marker in 1 Kings 9:1 (*wayehi*) points to the completion of all of Solomon's building projects, reasons of logic advise to include 1 Kings 9:1–9 as the explanation of the events depicted in 1 Kings 8:⁵ God appears to King Solomon in a theophanic dream or vision and confirms the consecration of the temple through his presence.⁶ The added admonition

---

3. See ch. 6, section 6.3 in connection with covenant.

4. Some scholars suggest a three-part division in 1 Kgs 8: first, the ark brought to the temple in vv.1–21; second, Solomon's prayer of dedication in vv.22–53; and, third, blessing, dedication, and feast in vv.54–66 (cf. Keil and Delitzsch, *1 and 2 Kings*, 3:117–18; de Vries, *1 Kings*, 122).

5. Similarly, Noth, *Könige*, 197, points to a connection between Solomon's prayer in ch. 8 and God's response in ch. 9 independently from any temporal connection; see also Walsh, *1 Kings*, 117; equally, de Vries, *1 Kings*, 120, in his commentary extends the structure from 1 Kgs 7:51b to 9:9. This extension could be justified given that God appeared twice to Solomon as in 1 Kgs 3:4–5 and 1 Kgs 9:1–9, both instances in the context of the king's covenantal fidelity. The third theophanic appearance in 1 Kgs 11:9–13 alludes to Solomon's covenantal infidelity and its consequences.

6. For the dedication of houses see Deut 20:5 and 28:30: it was normal in Israel to

expresses a warning: God would dwell in this temple and among his people as long as they keep their covenant, but censure disobedience by removing his presence from the temple and Israel from the land. Hence, we will concentrate on the section about the dedication of the first temple narrated in 1 Kings 8:1—9:1–9, which narrates God's presence in the context of his people's praise.[7]

1. The king assembled the leaders of Israel (1 Kgs 8:1–3); the priests and Levites carried the ark of the covenant of the Lord, symbol of divine presence, with its tent from the city of David to the temple on Mount Moriah (8:4).[8]

2. King and congregation offered animal sacrifices (8:5).

3. The priests brought the ark to its destined place into the Holy of Holies under the wings of the cherubim (8:6) followed by the explanatory remarks (8:7–9) that the ark contained only the stone tablets with the commandments of the Sinai covenant (8:9).

4. When the priests left the inner sanctuary, God's glory-cloud filled his house so that no priestly ministry was possible anymore (8:10–11). This phenomenon was explained by Solomon in terms of God taking his perpetual residence in the temple as promised (8:12–13).

5. Solomon offered blessings (blessing congregation in v.14 and blessing God in vv.15–21).

6. The king offered a prayer of supplication to God (8:22–53) and addressed words of blessing to God and congregation (8:54–61).

7. For the dedication ceremony of the temple, king and congregation offered animal sacrifices as peace offerings (8:62–64).

8. This was followed by a seven day public feast (1 Kgs 8:65–66).

9. After Solomon together with priests and Levites had accomplished the dedication, God appeared again to him confirming that he had

---

dedicate a house by taking residence there (cf. Hurowitz, *I Have Built*, 266–67).

7. Scholars attempted to solve a calendar problem in 1 Kgs 8:2: the dedication was dated in *Ethanim*, the seventh month—*Tishri* according to the Babylonian calendar—in a way that either the temple was dedicated in the seventh month before its total completion in the eighth, or that the ceremony took place eleven months later (cf. Montgomery, *Kings*, 187–88; also Robinson, *First Kings*, 94). According to 1 Kgs 8:2, the dedication of the temple was followed by the autumn harvest feast which usually took place in the seventh month marking the beginning of the New Year.

8. See 2 Sam 6:16.

consecrated the house by placing his presence there (his name, eyes, and heart) (9:3).

10. A divine admonition to keep the covenant was addressed to Solomon, combined with a warning (9:4–9).

The sequence of the events in 1 Kings 8 indicates human and divine interaction.[9] This is epitomized particularly in vv.10–11 where the ark is brought into the temple with sacrifices offered before and after, and the temple is filled with God's glory-cloud:

A1 Human action: covenant compliance by observing divine stipulations as to the ark of the covenant and sacrifice offerings to God (8:1–10)

   B1 Divine action: cloud filling the Lord's house (8:10–11)

     X No human action: no further priestly ministry (8:11)

   B2 Divine action (as explanation): God's glory in his house (8:11)

A2 Human action: Solomon blessing the congregation/God and offering prayers and praise followed by dedication ceremony and sacrifices (8:14–66)[10]

   B3 Divine action: God confirming the cloud as phenomenon of his abiding presence depending on the covenant obedience of his people (9:1–9).

This sequence of events depicts a frequent interaction throughout the entire chapter eight between human activity in terms of offerings, prayer and praise, and divine activity in terms of cloud and glory. These human-divine activities form a chiastic pattern:

A1–B1–X–B2–A2–B3 with divine glory and power in 8:10–11 forming a bracket, thus, emphasizing the centre of the chiasm, which pinpoints priestly powerlessness.[11]

Apparently, the sequence of events does not provide enough evidence to allow the conclusion that human activity in terms of God's

---

9. A: human activity, B: divine activity, X: centre of chiasm.

10. The ceremony of dedication was characteristic of later temple worship which consisted of offerings and also praise in the outer temple area (cf. Farrar, *First Kings*, 193).

11. Walsh, *Style and Structure*, 68, calls the structure in 1 Kgs 6–9 a "framing inclusion", but there are inclusions in a chiastic structure, too; for chiastic structures in Kings and Chronicles cf. Walsh, *Style and Structure*, 28–29.

people's prayer and praise can be considered an instrumental condition for divine action in terms of God's glory and presence entering his house. The repeated emphasis on covenant compliance rather suggests that human obedience is required for the Lord to dwell permanently in his temple and among his people.[12]

In this exegesis emphasis will be laid on 1 Kings 8:10–13 epitomizing human and divine interaction:

4.1.3 Exegetical Analysis: 1 Kings 8:10–13[13]

> **10**When the priests left the sanctuary, the cloud filled the house of the Lord so that the priests could not stand to minister on account of (literally: in front of) the cloud **11**because the glory of the Lord had filled the house of the Lord. **12**Then Solomon said: The Lord had promised to live in the thick cloud. **13**I have certainly built a grand house for you, a place for you to dwell forever.[14]

The first phrase in v.10, which is introduced by *wayehi* "and it happened," indicates a temporal direction.[15] The terms עָנָן "cloud" and כְּבוֹד־יְהוָה "glory of the Lord" are used here in an almost synonymous way to describe the presence of the Lord: "Cloud was the symbol of the divine presence. The word which was used to express that presence theologically was glory . . . The glory of the Lord was the outward indication of his presence and his nature."[16] Or, the cloud serves as a "visible sign of YHWH's hidden presence," while the glory is the sign of his "more immediate presence."[17] Although this distinction was originally applied to the tabernacle, it also

---

12. See chapter 6, section 6.3.2.

13. The Hebrew text follows BHS based on Leningrad Codex, the LXX is partly more restricted than the MT which reveals an expansion in vv.12–13; it is difficult to explain this textual characteristic as the cleaning process of a Greek translator, as Hurowitz, *I Have Built*, 262–64, does. Besides, since Wellhausen, 1 Kgs 8:1–11 has been understood to represent late priestly expansions; for differences between Greek and Hebrew textual versions see van Keulen, *Two Versions*, 151–80.

14. The English translation represents the author's translation based on the ESV, which applies to all subsequent Scripture citations.

15. The *wayehi*-construction of the verb *hayah* with a copulative *waw* (waw-consecutivum plus imperf.) followed by another verb in infinitive construct plus preposition serves a narrative purpose in temporal clauses (cf. Lambdin and von Siebenthal, *Bibel-Hebräisch*, 107; also Schneider, *Grammatik*, 212).

16. Robinson, *First Kings*, 96; see Lev 16:2b.

17. Hundley, *Keeping Heaven on Earth*, 46–47.

God's Glory-Presence in the Praises of His People in the Old Testament

relates to the temple. Both terms "cloud" and "glory" describe theophany, a metaphorical rhetoric expressing a specific form of divine presence which recalls Exodus 19:16; 24:16–18; 40:34–38; Leviticus 9:23–24; and Numbers 9:15–23.[18] The intertextual echoes in these texts reverberate the continuity of the Mosaic covenant: the Lord's presence is revealed *in* the Solomonic temple just as *on* the Mosaic tabernacle and *on* Mount Sinai.[19] The glory of the Lord marks this form of God's immediate presence.[20]

The verb in perfect *qal* מָלֵא "to fill" or "to be full of" conveys the Lord's presence filling the house like water filling a glass to the brim.[21] We will come back to the verbal metaphor of filling/infilling.[22]

The subordinate clause in v.11 "so that they were not able 'to stand to minister'" (MT: לַעֲמֹד לְשָׁרֵת with verbs in infinitive construct *qal* and *piel*) signifies that the Lord's presence was so powerful that the priests could not carry out their proper duties anymore, which was the offering of sacrifices. The subsequent explanatory clause tells the reason for the priestly powerlessness: "For the Lord's glory had filled the Lord's house" (LXX: καὶ δόξα κυρίου ἔπλησεν τὸν οἶκον). It was not priestly ministry which made the Lord's glory-presence enter the sanctuary, but the Lord's glory that rendered priestly service impossible: divine glory activity ruled out human sacrifice activity—what a key consequence![23] And what a

---

18. Brueggemann, *1 and 2 Kings*, 106; similarly, Kline, "Creation in the Image," 250–72, on God's theophanic glory; or Fretheim, *Suffering*, 79–84, on theophanies; Austin, *Glory of God*, 41–57, again, reduces the Lord's glory to divine attributes, which are somewhat limited in comparison with the Lord's glorious presence.

19. See also the textual parallels in 2 Chr 5:14 and 7:2; the theme of covenant continuity is also supported by Robinson, *First Kings*, 94, and Keil and Delitzsch, *1 and 2 Kings*, 3:122.

20. Hundley, *Keeping Heaven on Earth*, 54–55, asserts that 1 Kgs 8 has affinities with ANET accounts with regard to God/the deity entering the consecrated tabernacle/temple, which is indicated through his glorious presence.

21. For grammar analysis see Owens, *Analytical Key*, 441; Beall and Banks, *Parsing Guide*, 280–81.

22. See ch. 5, section 5.2.2, and ch. 6, section 6.2.

23. Robinson, *First Kings*, 95, claims that God's taking possession of the temple was a sign of acceptance of Solomon's offerings. Farrar, *First Kings*, 212–13, however, holds textual evidence in the OT often suggests that obedience, righteousness, and mercy are better than sacrifice; this would include covenant fidelity, which goes beyond a misuse or even proper use of the sacrificial system: e.g., 1 Sam 15:22; Mic 6:6–8; Amos 5:21–23; Isa 1:11–16; Jer 7:4–5; Ps 1:8–14; Ps 2:16–17; and Ps 11:6.

stark contrast to the anthropomorphic feeding and pampering which the gods received by their priests in the culture of the Ancient Near East![24]

The term עֲרָפֶל, "thick cloud" or "thick darkness" in v.12 relates to the intense and holy atmosphere of the invisible inner sanctuary, saturated with God's presence.[25] Thus, the threefold escalating terminology of "cloud," "glory of the Lord," and "thick darkness" in vv.10–12 intends to accentuate the fact that the Lord himself had entered with his presence the inner sanctuary of his new house. This interpretation is substantiated by the description of the Holy of Holies in vv.7–9 picturing the mercy seat on top of the ark, symbol of God's throne or footstool, which included the tablets of the covenant and was overshadowed by two cherubim. Moreover, given the obvious theme of covenant in Kings in general and in 1 Kings 8 in particular, it is plausible to infer that 8:9 (and 8:20–21) demonstrates continuity with the Sinai and Davidic covenants. Hence, the themes of covenant and divine presence complement and do not contradict each other in the context of ark and sanctuary.[26] On the contrary, the one determines the other. Besides, the king's prayer of supplication framed by praise in vv.15–61 repeatedly takes up the theme of the Lord's loyalty to his covenant in order for him to be revealed to his people and beyond Israel.

In v.13, the repetitive verbal construction בָּנֹה בָנִיתִי, infinitive with perf. of the verb "to build," expresses reinforcement and emphasis; hence, it emphasizes King Solomon as the master builder of this majestic home for God. Still, the text does not corroborate the idea that Solomon's acclamation expresses preference of his own house and dynasty to the Lord's house and temple. The emphasis supported by the subordinate clause "for you to dwell in" rather intends the previous events to be seen in the light of God fulfilling his promise by taking residence in this house built by Solomon, an interpretation which again sustains the idea of divine covenant fidelity.[27]

In this connection, the writer expresses intensification in v.13 by using the verb יָשַׁב "to dwell"[28] together with the adverbial addition עוֹלָמִים

---

24. Hundley, *God in Dwellings*, 263–71.

25. In the LXX, vv.12–13 are missing; this omission impacts on the interpretation in as far as the MT, in contrast to the LXX, expresses divine presence in cloud and house.

26. Contra Hurowitz, *I Have Built*, 267.

27. See also 2 Sam 7:13.

28. Walsh, *1 Kings*, 11, points out that the Hebrew verb יָשַׁב "to dwell" or "to be

God's Glory-Presence in the Praises of His People in the Old Testament 89

"continually"[29] following the verb שָׁכַן "to inhabit" in v.12:[30] the Lord who had said he would inhabit (provisionally) the thick cloud now has taken his abode (permanently) in the temple. The Lord who had "camped" in the tent has now been enthroned in his "permanent residence."[31]

It is true that the statement in 1 Kings 8:12–13 about the Lord's presence in his house (with parallel in 2 Chr 6:1–2) is balanced by 1 Kings 8:29 through Solomon's statement that Yahweh's presence in the temple is limited to that of "his name" alone. This language intends to avoid the impression that Yahweh's presence can be "pinned down" exclusively to the temple. In general, the so-called *shem* theology refers to the name as *representing* or *replacing* the divine person, but in this context God's name refers to his "concentrated" presence, which indicates metonymy.[32]

In connection with that, Joseph Robinson suggests that our understanding moves from the particular to the general, that is, if we meet the Lord in the temple, we become aware of his presence in every other place; however, only those who respond with "constant love" would experience this presence as blessing.[33] Similarly, Terence Fretheim proposes: "In providing vehicles for the divine presence, God acts not only for the sake of God's name . . . so that God could be as intimately and effectively present as possible with the people whom God loved."[34] This means, a transcendent God beyond time and space enters both in order to make his presence known to those he loves. Such understanding sees God's presence embedded in a loving covenant relationship with his people.

Last but not least, the term "house of the Lord," which is used instead of the term "temple," emphasizes the aspect of God's residing presence.[35] Besides, this home serves as a "vehicle of communication" for the

---

enthroned" also means '"to sit," which refers to Yahweh sitting on his throne and ruling in his temple; in any case, it relates to the Lord's permanent presence, whether as residence or rule.

29. In this context the addition עוֹלָמִים means "continually" rather than "eternally."

30. The verbal expression שָׁכַן "to inhabit" is used in the context of God dwelling among his people, and this not only temporarily.

31. See also Ps 132:8, 14; equally, 2 Chr 2:5 and 2 Chr 7:16–20 envisage a human-made building as divine dwelling place.

32. Janowski, *Gottes Gegenwart*, 128–29, perceives the *shem* terminology not in terms of "*Sublimierung*" [sublimation], but as "*Zentralisierungsformel*" [formula of centralization].

33. Robinson, *First Kings*, 103.

34. Fretheim, *Suffering of God*, 62.

35. A similar terminology can be found in Ezekiel: as long as the glory of the Lord

Lord to reveal his glorious presence and to commune with the people of his covenant.[36] In that respect, the house of the Lord (1 Kgs 8:13) is presented as a greater, better, more permanent tent of meeting or tabernacle in continuity with the Sinai covenant (1 Kgs 8:4, 9).[37]

Then, the priestly-pastoral emphasis of Solomon's prayer of supplication in section 8:22–61 cannot be ignored: the king appeals to the divine covenant partner to forgive the people's potential future sins.[38] If written from a posterior perspective, the sins against the divine covenant and its partner can be considered to have caused God to leave his house and his people to be led into Exile (v.46), or this represents a warning which already anticipates the Babylonian Exile.[39]

4.1.4 Summary

The sequence of events from 1 Kings 8:1 to 9:1–9 suggests God's people's covenant compliance is required for God to dwell permanently in his temple and among his people.

The text in 1 Kings 8, in particular in the Hebrew MT, does not corroborate the hypothesis that human activity can be considered an instrumental prerequisite for God's presence to appear. On the contrary, God's powerful glory rules out priestly sacrificial ministry. In other words, 1 Kings 8 does not provide evidence for the assumption that human prayer and praise are instrumental in bringing about God's glorious presence in his new house. All the same, in connection with the king's prayer they incite a divine reply as narrated in 1 Kings 9:1–9.[40] This issue will be further explored in the narrative in 2 Chronicles 5–7.

---

remains in the house of the Lord, the term "house" is preferred to that of "temple" (cf. Rochester, *Israel's Lament*, 135).

36. Brueggemann, *1 and 2 Kings*, 116–17; for covenant communication see, e.g., Num 7:89; and Exod 33:7b.

37. Farrar, *First Kings*, 175; see Exod 29:10; Num 17:7; 2 Chr 24:6; and Acts 7:44.

38. For blessings and penalties in connection with covenant see Lev 26 and Deut 28.

39. Sweeney, *1 and 2 Kings*, 140.

40. As has been pointed out by Hurowitz, *I Have Built*, 301; also Walsh, *1 Kings*, 117.

4.2 Divine Presence and Human Praise in 2 Chronicles 5–7: Temple Inauguration

4.2.1 Introduction

The title "Chronicles," which in Hebrew means "events of the days" or "annals," insinuates the purpose of the book to provide a historical narrative of events of the kings of Judah and Israel, whether as a parallel or alternative record; this theory was maintained in the past by scholars like Eichhorn and Keil.[41] Meanwhile, scholarship came to comprehend the purpose of Chronicles as an interpretive key to the historical events with a strong theological interest intended to unlock other historical books as well.[42] Accordingly, Scott Hahn, for example, considers Chronicles to represent a "theological and liturgical interpretation of Israel's history"—in other words, a liturgical remembrance of their history told with a prophetic intent to identify and explain God's people's present situation in the light of events recalled.[43] Similarly, Heiko Wenzel considers the purpose of Chronicles to represent an interpretation of the present events in the light of the past with an expectation for the future for God's people.[44] In particular 1 Chronicles 1:1–4 would reveal the hermeneutical purpose of Chronicles: to demonstrate continuity in the history of a people with their God. Equally, through the repetition of texts, Chronicles would through the textual density represent a link to the narratives of God—as in Kings—and the great narrative of God's faithfulness towards his people. Accordingly, the focus in Chronicles would be less on Israel's Exile, but more on the faithfulness of God to his people.

Anyhow, it has been generally agreed that the author of Chronicles relied on previous biblical sources as "building blocks," as Sara Japhet calls

---

41. The LXX title "the omitted things" refers to alternative material which was assumed to have been omitted from Samuel and Kings (cf. Klein, *1 Chronicles*, 1).

42. Dillard, *2 Chronicles*, xviii.

43. Hahn, *Kingdom*, 2–4: Hahn identifies covenant as a familial relationship of "one blood" or even a nuptial relationship of "one flesh" based on God's word and oath: the keeping of this covenant affects the identity of the covenant partners; and so, in such a relationship covenant and liturgy would be bound up together.

44. This comment is owed to Wenzel and his presentation "Wie viel Erzählung(en) braucht Geschichtsschreibung in der Chronik?" [How much Narratives Does Historiography Require in Chronicles] at the AfeT conference in Marburg, Germany, 2nd March 2020.

them.⁴⁵ Ralph Klein explains the differences between the Chronicler's *Vorlage* [model] and the MT by suggesting that the author used non-MT versions of the books of Samuel and particularly Kings while modifying his material skilfully.⁴⁶ There is no doubt that the chronicler also used extrabiblical sources, whether late postexilic material or earlier sources.⁴⁷

The chronicler's concern may have been the issue of restoration for the community returning from Exile—a restoration of hope, covenant, and God's presence through a restoration of temple and land. This concern can be seen to be supported by an emphasis on cult and temple worship, which, for some scholars, seems to point to a late provenance of the book; this dating, however, is disputed.⁴⁸

In any case, the key direction of the book has been considered to concentrate on the central section in the accounts of the kings David and Solomon from 1 Chronicles 10 to 2 Chronicles 9 highlighting two particular messages from God.⁴⁹ The first one refers to the divine promise of an eternal covenant with David and his dynasty (1 Chr 17:1-15) and the second to the corresponding divine confirmation to Solomon following his prayers and temple dedication (2 Chr 7:11-22); the second text is part of 2 Chronicles 5-7 and, therefore, of relevance. In both cases, covenant context is expressed. According to this perspective, the house of David and the house of the Lord are themes central to the chronicler's

---

45. Japhet, *1 and 2 Chronicles*, 14-16, mentions as preceding biblical sources in general the Pentateuch, the early Prophets, and Ezra-Nehemiah; she particularly considers the Book of Kings the most important of the chronicler's biblical sources, which could be seen from the chronicler's portrayal of Solomon's reign and also from explicit references to written sources, e.g., in 2 Chr 27:7; 16:11; 25:26; and in 2 Chr 20:34; 33:18; and 24:27 (cf. Japhet, *1 and 2 Chronicles*, 20).

46. Klein, *1 Chronicles*, 30-42, esp. 30, 39; he mentions as biblical sources Samuel, Kings, and Psalms, and points to similarities with the Qumran texts of Samuel.

47. Klein, *1 Chronicles*, 43-44; in support of this assumption, Japhet, *1 and 2 Chronicles*, 19, refers for earlier sources to tribal genealogies, census records, or monarchical passages as in 2 Chr 11:6-10, 18-20; for late postexilic material she mentions the organization of temple staff, the division system as in 1 Chr 23-27; and the genealogies of worship leaders as in 1 Chr 6:1-32.

48. 2 Chr 36:20-23 refer to Ezra 1:1-4, which deal with the restoration of temple, thus, providing one of the chronological and literary framing points; hence, some scholars inferred that the chronicler's lifetime coincided with that of Ezra in the postexilic period around the fifth century BCE (cf. Selman, *1 Chronicles*, 26); however, such positions were disputed by other scholars who maintain a date earlier than 539 BCE could be excluded (cf. Williamson, *1 and 2 Chronicles*, 15) and who situate the chronicler even beyond the lifetime of Nehemiah (cf. Japhet, *1 and 2 Chronicles*, 27).

49. Selman, *1 Chronicles*, 27, 44-46.

understanding of history as a story of divine-human covenant relationship.⁵⁰ Apparently, the author of Chronicles plays with the Hebrew term בַּיִת for "house" which can refer both to a dynasty for David and to a temple for the Lord. This history/story embraces on the one hand the Mosaic-Davidic-Solomonic covenant continuity, as narrated in the First Book of Chronicles, and on the other hand the frequent covenant infidelity of the divided Davidic dynasty up to its downfall, as depicted in most of the Second Book. Hence, like in Kings, covenant undoubtedly figures as a prevailing theme in Chronicles.

In connection with the theme of covenant, the theme of worship is emphasized by the author of Chronicles. As depicted in both texts (1 Chronicles 17 and 2 Chronicles 7), David and Solomon set up a system of regular worship and, as scholars have realized, divine revelation is connected with it on each occasion.⁵¹

The divine covenant with the Davidic dynasty was also a way for the Lord to demonstrate his kingdom rule among his people, another theme in Chronicles.⁵² Again, covenant and kingdom rule were connected with the temple as the centre of divine presence and with worship expressed through corporate, Levite-led praise and collective sacrifices.

4.2.2 Sequence of Events and Structure in 2 Chronicles 5–7

Having identified the main thrust of the book, the following section will concentrate on the narratives in 2 Chronicles 5–7 which represent a parallel to 1 Kings 8 elucidating the sequence of the events around the inauguration of the first temple in the context of human praise and divine presence.⁵³ These events will be summarized as follows:

---

50. Helberg, *Lord Reigns*, 93–94, explains this by going back to 2 Sam 7 that the Lord would build David a house and not the other way round because God desires to dwell in people and not in temples (see ch. 6 of this study, section 6.3).

51. Allen, *1–2 Chronicles*, 218–19.

52. Chronicles is not the only book which features the theme of the kingdom of God in the OT (see Psalms and Daniel), since the concept can be expressed in various ways without using the term; on the theme of the kingdom of God in the OT see, e.g., Bright, *Kingdom*, 1953:17–71, or Helberg, *Lord Reigns*, 10–11.

53. The classic division of the narrative by scholars like Keil and Delitzsch, *1 and 2 Kings*, 3:323–24, was a fourfold one: 1. transfer of the ark (5:2—6:11); 2. Solomon's dedicatory prayer (6:12–42); 3. the solemn sacrifice (7:1–10); 4. the Lord's answer (7:11–22); Keil and Delitzsch consider the first two acts as human dedication of the temple and the last two as divine consecration, which points to divine-human

1. After the Lord's house was completed (2 Chr 5:1),[54] the king assembled all the leaders of Israel, and the Levitical priests brought the ark and its tent from the city of David up to the temple (2 Chr 5:2–5).

2. King and congregation offered animal sacrifices (2 Chr 5:6).

3. The priests brought the ark into the inner sanctuary (2 Chr 5:7–10).

4. When the priests left the Holy of Holies (2 Chr 5:11) and the Levite musicians together with 120 priestly trumpeters worshiped God with vocal and instrumental praise in the temple (2 Chr 5:12–13ab), the house of the Lord was filled with the cloud, so that the priests could not keep ministering because of the Lord's glory in God's house (2 Chr 5:13c–14).

5. Then Solomon addressed the Lord (2 Chr 6:1–2) and the congregation with blessing (2 Chr 6:3) and praise, referring to the Lord's house and his own dynasty in the context of God's covenant fidelity (2 Chr 6:4–11).

6. The king offered a prayer of dedication and supplication to God (2 Chr 6:12–42).

7. Following this prayer, heavenly fire fell and consumed the offerings, and the glory of the Lord filled the house (2 Chr 7:1), so that the priests were not able to enter the temple because of that glory (2 Chr 7:2) and the people outside worshiped God in prostration (2 Chr 7:3).

8. King and congregation offered animal sacrifices (2 Chr 7:4–5), and instrumental Levite praise together with priestly trumpet praise was offered (2 Chr 7:6).

9. A seven-day consecration ceremony was succeeded by a seven-day feast and completed by a sacred assembly on the eighth day (2 Chr 7:7–10).

---

interaction. As in 1 Kgs 8, the textual markers in Hebrew in 2 Chr 5–7 witness to a narrative flow, as they frequently display narrative constructions with consecutive *waw* and the occasional "then" at the beginning of each sentence which are interrupted by copulative *wayehi* compositions with temporal meaning (see section 4.2.3).

54. Temporal indicators in 2 Chr 5:1–3 allow the inference that the building process of the temple was accomplished before the feast in the seventh month, which may support the flow of the argument that all had been done according to the Lord's instructions for him to be ready "to move in."

10. After the consecration, the Lord answered Solomon's prayer referring to promise and warning with regard to temple, dynasty, and land in the context of covenant (2 Chr 7:11–22).

The narrative dealing with the dedication of the temple and its corresponding events extends from 2 Chronicles 5 to 7. It has been understood as part of a chiastic structure, which even encompasses chapters 1–9, with the narrative of the temple dedication representing the centre of this chiasm.[55]

The description in 2 Chronicles 5–7 is more elaborate in terms of narrative action than in 1 Kings 8, whether regarding the events in general (e.g., 2 Chr 6:11b–13b), or the worship in particular (e.g., 2 Chr 5:11b–13a).[56]

The chronicler emphasizes that this worship involves the entire community and its representatives, especially Levites and priests.[57] The sequence of events reveals human and divine interaction in terms of human praise and divine presence in simultaneity:

---

55. E.g., Spawn, "Sacred Song," 51–58; esp. 53.

56. Spawn, "Sacred Song," 60–61, intends to contribute to a biblical theology of worship; he also means to apply the narrative of 2 Chr 1–9 to the contemporary renewal tradition.

57. More than the Book of Kings the chronicler is concerned with all Israel and its representatives (cf. Dillard, *2 Chronicles*, 41).

A1 Human action: covenant compliance concerning the ark of the covenant, symbol of divine presence (2 Chr 5:1–5 and 5:7–10), and animal sacrifices (2 Chr 5:6)

A2 Human action: vocal-instrumental praise by Levites with priests (5:12–13a–b)

    B1 Divine action: cloud filling the house of the Lord (5:13c)

        X1 No human action: priests not being able to minister (5:14a)

    B2 Divine action (as explanation): because of the Lord's glory in his house (5:14b)

A3 Human action: The king offering blessing to God and congregation, explaining events in the context of divine covenant fidelity (6:1–11), and offering prayers (6:12–42).

    B3 Divine action: heavenly fire consuming the offerings and divine glory filling the house (7:1)

        X2 No human action: priests were not able to enter the temple (7:2a)

    B4 Divine action (as explanation): because of the Lord's glory in his house (7:2b)

A4 Human action: people outside worshiping God (7:3)

A5 Human action: king and congregation offering animal sacrifices (7:4–5), and Levites and priests offering instrumental praise (7:6) followed by ceremony and feast (7:7–10)

    B5 Divine action: God answered the offerings, giving promise and warning (7:12–22).

The above human and divine interaction as human praise and divine presence succeeding each other form the following pattern in 2 Chronicles 5–7:

A1
A2
   B1
      X1
   B2
A3
   B3
      X2
   B4
A4
A5
   B5

Accordingly, one could infer that the entire narrative is structured as a chiasm with divine glory-presence in 5:13b–14 (B1 and B2) and 7:1–2 (B3 and B4), and God's glory (B2 and B3) framing Solomon's prayer as an *inclusio* (A3).[58] A simple chiasm would feature A–B–X–B–A with the emphasis placed on its centre, yet, the present structure is even more complex: the texts in 5:14a and 7:2a (X1 and X2) represent a dual chiasm which in both cases highlights priestly impotence in the face of divine potency rather than Solomon's prayer.[59] This emphasis suggests a radical corollary: divine glory-presence putting an end to priestly sacrificial ministry!

All the same, the account pictures human actions not only as sacrifices offered by priests, but also as praise offered by Levites, priests, and congregation in addition to the prayer and praise offered by the king. Apparently, human action in the form of praise is repeatedly depicted as interacting with divine action in the form of glory-presence. In chapter 5, the

---

58. Dillard, *2 Chronicles*, 41; like an *inclusio* a chiasm serves a literary emphasis; hence, scholars have debated whether a literary emphasis could describe two different events (Williamson, *1 and 2 Chronicles*, 216), which in this case would be a repeated glory-infilling of the temple, or one single event only (Dillard, *2 Chronicles*, 41; Keil and Delitzsch, *1 and 2 Kings*, 3:329). Still, the repetition creates the emphasis, and the repeated events are about praise!

59. Versus Dillard, *2 Chronicles*, 52.

praise which involves the Levitical choir and instrument band is narrated as *preceding* the infilling of the Lord's house with his glorious presence. In chapter 7, the praise which involves the entire congregation in prostration is narrated as *following* the heavenly fire coming down and the Lord's glory filling his house.

Moreover, covenant commitment is evidenced through allusions to human compliance with the divine covenant, such as the reference to the ark of the covenant (2 Chr 5:1–7a) and the description of the inner sanctuary with cherubim, ark, and law tablets of the Sinai covenant (5:7b–10). Covenant fidelity is also expressed through the entire priesthood having sanctified themselves (5:11) and the extravagant Levitic praise (5:12–13. Likewise, Solomon's prayer of dedication refers to the fulfilment of covenant promises (6:1–11), and his supplication even covers the potential covenant infidelity of the people (6:12–42). Finally, the Lord's explicit admonitions and strict warnings take up again the issue of covenant commitment (7:12–22, esp. v.14).

Consequently, the sequence of events and structure in 2 Chronicles 5–7 describe *human praise in a temporal correlation with divine presence, once before and once after the infilling of the Lord's house with his glory.* Hence, the facts allow for a consecutive interpretation of events: on one occasion, human praise had the effect of divine manifestations and, on the other, divine glory-presence had the effect of human praise while excluding priestly sacrifice ministry.

As a result, the evidence is not strong enough to infer from the above that God's people's praise can be considered *the* instrumental condition for God's presence to enter his house. Particularly the emphasis on covenant fidelity suggests that human obedience to the divine covenant is required for God dwelling permanently in his house and among his people.

Nonetheless, God's people's praise is mentioned twice in connection with God's glory-presence, namely in 2 Chronicles 5:13–14 and 7:1–3. These sections will be looked at in the exegetical analysis.

4.2.3 Exegetical Analysis: 2 Chronicles 5:13–14 and 7:1–3

2 Chronicles 5:13–14:
¹³*When the trumpeters and the singers in unison were to make themselves heard with one voice to praise and to glorify the Lord,*

> and when they lifted up their voice accompanied by trumpets and on cymbals and instruments of music, and when they praised the Lord saying, "He indeed is good for His loving-kindness is everlasting," then the house, the house of the Lord, was filled with a cloud **14**so that the priests could not stand to minister because of the cloud, for the glory of the Lord filled the house of God.

The sentence already starts in 5:11 with a coordinate clause in Hebrew introduced by וַיְהִי, a construction which points to the subsequent main clause implying a temporal coincidence:[60] "And it happened when the priests came forth from the holy place." This clause is interrupted by two parentheses, one in 5:11b explaining that all priestly divisions were present and sanctified, and the other in 5:12 describing the worship ensemble with the Levites' outfit, their stringed instruments, and the one hundred twenty priestly trumpeters. Some scholars interpret this clause in terms of a protasis which is taken up again in 5:13b to be followed by an apodosis in v.13c–14.[61]

In v.13, the *wayehi*-clause is followed by participial subjects plus preposition "as to the trumpeters and the singers," and verbs in infinitive construct plus preposition "to make themselves heard in unison as with one voice to praise and give thanks"; this construction serves to highlight the harmonious praise expressed through the phrases כְּאֶחָד and קוֹל־אֶחָד "in unison" and "as with one voice."[62]

Thus, in contrast to the author of Kings, the chronicler shows a particular interest in the Levites' musical worship (2 Chr 5:11–13). The vocal and instrumental praise by the Levites and priests, installed and stipulated by King David, is characterized by a holy commitment of all the representatives (5:11–12) and a harmonious unity (5:13).[63] Does this mean that the reason for God revealing his glorious presence can be

---

60. The *wayehi*-construction of the verb *hayah* with *waw-conversivum* or *consecutivum* plus imperf., followed by another verb in infinitive construct plus preposition, serves a narrative purpose in temporal clauses (cf. Lambdin and von Siebenthal, *Bibel-Hebräisch*, 107; also Schneider, *Grammatik*, 212).

61. Keil and Delitzsch, *1 and 2 Kings*, 3:325–26; Japhet, *1 and 2 Chronicles*, 580, notes that the parentheses refer to the preparations for the worship, but that the actual protasis, which relates to the beginning worship, is immediately followed by the apodosis, which relates to the infilling of the house with the cloud. This would demonstrate a correlation between presence and praise!

62. Keil and Delitzsch, *1 and 2 Kings*, 3:325.

63. See 1 Chr 23:5 (instrumental praise band of four thousand) and 1 Chr 25:1 (prophetic instrumental praise by the sons of Asaph, Heman, and Jeduthun).

found in his people's holy and harmonious praise? Martin Selman considers that worship to represent an example for God-filled praise: "When God's people set themselves apart for him to express heartfelt worship and praise, God will surely respond with some sign of his presence."[64] Similarly, Leslie Allen keeps emphasizing a subsequent correlation between temple worship and divine revelation:

> Worship is followed by God's revelation of Himself . . . In general terms the sequence is not an uncommon one. Those who bow their hearts before God in worship are in an attitude which is ready to receive new insights from God . . . Here, just as in 1 Kings 8:10–11, the divine revelation takes a material form. The temple is 'filled with a cloud' (5:13) which symbolizes God's 'glory'.[65]

In view of that, it may not be surprising that Kevin Spawn, a Pentecostal scholar, also perceives the "sacred song" to provide "a context for the filling of the temple with the glory cloud."[66] Still, he he would not go so far as to claim that the former produced the latter. Spawn phrases rather carefully, "The Chronicler has made us aware of an intimate link between song and presence."[67] At least, the text sustains that the reference to holy and harmonious worship is immediately followed by the reference to divine presence in vv.13c and 14.

The inserted quote in v.13b relates to Psalm 136, on of the praise psalms which served worship purposes; it was attributed to King David, who had also established the Levites' worship ministry (cf. 1 Chr 15 and 16) and had their instruments made for that purpose (cf. 2 Chr 7:6).[68] The Hebrew term חַסְדּוֹ "his faithfulness," as here in v. 13b, is used in praise songs to declare the Lord's covenant faithfulness towards his people, another hint of covenant setting. Therefore, a further motive for God revealing his glorious presence lies in his own faithfulness: because the Lord is good and faithful to his promises to the people of his covenant, he responds to their praise by revealing his presence.

The main clause to which the two subordinate clauses belong follows in v.13c: clouds were considered to manifest God's majestic

---

64. Selman, *1 Chronicles*, 320.

65. Allen, *1–2 Chronicles*, 223.

66. Spawn, "Sacred Song," 61–62, 51–68.

67. Spawn, "Sacred Song," 68.

68. See also Ps 107 and 118; it is agreed among scholars that the chronicler drew from psalms and not vice versa (cf. Williamson, *1 and 2 Chronicles*, 128).

God's Glory-Presence in the Praises of His People in the Old Testament 101

presence as a "visible vehicle."[69] Accordingly, the LXX in v.13c characterizes the cloud as representing the Lord's glorious presence, whereas the MT specifies the cloud through a genitive apposition as belonging to the Lord's house. In both cases, "cloud" serves as a metaphor which symbolizes the Lord's presence.[70]

Verse 14 represents a coordinate clause in Hebrew which can be interpreted in a consecutive way. It is followed by an explanatory clause, which describes the effects of the Lord's glorious presence: the כְּבוֹד־יְהוָה was so powerful that it brought any priestly service abruptly to an end; the priests could not stand to minister any more in the face of the cloud-presence of God because his glorious presence had filled his house. The MT uses the terms לַעֲמוֹד לְשָׁרֵת "to stand to minister," and the LXX uses the corresponding technical term λειτουργειν to express Jewish priestly ministry.[71] The textual echoes of the terms "cloud" and "glory" travel back to Exodus 40:34–35: after the work in the tabernacle was accomplished, Moses was not able to enter because of the Lord's glory filling the tabernacle. Here, the chronicler uses both terms quasi synonymously, whereas Exodus 40:35 differentiates that the cloud covered the tabernacle and the Lord's glory filled it.[72] These echoes even reach the New Testament resonating in Revelation 15:8 where the temple was filled with smoke and the glory of the Lord, and no one could enter the temple.

Solomon's prayer in 2 Chronicles 6 represents an intermission between the narrative of the Lord's presence entering the temple in chapter 5 and the narrative in chapter 7. The king's prayer and praise as described in 6:3–42[73] allude to God's covenant faithfulness in that he fulfilled his promises concerning the house of David and the house of the Lord. In

---

69. Keil and Delitzsch, *1 and 2 Kings*, 3:330.

70. Some scholars consider the apposition "house of the Lord" in the Hebrew text a gloss that had been omitted in the Greek translation (cf. Dillard, *2 Chronicles*, 40).

71. Concerning the term λειτουργειν, see ch. 2, sections 2.4.2 (Marshall, "How far," 217–18) and 2.6.2 (Wick, *Urchristliche Gottesdienste*, 22–26).

72. Japhet, *1 and 2 Chronicles*, 581; likewise, the terms "cloud" and "pillar of cloud" were used synonymously in Deut 31:15 to denote the Lord's presence and guidance in the wilderness; in Exod 19:9, the reference to God's presence in the cloud serves as a divine legitimation for Moses before the people; see also Isa 6:1–4 where smoke serves as metaphor to picture the Lord's glory-presence.

73. Physical postures of praise and prayer as depicted in 2 Chr 6 include turning to the altar as the place of sacrifice outside the inner sanctuary, kneeling, and lifting of hands.

addition, God's presence in his house is balanced by references to his presence in heaven.

2 Chronicles 7 deals with the closure of the dedication ceremonies of the temple and God's revelation to Solomon. And so, the divine manifestations in 7:1–3, a passage which is not found in 1 Kings 8, may be understood as God's answer to Solomon's prayer in chapter 6.[74]

While chapter 5 perceives the Lord's glory filling the temple, in addition to that, chapter 7 perceives the fire and glory of the Lord coming down.[75]

> 2 Chronicles 7:1–3:
> **1***As soon as Solomon finished praying, fire came down from heaven and consumed the burnt offering and the sacrifices, and the glory of the Lord filled the house.* **2***And the priests could not enter into the house of the Lord because the glory of the Lord filled the Lord's house.* **3***When all the people of Israel saw the fire come down and the glory of the Lord upon the house, they bowed down on the pavement with their faces to the ground and worshiped and gave praise to the Lord, saying, "For he is good, his steadfast love endures forever.*

Verse 1 starts with a copulative *waw* introducing a prepositional phrase with infinitive which points to a temporal correlation between the end of Solomon's prayers and the heavenly fire coming down.[76] This nexus between the two events implies that a human-divine process of communication and interaction was going on. Accordingly, the consumption of the sacrifices indicates a divine response and demonstrates that the Lord accepted the offerings—not only burnt offerings and fellowship offerings, but also the offerings of prayer and praise.[77] The Lord's fiery and consuming reply is reinforced by his glory filling his house. The

---

74. Japhet, *1 and 2 Chronicles*, 609.

75. This stance is shared by Keil and Delitzsch, *1 and 2 Kings*, 3:329–31: the repetition in 7:2 (see 2 Chr 5:14) would not insinuate that a second infilling of the temple with the Lord's glory took place in a way that the glory left while Solomon prayed, and then as a response to his prayer returned. The repetition would rather indicate that the same event is narrated from a different, more detailed perspective.

76. As concerns the Hebrew construction (verb in infinitive construct *piel* plus *ke* plus verb in infinitive construct *hitpael* plus *le*), the preposition *ke* is used to indicate that the two actions occurred simultaneously (cf. Owens, *Analytical Key*, 812; Schneider, *Grammatik*, 212).

77. Selman, *2 Chronicles*, 337, quoting Japhet, notes that both prayer and sacrifice took their place in worship "as two sides of the same coin."

construction signals that the threefold divine riposte escalates into a climax: fire coming down, sacrifices being consumed, and the Lord's house being filled with his glorious presence.[78] As a result, these theophanies have been perceived as divine consecration of the temple in response to its human dedication.[79]

On condition that the structure of the entire narrative is a dual chiasm, v.2 represents the centre of its second part with emphasis laid on priestly powerlessness being framed by divine presence (2 Chr 5:14 and 7:2); here in v.2, the priests were not able to go into the temple, whereas in 1 Kings 8:11 and 2 Chronicles 5:14 they were not able to stand to minister.

Japhet suggests a slightly different translation in v.3 claiming that a temporal subordinate clause would contradict the Hebrew syntax: "All the Israelites were watching as the fire came down . . . and they bowed low."[80] All the same, this would not exclude a temporal translation "seeing the fire come down they bowed low," or even a consecutive interpretation that the fire falling had the effect of their prostration. In any case, the correlation between the fiery divine presence and the prostrate human praise is evident.

Furthermore, another aspect is presented: whereas 2 Chronicles 5 presents only powerless priests in the temple while the Lord's glory fills his house, in addition to that, 2 Chronicles 7 portrays all the people prostrate in praise outside the temple when the Lord's fire came down.[81] Apparently, both instances report different human reactions in different locations depicted from different perspectives, whether to the same event or two different events. The question is whether 2 Chronicles 5 and 7 describe two different events of divine manifestations or observe the same theophanic event from two different perspectives. Japhet speaks of a "process of resumptive repetition" which, from a literary point of view,

---

78. Williamson, *1 and 2 Chronicles*, 222, understands this word order to be used in circumstantial clauses which describe the circumstances of the main action and not a new development. The second phrase may well be circumstantial and simultaneous to the first one. Yet, the third clause is intended to stress its subject and, thus, signals a climax.

79. Keil and Delitzsch, *1 and 2 Kings*, 3:328.

80. Japhet, *1 and 2 Chronicles*, 607.

81. See also Lev 9:23–24; Hurowitz, *I Have Built*, 268, claims that the chronicler "borrowed" the information that all the people witnessed the heavenly fire and glory coming down from the dedication ceremony of the tabernacle; this interpretation would signal a textual echo intended to express covenant continuity.

is "intended to express simultaneity of events."[82] However, this process could also be perceived as a subsequent recurrence.

The prostration וַיִּשְׁתַּחֲווּ prompted by the Lord's fiery glory is intensified through three adverbial expressions: they fell (1) on their faces, (2) to the ground, (3) on the pavement. A consecutive *waw* plus imperf. *hitpael* of the verb *shachah* respectively *chawah* "to bow down"[83] is used to describe *proskynesis*, a profound prostration of the body which in Judaism was meant to convey ultimate reverence towards God or the king (see Ps 45:11).

As already mentioned, the theophanies remind us of the phenomena demonstrated at Mount Sinai and the tabernacle.[84] They can be interpreted as textual echoes which insinuate covenant continuity starting with Moses up to David, only with the difference that on Mount Sinai the people responded with fear, while at the consecration ceremony in 2 Chronicles 7:3 they respond with prostration praise.[85]

In addition, the wording in 2 Chronicles 7:3 of God's people's praise celebrating the Lord's goodness (see Ps 136:1) exactly repeats the wording in 2 Chronicles 5:13 in the form of an *inclusio* which intends to emphasize God's covenant faithfulness. Because this phrase does not exist in 1 Kings 8, scholars concluded that it represents an addition to the *Vorlage* which the chronicler used.[86] Anyhow, the phrase demonstrates the importance the chronicler attributed to praise as an expression of the people's worship.[87]

2 Chronicles 7:11–14 continues with the divine promise of healing of the land in response to the repentant prayers of God's people.

---

82. Japhet, *1 and 2 Chronicles*, 610.

83. See Weingreen, *Grammar*, 120, on transposition of the first root-letter *shin* of *shachah* in *hitpael*; in contrast, Schneider, *Grammatik*, §39.5.2, sustains that the root is *chawah*.

84. Concerning theophanies see Exod 20:18 (thunder and lightning on Mount Sinai), Exod 24:16 (analogy of divine glory and cloud), Exod 40:34–35 (analogy of cloud covering tent, and divine glory filling it), and even Deut 5:5 (analogy of fire and the Lord's presence).

85. Japhet, *1 and 2 Chronicles*, 610.

86. E.g., Japhet, *1 and 2 Chronicles*, 608.

87. Allen, *1–2 Chronicles*, 218, explains that both David and Solomon, each in tabernacle and temple, had set up a system of regular worship to celebrate the Lord's goodness (e.g., 2 Chr 8:12–16).

4.2.4 Summary

The sequence of events suggests that 2 Chronicles 5–7 depict human praise in a temporal correlation with divine presence, once *before* and once *after* the infilling of the Lord's house with his glory, which allows for a consecutive interpretation: in one case, human praise precedes manifestations of divine presence, and in the other, divine glory-presence precedes human praise. The narrative structure of a dual chiasm emphasizes in both cases that priestly sacrifice service is suspended.

Similarly, the exegetical analysis in 2 Chronicles 5 validates that Levitical priestly praise, holy and harmonious, was followed by manifestations of divine presence, which again resulted in priestly powerlessness. The analysis in 2 Chronicles 7 suggests that on the one hand divine presence made priestly service stop and that God's presence stimulated his people's covenant praise on the other. In this case, the Lord's presence involved effects which imply a certain irony: powerless priests and praising people. This irony may balance a reciprocal correlation between presence and praise.

As a result, human praise cannot be considered *the* only precondition for divine presence because such a hypothesis would drive the interpretation of the textual witnesses in 2 Chronicles 5–7 too hard into the instrumental direction and neglect the aspect of covenant fidelity.

4.3 Similarities and Differences between 1 Kings 8 and 2 Chronicles 5–7

While 1 Kings 8–9 have been considered a literary *Vorlage* for 2 Chronicles 5–7, the events in Chronicles are described in a more detailed way than in Kings.[88] These details concern the sequence of events in general (e.g., 2 Chr 6:11b–13b) and the worship ceremonies in particular (e.g., 2 Chr 5:12–13a; also 2 Chr 9:6).

Sarah Japhet compares the literary unit of 2 Chronicles 5:2—7:22 with the parallel unit in 1 Kings 8:1—9:8. She maintains that the chronicler adopted the unit basically in its form with a few modifications, whether omissions (1 Kgs 8:50–53 replaced by 2 Chr 6:40–42; and 1 Kgs

---

88. In 2 Chr 5:13, the quote from Ps 136:1 about the people praising the Lord's goodness is repeated in 2 Chr 7:3, thus, forming an *inclusio*. This quote does not exist in 1 Kgs 8, therefore, scholars inferred that it represents an addition to the *Vorlage* (cf. Japhet, *1 and 2 Chronicles*, 608).

8:54–61 replaced by 2 Chr 7:1–3) or additions (2 Chr 5:11b–13a; and possibly 6:13; 7:6; 7:12b–15).[89]

There are more differences: 1 Kings 8 depicts the filling of the temple with the Lord's glory from one perspective only, which is reflected in 2 Chronicles 5. Then, 2 Chronicles 7 adds other elements: the falling of the fire and the consumption of the offerings. As we have seen, the structure of a dual chiasm in 2 Chronicles 5–7 highlights priestly powerlessness in the face of divine glory.

Moreover, in 2 Chronicles 7:3, the people's praise is depicted as a response to the manifestations of the Lord's presence narrated in 2 Chronicles 7:1–2. These manifestations follow again Solomon's prayer and praise in 2 Chronicles 6, which can be regarded as an interaction of human praise and divine presence. And then, unlike in Kings, the aspect of priestly holiness is particularly accentuated in Chronicles (2 Chr 5:11).

In sum, the main similarities between 1 Kings 8 to 9 and 2 Chronicles 5 to 7 concentrate on one perspective of the Lord's presence: the Lord's glory filling the temple (1 Kgs 8:10–11; 2 Chr 5:14; and 2 Chr 7:1–2). The variations concern the connection between human praise and divine presence:

1. Kings 8:10–11: no praise prior to this infilling;

2. Chronicles 5:13: the praise of the worship leaders is followed by the infilling of the temple with God's glory;

3. Chronicles 7:3: God's glory coming down on the temple is followed by the praise of all of God's people.

As a result, neither the sequence of events and narrative structure nor the exegetical results in 1 Kings 8 and 2 Chronicles 5–7 provide enough evidence which would us allow to infer that human praise offerings alone can be considered preconditional or instrumental in bringing about God's glorious presence in his house. As a matter of fact, God's powerful glory suspends priestly sacrifice ministry. In any case, 2 Chronicles 5–7 clearly show the chronicler's particular interest in worship.

In view of the above, one may be inclined to resume that 2 Chronicles 5–7 describe the same events as in 1 Kings 8, only from different perspectives. Still, the difference between 1 Kgs 8 and 2 Chron 5–7 in the description of the events of the dedication of the first temple could have another reason: 2 Chron 5–7 with the different and more detailed

---

89. Japhet, *1 and 2 Chronicles*, 573–74, 608.

account may open up an expectation of future events in the light of Israel's exilic presence.[90] Such expectation would aim at a greater glory of the Lord in another temple.[91]

In sum, these narratives do not support the idea that, without considering other aspects like covenant fidelity, human praise alone produced the manifestations of divine presence.

4.4 Human Praise and Divine Presence without Temple Context

To provide a detailed exegesis of Old Testament texts on human praise and divine presence without temple context would go beyond the frame of this study. Still, this section will look briefly at a potential correlation between both elements mostly outside the temple setting, whether in war context or in the context of spiritual and other conflicts.

Four Old Testament narratives reveal these conflict motifs in connection with human praise and divine presence: Joshua at Jericho in Joshua 6, Jehoshaphat facing a military challenge in 2 Chronicles 20, Elisha and the minstrel in 2 Kings 3, and David playing the harp in front of Saul in 1 Samuel 16. All of them evidence a variety of praise, whether vocal or instrumental. Having said that, one may question whether the blowing of the trumpets and the war cry of God's people at Jericho in Joshua 6 can be taken for battle praise. Similarly, it has been debated whether the instrumental play of David in front of a disturbed King Saul in 1 Samuel 16 or that of Elisha's minstrel in 2 Kings 3 can be considered worship. To be on the safe side, it would be reasonable not to exclude these options. In any case, the texts display that those "liturgical" expressions were followed by supernatural manifestations.

---

90. This idea is owed to Wenzel and his paper "Wie viel Erzählung(en)" on the meaning of narratives in connection with historiography in Chronicles at the AfeT conference in Marburg, Germany, 2nd March 2020.

91. This expectation of a greater glory is expressed in Hag 2:1–9; also Hab 2:14 or Isa 11:9; see ch. 6, section 6.2.3.

4.4.1 Joshua at Jericho in Joshua 6:20

Already Joshua 5:13–15 telling about Joshua's encounter with the "commander of the hosts of the Lord" serves as an introduction for the subsequent narrative:[92]

Joshua 6:2 relates God's promise of victory together with precise instructions for the city's conquest. These instructions involved the ark of the covenant, symbol of the Lord's presence (6:8), and required six days of marching once around the city (6:3), and on the seventh day seven times in the following order (6:4): armed men, seven priests with seven ram's horn trumpets being blown daily, followed by the ark with the rear guard (6:7–8); however, the battle cry of the people was meant to be heard on the seventh day only (6:9–10).

In Joshua 6:20, six verbal *waw*-consecutive constructions plus one *wayehi*-composition indicate the temporal flow of the narrative suggesting a consecutive interpretation:

> **20**So, the people shouted, and they [the priests] blew the trumpets; and [literally: it happened] when the people heard the sound of the trumpet, the people shouted a great shout, and the wall fell down flat [literally: under itself], so that the people went up into the city, every man straight ahead [literally: before him], and they took the city.

Keil and Delitzsch draw attention to the repeated reference to the number seven in Joshua 6:4 (seven priests, seven trumpets, seven days, seven marches), which is often used in Scripture as a symbol of divine attributes and works.[93] Furthermore, the divine promise of victory (6:2) and the presence of the Lord (6:8), embodied through the ark of the covenant (nine times in vv.4–13), imply divine involvement.[94] The priests' blowing of the *shofarot* trumpets[95] and the people's battle cry

---

92. On Josh 6 see Harstad, *Joshua*, 249–371, esp. 252: Harstad, referring to Josh 5:13–15, points out that these verses belong to the narrative in Josh 6 and that they offer an interpretive key through the "divine identity of 'the Commander of the host of the Lord.'"

93. Keil and Delitzsch, *Joshua*, 2:70–71.

94. See Exod 19:16 which describes the Lord's descent from Sinai accompanied by a "thick cloud" (the same term as in 1 Kgs 8:10) and a loud trumpet blast.

95. Keil and Delitzsch, *Joshua*, 2:69, relate the blowing of trumpets as a herald's call announcing the arrival of the Lord to establish his kingdom; this call would entail a holy convocation of Sabbath rest for his covenant people (as in Lev 23:24), or a Year of Jubilee with deliverance from bondage and oppression (as in Lev 25:9–10). Generally,

signal a call to war which is the Lord's, for instance, as with Gideon in Judges 7:19–22.[96] The outcome was a supernatural conquest manifested in judgment over the powers opposing the Lord's kingdom. Besides, the divine involvement in the military action is also implied through God's ban laid on the people to keep themselves from the things which are holy to the Lord (6:18–19, 21).

Of course, these brief comments do not represent an in-depth analysis, but they point to God's presence and action following his people's praise in a war context (6:20). If we regard the blowing of the trumpets as a call for battle and the war cry as a form of battle praise, the significance of their part in this victory cannot be ruled out. Evidently, the Holy War motif is connected with covenant setting, and battle praise could be considered one of the covenant stipulations to be followed. Still, it cannot be inferred that human praise was *the one and only* condition, instrumental in unleashing such divine military involvement.

4.4.2 Jehoshaphat in 2 Chronicles 20:22

Similarly, 2 Chronicles 20 describes in three sections how a military challenge—not a conquest to be achieved, but a defeat to be avoided—was handled. A great multitude of Moabites and Ammonites had come from Edom against King Jehoshaphat of Judah. The first section in 2 Chronicles 20 in vv.3–13 depicts how, in view of this challenge, Jehoshaphat and all the people of Judah—families included—sought the Lord in prayer and fasting. Jehoshaphat reminds the Lord of his faithfulness, explains the challenge, and pleads for divine help.[97] This prayer takes place on the temple premises (v.5). In fact, Jehoshaphat's prayer in vv.8–9 resembles that of King Solomon at the dedication of the temple (see 1 Kgs 8:31–53; 2 Chr 6:22–40), as had been pointed out by Leslie Allen: "In the temple system a prayer of need was regularly answered by a prophetic message in God's name."[98]

---

trumpets were blown to assemble the people, whether for departure or war (see Num 10:1–10; 2 Chr 13:14–18).

96. For the Holy War motif in connection with covenant see ch. 6, section 6.3.2; on God as holy warrior see Dozeman, *Joshua 1–12*, 325–32; Brueggemann, *Divine Presence amid Violence*.

97. Japhet, *1 and 2 Chronicles*, 788–89, comprehends the three-part structure in pairs of Jehoshaphat's prayer as a typical literary device of the chronicler.

98. Allen, *1–2 Chronicles*, 307.

Accordingly, the second section in vv.14–19 tells the outcome of this prayer: in v.17, the Spirit of the Lord came upon a Levite worshiper and caused him to prophecy that the battle would be the Lord's and so would be their salvation:

> Joshua 6:17:
> ¹⁷*You will not need to fight in this battle. Stand firm, hold your position, and see the salvation of the Lord on your behalf, O Judah and Jerusalem. Do not be afraid and do not be dismayed. Tomorrow go out against them, and the Lord will be with you.*

In this case, the people of Judah would not even have to fight, but only to position themselves (v.17a). Hugh Williamson, referring to von Rad, asserts that the appeal "fear not" and the promise of divine salvation and presence (v.17a, c) points to the concept of Holy War expressing God's involvement in the wars of his people.[99] Raymond Dillard also identifies Jehoshaphat's battle as a Holy War narrative where a lament ritual (vv.5–12) is followed by a priestly or prophetic oracle of salvation (vv.14–17).[100] Differently, Sara Japhet presupposes divine intervention in the wars of his people in general even beyond the strict literary genre of a Holy War narrative.[101]

This divine promise prompted in return the prostrate praise of Jehoshaphat and the entire people of Juda and Jerusalem (לְהִשְׁתַּחֲוֺת *shachah*, v.18) as well as the loud praise of the Levitic worship orchestra (לְהַלֵּל *hallal*, v.19). By faith the people anticipated this promised help thanking and praising the Lord for it.[102]

The third section in vv.20–23 starts with a word of admonition by Jehoshaphat, who then leads the people in worship on the battle field (v.20). Again, they offer praise—instead of battle cry as in Joshua 6—anticipating the fulfilment of the divine promise, which is described in detail: the Levite worshipers in holy attire (like in 2 Chr 5:12) preceded the armed men (unlike in Josh 6:13 where the armed men preceded the priests.) The content of their praise (*hallal*, v.21) reflects Psalm 136:1 (see 2 Chr 5:13 and 7:3) "give thanks to the Lord, for his loving-kindness is

---

99. Williamson, *1 and 2 Chronicles*, 297, 300.
100. Dillard, *2 Chronicles*, 154–55.
101. Japhet, *1 and 2 Chronicles*, 783.
102. Allen, *1–2 Chronicles*, 308, suggests that such anticipation by faith represented a traditional practice in temple procedure where lament was followed by thanksgiving.

everlasting." Thus, praise as a human response to the divine promise of salvation is repeatedly narrated in vv.18–22. The outcome of that praise is depicted in a temporal clause starting in v.22:

> 2 Chronicles 20:22–23:
> ²²*At the time when they began worshipping in jubilation (*רִנָּה *rinnah) and praise (*תְּהִלָּה *tehillah), the Lord set ambushes [literally: agents lying in wait] against the sons of Ammon, Moab and Mount Seir, who had come against Judah, and they were routed.* ²³*For the men of Ammon and Moab rose against the inhabitants of Mount Seir, devoting them to destruction, and when they had made an end of the inhabitants of Seir, they all helped to destroy one another.*

The text verifies a divine military intervention (v.22b) promised through prophecy (v.17), which brought about a supernatural victory for God's people, as their enemies exterminated each other (v.22c, 23). Thus, the Holy War motif points to a covenant setting in that God identifies with his people and considers his people's enemies to be his own enemies.

Similarly, in the military challenge of Israel facing the Egyptians at the Red Sea where Moses is reported to say in Exodus 14:14 "The Lord will fight for you, and you will be silent," the divine command "to be still" relates to the military activity of the people and not to their praise.

In response to the salvation accomplished, thanksgiving, blessing, and instrumental praise are narrated again in vv.26 and 28.

In view of the above, the divine war motif as a covenant theme is clearly evidenced in the narrative, as the text corroborates God's intervention on behalf of his people initiated through petition, promised through prophecy, prompted through praise, and fulfilled through a supernatural military victory.

In connection with that, 2 Chronicles 20 demonstrates a concern for faith and worship expressed through the emphasis on anticipatory praise. As a result, one can infer that repetitive praise together with faith in the faithful covenant God plays an influential role in the circumstances for divine presence to be manifested. For that reason, the military conflict represents a *test of the people's spiritual integrity rather than of their military capacity*. Hence, human praise cannot be considered the only requirement for divine presence to be manifested.

In sum, without going into exegetical details, the narratives in Joshua 6 and particularly in 2 Chronicles 20 imply a temporal or even consecutive connection between God's people's war cry and battle praise on the one hand, and manifestations of divine presence in the form of military conquest and victory on the other. This, however, occurs in covenant context where the spiritual integrity of God's people is tested. By the way, it is interesting to discover that in Qumran literature the Holy War motif has been spiritualized, and the anticipatory praise of the community of the light was expected to be supported by the praise of the angelic hosts to fend off the powers of the dark in spiritual warfare, as Daniel Falk points out.[103]

4.4.3 David and Saul in 1 Samuel 16:23

Scripture witnesses to three instances when the "evil spirit from God" came upon King Saul, and David played the harp: 1 Samuel 16:23; 1 Samuel 18:10; and 1 Samuel 19:9. However, only once in 1 Samuel 16, an association between this kind of instrumental music and its positive results is reported.

1 Samuel 16:14–16 already mention that the "therapeutic" effect of harp playing on the evil spirit which kept terrorizing Saul was known to Saul's servants. This is why they made David play before Saul. It has been suggested that the adjective "evil" in v.23 should be read as "injurious" in the sense of harmful and detrimental.[104] Hence, Joyce Baldwin identifies the evil spirit as "intermittent bouts of mental disturbance which required 'music therapy.'"[105] However, this interpretation may not suffice.

First, the evil force, which caused Saul to behave in a homicidal and raving manner (see 1 Sam 18 and 19), was characterized as of spiritual origin: רוּחַ־רָעָה מֵאֵת יְהוָה an *evil spirit from the Lord* after רוּחַ יְהוָה the *Spirit of the Lord* had departed from Saul (1 Sam 16:14). Accordingly, Keil and Delitzsch argue that this evil spirit was not merely a harmful mental disposition due to a certain depression, but "a higher evil power which took possession of him," a demon sent by God as a punishment for Saul.[106] For this reason, Keil and Delitzsch clarify that the genitive in Hebrew in

---

103. See Falk, "Prayer," 285–89, section "Worship as Warfare"; similarly, Vogel, *Heil des Bundes*, 268–78, expounds the role of hymnic praise in war in extracanonical liturgical texts such as 1QM and 1 and 2 Macc.

104. Baldwin, *1 and 2 Samuel*, 88–122.

105. Baldwin, *1 and 2 Samuel*, 123; nevertheless, Baldwin allows for a spiritual perspective in Saul's "reluctant compliance" towards God.

106. Keil and Delitzsch, *Joshua*, 2:170.

v. 23 "of/from the Lord" needs to be translated in the sense of "allowed by the Lord" to avoid confusing it with the Lord's Holy Spirit:

1 Samuel 16:23:
23And whenever the harmful spirit from God was upon Saul, David took the lyre and played it with his hand. So Saul was refreshed and was well, and the harmful spirit departed from him.

Second, 1 Samuel 16:23 witnesses to a twofold outcome of David's music: whenever the (evil) spirit from God (רוּחַ־אֱלֹהִים) came on Saul and David took the harp and played with his hand, Saul would be refreshed and well,[107] and the evil spirit (רוּחַ הָרָעָה) would depart from him.[108] The temporal phrase in Hebrew is introduced by *wehayah* with preposition *be* plus participle, which points to a repeated, consecutive interpretation:[109] each time when the spirit from God came to Saul and David played the harp, the evil spirit would depart from Saul. Again, the textual evidence also points to spiritual and not only to mental/emotional effects.

Hence, the "therapeutic charm" of David's music was most probably situated not only at a mental-psychological, but also at a spiritual level.[110] In other words, David's playing the harp may well have meant making music to God in a situation of spiritual conflict. Such potential praise hints at the divine war motif, which would certainly be more than medical music therapy.

In connection with that, 1 Samuel 10:5 and also 2 Kings 3:11, 15–16 refer to the music of harp and lyre as a means among prophets for them to come under the influence of the hand of the Lord and to prophesy. This was in the tradition of the Levites, who were known to be prophetic worshipers, and their temple worship with instrumental praise, as ordained by David and the Lord himself (e.g. 2 Chron 29:25). For those reasons, David's harp music in 1 Samuel 16 may have served as a "vehicle of worship" which hastened the evil spirit's departure.

---

107. In the MT, Saul is set in dative, twice with the preposition *le* "it would refresh *Saul* and it would be good *with him*."

108. In the MT, the adjective "evil" is missing in v.23a while present in v.23b, but the spirit is qualified as "of/from the Lord" (constructive genitive). In the LXX, the adjective "evil" is present in v.23ab, but the genitive attribute "of/from the Lord" is missing.

109. Schneider, *Grammatik*, §53.2.1.2.

110. Contra Baldwin, *1 and 2 Samuel*, 123–24.

4.4.4 Elisha and the Minstrel in 2 Kings 3:15

2 Kings 3 narrates that in a twice difficult strategic situation the prophet Elisha was asked to seek the counsel of the Lord: Joram, the king of Israel, facing a Moabite rebellion had sought the military help of Jehoshaphat, king of Judah, and of the king of Edom. After a week-long circuit march of the armies in the desert, they were lacking water (2 Kgs 3:7–9). In this twofold challenge, the kings went to get the prophet Elisha, who then made a minstrel play his instrument (v.15):

> 2 Kings 3:15:
> 15*"But now bring me a musician." And when the musician played, the hand of the Lord came upon him.*

As mentioned before, it has been questioned whether the minstrel's play means praise. Yet, the phrase "the hand of the Lord came upon him" (v.15b) points to the divine source of the subsequent prophetic revelation (v.16–19). Hence, the prophetic anointing can be seen as an empowerment to speak on God's behalf.[111] This allows the inference that the music which prompted the prophecy may also have been of a spiritual nature like meditative and prophetic worship: Keil and Delitzsch refer to 1 Samuel 16:16 underlining the meditative character of such music which helps the prophet "to become absorbed in the intuition of divine things."[112] Prophetic instrumental praise is also verified in 1 Chronicles 25:1 where the sons of Asaph, Heman, and Jeduthun were set apart for the ministry of prophetic worship. Accordingly, the musician being under this divine anointing received a specific revelation from God concerning the problem of water provision (vv.16–17) and the military challenge through the Moabites (vv.18–19):

> 2 Kings 3:16:
> 16*And he said, "Thus says the Lord, 'I will make this dry streambed full of pools.'* 17*For thus says the Lord, 'You shall not see wind or rain, but that streambed shall be filled with water, so that you shall drink, you, your livestock, and your animals.'* 18*This is a light thing in the sight of the Lord. He will also give the Moabites into your hand,* 19*and you shall attack every fortified city and every choice city, and shall fell every good tree and stop up all springs of water and ruin every good piece of land with stones."*

---

111. Williamson, *Sealed with an Oath*, 164.
112. Keil and Delitzsch, *1 and 2 Kings*, 3:304.

The phrase "he will also give the Moabites into your hand" (v.17) points to the divine origin of the ensuing victory, which implies covenant background: God's faithfulness to his covenant people causes him to identify with them in the military challenge, and he is fighting their enemies, who have become his own enemies, so that battle and victory belong to the Lord. This clearly evidences the Holy War motif, even if some military activity of the people was still required in this case to fend off the Moabite attack.

For those reasons, this narrative in 2 Kings 3 with human praise followed by manifestations of divine presence like prophecy and fulfilment testifies to the divine war motif in covenant setting.

4.4.5 Summary

In sum, the above narratives in Joshua 6, 2 Chronicles 20, 1 Samuel 16, and 2 Kings 3 suggest that God's people's praise instigated spiritual effects of a divine nature, whether in terms of a supernatural military conquest or a victory due to divine intervention through prophecy and fulfilment, or in terms of making an evil spirit leave. All the texts reveal the Holy War or a similar conflict motif in a covenant setting. Having said that, the divine war motif also occurs in texts without a correlation between human praise and divine presence, but with a similar covenant background, like God revealing himself as Lord (e.g. 1 Kgs 20:13 with King Ahab). Besides, we need to consider that not every narrative of such type implies a cause-consequence connection with an immediate triumphant outcome for God's people, as we see from the Book of Job or the fate of the first Christian martyr Steven in Acts 7. Hence, the above theory would have to be supported by further textual analysis, which, however, exceeds the frame of this study.

4.4.6 God's Presence in his People's Praise: Psalm 22:3

Traditionally, Psalm 22 has been considered a psalm of lament of David—possibly in the context of him being persecuted by Saul—given the characteristic elements of lament expressed in vv.1–2, 6–7, and 11–18.[113] And so, the utter lamentation in Psalm 22:1b is echoed in Jesus' cry on

---

113. Westermann, *Lob und Klage*, 50–51, 139.

the cross in view of God's apparent absence and desertion (quoted in Mt 27:46 and Mk 15:34).

Moreover, a characteristic element of lament psalms is that, despite the tension, eventually the lament is turned into thanksgiving and praise.[114] Accordingly, the MT[115] of Psalm 22 presents intermissions in the lament in vv.3 and 19 through a *waw adversativum* (וְאַתָּה "but you") which introduces each time a confession of faith appealing to God's covenant presence. Thus, Claus Westermann perceives these confessions of faith to indicate a change from lament to praise as in v.3.[116] Similarly, Peter Craigie suggests that the above textual signals be understood as "the essence of the covenant faith that those who trusted in the holy God would not be disappointed—hence the praise of Israel upon which God was enthroned."[117]

Apart from the completely different translation in the LXX[118] "but you *dwell in* the Holies, the praise of Israel,"[119] the predicate with preposition can also be rendered differently: "You who are *enthroned upon* the praises of Israel." In the Hebrew text, the participle יֹשֵׁב (*qal* of יָשַׁב) in the transitive verbal construction is followed by a noun in accusative without preposition.[120] A similar phrase without preposition יֹשֵׁב הַכְּרֻבִים "being enthroned (above) the cherubim" is found in 1 Samuel 4:4; Psalm 80:1; Psalm 99:1; and Isaiah 37:16.[121] Keil and Delitzsch explain Psalm 22:3 quite beautifully: "The songs of praise, which resounded in Israel as the memorials of His deeds of deliverance, are like the wings of the cherubim,

---

114. See Westermann, *Lob und Klage*, 60; on the tension between lament and praise in psalms including Ps 22 also more recently Rechberger, *Von der Klage*, 41–42, 148–49.

115. In the LXX and English versions vv.3 and 19; the MT already counts the introduction as v.1, which explains the different verse count in the translations.

116. Westermann, *Lob und Klage*, 54.

117. Craigie, *Psalm 1–50*, 199; similarly Goldingay, *Psalms*, 1:323.

118. It is possible to place the *atnah* under *yoshev*, which results in the different translation of the LXX (cf. Craigie, *Psalm 1–50*, 196, footnote 4a): σὺ δὲ ἐν ἁγίοις κατοικεῖς, ὁ ἔπαινος Ισραηλ.

119. Rechberger, *Von der Klage*, 148, referring to Gese and Kraus, recommends the singular reading of praise based on MT variants or LXX.

120. Keil and Delitzsch, *Psalms*, 5:312, identify the construction without preposition as an accusative of the verbs of dwelling and tarrying; they seem to use both translations synonymously; on *yashab* see also exegetical analysis of 1 Kgs 8:13 under section 4.1.3 of this chapter.

121. Buhl, *Gesenius*, 323.

upon which His presence hovered in Israel."[122] So, the verbal expression above reverberates God's presence, which is symbolized by the ark in the sanctuary with the cherubs' wings (cf. 1 Kgs 8:6 and 2 Chr 5:7). This intertextual link would justify the translations "You are *enthroned above* the praises of Israel" or "You *dwell in* the praises of Israel."

As a result, it can be inferred that, even without going into further exegetical analysis, the MT in Psalm 22:3 proposes a correlation of God's presence and God's people's praise, probably with the latter inviting the former.

4.5 Human Praise and/or Divine Presence?

Given our purpose to investigate a connection between human praise and divine presence, we will not deal comprehensively with biblical concepts of either worship or divine presence, but texts will be referred to mainly where these elements occur together.

4.5.1 Examples of Praise in the Psalms

In general, in the psalms praise and thanksgiving were considered offerings pleasant to God or still better than that (see Pss 50:23 and 69:30–31). Even before the times of King David, psalms were used as worship songs in Israel for the people to praise their God remembering his acts of deliverance. They joyfully celebrate the Lord's faithfulness and tell of his mighty deeds like the pilgrim psalms from 120 to 134.[123]

Similarly,[124] 2 Chronicles 5:13 and 7:3 and also 2 Chronicles 20:21 hold a citation from Psalm 136: this psalm, which represents a characteristic example of praise psalms, repeats in each one of its verses the phrase "for his loving-kindness is everlasting" with the Hebrew term חַסְדּוֹ "his faithfulness" as a hint of covenant context.[125]

Likewise, Psalms 145–150 comprise typical examples of exhortation to praise. According to Westermann, particularly Psalms 148 and 150 belong to the "imperative psalms" with the exhortation to praise.[126] In

122. Keil and Delitzsch, *Psalms*, 5:312.
123. Westermann, *Lob und Klage*, 61.
124. See section 4.2.3 of this chapter.
125. Also Pss 107 and 118:2, 3, 4, 29.
126. Westermann, *Lob und Klage*, 98–99.

a similar way, the Davidic Psalm 145 reveals voluntative ("I will praise") and jussive ("they shall praise") forms of invitation to worship the Creator God and to celebrate Israel's faithful king.[127]

Psalms 145–50 also contain exhortations to praise Yahweh as Creator, king, and covenant God framed by the call הַלְלוּ־יָהּ which marks the final collection of praise psalms.[128]

In sum, these classic praise psalms contain exhortations addressed to God's people to praise their Lord in the context of a personal and corporate covenant relationship with him. Therefore, such worship and praise surpasses "the relational phenomena between the created and the Creator," as Timothy Pierce states, since it refers to a bond between the people and their God.[129]

All the same, there is hardly any evidence in Psalms—except for Psalm 22:3—that points to a connection between God's people's praise and God's presence.

4.5.2 God's Glory in his Temple: Ezekiel 10, 11, and 43

The book of Ezekiel deals with the "crisis of God's presence," as Herrie van Rooy aptly remarks.[130] This crisis pictured in visions by the prophet Ezekiel is overall about the Lord's glory departing from the temple, the land, and the people of his covenant and, hence, is a crisis of judgment.

That the Lord's glory כָּבוֹד and his presence are used synonymously in Ezekiel can be seen, for example, from Ezekiel 9:3. Another term is רוּחַ *ruah* "Spirit" as in Ezekiel 11:19 and 37:14, but there, it conveys God's breath of life rather than his presence. Besides, the term *ruah* "Spirit" is used in Ezekiel not as frequently as the term *kevod* "glory" which denotes the Lord's presence departing from and returning to temple, people, and land. Another term in Ezekiel 37:27 is מִשְׁכָּן *mishkhan* "dwelling place" based on the root *shakhan* "to dwell" which expresses that God wants to dwell among his people.

Relevant passages about God's glory-presence departing are found in Ezekiel 10 and 11: they deal with prophecies of God's judgment against his people who have sinned against their God. These messages of warning

---

127. Allen, *Psalms 101–150*, 298–99.
128. Allen, *Psalms 101–150*, 302.
129. Pierce, *Enthroned*, 3.
130. Van Rooy, "Ezekiel," 148.

are consistent with those in 1 Kings 8 and 2 Chronicles 5–7. On the contrary, Ezekiel 43 deals with prophecies of restoration as to worship and the Lord's glory in his temple.[131] Consequently, judgment is identified with the departure of the Lord's glory-presence and restoration with the return of this presence.

At first, in Ezekiel 10:3, the prophet's vision describes the cloud of the glory of the Lord filling the inner court; similarly, v.4 pictures the house of the Lord being filled with the cloud and the court being filled with the brightness of his glory, but without praise context. Then, in Ezekiel 10:18, the vision portrays the glory of the Lord leaving his house; likewise, Ezekiel 11:23 depicts the glory of the Lord departing from the the city of Jerusalem. The reason for this prophesied and executed judgment is the covenant infidelity of the Lord's people. Nevertheless, this crisis is not without a chance, which is epitomized by the promise of restoration after their repentance, corporately and individually:[132] a "new heart surgery" for God's people and a restoration of God's presence in temple, city, and land (Ezek 11:19–20). Hence, the "crisis of God's presence" is resolved by a return of the glory of the Lord.[133] Accordingly, Ezekiel 43:4–5 describe how the glory of the Lord fills the house of the Lord; or, Ezekiel 44:4 pictures how Ezekiel prostrates himself in view of such divine glory. Ezekiel 43:12 makes clear that this hoped-for restoration is envisioned in the context of a holy dwelling place for God and, thus, a holy covenant relationship with his people. John Levison even identifies an "Edenic restoration" of the temple in Ezekiel's visions in Ezekiel 40–48.[134] In connection with that, Volker Gäckle explores an early metaphorization of the term temple and its theology.[135]

As a result, these prophetic messages of warning against judgment and hope for restoration in Ezekiel are pictured against the background of a holy covenant relationship between God and his people as in Kings and

---

131. Kilchör, *Wiederhergestellter Gottesdienst*, deals with the restoration of Israel's worship in Ezek 40–48 and, in connection with that, the eschatological expectation of the temple restored in greater glory.

132. Van Rooy, "Ezekiel," 142–44, in unison with von Rad and Kaminsky, highlights the new aspect of individual responsibility in Ezekiel (9:4 and 18:1–4).

133. Van Rooy, "Ezekiel," 134.

134. Levison, *Filled with the Spirit*, 211–12, contra Block, "Eden: A Temple," 21: Block, referring to Ezek 47:1–12, admits that there may be Edenic features reflected in temple imagery, but not vice versa; see ch. 6, section 6.2.1.

135. Gäckle, *Allgemeines Priestertum*, 110–11.

Chronicles. There is no sufficient evidence of a connection between the Lord's presence and his people's praise in Ezekiel, except for three instances in Ezekiel 3:23; 43:2–3; and 44:4: there, the Lord's glory prompts the prophet's prostration, whether outside or inside the temple. For the rest, there are only subtle references to worship in terms of cultic stipulations as in chapters 40–48 (e.g., Ezek 46:3). As will be further revealed, worship and its expressions of praise occur in the life-setting of a holy divine-human relationship. This relationship is characterized by divine faithfulness to the covenant promises on the one hand and human faith in and obedience to the covenant God on the other. If this relationship is damaged, judgment is inflicted as a consequence, yet, with the hope of restoration.

4.6 Summary

As has been verified in the structural and exegetical analyses of 1 Kings 8, divine glory is portrayed as prompting human praise and bringing priestly ministry to an end. The textual evidence demonstrated that *without covenant fidelity* there is no connection between human praise and divine presence.

The structural analysis of 2 Chronicles 5–7 revealed that human praise holds a temporal correlation with divine presence, once before and once after the infilling of the Lord's house with his glory. The exegetical analysis in 2 Chronicles 5 validated that holy Levitical and priestly praise is superseded by divine glory-presence filling the house of the Lord. The exegetical analysis in 2 Chronicles 7 corroborated that divine manifestations, such as fire and glory filling the temple, were followed by "pause and praise"—pause of the priestly sacrifice ministry and praise of the people. The irony of the Lord's presence producing powerless priests and praising people may balance a reciprocal correlation between divine presence and human praise.

As a result, in view of the covenant aspects demonstrated in both narratives, human praise cannot be considered *the* precondition for divine presence either in 1 Kings 8 or in 2 Chronicles 5–7.

Even narratives mostly without temple context imply covenant setting through the divine war motif, although they demonstrate a consecutive correlation between God's people's praise and manifestations of divine presence in battle context as in Joshua 6 and 2 Chronicles 20. Similarly, the narratives in 1 Samuel 16 and 2 Kings 3 support the idea of worshipful music with spiritual side effects, whether in terms of making an evil spirit leave or releasing divine salvation through prophecy and fulfilment.

Undoubtedly, Psalm 22:3 with God dwelling in or being enthroned upon his people's praises testifies to a tangible link between God's people's praise and God's presence in the context of covenant relationship. Covenant relationship is also implied in the praise psalms, although there is little evidence of a connection between human praise and divine presence. The case is similar with Ezekiel, a book which portrays the departure of the Lord's presence in judgment and the return of his presence in restoration, but overall not in the context of praise.

Thus, the inquiry in this chapter prepares the ground for exploring relevant passages of the New Testament. In the next chapter, New Testament texts from the Book of Acts and the Letter to the Ephesians which portray initial and repetitive infillings of God's new people with Holy Spirit in the context of their praise will be probed concerning a correlation between this form of divine presence and human praise.

5.0

God's Spirit-Presence and God's People's Praise in the New Testament

In the Old the New lies concealed, in the New the Old is revealed.

—LATE MEDIEVAL RHYME

THE LAST CHAPTER EXPLORED passages about divine presence and human praise with God dwelling among his people Israel through his glory in a new temple. This chapter will explore passages about divine presence and human praise with God dwelling in his new people through his Holy Spirit, corporately and individually.

After a general introduction, in the first part of this chapter narratives from Acts 2 (2:1–4) and Acts 10 (10:44–46 with reference to 11:15–18) will be explored, texts which depict the praise of God's people in connection with their initial reception of the Holy Spirit. This bestowal is described as their "being filled with Holy Spirit," "being baptized with Holy Spirit," or the "Holy Spirit being poured out"—key concepts in Acts to describe divine presence. Again, the structural analyses will take into account sequence of events and literary structure, and the exegetical analyses will consider aspects of grammar and semantics. The question asked in these explorations is whether God's Holy Spirit inspired his people's praise upon their reception and whether their praise also instigated manifestations of God's Spirit-presence in return. Hence, this part will investigate whether and in which ways the above texts witness to a consecutive connection between divine Spirit presence and human praise. For that reason, other aspects or texts beyond this issue will not be considered.

The second half of this chapter will concentrate on texts dealing with the new Christians being refilled with Holy Spirit or other divine manifestations in the context of their praise. The relevant narrative texts are taken from Acts 4 (4:24–31), Acts 16 (16:25–26), and an exhortatory text from Ephesians 5 (5:18–20). The question asked then is whether God's people's prayer and praise instigated their refilling with Holy Spirit or other manifestations of divine presence. Accordingly, that part will investigate whether and in which ways these texts witness to a consecutive connection between human praise and divine presence. Again, aspects or passages beyond this question will not be taken into consideration.

5.1 General Remarks on Luke-Acts

Scholars have acknowledged an authorial unity between the Book of Acts and the Gospel of Luke, but views differ a lot whether historical, theological, literary, narrative, or other levels of unity are concerned.[1] By and large, scholarly theories on that unity are owed to various reasons: first, general historical relations have caused Luke-Acts to be read as a history of Christian origins;[2] second, particular theological relations between both books, for example, the salvation for God's people now including Jews and Gentiles has been perceived as the fulfilment of Old Testament promises to which both books refer;[3] and, third, in connection with that, the gift of the Holy Spirit has been considered a thematic link connecting Luke and Acts.[4] For those reasons, issues of literary and other unity between the two books matter a lot. The various ways in which the Holy Spirit is portrayed in Acts are also highly significant. The present approach supports both a literary-narrative and historical-theological unity within diversity for Luke-Acts. William Shepherd Jr. believes the purpose of the

---

1. Parsons and Pervo, *Rethinking the Unity*, 115, identify at least five different levels of unity; see also Powell, *What are They Saying*, 5–9; Bird, "Unity of Luke-Acts," 3–16; Verheyden, "Unity," 45–56; Bock, *Luke and Acts*, 55–62.

2. This aspect is pointed out by McCollough in connection with what he terms as "sequential reading" in *Ritual Water, Ritual Spirit*, 45–62, 79–80. On Luke's travel report as a historical document see Baum, *Lukas als Historiker*, 203–63.

3. E.g., Isa 61:1 and Luke 4:18–19; Ezek 36 and Luke 24:44–49; Joel 2 and Acts 2, 10, 11.

4. Marshall, *Luke*, 200; Bock, *Luke and Acts*, 55–61.

discourse in Acts is to portray the Spirit as a divine character in an indirect, narrative way.[5] Ju Hur reaches beyond this narrative purpose by identifying the Spirit as a divine agent.[6] He advocates the method of a "dynamic biblical narrative criticism" emphasizing that "we need to look at the narrative of Luke-Acts as a final literary form in order to understand its presentation or function of the Holy Spirit."[7] One may go even one step further by looking into an interaction between divine and human agents.[8] This interaction will reveal its dynamics in the next section on structure analysis, which will, again, be followed by the exegetical analysis.

5.2 The Initial Spirit-Infilling and Praise of God's New People: Acts 2

5.2.1 Sequence of Events and Structure

This section elucidates the temporal sequence of events as narrated in Acts 2 portraying the beginning of God's new people (vv. 1–4) who, at first, consist of Jews mainly. The stage for the events is already set in Acts 1:12–14.

1. Following the ascension of Jesus, the eleven male disciples, some unnamed female disciples, and members of Jesus' family were gathered together (Acts 1:12–14; Luke 24:49–52).

2. Such gatherings of prayer and praise used to take place in Jerusalem just like on the day of Pentecost (Acts 2:1).[9]

3. Sudden manifestations of God's presence appeared, illustrated through the metaphors of wind and fire (2:2–3).

---

5. Shepherd, *Narrative Function*, 248–50; on narrative criticism in Luke-Acts see ch. 3, section 3.5.5.

6. Hur, *Dynamic Reading*, 33, 114.

7. Hur, *Dynamic Reading*, 34, 28–29.

8. This is what distinguishes Hur from Shepherd's narrative literary-critical approach.

9. Barrett, *Commentary*, 1:112, referring to Schille, deems the purpose of these meetings to be common worship, whether in smaller or larger settings; three favorite places beyond the private homes were the Mount of Olives, the temple mount, and the so-called "upper room" of a place which was considered a house of prayer. Peterson, *Acts*, 132, refers to the temple as "house of prayer," but assumes a house-setting for Pentecost first which then led to a more "public arena."

4. Subsequently, all the disciples were filled with the Holy Spirit and declared God's wonders by praising him in other tongues (2:4, 11).

The above events in Acts 1 and 2 reveal divine and human interaction: divine Spirit-presence depicted in metaphorical terms is preceded by prayer and followed by praise. The temporal association is epitomized in Acts 1:14, where the disciples were gathered together in one place for the purpose of prayer, and Acts 2:4, 11, where the disciples were filled with Holy Spirit and then praised God in other tongues:

A1 Human action:[10] the disciples observed Jesus' stipulations as to their staying in Jerusalem until they would be "clothed with power from on high" (Luke 24:49). While in prayer they were "waiting for the promised gift," namely to "be baptized with Holy Spirit" (Acts 1:4–5).

B1 Divine action: the sound like of a violent wind blowing from heaven filled the entire house (Acts 2:2).

B2 Divine action: tongues like of fire appeared and rested on each one of the disciples (2:3).

B3 Divine action: all of them were filled with the Holy Spirit (2:4a).

A2 Human action: they spoke in other tongues (2:4b) and praised God by declaring his miracles (2:11b).

This sequence of events in Acts 1 and 2 represents an *inclusio* with human action as prayer and glossolalia-praise which frames and emphasizes divine action as a twofold theophany and Spirit-infilling:

A1
  B1
  B2
  B3
A2

Thus, glossolalia praise is narrated as immediately following a threefold manifestation of divine Spirit-presence highlighted through repetition. And so, it can be inferred that divine presence in the form of an initial infilling with Holy Spirit must have instigated this praise. Yet, the sequence of events does not justify the reverse assumption. It is true,

---

10. For reasons of convenience the term "action" was chosen: A = human action, B = divine action.

prayer is narrated in the context preceding these manifestations at Pentecost, but this can also be interpreted in terms of covenant commitment.

In the exegetical analysis of Acts 2:1–4, the influence of divine Spirit-presence on human praise will be further explored. Especially v.4 characterizes this divine and human interaction.

5.2.2 Exegetical Analysis: Acts 2:1–4

> ¹*When the day of Pentecost came to an end, they were all together in one place.* ²*Suddenly a sound like the blowing of a mighty wind came from heaven and filled the entire house where they were sitting.* ³*They saw what seemed to be tongues of fire that separated and came to rest on each one of them.* ⁴*All of them were filled with Holy Spirit and began to speak in other tongues as the Spirit enabled them.*

The subordinate clause in v.1 expresses through the verbal construction ἐν τῷ συμπληροῦσθαι "when was fulfilled"[11] a temporal coincidence between the day of Pentecost and the disciples' prayer gathering conveying the idea of temporal fulfilment. This moment in time not only denotes the end of the fifty-day interval between Passover and Pentecost, but also happens to be the fiftieth day after Jesus' ascension. Moreover, Pentecost designates the so-called Feast of Weeks, a Jewish harvest festival of the first fruit (Lev 23:10).[12] At that time, it was celebrated as one of the three great pilgrimage festivals of Judaism which inundated Jerusalem with a crowd of Diaspora Jews.[13]

---

11. Verbal construction in infinitive passive as part of *aci*; Bauer, *Griechisch-Deutsches Wörterbuch*, 1555, holds that, given the grammatical signals ἐν τῷ in connection with *aci* a temporal fulfilment is implied, whether as time span or specific date (also Haubeck and von Siebenthal, *Neuer sprachlicher Schlüssel*, 616); Zerwick, *Biblical Greek*, §187, affirms that the regular use in the temporal sense may be due to Hebrew influence (also Zerwick and Grosvenor, *Grammatical Analysis*, 352); similarly, Metzger, *Textual Commentary*, 289, sees in this Bezan version of the "unusual Greek" the result of translation from Aramaic.

12. Bruce, *Acts*, 113–14, explains that the first fruit were offered by the Israelites in remembrance of their Exodus from Egypt (Lev 23:9–16). Following this first offering at Passover—the Hebrew term *omer* means "sheaf" referring to the first sheaf—they had to count seven weeks or fifty days—*pentecostae* in Greek—until the next offering of the first fruit at the Feast of Weeks—*shavuot* in Hebrew (see Num 28:26).

13. Keener, *Commentary*, 1:193.

God's Spirit-Presence and God's People's Praise in the New Testament 127

Later in Judaism, Pentecost was associated with the giving of the law. Consequently, scholars have maintained that, just as the gift of Torah was considered an act of divine revelation which resulted in a covenant between God and his people, the Christian Pentecost became a new act of divine revelation through the Holy Spirit which also resulted in a new covenant between God and his new people.[14] Accordingly, James Dunn clarifies that almost every Jew or proselyte at that time must have perceived the sending of the Spirit as the giving of the "new Torah" written on the tablets of their hearts.[15] And so, in line with Jewish eschatology, the gift of the Spirit was considered one of the significant signs of the "new age." This idea of a "new Torah" has been debated. For example, C. K. Barrett rejects this concept as too late,[16] and Max Turner argues that Luke does not portray Pentecost as the beginning of the "new age" of salvation or as a new covenant, but as the fulfilment of the one made to Abraham.[17] For now, scholars tend to support the idea of a new, eschatological age of salvation.[18] This seems to be legitimate in view of the biblical support, e.g., the MT in Jeremiah 31:31 talks about בְּרִית חֲדָשָׁה or, the LXX about διαθήκην καινήν, a new covenant.

In any case, for Luke, Pentecost points to the Sinai covenant given the theophanic allusions he uses (Acts 2:2–3). Also, this feast heralds God's "renewed" or new covenant people, as textual signs suggest the fulfilment of eschatological promises for God's people:

1. Jesus' promise in Luke 24:49 of the disciples' "being baptized in Holy Spirit" is narrated as being fulfilled in Acts 1:5.
2. The "outpouring" of God's Spirit promised in Joel 2:28–29 (cf. Isa 32:15 and 44:3; also Ezek 39:29b) is narrated as being fulfilled in Acts 2:16–18.

In Acts 2:2a, the verbal form ἐγένετο "it happened" (aorist of γίνομαι)[19] plus καὶ combined with the adverb ἄφνω "suddenly" introduces an immediate, supernatural event, namely a theophany depicted in the

---

14. Dunn, *Baptism*, 49.
15. Dunn, *Baptism*, 46–49.
16. Barrett, *Acts*, 1:111.
17. Turner, *Power from on High*, 353.
18. Bock, *Luke and Acts*, 220.
19. Culy and Parsons, *Acts*, 23.

form of a simile:[20] ὥσπερ "like" the sound of a strong πνοή "wind"[21] rushing from heaven came and filled the entire house. The Greek syllable *pnef* or the verb *pne(f)o* originally referred to such an energy-laden movement of the air which led to the nouns πνοή "wind" (2:2)[22] and πνεῦμα "s/Spirit" (2:4). This πνοή is associated in the LXX with the God-given "breath of life" in Genesis 2:7.[23] In v.2b, the verb ἐπλήρωσεν "filled" (aorist active) provides a metaphorical reference point for the disciples' being filled with Holy Spirit in v.4.

Likewise, the subsequent divine manifestation in Acts 2:3 is illustrated through another simile: "Divided tongues *like* of fire appeared to them and rested on each of them." Metaphors of wind, fire, and smoke are used in the Old Testament to refer to divine appearances emulating the theophanies with Moses and the Israelites at Mount Sinai (Exod 19:18–20).[24] In the same way, fire is mentioned in 1 Kings 8 and 2 Chronicles 7. Fire symbolizes God's holiness and, as a consequence, also represents his cleansing and judgment.[25] Besides, scholars have highlighted in connection with concepts of רוּחַ in the OT that theophanies in the form of breath and wind can be perceived by their effects.[26] Thus, one may infer that Luke used wind and fire in the form of metaphorical similes to epitomize the *effects* of the Holy Spirit: "the *sound* like of a mighty wind" in v.2a (see also John 3:8), or "the *shape* like of divided fire tongues" in v.3. At this point, a brief foretaste of metaphors and their interpretation seems appropriate. We will still come back to this topic in the next chapter.[27]

Paul Ricoeur, the renowned "master of metaphors" and their interpretation, criticizes classical rhetoric theory in that it defined metaphor as a figure of discourse "which represents the extension of meaning of

20. A simile is a type of metaphor in which the association is made through "like" or a corresponding word; while a simile refers to a comparison, a metaphor refers to a direct equation (cf. Cotterell and Turner, *Linguistics*, 299–307).

21. Keener, *Acts*, 1:800, points out that Luke uses a rare term for wind.

22. Bauer, *Griechisch-Deutsches Wörterbuch*, 1363.

23. Keener, *Acts*, 1:800.

24. 1 Kgs 19:11; Isa 6:1–4; Isa 66:15; and Ezek 1:4; on Spirit in the OT cf., e.g., Averbeck, "Breath," 25–37; see also ch. 4 of the present study, section 4.2.3.

25. Barrett, *Commentary*, 1:114, refers to fire as symbolizing divine cleansing and purification (see Ps 50:3); also Keener, *Acts*, 1:804.

26. Averbeck, "Breath," 36; Thiselton, *Holy Spirit*, 4; see Dreytza, *Theologische Gebrauch von RUAḤ*, 125–45, 198–235; on the use of *ruaḥ* see also Hildebrandt, *OT Theology of the Spirit of God*, 1–27.

27. See section 6.2.

God's Spirit-Presence and God's People's Praise in the New Testament 129

a name through deviation from the literal meaning of words" on the basis of resemblance.[28] He does not want to see a metaphorical utterance reduced to the semantics of words, but to involve the semantics of a sentence or even discourse, nor does he locate the reason for this deviation in resemblance. On the contrary, Ricoeur insists that this divergence involves a "shock engendered by two incompatible ideas" and that a metaphor entails reducing this shock.[29] For that reason, a metaphor encompasses a literal (vehicle) and a figurative side (tenor) embodying together this tension and generating its result which equals a "creative act" and a semantic innovation.[30]

Following Ricoeur's theory, the *sound of wind* and the *shape of fire tongues* generates a tension between the ideas of wind/fire on the one hand and divine Spirit on the other, and by doing so they create innovative meaning. Such a model of dynamic interpretation seems suitable, since the Book of Acts depicts the bestowal of God's Spirit through dynamic, verbal metaphors which perceive the reception of the Holy Spirit from different angles of view:[31]

1. "You shall be baptized with Holy Spirit" (Acts 1:4–8 cf. 11:16); this verbal metaphor appears only twice in Acts and once in Luke (Luke 3:16;[32] also Matt 3:11; Mark 1:8; John 1:33; 1 Cor 12:13);
2. "I will pour out of my Spirit,"[33] "He poured out" (Acts 2:16–18, 33; 10:45; cf. Isa 44:3–4 and Joel 2:28);
3. "They were all filled with Holy Spirit" (Acts 2:4), "You will be filled with Holy Spirit" (Acts 9:17), "They were filled with Holy Spirit" (Acts 13:52; cf. also 4:8, 31);
4. "The Holy Spirit had (not yet) fallen on them" (Acts 8:16; 11:15).

---

28. For literary discourse and the "surplus of meaning" of metaphors see Ricoeur, *Interpretation Theory*, 45–70.

29. Ricoeur, *Interpretation Theory*, 51–52.

30. Cotterell and Turner, *Linguistics*, 299–302, esp. 300.

31. Atkinson, *Baptism in the Spirit*, 126, referring to Turner, points out that in Luke's time these metaphors may still have been "fluid" and not yet technical terms; see also the useful diagram by Hamilton, *God's Indwelling Presence*, 198, on metaphors of Spirit-reception.

32. Luke 3:16 adds "baptism in Spirit and fire."

33. Salter, *Power of Pentecost*, 6, explains the preposition followed by genitive in the phrase ἐκχέω ἀπὸ τοῦ πνεύματός as partitive governed by the verb, which does not specify the quantity of the infilling etc.

In addition to these co-referential verbal metaphors, there are simple verbs in connection with Holy Spirit, such as "to receive" (Acts 2:33, 38), "to give" (11:17), and "to come upon" (1:8) which mostly, but not exclusively, refer to an initial Spirit reception.

In view of the above, it seems logical to propose that Luke uses two verbal metaphorical similes—the house being filled with something like wind (v.2) and tongues like flames of fire resting on each individual (v.3)— as vehicles to illustrate the bestowal of the Holy Spirit as tenor (v.4): just as the house of meeting was filled with wind, the disciples were filled with Holy Spirit;[34] and just as the divided fire tongues came to rest on each individual, every person came to receive the Holy Spirit.[35] This reminds us of the Lord's house being filled with his glory (1 Kings 8 and 2 Chr 5–7).

As a matter of fact, Luke uses four times in Acts the metaphorical concept of the verb πλήθω in connection with people being filled with Holy Spirit (Acts 2:4; 4:8, 31; 9:17).[36] This metaphor has been considered by scholars to be characteristic of Luke-Acts.[37] Darrell Bock specifies that references to "being filled with Holy Spirit" appear in Acts, while they are largely absent from Luke's Gospel.[38] The term "Holy Spirit" is used without the definite article like a personal name, which could refer to God's presence through the Holy Spirit.[39]

---

34. Concerning a metaphorization of temple terminology in Luke-Acts see Gäckle, *Allgemeines Priestertum*, 310–13.

35. Similarly, Levison, *Filled with the Spirit*, 330, describes the association of Spirit-infilling and fire as "tandem partners that effect and accent the inspired state."

36. Verb in aor. passive plus noun in genitive of quality: Haubeck and von Siebenthal, *Neuer sprachlicher Schlüssel*, 617, and Zerwick and Grosvenor, *Grammatical Analysis*, 353, interpret this form as "to cause something to be full" in connection with Holy Spirit. Louw and Nida, *Greek-English Lexicon*, 1:598, explain it as an intensification of the verb πληρόω, "to cause something to be completely full"; scholars differ on the verb form in 2:4: Peterson, *Acts*, 132, and Culy and Parsons, *Acts*, 25, refer to πίμπλημι. On Spirit-infilling in Acts, esp. in 2:4, see Levison, *Filled with the Spirit*, 326–47, esp. 361.

37. Turner, *Power from on High*, 165–69; for metaphors of Spirit infilling in Luke-Acts see also Braun, "Concept," 44–87, esp. 58–60: the LXX renders 70 forms of the Hebrew verb *malē'*, with πληρόω; out of 87 times in the NT forms of the verb πληρόω occur 9 times in Luke's Gospel and 16 times in Acts.

38. Bock, *Luke and Acts*, 212.

39. Haubeck and von Siebenthal, *Neuer sprachlicher Schlüssel*, 617. In contrast, Haya-Prats, *Empowered Believers*, 13, referring to Proksch, explains the lack of article as a typical prophetic formula to "refer to a more general and Old Testament sense of the Spirit." This, however, may only be correct in as far as the fulfilment of OT promises is concerned.

God's Spirit-Presence and God's People's Praise in the New Testament 131

The adding of the suffix *ma* to the root *pne(f)* creates the verbal noun *pneuma* which in Greek originally denoted substance, event, and effect: moved air as a specific, material substance with emphasis on the effective power of this movement.[40] Thus, among the literal meanings of the term *pneuma* are breath, air, and wind filled with an intrinsic power, and among the figurative meanings are spirit and divine Spirit as a "wind from heaven." So, in classical Greek, *pneuma* referred mainly to a dynamic physical substance which was also applied to spiritual realities. However, the Greek concept of divine Spirit as material substance has been disputed on the basis that it cannot be applied to Jewish biblical texts.[41] This argument was brought to the fore by Craig Keener and Volker Rabens.[42] Particularly Rabens elucidated that, partly because of a misconception of metaphorical language, a material Spirit concept in Hellenism has falsely been read into Jewish texts.[43] This is why Rabens is opposed to a material concept of divine Spirit in Pauline texts and why he replaces it with a model of "relational transformation and empowering."[44] That caveat may also affect potential misconceptions of the Spirit in Acts. Then, the question is whether a relational concept, which includes soteriological and empowering aspects of God's Spirit, can also be applied to Acts and other books. Hence, we have tested in as far as such a relational concept applies to the interaction between God's presence and his people's praise in the context of covenant relationships.[45]

As has been mentioned, the verbal metaphor of an initial "infilling" of the disciples with Holy Spirit is also referred to as "being baptized with Holy Spirit" or "Spirit-baptism," but from a different metaphorical reference point (Luke 3:16; Acts 1:5). Henry Lederle maintains that "being baptized with" and "being filled with Holy Spirit" are synonymous

---

40. Kittel, *Theologisches Wörterbuch*, 6:33–37.

41. The LXX translates *ruaḥ* in the OT 277 times with *pneuma*, referring besides the Spirit of God to wind and breath as utterances of human energy of life (see Kittel, *Theologisches Wörterbuch*, 6:366). In the NT, *pneuma* is used 379 times, partly repeating the OT use of *ruaḥ*, but mainly introducing a new domain of meaning for God's Spirit as gift of the Father and the Son for the church (cf. Kremer, "Pneuma," 3:117–23, esp. 118); in Acts, references to the Spirit are almost four times as many as in Luke with six references in Acts 2 only (cf. Kittel, *Theologisches Wörterbuch*, 6:401–13); also Braun, "Concept," 59.

42. Keener, *Acts*, 1:799; Rabens, *Holy Spirit*, 25–79.

43. Rabens, *Holy Spirit*, 43–52.

44. Rabens, *Holy Spirit*, 123–45.

45. See ch. 6, section 6.3.

expression to denote the initiatory experience.[46] However, on the other hand, he would understand "Spirit-baptism" as the "open-end" charismatic dimension of the normal Christian life and the term "infilling" as the ongoing experience.[47] To clarify, in our investigation, we tend to use the term "infilling" for the initiatory Spirit bestowal and reserve the term "refilling" for any subsequent Spirit-reception.

This brings us to the lively debate among non-Pentecostals or non-Charismatics on the one side and Pentecostals, Charismatics, and neo-Pentecostals on the other side about what this baptism in the Spirit involves, a discussion maintained particularly in the Anglophone scholarly world over the last four decades.[48] Suffice it to point to some of the main protagonists: on the one side, Dunn explains his view on "Spirit-baptism" in terms of conversion-initiation and criticizes Pentecostal positions as "second blessing" theories.[49] On the other side, classic Pentecostal scholars like Ervin, Stronstad, Shelton, and Menzies focus on the empowering aspect of Spirit-baptism.[50] Similarly, Baumert, a representative of the Catholic renewal movement, favors the Pentecostal two-stage model over against a sacramentalist interpretation of Spirit-baptism.[51] A third party seeks to reconcile soteriological and empowering aspects, among them the originally Pentecostal Turner and, more recently, the Pentecostals Macchia and Atkinson.[52]

Regarding method, Hur criticizes scholars from Dunn via Menzies to Turner for almost always using historical-critical methods like

---

46. Lederle *Treasures Old and New*, 224.

47. Lederle, *Treasures Old and New*, 224–26, talks about Spirit-baptism in terms of Spirit-infilling (integrative view).

48. This is why German contributions, though not irrelevant, have not been focussed upon in this study; e.g., Wenk, *Community-Forming Power*, concentrates on the socioethical role of the Spirit in Luke-Acts. As to contemporary scholarship, Thiselton, *Holy Spirit*, 394–467, refers to influential authors from France, Germany, Greece, and Russia, e.g., Congar, Gunkel, Horn, Moltmann, Pannenberg, Schweizer, Losski, Zizioulas et al., with the first one representing Catholic and the two latter ones representing Eastern Orthodox traditions.

49. Dunn, *Baptism*.

50. Ervin, *Conversion-Initiation*; Stronstad, *Charismatic Theology*; Stronstad, *Prophethood*; Shelton, *Mighty in Word and Deed*; Menzies, *Empowered*.

51. See Baumert, "Charism," 147–79, esp. 147.

52. Turner, *Power from on High*; Macchia, *Baptized in the Spirit*; Atkinson, *Baptism in the Spirit*.

redaction criticism.⁵³ Nevertheless, despite Hur's different method of a "dynamic biblical narrative criticism," his understanding of the role of the Spirit in Acts as comprising salvation and empowering is similar to Turner's. Interesting representatives of the late twentieth and early twenty-first century affected by "postmodern pluralism" are Yong and Kärkkäinen:⁵⁴ Yong travelled from Pentecostalism via Evangelicalism to Eastern Orthodoxy combining the Spirit approaches of the three, and Kärkkäinen combines his Pentecostal inheritance with Lutheran Protestantism.⁵⁵

Lederle's "integrative theology" of Spirit-baptism represents an earlier attempt to avoid a split-up of Spirit-reception into several stages and to evade an experiential pneumatology.⁵⁶ There has been consent among scholars that Luke understands the Holy Spirit in Acts as a "Spirit of prophecy," yet, the content of this concept has remained a debated issue as concerns soteriological and empowering aspects. Menzies thinks of a "Spirit of prophecy" as an additional empowering gift on top of salvation.⁵⁷ Differently, Turner identifies the concept of a Spirit of prophecy in rabbinic Judaism, which he thinks to have influenced Luke-Acts, but to have been complemented by a messianic, ethical-soteriological aspect.⁵⁸

Whatever the view on "Spirit-baptism" is,⁵⁹ the debate makes clear that the reception of the Holy Spirit, whether in terms of "being filled with" or "being baptized with Holy Spirit," involves ethical-soteriological aspects of covenant background, which is of consequence for this investigation.

Coming back to the Spirit-infilling of the disciples, F. F. Bruce asserts that the earliest Old Testament precedent for such infilling with inspired side effects is Numbers 11:25.⁶⁰ However, the Lord coming down in a cloud took the Spirit that was upon Moses and placed him *upon* and not

53. Hur, *Dynamic Reading*, 279–80.

54. Yong, *Discerning the Spirit(s)*; Kärkkäinen, *Pneumatology*.

55. Thiselton, *Holy Spirit*, 453.

56. Lederle, *Treasures*, 218, distinguishes between one-stage, two-stage, and three-stage Pentecostals (which also applies to Neo-Pentecostals and Charismatics): the one-stage concept refers to Spirit-initiation with tongues as part and parcel, the two-stage concept distinguishes between conversion-initiation and empowering with tongues as evidence of the "second blessing," and the three-stage concept relates to conversion-initiation, sanctification, and empowering.

57. Menzies, *Empowered for Witness*.

58. Turner, *Power From on High*, 82–137; also Turner, "Spirit in Luke-Acts," 75–101 where he refers to the concept of a Spirit of prophecy.

59. See also the summary by McCollough, *Ritual Water, Ritual Spirit*, 5–42.

60. Bruce, *Acts*, 114.

within the seventy elders, which caused them to prophecy. Accordingly, James Hamilton Jr. emphasizes that God's presence in the Old Testament was *with and not in* his people.[61] Indeed, God's presence in the New Testament was *within* his new people, individually and corporately.[62] Under the former covenants, God's presence dwelling among his people was bound to specific places like the temple, and his presence empowering kings, priests, and prophets was bound to their specific tasks. God could operate on the hearts of his people through his Spirit while not dwelling in individuals. However, under the new covenant, God inhabits every one of his people through his Spirit. Therefore, this new way of *indwelling divine presence* enunciates a certain discontinuity between the Testaments, a significant corollary for our exploration.[63] We will return to the metaphor of Spirit-infilling in connection with the metaphor of divine indwelling later in the chapter on biblical theology.[64]

This new indwelling presence of God's Spirit resulted in inspired utterance for the disciples, although it cannot be reduced to that. They started to speak in other tongues (glossolalia), which most probably refers to the foreign languages spoken by the Diaspora Jews present at Pentecost. This instance points to a global scope that involves "every nation under heaven" (Acts 2:4–11; also 10:46 and 19:6). For the disciples, other "tongues" were new, unlearnt languages (xenolalia), since they were only enabled by the Holy Spirit to express themselves (2:4b). Consequently, some scholars thought this phenomenon equals a miracle of speech, which can be seen as a reversal of the judgment at Babel (Gen 11:1–9) when God came down to confuse the tongues of the nations.[65]

---

61. Hamilton, *God's Indwelling Presence*, 25–56.

62. Hamilton, *God's Indwelling Presence*, 25, referring to Janowski, looks at the contrast between a "*shekhinah* theology" in the OT and a "theology of indwelling" in the NT: he points out that the OT uses prepositions like *be* in the sense of *al*, *betokh*, and *bemidbar* which relate to God's presence *with* and *among* his people (*God's Indwelling Presence*, 25–55), but not *in* each individual. Still, the term *shekhinah*, which relates to the glory-cloud accompanying God's people in the wilderness, is not a biblical, but a doctrinal term from rabbinic literature, since the term itself does not occur in the Hebrew Bible.

63. Hamilton, *God's Indwelling Presence*, uses the term "indwelling" in a similar sense; on the idea of indwelling see also Kaiser, "Indwelling Presence," 308–15.

64. See ch. 6, section 6.2.

65. Dunn, *Jesus and the Spirit*, 148–52, moderates his position through the remark that those present at Pentecost thought it was glossolalia; also Carson, *Showing the Spirit*, 138–39.

This represents a traditional earlier view. Others support the theory of a miracle of hearing, while others again do not take sides.⁶⁶

In Acts 2:15–16, Peter gives the explanation for the phenomenon of xenolalia, first, through negation and, second, through affirmation. McCollough qualifies the phenomen of xenolalia as the "solitary referent for Peters discourse."⁶⁷ The γὰρ introduces Peter's explanation in Acts 2:15 where he juxtaposes wine and Spirit, as Bock points out referring to Luke 1:15 and Eph 5:18.⁶⁸ The point of comparison serves to explain the origin of the phenomenon: *not intoxicated by wine, but inspired by Spirit*. For Levison, this is the first level of interpretation; he discerns two deeper levels:⁶⁹ a second level, seen against the background of Bacchic rituals, would interpret the disciples *to be seen as drunk and inspired*, and a third level would explain them *to be falsely believed to be inspired, as they appear to be drunk*. This represents an overly differentiated interpretation, hence, the first level may suffice. For Levison, the first interpretation is supported by the verb ἀποφθέγγεσθαι "to declare plainly" in Acts 2:4 which he explains in terms of inspired proclamation of scriptural truths and not in terms of praise.⁷⁰

Then, Peter refers to the Jewish interpretation mode of *pesher* "this is that."⁷¹ Darrell Bock mentions the similarity in Jewish *pesher* style and also refers to the Jewish method of *gezerah shewa*, a method of connecting two passages through one term, i.e., Acts 2 would connect with Joel 2 though the term "pour out," which would indicate a universal distribution of God's Spirit on all people.⁷² Equally, Robert Wall perceives an extended narrative from Acts 2:22—15:12 reflecting Joel 2:28–29.⁷³ By quoting in Acts 2:17–21 from Joel 2:28–32, Peter explains tongues in light of the fulfillment of Joel's promise, which refers to the outpouring of God's Spirit. The universal distribution of divine Spirit-presence involves prophetic empowerment, such as prophecies, visions, and dreams for each individual among God's people. The phenomenon of speaking in

66. Thiselton, *Holy Spirit*, 54, refers to Carson for glossolalia and to Montague for the miracle of hearing.
67. McCollough, *Ritual Water, Ritual Spirit*, 35.
68. Bock, *Luke and Acts*, 111.
69. Levison, *Filled with the Spirit*, 333–35.
70. Levison, *Filled with the Spirit*, 357–61.
71. Peterson, *Acts*, 138–40.
72. Bock, *Acts*, 11, 16.
73. Wall, "Israel and the Gentile Mission," 443.

tongues, which is not mentioned in Joel, is seen to be part of this prophetic equipment.

Still, Peter's references to Joel's promise need to be seen against the background of repentance in view of judgment, salvation/restoration, and prophetic empowerment, as Larry McQueen elucidates.[74] First, Joel issues a call for lament and repentance (Joel 1, also 2:12–17), which is reinforced through references to the coming day of judgment (Joel 2:1–11). This call is echoed in Peter's appeal for repentance (Acts 2:38); it also resonates with John's call for repentance who baptized in water, a ministry preceding the ministry of the risen Jesus Christ who baptizes in Holy Spirit (Acts 1:5); besides, this call is anticipated in Luke's reference to a "baptism in Spirit and fire" (Luke 3:16–17).[75] Second, Joel gives assurance of salvation and restoration for people and land (Joel 2:18–27).[76] Third, and only then, prophetic empowerment in terms of prophecies, visions, and dreams is promised for each individual among God's people (Joel 2:28–29). This ethical-soteriological background in Joel certainly involves covenant.

In addition, Peter in his speech in Acts 2:22–39 points to a Davidic Messiah and king (Acts 2:29–31 with quote from Ps 17:8–11b and Ps 110:1) whom he identifies as Jesus of Nazareth (Acts 2:22–24, 32): Christ, the "Anointed One" and "Baptist in Holy Spirit," received from the Father and poured out the Holy Spirit (2:33),[77] a gift to be received by all who repent (2:38, 39). Jesus is the name they must call for forgiveness of sins (2:38), and this is the name the disciples, empowered by the Spirit,

---

74. McQueen, *Joel and the Spirit*, 56; in connection with that, Bock, *Luke and Acts*, 221, presumes an earlier Jewish tradition prior to Joel.

75. Luke 3:16–17 adds "and fire" to the disciples' being baptized in Spirit: accordingly, Turner, *Power from on High*, 175–87, explains a "baptism in Spirit and fire" as representing two sides of the same coin: purification for the repentant and judgment for the unrepentant; Bock, *Luke and Acts*, 214–18, evaluates the "fire debate": he remarks that Peter in his speech in Acts 2 refers back to Luke 3:16–17, which would, again, allude to a purging process mentioned in Isa 4:4.

76. Keener, *Spirit in the Gospels and Acts*, 191, maintains the disciples assumed that, due to the eschatological character of both Spirit and kingdom, "a promise concerning the Spirit implied the imminent restoration of Israel" (Acts 1:6). Salter, *Power of Pentecost*, 29–36, esp. 34, referring to Turner, draws attention to restoration motifs used in Acts 2, but he seems to connect them with Exodus and Davidic motifs rather than with the background in Joel (also Turner, *Power from on High*, 279).

77. Brawley, *Centering on God*, 88, notes that the Spirit's outpouring represents a sign of approval of Jesus' kingship: "In the narrative schema of the kingship of Jesus, the pouring out of the Spirit sanctions the resurrection and exaltation of enthronement."

God's Spirit-Presence and God's People's Praise in the New Testament 137

proclaim beginning in Jerusalem "until the ends of the earth" (Luke 24:47–49). Hence, the function of the Spirit is Christ-centered and not self-centered. His role is to point to Christ Jesus (Acts 1:8) who, again, came to reveal the Father (John 12:45; 14:9). As a consequence, this new divine Spirit-presence opens up a new form of relationship with the triune God. How through the bestowal of God's Spirit his people also share in the inner-Trinitarian relationship will be further explored.[78]

Coming back to the phenomenon of glossolalia, the role of speaking in tongues as the "initial evidence" of a "Spirit-baptism" developed into a doctrine among the upcoming Pentecostal movement since the beginning of the twentieth century. However, it has been a disputed matter among scholars up to now whether the biblical text presents the Pentecost phenomenon of tongues as *the* paradigmatic initial evidence.[79] Without entering into that debate suffice it to say Acts 2 narrates this phenomenon as part and parcel of the experience of the disciples as a way to express their worship. The relevance for this study is that, just as the tongues of fire rested on each of the disciples, each of them was given a new tongue "to declare the wonders/mighty works of God" (Acts 2:11). This declaration has been considered tantamount to praise, as Howard Marshall asserts.[80] Likewise, John Polhill speaks of a "praise language."[81] Similarly, Craig Keener writes: "Acts 2:46–47 shows that a further feature of the Spirit-filled community was continuing worship."[82]

For those reasons, one may conclude that God dwelling in each individual of his people through this Spirit-infilling instigated their praise in new, unlearnt tongues.

5.2.3 Summary

The results of the structural analysis of Acts 2 and the exegetical analysis of Acts 2:1–4 corroborate that divine presence instigated human praise. The initial infilling of God's people with his Holy Spirit literally "inspired" their xenolalia worship. This new Spirit-presence in each individual of God's new people is portrayed by two verbal metaphorical

---

78. See ch. 6 of this study, section 6.5.
79. Turner, *Power from on High*, 357–58.
80. See Marshall, "Worshipping Biblically," 146–61, esp. 159; also Bruce, *Acts*, 115.
81. Polhill, *Acts*, 99.
82. Keener, *Spirit in the Gospels and Acts*, 200.

similes, wind and fire—wind filling the entire house picturing the Spirit-infilling of the disciples and fire tongues resting on each individual depicting their glossolalia. This divine Spirit-presence at corporate and individual levels evidently prompted the praise of the disciples. However, there is no evidence for the reverse assumption that prayer/praise provoked this Spirit-infilling.

Moreover, it has been demonstrated that the xenolalia praise following the Spirit-infilling in Acts 2:4 is associated with allusions to Joel's background in Acts 2:17–21 and references to a Davidic messiah in Acts 2:22–40. The quotations from Joel (Joel 2:28–32a) reveal elements of repentance, salvation, and empowerment which *can be discerned* as "three-in-one," but *must not be divorced* from each other. The messianic references (Ps 17:8–11b and Ps 110:1) express a Trinitarian aspect in the divine-human relationship, now focused on Jesus Christ and bestowed through the Holy Spirit. This substantiates a covenant background for the initial infilling with God's Spirit of God's people in the context of their praise. Although the author of Luke-Acts does not use temple/house of God terminology, the textual connotations reverberate 1 Kings 8 and 2 Chronicles 5–7 with the initial infilling of God's newly-built temple with his glory-presence in his people's praise. We will return to the temple imagery later on in connection with the metaphor of the divine indwelling in the chapter on biblical theology.[83]

5.3 The Initial Spirit-Infilling and Praise of God's New People: Acts 10 and 11

The chapters between Acts 2 and Acts 10 portray the transition of the gospel from a Jewish to a Gentile environment in the face of opposition and persecution. The initial Spirit-infilling of new believers followed by their praise comes into play again in Acts 10 and 11, while a repeated Spirit-infilling following prayer and praise already appears in Acts 4 and 16.

Accordingly, as Acts advances, Luke reports healings and an increasing persecution of the apostles, for instance, that of Stephen (Acts 7). Steven, full of the Holy Spirit and beholding the glory of God (7:55), was stoned and breathed his last praying for his persecutors (7:59–60), but no praise is reported. The ensuing persecution involves the scattering of the young Christian community and furthers the spreading of the gospel

---

83. See ch. 6, sections 6.2.1 to 6.2.4.

God's Spirit-Presence and God's People's Praise in the New Testament   139

from Jerusalem to Judea, Samaria, and even Ethiopia (Acts 8). The Samaritans received the Holy Spirit through the apostles laying their hands on them, but no praise is indicated (8:17). On the contrary, the former sorcerer Simon had purchase in mind instead of praise because he intended to buy with money the ability of such "Spirit-transfer" (8:18–19). Then, when the passionate persecutor and Jew Saul was turned into the faithful follower of Jesus and Gentile missionary Paul, he prayed (Acts 9:11) and was prayed for in order to be filled with the Holy Spirit (Acts 9:17), but no praise is narrated in that case either. However, in Acts 10 and 11, as the largely Jewish community of new believers is extended to include Gentiles, their initial Spirit-infilling is narrated to have instigated praise, also among the Jews.

Thus, the following section will examine the narratives in Acts 10 and 11 regarding a connection between divine presence in the form of an initial Spirit-infilling and the praise of God's extended people. Again, we will test whether this mode of divine presence indeed prompted human praise. Possible similarities with Acts 2 will be considered.

5.3.1 Sequence of Events and Structure in Acts 10 and 11

The chronological sequence of events in Acts 10 and 11 portrays that Gentiles were incorporated into God's people. Especially the first narrative contains elements of divine Spirit presence and human praise.[84]

1. The God-fearing and charitable Roman officer Cornelius was in prayer (10:1–2).

2. During that time, Cornelius was given a divine vision: a divine messenger affirming that God had remembered Cornelius' prayers and gifts gave a command (10:3–6, 22, 30–32; 11:13–14).

3. Cornelius obeyed the divine command to send for Simon Peter, the disciple and apostle (10:7–8).

4. Peter was in prayer (10:9; 11:5a).

5. During that time, Peter, getting hungry, also received a divine vision: a variety of clean and unclean animals was set before him with the divine command to eat. He refused.[85] The command was reinforced

---

84. Paraphrase and summary of events.
85. For clean and unclean animals see Lev 11, according to which the animals in

through a threefold repetition (10:10-16 and 11:5-10). The vision with command clarified the subsequent divine command given to Peter (10:17-20; 11:11-12a).

6. Peter obeyed this command to go to the home of Cornelius (10:21-29; 11:12b).

7. Cornelius told Peter about his vision, which provides an opening for Peter's message (10:30-33; 11:13-14).

8. Peter shared the lesson he had learnt, i.e., the metaphorical illustration had demonstrated to him that in God's sight there is no impurity with Gentiles; then, he gave his message (10:34-43; 11:15a).

9. While Peter was speaking, the Holy Spirit "fell" on the Gentile auditors (10:44; 11:15b). Their subsequent glossolalia praise caused the Jews to infer that the Holy Spirit had also been "poured out" on Gentiles (10:45-46) and they had now been "baptized" with the same Holy Spirit (11:16-17).

Luke's report in Acts 10 prepares in a powerful way for the imminent inclusion of Gentiles into God's people. Peter's triple metaphorical vision in 10:10-16 serves as an emphatic vehicle to illustrate the inclusion of Gentiles into God's people as tenor:[86] just as "food from heaven" is declared clean in God's sight, Gentiles are declared clean, too (Acts 10:28, 34, 35, 47-48). This is in sum the lesson the Jew Peter declares to have learnt and which he spells out in detail.[87]

---

the cloth of Peter's vision were "mixed." Following the Torah, this ritual distinction cannot be transferred to humans, but the transfer of distinction is due to the Jewish *halakhah*: Gentiles were considered ritually "unclean" people; a house belonging to them was also "unclean". Therefore, entering such house would make a Jew "unclean" as well, which was not forbidden, but required cultic cleansing. Peter's reluctant reaction shows that he is still prejudiced. God challenged his sociocultural prejudices and those of his fellow Jews. This argument is owed to Baltes and his presentation on ritual purity in Acts 10 at the AfeT conference in Marburg, Germany, 29th February 2016 (Baltes referred to *Mishna mOhol* 18:7 and Josephus, *Bell.* 2:150). Bock, *Acts*, 390, presents a similar argument by referring to Polhill, *Acts*, and Bruce, *Acts*, contra Jervell, *Apostelgeschichte*: Bock maintains that the issue is about people and not food; however, in Peter's vision, food imagery is used metaphorically to refer to people.

86. See the excursus on metaphors in the exegetical analysis of Acts 2 in section 5.2.2.; see Jesus' remark in Mk 7:19c where he declared every food to be clean.

87. Peter's lesson is depicted in detail: at first, he learnt through a divine vision that Gentiles were not unclean before God (10:28). Then, he comprehended that God-fearing Gentiles were even welcomed into his people by God himself (10:34). In the end, Peter confirmed this insight through the order to get them baptized into water,

Craig Keener's understanding of Peter's vision draws out this universal aspect:[88] the heavens opening is understood as relating to God's dwelling place and/or divine revelation; and the four ends of the cloth coming down on earth is perceived as referring to the "universality" of all peoples. Consequently, as God's people Israel were extended to embrace Gentiles from "the ends of the earth," the house of the Lord at Jerusalem was also enlarged in a metaphorical way to reach "the ends of the earth."[89] Until then and there, God has dwelt *among* his people through the Jerusalem temple being filled with his glory-presence, which prompted his people's praise. From here and now on, God is dwelling *in* his extended people through their being filled with his Spirit-presence, which also prompts his people's praise. Correspondingly, Volker Gäckle observes a process of metaphorization from the Old to the New Testament during which cultic terms like priesthood and temple are redefined in connection with Jesus Christ.[90] Thus, the term "temple" as God's earthly dwelling place and place of human-divine communication from Genesis to Revelation would undergo a metaphorical redefinition.[91] Luke's emphasis on temple terminology in his Gospel is evident, and so is a redefinition of this term in Acts: in the beginning of Acts, Luke presents the temple more positively as a meeting place for the new believers; however, as the book moves on and reports the increasing persecution of the young Christian community through the Jewish authorities, the existing temple tragically loses its meaning, which inevitably leads to a redefinition of the term "temple."[92] In view of the above, the metaphorical connotations

---

the same ritual Jewish believers in Jesus had undergone (10:48 and 2:38).

88. Keener, *Acts*, 2:1776.

89. Similarly, Walton, "Tale of Two Perspectives," 149, describes a change from a "localized view" of God dwelling in the temple to a "universalized view" by concentrating on the theme of temple in biblical theology; likewise, Beale, *Temple and the Church's Mission*, follows the theme of metaphorical temple in terms of God's dwelling place from Eden to Revelation; see ch. 6, section 6.2.4.

90. Gäckle, *Allgemeines Priestertum*, 9–17.

91. Gäckle, *Allgemeines Priestertum*, 142–77, esp. 161–67, also mentions tendencies in Jewish apocalyptic literature expressing criticism of the existing temple and expectancy of a new, eschatological temple.

92. Gäckle, *Allgemeines Priestertum*, 310–13, explains that the coming of Jesus leads to a salvation-historical *Relativisierung* [relativization] of the temple as the central Jewish institution, which represents the beginning of a metaphorical redefinition of the term.

clearly resonate the house of God motif and its extension, although Luke avoids the metaphorical term temple to describe God's extended people.[93]

Further weight is added through repetition in Acts 11 with Peter's apology in front of his fellow Jews in Jerusalem in favor of the Gentile believers at Caesarea. This apology is reinforced through Peter's emphasis on God's intervention in teaching this lesson to him.[94] Those apologetic undertones in Luke's narrative intend to express that God himself is at the heart of action preparing a way for the Gentiles' Spirit reception and praise.[95]

Now we come to the context of Peter's vision. The events in Acts 10 and 11 display an interaction between human prayer[96] and divine visions on each side, the latter of which include divine commands addressed to Peter and Cornelius. The God-fearing Gentile Cornelius[97] and the Jewish believer Peter obeyed their visions and commands.[98] This divine-human communication represents the background for the events condensed in 10:44–46 and 11:15–17, which epitomize divine and human interaction: divine action in terms of the "Holy Spirit falling" on the Gentile listeners and human action in terms of speaking in tongues and magnifying God:

---

93. The term ἐκκλησία occurs for the first time in Acts 5:11; see Paul's temple terminology in 1 Cor 3:16 and 6:19; or 2 Cor 6:19 and Eph 2:21 (cf. Gäckle, *Allgemeines Priestertum*, 361–83); see also ch. 6, section 6.2.3.

94. The divine voice from Heaven spoke to Peter in his vision (11:7–10) telling Peter to go to Cornelius' home (11:12); then, he was reminded of the Lord's promise concerning Spirit-baptism (11:16 and 1:5) and in the end, he witnessed to his fellow Jews that God had given the same gift to Gentiles (11:17) and the same repentance to life (11:18).

95. Peterson, *Acts*, 343–48; the same apologetic undertone is found in Acts 15:7–10; see the analysis by Haya-Prats, *Empowered Believers*, 250, regarding parallels between Acts 10, 11, and 15.

96. Keener, *Acts*, 2:1750, notes that there is a general emphasis on prayer in Luke-Acts; here, prayer is immediately followed by divine manifestations.

97. Keener, *Acts*, 2:1750–53, points out that Cornelius could not have been a Jewish proselyte, since Luke does not use that term, and so he must have been a sympathetic "God-fearer" rather than a convert.

98. Complementary or doubled visions add force and divine authority to their weight (cf. Keener, *Acts*, 2:1760).

God's Spirit-Presence and God's People's Praise in the New Testament

A1 Human action: reverence expressed through the prayer of Cornelius (10:2)

   B1 Divine action: divine vision and command given to Cornelius (10:3–6; 11:13–14)

A2 Human action: obedience to divine command by Cornelius (10:7–8, 33; 11:11)

A3 Human action: covenant observance expressed through Peter's prayer (10:9)

   B2 Divine action: divine vision and command given to Peter (10:10–20; 11:5–12)

A4 Human action: obedience to divine command by Peter (10:21–29, 34–43; 11:12b, 15–17)

   B3 Divine action: "coming/falling" of divine Spirit (10:44; 11:15): the Holy Spirit "was poured out" on the Gentile listeners (10:45), they were "baptized with Holy Spirit" "receiving the same gift" as the Jewish believers (11:16–17)

A5 Human action: glossolalia praise through Gentile believers (10:46)

A6 Human action: praise through Jewish believers because of the Gentiles' repentance to life (11:18).

The above sequence of events with divine-human interaction results in the pattern of a repetitive *inclusio*:

A1
   B1
A2
A3
   B2
A4
   B3
A5
A6

or, if reduced to the condensed picture in 10:44–46:

B3 divine action as the coming of the Holy Spirit, and **A5 human action** as glossolalia praise.

Thus, in the broader picture, the coming of the Holy Spirit is embedded in an *inclusio* of human prayer, obedience, and praise. In the condensed picture, human praise immediately follows this coming of the Spirit. The Gentiles' glossolalia praise subsequent to their Spirit reception is mentioned only in Acts 10 (10:44–46), whereas the Jews' praise subsequent to the Gentiles' repentance and Spirit reception is referred to only in Acts 11 (11:15–18). Hence, in the exegetical analysis the first of these passages will be focussed on and supplemented with references to the second one. For the moment, one may suppose that manifestations of divine Spirit-presence provoked human praise in more ways than one.

5.3.2 Exegetical Analysis: Acts 10:44–46 (11:15–18)

Acts 10 presents Luke's direct report as narrator of the Cornelius episode, whereas Acts 11 presents Luke's indirect report with Peter as narrator.

> Acts 10:44–46:
> **44** *While Peter was still speaking these words, the Holy Spirit fell on all who heard the message.* **45** *And the believers from among the circumcised who had come with Peter were astonished, because the gift of the Holy Spirit had been poured out even on the Gentiles.* **46** *For they heard them speaking in tongues and extolling God.* 11:15: *'As I began to speak, the Holy Spirit came on them as he had come on us at the beginning.* **16** *Then I remembered what the Lord had said: 'John baptized with water, but you will be baptized with Holy Spirit.'* **17** *So, if God gave them the same gift he gave us who believed in the Lord Jesus Christ, who was I to think that I could stand in God's way?"* **18** *When they heard this, they had no further objections and praised God, saying, "So then, even to Gentiles God has granted repentance that leads to life."*

In Acts 10:44, the phrase ἔτι λαλοῦντος τοῦ Πέτρου . . . ἐπέπεσε τὸ πνεῦμα τὸ ἅγιον expresses a temporal correlation between Peter witnessing to Jesus Christ and the "falling" of the Holy Spirit on those listening.

In the corresponding verse in 11:15, Peter puts the Gentile auditors on an equal par with the Jews in Acts 2:2: "The Holy Spirit came on them as he had on us." Even though Peter had just begun speaking, he must have shared enough of his message for his hearers to take it in before suddenly the *Holy Spirit came on them*. Scholars maintain that this verbal metaphor reflects Old Testament language indicating empowerment for prophecy for God's people like in Numbers 11.[99] These veterotestamental allusions signal a continuity of the spiritual experience. Besides, the phrase "The Holy Spirit came on them as he had on us" refers to another continuity: the same Holy Spirit that had been with the Jewish believers at Pentecost and provoked their praise now came on the Gentile believers and provoked their praise as well. This continuity of Spirit reception affects the connection between divine Spirit-presence and human praise, too.

In Acts 10:45, Luke refers to Peter's Jewish companions as "circumcised believers" in the Lord Jesus Christ. This was perhaps to emphasize that they were not simply Jews, who were circumcised in any case, but very conservative Jewish believers with strong reservations, as scholars have pointed out.[100] Yet, they could also have been Jews who had come to faith in Jesus having received the Holy Spirit. They ἐξέστησαν "were put out with astonishment"[101] in view of the gift of the Spirit ἐκκέχυται "poured out"[102] upon the Gentiles. It is no coincidence that Luke uses the same outpouring metaphor as in Acts 2:17, thus, emphasizing that even uncircumcised and non-proselyte Gentiles received the same Spirit as the Jews at Pentecost. This is why this outpouring has been called the "Pentecost of the Gentiles."[103] Besides, Acts 2:17 connects the outpouring metaphor with the object "on all flesh," which relates to the universality of all nations beyond Israel.

In the corresponding verse in 11:16, Peter affirms the equal footing of believing Gentiles with believing Jews through the same baptismal terminology "You will be baptized with Holy Spirit" reverberating Acts 1:5. Hence, both Spirit metaphors in Acts 10:45 and 11:16 are intended to highlight God's acceptance of Gentiles and their inclusion into his people, which is again supported by the fact that their Spirit-baptism even preceded their water-baptism. Both baptisms clearly reveal an initiatory momentum.[104]

In Acts 10:46, Luke explains the Gentiles' glossolalia praise as the audible sign of the gift of the Holy Spirit: their magnifying God in other tongues is ascribed by the Jewish auditors to the Gentiles' prior reception

99. Keener, *Acts*, 2:1810.

100. Polhill, *Acts*, 266; Culy and Parsons, *Acts*, 215, translate "the faithful from the circumcision"; one could also translate "the believers from among the Jews," as this expression could refer to those among the Jews who had come to faith in Jesus.

101. Aorist active of ἐξίστημι; cf. Culy and Parsons, *Acts*, 215.

102. Perf. passive of ἐκχέω.

103. Bock, *Acts*, 400, referring to Bruce.

104. McCollough, *Ritual Water, Ritual Spirit*, 191.

of the Spirit because they could identify this phenomenon on the basis of their own analogous experience at Pentecost (cf. Acts 2:4b).[105] The verb μεγαλυνόντων "to magnify"[106] denotes praise with God as object (Luke 1:46; Acts 19:17).[107] Therefore, Luke's argument in favor of the Gentiles' inclusion into God's people draws on the evidence of their Spirit reception, both visible and audible in their praise of God, a result which verifies a consecutive correlation between divine Spirit-presence and human praise.

In 11:17, Peter applies the phrase "God gave the same gift" as an argument: since God took initiative in bestowing the same Spirit gift, this divine action ought not to be opposed by humans. The verb κωλύω suggests the idea of opposition to God.[108] The God-fearing Gentiles around Cornelius in Caesarea had received the same gift as the Jewish believers in Jerusalem before. They had come to the same faith in the same Lord Jesus Christ. Their μετάνοιαν εἰς ζωὴν "repentance that leads to life" (11:18) indicates even more their "clean" status before God and their acceptance by him. Therefore, the Jews should not refuse their acceptance either.

This line of reasoning convinced Peter's Jewish fellow believers after all so that in return they praised God about this repentance that God had granted to Gentiles. The argument served not only Peter's apologetic purpose, but also Luke's pedagogic purpose.[109] While in Acts 10 the Gentiles' praise is highlighted as a consequence of their Spirit-reception, in Acts 11 the Jews' praise is reported as a result of the Gentiles' repentance. The praise of both groups of believers is narrated as following divine manifestations, whether in terms of the outpouring of the Holy Spirit or the God-given repentance made visible in this outpouring. In the first case, the connection between divine presence and human praise is more direct, and in the second case rather indirect. In sum, it can be inferred that in these narratives divine Spirit-presence is reported to have initiated human praise in more ways than one.

---

105. Scholars speak of a "Gentile Pentecost" which did not occur according to a set sequence, but with the Holy Spirit coming before water (cf. Polhill, *Acts,* 264).

106. Present active participle of μεγαλύνω; Culy and Parsons, *Acts,* 215, explain the double genitive construction as complement of ἀκούω.

107. Barrett, *Acts,* 1:529–30.

108. Polhill, *Acts,* 267.

109. Keener, *Acts,* 2:1817

5.3.3 Summary

Luke depicts the Gentiles' glossolalia praise as a distinct sign of the outpouring of the Holy Spirit (Acts 10:46), as their magnifying God in other tongues is ascribed to their reception of God's Spirit-presence. The Spirit reception and praise are reported as indicative of the Gentiles' inclusion into God's extended people. This extension evokes the idea of God's dwelling place being enlarged to include "the ends of the earth," although no temple/house metaphor is used. In Acts 10, the Gentiles' praise in Cornelius' house is highlighted as a consequence of their Spirit reception, whereas in Acts 11, the Jews' praise is reported as a result of the God-given repentance of these Gentiles. The praise of both groups is narrated as following divine manifestations. This is confirmed through the same "outpouring" terminology in Acts 10:46 as in 2:17 and the same baptismal terminology in Acts 11:16 as in 1:5. As a result, it can be inferred that divine Spirit-presence is narrated as having prompted human praise in more ways than one.

Acts 12–20 again testify to expanding evangelization activities of the apostles, but no explicit mention is made of an initial Spirit-infilling in connection with human praise. The Ephesians, who had known nothing of the Holy Spirit and a baptism in the name of Jesus, received both (Acts 19); no reference to praise is made, only to prophetic utterance (Acts 19:6–7), although Acts 19 displays the same outpouring terminology as in Acts 2 and 10.

While the preceding sections on Acts 2, 10, and 11 dealt with a consecutive correlation between an initial Spirit-infilling and human praise, the following sections will look into a reverse relationship between human praise and repeated Spirit-infillings in Acts 4, Acts 16, and Ephesians 5.

5.4 Human Praise and Spirit-Refilling in Acts 4

Here, we will test whether human praise instigated manifestations of divine presence like repeated Spirit-infillings of God's people.

5.4.1 Sequence of Events in Acts 4

Luke's report in Acts 4 witnesses to the spreading of the Gospel in the context of the beginning persecution of the new community. The events recount the apostles' bold and Spirit-filled testimony in the face of opposition from their own Jewish authorities:

1. Peter and John were teaching and proclaiming Jesus as resurrected from the dead, who was rejected by Jews and pagans (4:1–2).
2. The priests, the captain of the temple, and the Sadducees, greatly disturbed, threw them into prison (4:3).
3. Yet, many who heard the message came to faith (4:4).
4. The members of the Sanhedrin at Jerusalem—rulers, elders, and scribes—interrogated Peter and John (4:5–7).
5. Peter, filled with the Holy Spirit, responded boldly explaining the healing of the lame (3:7–8) in connection with Jesus Christ of Nazareth, rejected by the leaders of his people, but raised from the dead by God (4:8–14).
6. After some consultations, the High Council warned them against proclaiming that name any further (4:15–18).
7. Still, Peter and John made their allegiance to God clear (4:19–20).
8. They were threatened, but released due to the people's approval of the healing of the lame (4:21–22).
9. Hearing their report, the new Christian community offered prayer to God praising him and pleading for boldness and miracles (4:23–30).
10. Subsequently, the meeting place was shaken (4:31a), and all of them were filled with the Holy Spirit (4:31b; cf. 4:8).
11. They spoke God's word boldly (4:32; cf. 4:5).[110]

The narrative describes the prayer, praise, and petition of the Christian community. The prayer was succeeded by an earthquake and their being refilled with God's Holy Spirit, which caused them to speak the Good News boldly. Similarly, Spirit-infilling and boldness in preaching are already indicated prior to these events:

---

110. Paraphrase.

God's Spirit-Presence and God's People's Praise in the New Testament   149

A1 Human action: proclamation of the Good News about Jesus through Peter and John

A2 Human action: arrest of the apostles

A3 Human action (divine influence implied): new believers came to faith

A4 Human action: interrogation through the Sanhedrin

A5 Human action (divine influence implied): Peter's bold and Spirit-filled testimony about Jesus of Nazareth

A6 Human action: High Council warning against further proclamation of the name of Jesus

A7 Human action: covenant obedience of the apostles

A8 Human action: further threats, but release

A9 Human action: prayer with praise and petition of the community

   B1 Divine action (implied): earthquake and Spirit refilling

A10 Human action: preaching with boldness.

Accordingly, the following pattern of interaction between human and divine activities can be identified:

A1
A2
A3
A4
A5
A6
A7
A8
A9
   B1
A10

   or, if reduced to Acts 4:23–31:]

A9
   B1
A10

Hence, in the former case, these actions take the shape of an extended *inclusio*. In the latter case, they form a condensed *inclusio* with human activity framing divine activity.

On the one hand, Peter's Spirit-filled testimony (4:8) and the brave courage of Peter and John (4:13), which precede the collective prayer, already suggest divine impact. On the other hand, the prayer of the young Christian community with praise and petition (4:25) immediately precedes the manifestations suggesting divine impact, i.e., seismic activity and their being refilled with Holy Spirit (4:31). Again, these manifestations of divine presence are immediately ensued by courageous preaching (4:32). Therefore, the facts already insinuate a certain consecutive relationship between human prayer/praise and divine Spirit-presence on the one hand and Spirit-refilling and bold witness on the other.

Moreover, covenant context is conveyed in Acts 4:13, 19: Peter and John "had been with Jesus" and decided for themselves "to obey God" rather than the rulers, elders, and teachers of the law.

5.4.2 Exegetical Analysis: Acts 4:24–31

> **24**And when they heard it, they lifted their voices together to God and said, "Sovereign Lord who made the heaven and the earth and the sea and everything in them, **25**who through the mouth of our father David, your servant said by the Holy Spirit, 'why did the Gentiles rage, and the peoples plot in vain? **26**The kings of the earth set themselves, and the rulers were gathered together against the Lord and against his Anointed' **27**for truly in this city there were gathered together against your holy servant Jesus whom you anointed, both Herod and Pontius Pilate, along with the Gentiles and the peoples of Israel, **28**to do whatever your hand and your plan had predestined to take place. **29**And now, Lord, look upon their threats and grant to your servants to continue to speak your word with all boldness, **30**while you stretch out your hand to heal, and signs and wonders are performed through the name of your holy servant Jesus." **31**And when they had prayed, the place in which they were gathered together was shaken and they were all filled with the Holy Spirit and continued to speak the word of God with boldness.

Verse 24 starts with a participial subordinate clause followed by a main clause, which expresses temporal coincidence.[111] The young Christians

---

111. This reading is questioned by Culy and Parsons, *Acts*, 75–76, on the basis

hearing the Spirit-filled, courageous testimony of Peter and John in view of threats unanimously went into worshipful prayer. Two Western textual versions, among them Codex Bezae, add "And when they realized the *energeia* of God";[112] hence, these accounts refer to a powerful working of God already prior to the worshipful prayer. Such relation, though sparsely testified, is interesting and relevant for the divine-human interaction.

All of the disciples raised their voices in unanimity addressing the Lord as ruler and Creator God of Heaven and earth, which was a common title for God in Jewish prayers.[113] The Greek noun δέσποτα in vocative meaning "sovereign Lord" or "ruler" is rarely employed in the LXX, mostly as equivalent of the Hebrew term Yahweh/*ădonāy*.[114] Invoking God as sovereign Lord and Creator of the universe at the beginning of their unanimous prayer is tantamount to praise in the form of acclamation.

This opening praise is continued in vv.25–28 through the *pesher* interpretation of a quote from the Davidic Psalm 2:1–2 in light of the opposition Jesus had experienced and they are experiencing:[115] religious and political leaders, Jews and Gentiles alike, as well as their own people conspired and still keep conspiring against the Lord and his Anointed One, Jesus, whom they crucified.[116] This means that the hostility directed against the new Christian community actually aims at the sovereign Lord himself and his Messiah Jesus. In that respect, the new followers of Christ tread the path of their messianic master. They are convinced that their adversaries can only do to them what the Lord himself "in his plan had predestined to take place." They consider this plan already announced

---

that the writer would not use a pronominal article with an adverbial participle at the beginning of a sentence.

112. Barrett, *Commentary*, 1:243–44; in contrast, Metzger, *Textual Commentary*, 321, refutes this reading because Luke would use the term *energeia* nowhere else.

113. Keener, *Acts*, 2:1166–67.

114. The Greek term δέσποτα is used six times in the NT, twice by Luke and once of God here in v.24; as part of the Christian liturgy by the end of the first century CE, this term may already have belonged to Luke's "liturgical memory" (cf. Keener, *Acts*, 2:1166). Culy and Parsons, *Acts*, 76, explain this term intends to convey that God is in control of everything he created including the Jewish authorities.

115. Keener, *Acts*, 2:1169–1171.

116. The term "Anointed One" refers to the Spirit endowment Jesus received at his baptism, which makes clear that this is not just an alternative name for Jesus, but his messianic title (cf. Bruce, *Acts*; 157–58).

in Psalm 2 through their ancestor David being the "mouth piece" of the Holy Spirit (Acts 2:25).[117] Their remembrance of the Lord's universal sovereignty spurs their reverential exaltation which culminates in this explanatory acclamation and leads to a precise petition. Thus, their praise and prayer express faith in a sovereign Lord who is in control of everything, an indirect pointer to covenant context. In addition, this setting of conflict recalls the Holy War motif, again a covenant marker where God considers his people's enemies to be his own enemies.

Their specific petition starts in v.29: as followers who identify themselves with their messianic master they ask for boldness in spreading his Good News in the face of opposition. Likewise, they ask for divine confirmation of this message through healings, signs, and wonders. Clearly, they expect Jesus to perform these miracles "by his hand"[118] and "through his name," i.e., in person, to validate their gospel message.

In v.31, the participle δεηθέντων[119] signals a temporal sequence: after they had finished their prayer, a series of manifestations set in which can be attributed to divine origin, also because the seismic activity is narrated together with Spirit-refilling. C. K. Barrett suggests that the shaking of the place matches the theophanic metaphors of wind and fire in Acts 2, but this has been debated.[120] Still, the repeated infilling of each individual with God's Holy Spirit undoubtedly echoes the initial Spirit-infilling in Acts 2. Thus, these verbal echoes generate a continuity revealing that divine presence through Spirit-infilling cannot be reduced to an initial, unique event. The echoes may also imply a continuity regarding prayer and praise succeeded by repeated Spirit-infillings. Craig Keener remarks that often in Luke-Acts prayer invites the coming of the Spirit.[121] Besides,

---

117. Bruce, *Acts*, 156; see Peterson, "Motif of Fulfilment," 98. The majuscule D and the Syrian Peshitta, one of the oldest versions, read twice the preposition *dia* plus genitive object, which allows for a dual authorship by the Holy Spirit and David; however, the textual version with only one *dia* referring to the Holy Spirit is well testified by at least five other main majuscules, among them P^{74}, ℵ, and A; the loss of one *dia* could have been caused by textual corruption through copying (cf. Metzger, *Textual Commentary*, 322–23).

118. Culy and Parsons, *Acts*, 79, perceive the infinitive construction as an idiomatic expression meaning "to show one's power"; therefore, they translate "as you stretch out your hand" and interpret it as another prayer request.

119. Aorist deponent participle of δέομαι in genitive absolute; cf. Culy and Parsons, *Acts*, 79.

120. Barrett, *Acts*, 1:249.

121. Keener, *Acts*, 2:1174; as in Luke 3:21–22; 11:13; or in Acts 1:14; 8:15; 9:11, 17;

Spirit-infillings can be given for special purposes.[122] And speaking God's Word boldly in the face of opposition can be perceived as such an effect (vv. 29, 31).[123] Therefore, Acts 4:31 clearly corroborates the effect of human prayer and praise on manifestations of divine presence and even implies a reciprocal correlation.

5.4.3 Summary

The sequence of events in Acts 4 suggests an evident influence of human prayer and praise on manifestations of divine presence, especially since these are sandwiched between worshipful prayer and bold preaching. Similarly, the exegetical analysis of 4:24–31 verifies that the reverential exaltation of God as sovereign ruler and Creator of the universe, which culminates in an explanatory acclaim and blends into a precise petition, has a powerful effect: manifestations of divine presence such as seismic activity and a renewed Spirit-infilling of the believers. Such divine manifestations create verbal echoes which resonate with Acts 2. Hence, the results in Acts 4 confirm a consecutive connection between human praise/prayer and divine presence with the former having a powerful effect on the latter. Having said that, not every conflict narrative reveals a triumphant outcome, as we see from the first Christian martyr Stephen in Acts 7.

5.5 Human Praise and Divine Presence in Acts 16

As has been demonstrated in Acts 10 and 11, the Christian community was extended to include Gentiles whose initial Spirit-infilling was followed by glossolalia praise just as in Acts 2. Chapters 12–20 testify to expanding evangelization activities of the apostles in the face of expanding persecution, frequently depicted in the context of prayer, praise, and divine manifestations.[124] As to expanding evangelization, the worship of the Christians in Antioch is followed by instructions of the Holy Spirit concerning their

---

10:30, 44–46, and 19:6.

122. Barrett, *Acts*, 1:250.

123. On a slightly different note, Rapske, "Opposition to the Plan," 247–48, points out that this emboldened preaching, just as that of Steven in Acts 6:10 and that of Paul in 9:17, is a sign of Spirit-infilling promised by the Lord in Luke 12:11–12.

124. That this link also works in the negative becomes obvious in Acts 12:23 where Herod suffers an "angelic knock-out" because he had not given God the praise and glory due to him.

evangelization work (Acts 13:2). As to expanding persecution, the church's prayer on behalf of the imprisoned Peter is followed by Peter's miraculous release through angelic intervention (Acts 12:5–11). This episode in Acts 12 echoes Acts 4, as concerns the effect of human prayer and praise on divine manifestations in persecution context, and prefigures Acts 16 with a similar context. Again, the question will be raised whether human praise prompted manifestations of divine presence.

5.5.1 Sequence of Events in Acts 16

1. The apostle Paul and his companions were edifying the churches in the Greek diaspora building up their faith and numbers (16:5). Then, the Holy Spirit prevented them from preaching in the province of Asia and, likewise, the "Spirit of Jesus" hindered them from entering Bithynia (16:6–7). Instead, Paul was instructed in a divine night vision to go to Macedonia, a region which belongs to what is now called Europe (16:9–10).

2. Following their proclaiming the gospel there, the first Christian church in Europe was born in Philippi, Macedonia, in the house of a new believer called Lydia (16:11–15).

3. Persecution in the shape of severe beating and imprisonment set in as a consequence of Paul driving out a lucrative fortune-telling spirit from a slave girl (16:19–24).

4. When Paul and Silas, their feet fastened in the stocks, were singing hymns to God, their nocturnal praise concert with the prisoners as audience was succeeded by a sudden, violent earthquake. As a result, the prison doors flew open, and the chains came loose (16:25–26).

5. This shaking caused the repentance of the prison keeper and his household (16:27–34).

6. The Philippi account ends with the apostles being officially escorted from prison by the authorities and, again, with their encouraging the local Christian community (16:35–40).[125]

The above events culminate in the devoted praise of the apostle Paul and his companion Silas. Their hymnic worship results in an earthquake,

---

125. Paraphrase and summary.

which could be interpreted as divine intervention.[126] In any case, the supernatural manifestations and their effects brought about not only their release, but also the repentance of the jailor. The human-divine interaction can be seen from the following structure:

A1 Human action: edification of churches through the apostles
   B Divine action: threefold divine intervention:
   B1 first, explicitly through the Holy Spirit
   B2 second, explicitly through the "Spirit of Jesus" and
   B3 third, implicitly through a divine vision
A2 Human action: evangelization through the apostles at Philippi
A3 Human action (divine power implied): exorcism through Paul
A4 Human action: imprisonment of the apostles
A5 Human action: hymnic praise of the apostles
   B4 Divine action (implied): seismic activity
A6 Human action: repentance of jailor
A7 Human action: release of the apostles.

Thus, the following pattern in the shape of a twofold *inclusio* can be identified:

A1
   B1
   B2
   B3
A2
A3
A4
A5
   B4
A6
A7

   or, if reduced to Acts 16:25–26 only:

---

126. Spencer, *Acts*, 168, expresses that the suffering prisoners in their yet joyful praise were anticipating divine intervention.

A5 (human praise) and **B4** (implied theophanic manifestations). Still, they were followed again by **A6** (human repentance) and **A7** (release).

In the first case, human activities (evangelization) framing three divine activities (revelation) form an *inclusio*. In the second case, human activities (imprisonment due to exorcism, prayer/praise, repentance, release) framing divine activity (earthquake) form another *inclusio*. In the second *inclusio*, prayer and praise are followed by supernatural manifestations. This allows the provisional inference that worship may have had an immediate effect on the presumed manifestations of divine presence in action. Therefore, the relevant verses 25–26 will be looked at more closely in the exegetical analysis.

5.5.2 Exegetical Analysis: Acts 16:25–26

> ²⁵*When towards midnight Paul and Silas were praying and singing hymns to God, the other prisoners were listening to them.* ²⁶*Suddenly there was such a violent earthquake that the foundations of the prison were shaken. At once all the prison doors flew open, and everyone's chains came loose.*

The first part of v.25 is the auxiliary clause with the main clause in the second part: the auxiliary clause begins with προσευχόμενοι "praying"[127] and continues with ὕμνουν "they were singing praise";[128] the main clause begins with ἐπηκροῶντο "they were listening".[129] This verbal construction indicates a process of prayer and hymnic praise said and sung by the apostles and listened to by the prisoners. This worship concert took place immediately before a series of powerful supernatural events set in.

Verse 26 shows the reverse structure: the first part is the main clause with the auxiliary clause in the second part: the main clause starts with a temporal adverb ἄφνω "suddenly" plus ἐγένετο "it occurred"[130] to convey that abruptly a great earthquake happened; the auxiliary clause depicts its consequences starting with σαλευθῆναι "to be shaken",[131] which relates to the result of this shaking on the prison walls and foundations. The

---

127. Participle present deponent pl. of προσεύχομαι.
128. Finite verb imperf. active of ὑμνέω.
129. Finite verb imperf. deponens of ἐπακροάομαι; for the analysis see Culy and Parsons, *Acts*, 318.
130. Finite verb aorist deponent of γίνομαι.
131. Verb aorist infinitive passive of σαλεύω.

following two finite verbs in aorist passive, which are specified by a second temporal adverb παραχρῆμα "immediately," can be understood either as continuing the auxiliary clause or as starting a new main clause, which does not change the meaning: the first verb ἠνεῴχθησαν "were opened"[132] relates to the prison doors, the second verb ἀνέθη "were loosened"[133] concerns the fetters of the prisoners. Thus, this construction portrays the instant liberating effects of this sudden seismic event (see Acts 12:7 with Peter's miraculous release from prison).

The chiastic structure of the two clauses underscores the immediate temporal connection between the nocturnal praise of Paul and Silas and the ensuing earthquake. Their devoted praying and singing hymns to God expected a divine response of some kind (see Eph 5:19),[134] which evokes Acts 4. That the supernatural manifestations were of divine origin, however, has not found unanimous support. C. K. Barrett, e.g., argues that Luke does not directly attribute the earthquake to divine providence.[135] In contrast, Craig Keener attributes divine vindication in the form of an earthquake to prayer and praise, whether in Acts 4 or Acts 16.[136] Similarly, John Polhill and Eckhard Schnabel maintain that seismic activity was nothing new at all in that region, but rarely experienced more timely, which points to divine intervention, albeit not explicitly stated.[137]

In connection with that, covenant context is conveyed through the apostles' committed and "faith-ful" prayer and praise in suffering and also through the jailor's God-fearing attitude of repentance and instant baptism.[138] Anticipatory praise in a situation of persecution and conflict reminds of the veterotestamental Holy War narratives where God identifies with his people and intervenes supernaturally.[139]

---

132. Verb ἀνοίγω.
133. Verb ἀνίημι.
134. Keener, *Acts*, 3:2490, 3:2494, mentions both references.
135. Barrett, *Acts*, 2:794.
136. Keener, *Acts*, 3:2490, 3:2494–97.
137. Polhill, *Acts*, 354; Schnabel, *Acts*, 689.
138. Barrett, *Acts*, 2:793.
139. See ch. 5, sections 4.4.1–4.4.3.

5.5.3 Summary

The sequence of events in Acts 16 reveals that human worship was immediately succeeded by an earthquake and its liberating effects in more ways than one, which allows to deduce a divine intervention. The exegetical analysis confirms that a process of prayer and hymnic praise said and sung by the apostle Paul and his companion Silas was taking place immediately before a powerful seismic activity set in. Their praise in suffering expressed faith in their Lord, which allows assuming a divine origin of these manifestations; it certainly demonstrates covenant context and echoes the divine war motif. The connection between prayer/praise and theophanic manifestations is evident, although no refilling with Holy Spirit is reported in this case. It can be inferred that human praise instigated divine presence in action through supernatural manifestations.

The next section will deal with a text from the Epistle to the Ephesians on divine presence in the form of a recurring Spirit-infilling, which is encouraged to be pursued in connection with praise.

5.6 Human Praise and Spirit-Refilling in Ephesians 5

Ephesians belongs to a different literary category, the paraenetic genre. Ephesians 5:18–20 was selected because these verses address an invitation to God's people for them to be filled with Holy Spirit offering praise and thanksgiving to God. Again, the question asked of this text is whether God's people's praise prompts divine presence in the form of Spirit-infilling.

5.6.1 Literary Co-Text of Ephesians 5

In the beginning, the author of Ephesians establishes a foundation for his paraenesis.[140] The three-part introduction in the first chapter reflects the structure of the epistle: prescript (Eph 1:1–2),[141] praise of God's salvation

---

140. Issues of authorship have been much debated. Fowl, *Ephesians*, 9–10, summarizes the pros and the cons aptly: "The text is canonical, Paul is not"; yet, he adds "Those involved in the formation of the NT canon took Ephesians to be authentically Pauline." Fowl does not consider Pauline authorship to be a decisive matter. Nevertheless, if Pauline authorship is suggested by the text itself (Eph 1:1; Acts 19, 20), this, indeed, is a relevant matter.

141. Some major majuscules omit the address while the majority has it; hence, it is

God's Spirit-Presence and God's People's Praise in the New Testament 159

(1:3–14), and grateful petition (1:15–23). Already in this introduction, the corporate nature of this salvation is announced: the fullness of Christ dwelling in the church (1:23).

In the second chapter, the letter portrays the new life in Christ as a free gift of grace (2:1–10): Christ uniting Jews and Gentiles in his "body" (2:16), a "building" and "holy temple," a "dwelling" for God through his Spirit (2:21–22). In connection with that, Timothy Gombis holds that "Just as God dwelt in the temple in the Old Testament, so now the church is the new temple of God, the place where his presence dwells," and that the Holy Spirit is the means by which God's presence is mediated to his people.[142]

Having established this basis, the author argues in the third chapter of Ephesians in favor of his own mission among Gentiles (3:1–13), which leads him to intercede on behalf of the believers (3:14–21) for them to be edified (3:16) and united in the faith and love of Christ (3:17–18) and for God to be glorified (3:21).

Accordingly, the unity of the body of Christ and the edification of his temple through the charismata of the Holy Spirit (4:1–16) serve as a motivation for the author's appeal addressed to the young Christians in the fourth chapter: they are meant to "undress" their old self and life (4:17–24) and to "put on" the new self and life (4:25–32).

Similarly, in the fifth chapter of Ephesians, the love of the heavenly Father to his children (5:1) and the sacrificial love of Christ (5:2) serve as motivation for a series of negative (5:3–7, 11–12) and positive (5:8–10, 13–14) exhortations addressed to the Christian believers. For example, "You are light, therefore live in the light" (5:8). The works of the light are spelled out as goodness, righteousness, and truth (5:9), in contrast to the works of darkness, which are meant to be uncovered (5:13–14).[143] These admonitions are summarized in the admonition to the believers not to be foolish, but to lead their life wisely (5:15–17).

This co-text immediately preceding Ephesians 5:18–20 affects the interpretation of this text: God's people are being exhorted not to get drunk with wine, but to allow themselves to be filled with the Spirit,

---

plausible that the letter has also been sent to recipients beyond Ephesus (cf. Lincoln, *Ephesians*, 1–2).

142. Gombis, "Fullness of God," 261.

143. Lincoln, *Ephesians*, 326–31, advocates that the imagery of light and darkness suggests baptismal paraenesis; Barth, *Ephesians*, 600, stresses the ethical, existential, and cultic meaning of these terms. As to the light-darkness contrast, Schnackenburg, *Epheser*, 219–30, refers to Qumran literature such as 1QM and 1QS.

encouraging each other with Spirit-inspired songs, offering whole-hearted praise to the Lord through Christ, and giving thanks to the Father. This multi-facetted instruction mentions Spirit-refilling and Spirit-inspired praise alongside each other in imperative mode.

Ecclesial-marital directives follow (5:21–32) and, then in the sixth chapter, family codes, household codes (6:1–9), and instructions for spiritual combat (6:10–20). Accordingly, the mutual submission, including that of wives to husbands (5:21–33), is based on Christ's dedication to the church. Similarly, the submission of children to their parents and of slaves to their masters is expected on the same basis (6:1–9). Likewise, the spiritual combat required of the believers is seen against the background of the gospel of Christ and his heavenly armor (6:10–20).[144]

In view of the above, literary co-text and structure prove to be quite different from that of the narratives examined up to now, which may be due to the paraenetic genre of the epistle. Again and again, the epistle presents divine soteriological realities as motivation for human activities which are requested through positive and negative admonitions. These admonitions appear in contrasting pairs: old life versus new life, light versus darkness, foolishness versus wisdom. As a result, in these paraenetic passages, divine indicative precedes human imperative.[145] The interaction between the given divine actualities and the desired human activities implies a relational covenant context.

5.6.2 Exegetical Analysis: Ephesians 5:18–20

> [18]*And do not get drunk with wine, for that is debauchery, but be filled with (the) Spirit,* [19]*addressing one another in psalms and hymns and spiritual tunes, singing and making melody to the Lord from your heart,* [20]*giving thanks always and for everything to God the Father in the name of our Lord Jesus Christ.*

Verse 18 presents the last of three negative-positive imperative pairs from vv.15–18. In the third pair, the negative imperative (present passive of μεθύσκω) "do not be/get yourselves drunk with wine" is contrasted with the following positive imperative (present passive of πληρόω)

---

144. For a semantic structure analysis see Braun, "Erfüllung," 14–15.

145. Similarly, Lincoln, *Ephesians*, 293–94, identifies a pattern of exhortation followed by motivation and, again, exhortation forming a circle; likewise, Barth, *Ephesians*, 588, asserts that Paul's paraenesis is based on the Good News of God's grace.

"but get yourselves filled with Spirit." The phrase ἐν ᾧ ἐστιν ἀσωτία "in which is debauchery" describes dissipation and refers to a state resulting from excessive wine consumption and not just to wine itself.[146] The instrumental dative object οἴνῳ "with wine" complements μὴ μεθύσκεσθε "do not get drunk," just as the instrumental dative object with preposition ἐν πνεύματι "with Spirit" complements πληροῦσθε "get filled."[147] S. M. Baugh explains that the critical editions set ἐν in brackets and that the dative πνεύματι would have been sufficient for the interpretation.[148] Nonetheless, since majuscules like P[46] or B and also reliable minuscules include the preposition, and also a parallel text in Col 3, this reading can be considered legitimate. Timothy Gombis suggests that ἐν signals an instrumental direction in terms of the Holy Spirit mediating the fullness and presence of God in Christ.[149] In a similar way, ἐν πνεύματι in John 4:23 refers to the Holy Spirit motivating and mediating the true worship of the true worshipers to the father.

The present form of the two imperatives above suggests an iterative, tolerative reading, which can be translated "do not keep getting yourselves inebriated with wine, but let yourselves continually be filled with Spirit."[150] Thus, the text refers to *a repetitive, constant Spirit-infilling*. Besides, the plural indicates a corporate rather than an individual level, as Timothy Gombis points out, anxious to avoid individualistic tendencies.[151] Still, both aspects are not mutually exclusive, but condition and complement each other.

As to the context of the wine-Spirit contrast, Andrew Lincoln refers to Philo, who identified drunkenness with spiritual folly and the "sober inebriation" of the "God-possessed soul" with spiritual wisdom.[152] This allusion is supported by the dualism "folly-wisdom" mentioned afore, as Stephen Fowl reminds us.[153] In connection with that, S. M. Baugh

---

146. Larkin, *Ephesians*, 124.

147. Or a dative of means (cf. Larkin, *Ephesians*, 124). For a history of interpretation Gombis, "Fullness of God," 260, refers to Hollis, "Become Full," 8–16.

148. Baugh, *Ephesians*, 445.

149. Gombis, "Fullness of God," 267.

150. Both middle imperatives suggest a reflexive, tolerative, and repetitive interpretation.

151. Gombis, "Fullness of God," 262.

152. Lincoln, *Ephesians*, 344 (cf. Philo, *De Ebr.*, 146–48); see also the parallel on the dualism "drunk-sober" in 1 Thess 5:7b–8.

153. Fowl, *Ephesians*, 177.

mentions wisdom literature referring to Proverbs 23:31.[154] Peter Gosnell perceives meal settings as the context where drunkenness occurred, a state to be avoided.[155] And Graham Cole consults Calvin who refers to excessive drinking to use it as a contrast to the "'exhortation' to 'deep drinking' with regard to the Spirit."[156] Cleon Rogers, referring to Acts 2:13, 15, evokes the Dionysian cultic orgies of the time which aimed at an idolatrous, spiritual intoxication through excessive, vinic inebriation.[157] Baugh, referring to Moritz et al., is sceptical of the Bacchic rites as a way "to cause Dionysius to enter and fill the worshiper's body," which Baugh considers a "theological romanticism."[158] Still, the contextual hint should not be disregarded altogether as a contrasting interpretive help.

Gombis clarifies that this "fullness in Spirit" requested in Ephesians 5:18 is perceived in Ephesians 1:23 in connection with the "fullness of Christ" as God's presence dwelling in the church;[159] he observes that the Old Testament as well refers to divine presence through "fullness" language as in Ezekiel 44:4 or Jeremiah 23:24. This observation is also corroborated by 1 Kings 8 and 2 Chronicles 5–7, narratives which obviously use filling language regarding the Lord's glory in his house.

Verse 18 is made of two main clauses, the second one of which is specified by three subordinate participial clauses in vv.19 and v.20 including four present participles (to be followed by another participial clause in v.21):

1. λαλοῦντες ἑαυτοῖς ψαλμοῖς καὶ ὕμνοις καὶ ᾠδαῖς πνευματικαῖς "speaking to one another with songs, praises, and spiritual tunes."

    The active present participle λαλοῦντες "speaking/encouraging" is complemented by the reflexive pronoun ἑαυτοῖς "each other" as dative object, which suggests a reciprocal meaning, and three adverbial qualifications in instrumental dative.[160] This syndetic listing of nouns at first sight appears to refer to synonymous attributes,

---

154. Baugh, *Ephesians*, 451.

155. Gosnell, "Ephesians 5:18–20," 363–71; the reference to Gosnell is owed to Baugh, *Ephesians*, 463.

156. Cole, *Engaging*, 110–11.

157. Rogers, "Dionysian Background," 249–57, esp. 256.

158. Baugh, *Ephesians*, 452.

159. Gombis, "Fullness of God," 260–61.

160. Larkin, *Ephesians*, 125.

since they all pertain to festive songs of praise.[161] However, at a closer look they reveal different interpretive shades:

- ψαλμοῖς as praise songs sung and (originally) played,
- ὕμνοις as festive praise (secular and cultic), and
- ᾠδαῖς (πνευματικαῖς) as (Spirit-inspired) poetic songs to celebrate God's glory.[162]

The adjective πνευματικαῖς, although missing in some manuscripts, is verified in significant majuscules; hence, it may specify not only the last, but all three nouns and makes sense as a counterpart of the previous phrase ἐν πνεύματι.[163]

The phrase "songs inspired by the Spirit" has been the topic of scholarly debate.[164] Lincoln, for example, dissents that the focus of these songs is praise of God, but they would concentrate rather on edification, instruction, and exhortation of the assembly.[165] In aid of his idea, he refers to Colossians 3:15–20 from which the writer of Ephesians is assumed to have drawn. Similarly, Block tends to interpret this phrase exclusively in terms of singing Scripture to each other, although he admits that these Spirit-inspired songs in Ephesians 5:19 direct people to Jesus.[166] However, both relational aspects of worship—edification of the assembly and praise offered to God—are not mutually exclusive, "since a Christian's praise has a dual object," as Fowl asserts.[167] In any case, the Ephesians were invited to give expression to their identity as God's dwelling place in the Spirit.[168]

Concerning the parallel in Colossians 3:15–17, John Callow in his semantic structure analysis identifies vv.15–16 as belonging together and v.17 as a "general exhortation," which includes all

---

161. Scholars have suggested that these three terms cover in an inclusive way all the singing that goes on in worship (cf. Larkin, *Ephesians*, 125, referring to Best).

162. Braun, "Erfüllung," 33–39.

163. Schnackenburg, *Epheser*, 10:243; Larkin, *Ephesians*, 126.

164. Although Block in his biblical theology of worship, *Glory of God*, generally allows for the help of the Holy Spirit in praise, he does not say much on the Spirit's role in worship, as also Foreman points out (review of Block's *Glory of God*, 97–99).

165. Lincoln, *Ephesians*, 345.

166. Block, *Glory of God*, 189, 234, 359.

167. Fowl, *Ephesians*, 177.

168. Baugh, *Ephesians*, 455.

previous ones starting with Colossians 2:6.[169] He perceives the three independent imperative verbs followed by participles (at syntactic level) to represent three independent exhortative head propositions described by means and circumstance (at semantic level). Thus, teaching and admonishing each other (means) while singing praise (circumstance) leads to Christ's word dwelling in the believers (Col 3:15–16). In analogy to that, one may infer that edifying each other through songs (means) while praising the Lord (circumstance) leads to God's Spirit filling the believers (Eph 5:18–20).[170] Still, the construction Callow refers to in Colossians 3:12–17 is slightly different from the one in Ephesians 5:18–20.[171] Colossians 3:18 on the submission of wives marks the beginning of a new section, which could support a break in the flow of argument in Ephesians 5:21 at this point as well.[172] Nevertheless, Baugh (2016:459f) warns against letting one passage settle the interpretation of the other.

In addition to that, the question has been asked whether this hymnic edification and God-praise enthused by the Spirit covers not only familiar or spontaneous praise songs prompted by the Spirit, but also glossolalia praise. By drawing on 1 Corinthians 14:15, Gordon Fee thinks of a "charismatic hymnody" and of "Spirit-inspired singing," both familiar and spontaneous, for teaching and mutual admonishing in addition to praise.[173] Undeniably, in 1 Corinthians 14:14–15, Paul compares ψαλῶ τῷ πνεύματι "praise in/by means of the Holy Spirit" with ψαλῶ τῷ νοΐ "praise with one's mind" recommending praise in both ways. Additionally, Paul encourages the church in 1 Corinthians 14:26 to contribute a tongue separately from its interpretation. Scholarly opinion has not been unanimous on this issue, also in view of the fact that Paul prefers prophecy to uninterpreted tongues in church worship (see 1 Cor 14:6–13). In

---

169. Callow, *Semantic Structure Analysis*, 189–98.

170. Similarly Fee, *Paul, the Spirit*, 156–59, on the parallels between Eph 5 and Col 3.

171. Callow, *Semantic Structure Analysis*, 193.

172. On mutual submission Baugh, *Ephesians*, 460, referring to Walden and Helton, emphasizes that submission is not absolute, but relative with regard to people and the area of submission, and that its meaning depends on the semantic relationships in the discourse.

173. Fee, *Paul, the Spirit*, 160, 168; cf. also Fee, *God's Empowering Presence*, 718–23; Dunn, *Jesus and the Spirit*, 238–39, and Lincoln, *Ephesians*, 346.

any case, Ephesians 5:19 refers to all Spirit-inspired singing, which does not explicitly exclude glossolalia.

2. and 3. ᾄδοντες καὶ ψάλλοντες τῇ καρδίᾳ ὑμῶν τῷ κυρίῳ "singing and praising the Lord from your heart."

The two participles in present active mode are accompanied by an adverbial qualification plus dative object. Both predicates reverberate the previous nouns reinforcing their meaning: praise said and sung "from your heart," i.e., the innermost being and core of one's personality. This interpretation rules out the meaning "inwardly in your heart," but denotes sincerity and integrity.[174] Similarly, Larkin identifies a dative of means dismissing a dative of sphere.[175] Thus, in v.19, the vertical aspect of personal, wholehearted praise addressed to the Lord accompanies the horizontal aspect of corporate, mutual edification mentioned in v.18b.[176]

4. εὐχαριστοῦντες πάντοτε ὑπὲρ πάντων ἐν ὀνόματι τοῦ κυρίου ἡμῶν Ἰησοῦ Χριστοῦ τῷ θεῷ καὶ πατρί "giving thanks always for all things in the name of our Lord Jesus Christ to God the Father."

The participle in present active mode is accompanied by the adverbial qualification πάντοτε indicating temporal direction plus prepositional object ὑπὲρ πάντων, both of which may simply suggest alliteration. They are followed by the adverbial qualification ἐν ὀνόματι, which indicates instrumental direction, plus genitive attributes, and dative object. And so, the name and person of our Lord Jesus Christ is presented as the mediator for the thanksgiving to be addressed to God the Father. This looked-for gratitude to the Father through Jesus adds to the Spirit-inspired praise, which implies a Trinitarian dimension. Block emphasizes that although the Spirit "drives" the worship, he would not receive worship himself.[177] We will return to this argument in the next chapter.[178]

The interpretation of the above participles has only occasionally been the focus of scholarly work. Timothy Gombis, e.g., in his article

---

174. On the requirements of our worship to God see also Block, *Glory of God*, 55–80.
175. Larkin, *Ephesians*, 126.
176. Lincoln, *Ephesians*, 346.
177. Block, *Glory of God*, 50–53.
178. See ch. 6, section 6.5.1.

advocates interpreting these participles in the context of the letter which highlights the full presence of God in Christ dwelling in the church through the Spirit.[179] Thus, the request for Spirit-infilling with the ensuing participles would have to be interpreted against this background.

The following options reveal five ways in which the participles might be interpreted:[180]

1. *imperative and/or coordinated*: be filled with the Spirit, *(and) sing praise, (and) give thanks* to the Lord

2. *modal and/or temporal*: be filled with the Spirit, *as you sing praise*

3. *final*: be filled with the Spirit *in order to sing praise*

4. *consecutive*: be filled with the Spirit *so that you sing praise*

5. *instrumental*: be filled with the Spirit *by means of singing praise*.

An *imperative* interpretation turns these participles, which depend on the main hortative proposition "be filled with the Spirit," into coordinate imperatives. Then, semantically they would count as imperative predicates of a new main clause. The advantage of this option lies that it is frequently testified in other instances.[181] Another advantage would be that it does not confine the manner of the Spirit-infilling; yet, not specifying the manner could also be a disadvantage. A *modal and/or temporal* interpretation represents the most general way of interpreting the participles as to the manner of this requested Spirit-infilling which encompasses, but does not exclude other interpretive shades. In this case, the participles are converted into coordinate predicates in indicative mode of three subordinate clauses.[182] A *final* interpretation, which aims at a

179. Gombis, "Fullness of God," 259–71 esp. 271, refers to Schreiner, Gnilka, and Schlier who hold a similar position as Gombis, but remain unclear as to how this Spirit-infilling is to be achieved.

180. Conjunctive participle as equivalent of an adverbial clause and categories are: "final," "instrumental," "modal," "temporal," "co-ordination with καί," "imperative" (cf. BDF §§418–419); the last "consecutive" category has been added by the present writer; BDF §468, remark that "Paul is fond of continuing a construction begun with a finite verb by means of co-ordinated participles, sometimes in a long series," or using a participle in place of a finite verb in an imperatival sense; specifically regarding Eph 5:21, they assert that ὑποτασσόμενοι in v.21 "is smoother, yet greatly detached from the finite verb and already approaching the imperatival usage."

181. BDF §468.

182. This interpretation is also favored by Haubeck and von Siebenthal, *Neuer sprachlicher Schlüssel*, 165–65.

goal, represents a more limited option, since it restricts Spirit-infilling to the aim and purpose of praise. Similarly, a *consecutive* direction is more restricted, since it limits Spirit-infilling to the result and effect of praise.[183] An *instrumental* way of interpreting these participles answers the question of how this desired Spirit-infilling is to be achieved: by way of praise. This could be understood positively as explaining praise as a means and instrument, or negatively in terms of (mis-)using praise as a means for a purpose.[184] The latter gets perverted when praise is misused as a "master key" to Spirit-refilling: Spirit-presence through the instrument of praise As Gombis makes clear: "The five participles do not lead to the filling by the Spirit, rather they indicate the means by which the command is carried out."[185]

As a result, a *modal* interpretation or, if at all, a *positive, instrumental* one represent balanced readings: "be filled with the Spirit, *as you sing praise*." The other options tend to be too specific, since the Spirit-infilling would depend on praise (or also on mutual submission as in v.21). Or, praise would be reduced to a means for the purpose of Spirit-infilling. Or, Spirit-infilling would be restricted to a method which leads to praise. To put it bluntly, praise is not like a coin to be inserted into a "praise machine" in order to get out a fresh dose of Spirit-infilling. The Holy Spirit is not to be abused like a dosage of drugs. God's Spirit-presence is not meant to be conveyed in a mechanism of praise performance, but as part and parcel of an unadulterated and holy covenant relationship with God and one another. This is beautifully expressed in the quote by Timothy Gombis:

> The church is to be the temple of God, the fullness of Christ by the Spirit by being the community that speaks God's word to one another, sings praises to the Lord, renders thanksgiving to God for all things in the name of the Lord Jesus Christ, and lives in relationships characterized by mutual submission.[186]

---

183. Accordingly, Block, *Glory of God*, 232, perceives music as an "outlet" indicating a person's infilling with the Spirit. Baugh, *Ephesians*, 454, mentions a similar interpretation by Wallace referring to the result of this Spirit-infilling.

184. See also Wick in ch. 2 of this study, section 2.6.5.

185. Gombis, "Fullness of God," 270.

186. Gombis, "Fullness of God," 271.

5.6.3 Summary

The literary structure of Ephesians verifies that repeatedly the text pinpoints the given divine actualities as a motivation for the anticipated human activities which are invited through positive and negative exhortations. So, the "divine indicative" is presented as a motivation for the "human imperative." In the flow of this argument in Ephesians 5, wisdom in contrast to folly is associated with looked-for edification and praise, thanksgiving and holy living, which implies covenant background.

The exegetical analysis of Ephesians 5:18–20 demonstrates that Spirit-infilling is invited in association with mutual, hymnic edification through familiar and spontaneous praise songs which are offered to God from the core of one's personality, all enthused by the Spirit, together with thanksgiving presented to God the Father through Jesus Christ. Thus, the vertical aspect of whole-hearted, individual, and corporate praise, which involves a relationship with the triune God, complements the horizontal aspect of mutual edification, which involves relationships at church level.

A modal/instrumental interpretation of the relevant participles enables a balanced reading. Other options prove to be too specific, although some of their connotations may be involved.

In sum, a constant and repeated Spirit-infilling is invited in connection with worship and thanksgiving. How this Spirit-infilling is to be achieved can be summed up in the formula "Spirit-refilling in the milieu of praise," which implies a reciprocal correlation between presence and praise.

5.7 Summary and Conclusion

As has been corroborated, Acts 2 provides a hermeneutical key for other Spirit narratives in Acts which involve both Jews and Gentiles: divine Spirit-presence literally "inspired" human praise, as the initial Spirit-infilling as a form of divine presence prompted glossolalia praise, while there is no proof for the reverse. This connection is seen against the background of a human-divine relationship which in Acts 2 comprises human repentance, divine salvation, and prophetic empowerment through the Davidic Messiah Jesus Christ. These distinct elements can be discerned as "three-in-one," but must not be divorced from each other. The initial infilling of God's new people with his Spirit-presence echoes the initial infilling of God's new temple with his glory-presence in 1 Kings 8 and 2 Chronicles 5–7.

Equally, in Acts 10 and 11, the Gentiles' glossolalia praise is depicted as the manifest sign of the outpouring of the Holy Spirit (Acts 10:46). Here, the divine Spirit-presence is clearly narrated as having prompted human praise. Given the same outpouring and baptismal terminology as in Acts 2, this initial Spirit bestowal is reported as indicative of the Gentiles' inclusion into God's people or as the extension of God's house. Although Luke does not explicitly use temple metaphors, the concept of metaphorical divine dwellings is alluded to, as shall be substantiated in the subsequent chapter.

The events in Acts 4 reveal that earthquake and Spirit-refilling are sandwiched between prayer with praise and bold preaching. Similarly, the exegetical analysis attests that a reverential exaltation of God together with explanatory acclaim and precise petition bring about a powerful outcome in the form of an earthquake and a repeated Spirit-infilling. The implied theophanic manifestations and the manifest Spirit-infilling create verbal echoes and, thus, a continuity with Acts 2, although a reverse correlation between divine Spirit-presence and human praise is not testified. Hence, the results in Acts 4 validate a connection between human praise and divine Spirit-presence with the former instigating the latter. Besides, they hint at covenant background and remind of the Hoy War motif.

Likewise, the sequence of events in Acts 16 communicates that worship was immediately succeeded by an earthquake with "liberating" effects in more ways than one. The exegetical analysis allows the inference that a process of hymnic praise said and sung by the apostle Paul and his companion was influential in bringing about this powerful seismic event. Their faith expressed through praise in suffering expected divine intervention, which allows to infer a divine origin of the manifestations; besides, it suggests a covenant context and echoes the divine war motif. Therefore, the connection between prayer/praise and manifestations of divine presence is evident, although no Spirit-refilling is stated in this case.

The Letter to the Ephesians, characterized by a paraenetic literary genre, reveals that divine activities are presented as a motivation for anticipated human activities, which are requested through negative and positive imperative pairs, like folly versus wisdom. Accordingly, the literary structure in chapter 5 suggests that wisdom is related to Spirit-infilling, worship, thanksgiving, and a holy living, which hints at covenant context. The exegetical analysis of Ephesians 5:18–20 verifies that Spirit-infilling is invited in association with mutual, hymnic edification through praise songs, all enthused by the Spirit and offered from the core of one's personality together with thanksgiving to God the Father through Jesus Christ the Son. How this Spirit-infilling is to be achieved can be summed up in the formula "Spirit-refilling in the milieu of praise." This involves a reciprocal correlation between presence and praise and testifies to covenant relationships at horizontal and vertical levels.

In sum, from the textual analyses of the Book of Acts and the Letter to the Ephesians the following results can be inferred: there is a connection between divine presence in the form of initial Spirit-infilling and human praise with the former prompting the latter. Vice versa, there is also a connection between human praise and Spirit-refilling, and/or theophanic manifestations with the former instigating the latter. Both directions are portrayed against the background of covenant relationship, which will be further explored.

The exploration in the Old and New Testaments leads to a biblical theology perspective in the next chapter which seeks to identify potential intertextual themes.

6.0

Results from a Biblical Theology Perspective: Three Intertextual Themes and Related Issues

Biblical Theology is more than the sum of Old Testament and New Testament.

—FRANCIS WATSON

THE OVERALL QUESTION POSED in this project is about a connection between God's presence and the praises of his people. In the attempt to answer this question, the investigations of texts from the Hebrew Bible, i.e., the First or Old Testament, and the Greek Bible, i.e., the Second or New Testament, have identified cases in which such correlation is validated: God's presence prompting his people's praise and human praise initiating manifestations of divine presence.

This chapter will pay attention to these results from a biblical theology perspective so that the witnesses of both Testaments can be heard "in concert."[1] Echoes from the Old Testament are heard together with those from the New and vice versa. Some reverberations resonate more fully in the New Testament, as revelation has progressed and textual meaning has been unpacked more fully. And so, the voices from both Testaments may sound differently when heard together, just as biblical theology is more than the sum of Old Testament plus New Testament, as Francis Watson rightly pointed out.[2] Thus, reverberations run back and forth

---

1. Childs, *Biblical Theology of OT and NT*, 78, 85; see ch. 2 of this thesis, section 3.2.3.
2. Watson, *Text and Truth*, 8.

and allow existing analogies and themes to be discerned, separately and together. In connection with that, the term intertextuality is used here to denote intertextual links in the form of insinuations resonating between texts from both Testaments. In this "biblical-theological concert" the following three intertextual themes can be identified in the texts analyzed:[3] first, *the connection between divine presence and human praise*, second, *the divine indwelling*, and third, *the divine-human covenant relationship*.

Potential analogies will be uncovered starting with the connection between divine presence and human praise. This connection involves literal and metaphorical dwellings filled with divine glory or Holy Spirit, as well as the divine-human covenant relationship. Contraindications regarding such connection, such as idolatry and rebellion, will be pinpointed. Queries about worship and praise, as well as Trinitarian worship will be addressed, as our worship depends on our perception of the triune God and of the divine nature of the Holy Spirit. The areas outlined above involve issues of divine personhood, human personhood, and relationality, as in the concepts of perichoresis and *imago Dei*, which have their place in a systematic theology setting. On a concluding note, a minor philosophical reflection will be presented. Scholarly debates will only be touched on where relevant, but not handled exhaustively.

6.1 The Connection between Divine Presence and Human Praise

6.1.1 Intertextual Links between 2 Chronicles 5–7, Acts 2 and 10/11, Acts 4 and 16, and Ephesians 5

As already mentioned, 1 Kings 8 witnesses to a one-sided connection only, while 2 Chronicles 5–7 testify to a reciprocal relationship between human praise and divine presence. In the latter narrative, the worship events are pictured in detail: to recapitulate briefly, a huge Levite vocal and instrumental orchestra with priests playing trumpets offered praise to the Lord before God's glory-cloud filled his house, which prevented further priestly sacrifice ministry. Thus, *human praise initiated divine presence*, which, again, inspired the King's prayer and praise. Subsequently, fire fell, consumed the sacrifices, and *the glory of the Lord filled the house*. The priests could not reenter the temple while the people outside started

---

3. On intertextuality see ch. 3, section 3.5.5.

worshiping: now, *the divine manifestations* are reported to have *initiated human prayer and praise* while having prevented priestly sacrifice. This reciprocal relationship between divine presence and human praise can be perceived in terms of a "glorious circle" as opposed to a "vicious circle":[4]

Chart 2:   Glorious circle or 'circulus gloriosus'

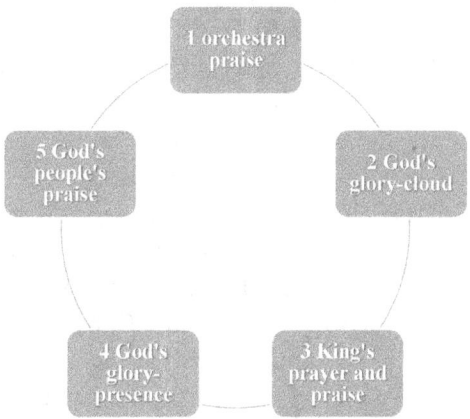

Orchestra praise → God's glory-cloud → King's prayer and praise → God's glory-presence → God's people's praise ...

The theophanies in 2 Chronicles 7:1–3 with fire coming down and divine glory filling the house are echoed in Acts 2:3–4a with fire tongues coming on every one of the disciples and Holy Spirit filling them all.[5] The reverberations of 2 Chronicles 5–7 and Acts 2 heard together reveal analogies and intertextual links in more ways than one: first, divine presence filling the dwelling (2 Chr 5, 2 Chr 7, also 1 Kgs 8, and Acts 2) and, second, fire and glory (2 Chr 7), fire tongues and Holy Spirit (Acts 2); *in both cases divine presence inspired human praise* (2 Chr 7 and Acts 2). Still, in Acts 2, in contrast to 2 Chronicles 5–7, the correlation is only one-sided and not reciprocal.

Equally, in Acts 10 and 11, the initial Spirit-infilling of new, non-Jewish believers prompted their glossolalia praise, which was declared

---

4. A friend with a background in physics gave explanation that in physics such a model would be rather called a helix because of its open spiral; still, a *circulus gloriosus* renders the play on words.

5. Selman, *2 Chronicles*, 2:350, already indicated that parallel.

the manifest sign of their reception of the Holy Spirit (Acts 10:46; 11:16). Once more, *divine Spirit-presence inspired human praise*. Reverberations of that theme can be heard in Acts 2 and 2 Chronicles 7. They evidence a twofold intertextual link: first, the glory of the Lord and the Holy Spirit appear as different modes of divine presence and, second, the glory of the Lord and the Holy Spirit both prompt human praise.

In contrast, in Acts 4 the prayer and praise of the young Christian community were succeeded by the shaking of the place and their repeated Spirit-infilling. Thus, *human prayer/praise was influential in bringing about the Spirit-refilling and earthquake*, which were both attributed to divine origin. On the one hand, these theophanies point to an intertextual link between Acts 4:31 and 1 Kings 8:11; 2 Chronicles 5:14; as well as 2 Chronicles 7:1–3 regarding the infilling of the house with divine glory. On the other hand, they propose an intertextual link with Exodus 19:18b concerning the theophanic shaking at Mount Sinai.[6] Another link is evident between Acts 4 and 2 Chronicles 5 regarding a *reverse correlation with human praise initiating divine presence*. Some may hear this echo also in Revelation 15:1–8 with the conquerors in Heaven praising God, and the heavenly temple being filled with divine glory. Yet, the events there are embedded in eschatological visions of God's wrath being poured out on earth: the infilling of the heavenly temple with smoke from the Lord's glory occurs in the context of judgment, which can be interpreted as a negative covenant signal. Although much praise is portrayed in Heaven, much of this occurs in such negative context. Having said that, we need to point out that our project concentrates on human praise on earth rather than in Heaven.

In Acts 16, a process of hymnic praise sung by Paul and Silas in prison was succeeded by a strong earthquake with liberating effects in more ways than one, which, again, has been attributed to divine origin. Once more, *human praise initiated manifestations of divine presence*. Yet, here no refilling with Holy Spirit is mentioned. The seismic activity in Acts 16 recalls besides Acts 4 also Exodus 19.

In Ephesians 5:18–20, the believers' infilling with Holy Spirit is invited in association with hymnic edification and praise songs enthused by the Spirit, offered sincerely and gratefully to God the Father through Jesus Christ. Here, the connection is more of a general kind: *a Spirit-refilling in the milieu of praise*. There is no explicit evidence of praise prompting

---

6. A similar link occurs in Rev 11:19 and Rev 16:18 with earthquakes, but in the context of judgment.

a Spirit-infilling, but the echoes reverberate softly and reciprocally. The intertextual links are tied with a loose knot which may attach Ephesians 5 to texts with literal or metaphorical divine dwellings in praise context such as 2 Chronicles 5 or Acts 4.[7]

In view of the above, texts with literal and nonliteral temple context verify intertextual links which witness a connection between presence and praise. This theme emits echoes, whether divine presence inspiring human praise or human praise initiating manifestations of divine presence. Still, the correlation does not work reciprocally in every instance. Besides, the link also occurs in texts without literal temple context, but always with covenant background.

6.1.2 Intertextual Echoes of a Connection without a Literal Temple Context

The narratives in Joshua 6 (without temple context) and 2 Chronicles 20 (with and without temple context) revealed: *God's people's praise invited manifestations of divine presence in battle context*. This connection, which implies covenant background and the Holy War motif, resonates in Acts 4 and Acts 16, passages with covenant background which likewise reveal a context of persecution and conflict, whether spiritual or other, and, thus, echo the divine war motif.[8]

Similarly, the narratives in 1 Samuel 16 and 2 Kings 3 (without temple context) support the theme of *worshipful music with spiritual side effects*, whether in terms of making an evil spirit leave or releasing prophecy and divine salvation in battle context. An equivalent intertextual link exists with Acts 4 and Acts 16 with worship entailing theophanic side effects of a spiritual and/or seismic nature.

In sum, these intertextual echoes result in a "symphony" with reverberations emerging from Joshua 6, 2 Chronicles 20, 1 Samuel 16, and 2 Kings 3 in the Old Testament and reaching Acts 4 and Acts 16 in the New.

Psalm 22, a Davidic psalm of lament without temple context, reveals an intertextual nexus in v.3 with God dwelling in the praises of his people, and this independently from a man-made house as a divine dwelling.[9] In that respect, the link may connect Psalm 22:3 with Joshua

---

7. As to worship in Spirit and in truth invited by Jesus see also John 4:24–26.
8. See section 6.3.2 of this ch.
9. Ch. 4, section 4.4.4.

6 and 2 Chronicles 20, 1 Samuel 16 and 2 Kings 3. Of course, the theme of God dwelling in his people's praise also affects New Testament passages without a literal temple context, like Acts 4, Acts 16, and Ephesians 5, but with a metaphorical divine dwelling (see table 3 below).

Chart 3: Table on intertextual links with a connection between presence and praise

	1 Kgs 8–9	2 Chr 5–7	Josh 6	2 Chr 20	1 Sam 16	2 Kgs 3	Ps 22	Acts 2, 10	Acts 4, 16	Eph 5
Divine glory filling temple	x	x								
Supernatural phenomena:										
fire	x	x								
shaking			x						x	
spiritual/physical deliverance					x				x	
divine intervention/ victory			x	x	x	x			x	
Divine presence/ Spirit-infilling							x	x	x	xx
sacrifices	x	xx			x					
Praise	x	xx	x	xx			x	x	x	xx
Anticipatory/ prophetic praise			x	x	x	x			x	

6.1.3 Summary

As a result, in all the above texts the connection between divine presence and human praise has been confirmed. The thematic analogy is perceptible, whether in terms of divine presence inspiring human praise or human praise instigating manifestations of divine presence, or reciprocally as a *circulus gloriosus*.

Furthermore, echoes of this intertextual theme have been substantiated in texts of both Testaments independently from a literal temple, but often in connection with nonliteral divine dwellings and always with covenant background. Therefore, we will at first delve into metaphorical concepts of divine dwellings.

6.2 The Divine Indwelling: The Infilling of God's House with his Presence

This section deals with passages from both Testaments which refer to metaphorical divine dwellings by focusing on the texts analyzed so far, which means the selection is not exhaustive. Then again, not all the references involve a context of praise. Before embarking on metaphorical divine dwellings in both Testaments and the intertextual theme of the divine indwelling with a corresponding metaphorical interpretation, a brief excursus on modes of divine presence and temple symbolism will be offered.

6.2.1 Modes of Divine Presence

As mentioned before, God's general presence in Creation is distinguished from his specific presence among his people Israel in the Hebrew Bible, and again from his indwelling presence in his new people in the Greek Bible. At times, scholars have highlighted one mode of divine presence over against the others, or sought ways to link them:

Samuel Vollenweider, referring to Janowski, maintains that the idea of God dwelling among his people is connected with the *shekhinah* motif, a way in Judaism to express God's presence and glory among his people.[10] However, only variations of this verbal stem occur in the Hebrew Scriptures and not the noun *shekhinah* itself.

Robert Johnston complains that evangelicalism has emphasized the particular revelation of God in salvation at the expense of his general revelation in Creation.[11] For Johnston, divine Spirit-presence is the connecting link between both.[12] This, however, does not do justice either to the different modes of divine presence or to the motif of the divine indwelling.

Equally, James Arcadi connects God's general presence with his specific presence: God's specific presence means God acting at a specific location, and God's omnipresence means God acting at all locations.[13] This assumption is correct, but again does not do credit to the indwelling motif.

---

10. Vollenweider, "Göttliche Einwohnung," 203-4.

11. Johnston, *God's Wider Presence*, 10-11; Ash and Kreider, review of *God's Wider Presence*, 239-40.

12. Johnston, *God's Wider Presence*, 199.

13. Arcadi, "God Is where God Acts," 631-39.

In a similar, but more specific way, Tom Austin perceives God's glory as the basic attribute of his person and presence represented both in Creation and salvation.[14] Still, the term glory per se does not represent the divine indwelling in terms of the Lord's glory filling his house, or represent all the aspects of his presence in salvation. This is why it could be helpful to discern the different modes of divine presence with reference to the motif of the divine indwelling.[15]

In connection with that, the question of an "incarnational analogy" arises.[16] Is there an analogy between the incarnation of God taking on human flesh through Christ and dwelling in him, and God filling the believers with his Spirit and dwelling in them? The answer is both positive and negative. Yes, there is an analogy because in both instances metaphorical and still material dwellings are filled with divine presence. An analogy can legitimately be discerned between the work of the Spirit in Jesus Christ incarnate and in the believers and their bodies.[17] Whether this be Mary's womb as a holy receptacle of the divine Son, or Jesus' physical body, or the believers as a holy habitation of the divine Spirit, in each case "the Spirit gives a body to Christ," as Eugene Rogers elucidates: he identifies a pattern that is based on intimate relationship and lives "in the incorporation of others into its pattern."[18] Accordingly, one may even postulate an analogy between the mutual, inner-Trinitarian indwelling of Father, Son, and Holy Spirit, which the Church Fathers called "perichoresis," and the mutual indwelling of God and the believers.[19] The mutual indwelling within the Trinity opened up to include humans, an insight supported by characteristic texts in both Testaments from Genesis 1 to John 17.[20] We will back to this relational aspect in connection

---

14. See Austin, "Glory of God," 41–57.

15. On different modes of divine presence and their terminology see Hamilton, *God's Indwelling Presence*; on different opinions on the indwelling Holy Spirit in the OT see Hamilton, "Old Covenant Believers," 37–54; Kaiser, "Indwelling presence," 308–15, argues contra Hamilton that the OT believers were already indwelt by the Holy Spirit; see also Lampe, *God as Spirit*, esp. section "God as Spirit and the Holy Spirit," 206–28, where he elucidates God's presence as Spirit-presence.

16. See section 6.2.3.

17. Rogers, *After the Spirit*, 208–9.

18. Rogers, *After the Spirit*, 208–11.

19. Torrance, *Worship*, 27; see also section 6.5.1 of this ch.

20. Letham, *Holy Trinity*, 155–56; see, e.g., John 10:38 with Jesus saying "The Father is in me and I in him", John 15:4 on the vine and the branches concerning Jesus and the believers, and John 17:23 with Jesus talking to the Father about the believers

with the theme of covenant relationship.[21] In that respect, the perichoretic unity between the triune God and the believers reveals a certain "incarnational" analogy in terms of the divine indwelling. On the other hand, no, there is not such analogy because there is only one incarnation, namely that of Jesus Christ, with the purpose of reconciling the Creation to the Creator.[22] Accordingly, scholars have perceived incarnation in connection with salvation and the restoration of the *imago Dei*, i.e., the divine image in humankind.[23] The relational aspect of the *imago Dei* will also be taken up again.[24]

6.2.2 Scholarly Debate: Temple Symbolism in Cosmic Context

The present writer was first confronted with the theme "temple" in biblical theology through the biblical theology study group of the Tyndale Fellowship conference at Cambridge, UK, in 2001. The content of this event is reflected in the volume of essays published by T. Desmond Alexander and Simon Gathercole.[25] Further impact is due to the work by Greg Beale on temple and the church.[26] Moreover, in the last two decades scholars have discussed the cosmic context of temple symbolism. They have debated whether Eden as a microcosmos of Creation anticipated tabernacle and temple and whether the first man-made temple represented Heaven and earth.[27]

In fact, already in Scripture (Gen. 3:8), Eden is considered a place of divine presence and divine-human communication where God walked and talked to Adam and Eve.[28] Then, this symbolism was not far-fetched in view of the culture of the Ancient Near East: temples were perceived as "meeting points of Heaven and earth" and represented "the vertical

---

"I in them and you in me."
- 21. Section 6.5.1.
- 22. Moritz, "Deep Incarnation," 436–43.
- 23. Moritz, "Deep Incarnation," 436–37.
- 24. Section 6.5.1.
- 25. Alexander and Gathercole, *Heaven on Earth*.
- 26. Beale, *Temple and the Church's Mission*.
- 27. See Barker, *On Earth*, also Beale, *Temple and the Church's Mission*, and Alexander and Gathercole, *Heaven on Earth*. Beale et al. concur with Barker in the concept of temple representing Heaven and earth. Barker, *On Earth*, 73–80, finds even more evidence of this temple theology in noncanonical material such as Qumran texts.
- 28. Renwick, *Paul, the Temple*, 25–46, esp. 27.

and horizontal cosmic axis" and, thus, sites of divine-human communication.[29] Accordingly, Greg Beale holds that "Eden was the first archetypal temple upon which all of Israel's temples were based."[30] Similarly, Margaret Barker believes the entire temple to represent the Garden of Eden and the created world, and the Holy of Holies to symbolize Heaven as the place of God's presence.[31] Thus, symbols of Heaven and earth in the temple would merge representing "on earth as it is in Heaven."[32] Also, the temple rites were "Heaven on earth," which naturally includes praise. Acordingly, Crispin Fletcher-Louis states that the cult in tabernacle and temple was a mirror image of Creation: "Tabernacle and Temple are organized to reflect Israel's understanding of the structure of the cosmos, and the worship and rituals of the cult actualize and guarantee the God-intended order and stability of creation."[33] Or, John Levison perceives Eden and temple to be "spaces that overlapped or even coincided with one another" arguing in favor of an Edenic restoration of Jerusalem and the temple by using Ezekiel 47 as an example.[34] Moreover, it has been maintained that the "garden-temple" Eden involves the predisposition of expansion: through the metaphor of expanding landscapes, Old Testament texts would depict God's people Israel as a divine habitation in growth.[35] And in the end, the "garden-temple" Eden of Genesis 2 finds its eschatological consummation in the arboreal "city-temple" of Revelation 21, as Beale sums up: "Eschatology not only recapitulates the protology of Eden, but escalates it."[36]

In contrast, Daniel Block explains such temple symbolism in terms of a "nonreciprocating equation":[37] he questions the view that Eden or the cosmos represent a temple, while he admits that tabernacle and

29. Hundley, *Gods in Dwellings*, 136.
30. Beale, *Temple and the Church's Mission*, 79–80, 66–80.
31. Barker, *On Earth*, 8.
32. Barker, *On Earth*, 30, 49–50.
33. Fletcher-Louis, "God's Image," 82.
34. Levison, *Filled with the Spirit*, 213; and Beale, "The Final Vision," 205–6, also point to extrabiblical literature such as Jubilees 8:19; similarly, Beale mentions 4Q418; both texts identify Eden in connection with temple.
35. Beale, *Temple and the Church's Mission*, 123–67; see also section 6.2.2.
36. Beale, *Temple and the Church's Mission*, 368.
37. Block, "Eden: A Temple," 20–25, esp. 21, buttresses his argument by using Isa 66:1–2; Ps 132:7–8, 13–14 or pointing to Ezek 43:1–12 and Hebrews 8 and 9; these texts speak of God's dwelling place in Heaven and its earthly microcosmic replica.

temple involved Edenic features.[38] Block concedes that Eden represents a kind of organic place of meeting and relationship between God and humans, who were entrusted with the guardianship of Creation. That this was reflected in some of the temple symbols would, however, not make Eden into a "sacred shrine."[39] Block refers to Revelation and its climactic visions of a restored cosmos as no return to Eden, but as a "transformation of the original home of humanity" (Rev 21–23, esp. 21:2–23).[40] All the same, just as a gentle reminder, echoes of intertextual themes run between both Testaments and have the potential to resonate reciprocally.[41] Hence, Genesis 2 may well witness to a divine garden sanctuary with the propensity of future expansion and with features reflected in tabernacle (Exod 26), temple (1 Kgs 6 and 2 Chr 3), and, last of all, in the new "city of the *eschaton*" (Rev 21).

This brief outline of the contemporary discussion illustrates how relevant literal and nonliteral, i.e., metaphorical concepts of divine dwellings are for an accurate comprehension of the various modes of God's presence.

6.2.3 House of God and Other Metaphors in the Old Testament

The term "house of God" occurs in several of the texts to designate God's abode in a literal sense. Other texts refer to "house" and "tabernacle" as divine dwellings in a metaphorical sense or even to the Lord's presence as a city temple (Ezek 48:35).

First of all, neither 1 Kings 8 nor 2 Chronicles 5–7 use the term "temple" (הֵיכָל), but "house of the Lord" (בֵּית יְהוָה) to refer to the first temple filled with God's glory. Thus, 2 Chronicles 7:16 applies the term בַּיִת "house" referring to the Solomonic temple as the divine dwelling place. Moreover, in 1 Chronicles 17:4, 10 (cf. 2 Sam 7:5–16), this term allows a play on words: David is not meant to build a "house for the Lord," but the Lord promises to build a "house for David."[42] The latter house means a future royal family for David and an eternal messianic dynasty

---

38. Block, "Eden: A Temple," 3–29.
39. Block, "Eden: A Temple," 21, contra Beale, "Final Vision," 199.
40. Block, "Eden: A Temple," 29; also Rev 7:15; 11:19; 14:15, 17; and 15:5—16:1, 17.
41. See ch. 3, section 3.2 on Childs, particularly 3.2.2.
42. See also Rudnig, "König ohne Tempel," 426–46, on house terminology in 2 Sam 7.

for God, which is reflected in the prophetic promise in Amos 9:11 about "the fallen hut of David" to be restored.[43] Hence, the concept of בַּיִת is open for a metaphorical use in more ways than one.

Equally, a metaphorization of house terminology was observed in the Book of Ezekiel. In Ezekiel 37:11, for example, the term בַּיִת "house" is used for Israel.[44] Then, Ezekiel's prophetic visions of the new temple area in Ezekiel 40–48 use in most cases בַּיִת to describe a temple filled with divine glory which likely foreshadows the eschatological city of Revelation 21.[45] Similarly, Ezekiel 37:27 refers to a metaphorical dwelling place (מִשְׁכָּן "dwelling" or "tabernacle") indicating that God will have his dwelling among his people.[46] Likewise, Ezekiel 43:7, 9 express this idea by using the same root שָׁכַן "to dwell."[47] And Ezekiel 48:35 states that the name of the new eschatological city Ezekiel saw in his vision is יְהוָה שָׁמָּה "the Lord is there," which is echoed in Revelation 21:22.

In addition to that, divine dwellings tend to involve the tendency of expansion. Already the Old Testament uses the metaphor of expanding landscapes to portray God's people as a divine habitation in growth.[48] In analogy, the temple is seen with an inherent propensity to expand in a metaphorical way. Likewise, God's presence in the form of eschatological divine glory has the propensity to expand, which is evidenced in passages like Numbers 14:21 predicting that all the earth be filled with the glory of the Lord (cf. Isa 6:3). Also, Habakkuk 2:14 prophesies that the earth will be filled with the knowledge of the glory of the Lord, as the waters cover the sea (cf. Isa 11:9).[49] Equally, Haggai 2:9 prophetically anticipates a greater glory of the new temple. What could be the greater glory of this new temple, and how could this greater divine glory cover the earth like

---

43. Ch. 4, section 4.2.

44. Ch. 4, section 4.5.2.

45. Block, *Ezekiel*, 506, contra Beale, Spatafora et al.: Block opposes the view of an eschatological temple pictured in Ezekiel's visions.

46. Beale, *Temple and the Church's Mission*, 367, points to a link between Lev 26:11 and Ezek 37:27; similarly, Joel 3:17 and Zech 8:3 confirm that the Lord dwells in his city Jerusalem and on his holy mountain Zion.

47. Also Exod 29:45; Num 35:34; 1 Kgs 6:13; Isa 57:15; Zech 2:10, 11; and Ps 43:3; cf. Renwick, *Paul, the Temple*, 29–30; also Janowski, *Gottes Gegenwart*, 123–27.

48. E.g., Num 24:5–7; Isa 54:1–3; Jer 3:16–18; Zech 1:16; and 2:1–5, 10–13; Beale, *Temple and the Church's Mission*, 123–67, mentions even more texts that describe Israel as a growing landscape, but without the explicit reference to a divine dwelling.

49. Differently, Hab 3:3b witnesses that God's glory covered the Heaven and his praise filled the earth.

water? The new temple apparently relates metaphorically to God's new people expanding to the ends of the earth, which equals greater divine glory, as they take God's glorious Spirit-presence with them. This is how the knowledge of God's presence may fill the earth.[50] This eschatological, global divine presence in the mentioned texts is also pictured in figurative terms of a river of living water flowing forth from the temple and filling the land (Ezek 47 pointing to Rev 22).

In view of the above, it can be inferred that a metaphorical use of the term house or divine dwelling place etc. is already intrinsic to the Old Testament and does not start with the New Testament,[51] as demonstrated in table 4:

Chart 4: Table on house of God metaphors et al. in the Old Testament

	House of the Lord	House of Israel	Family, dynasty	Fallen hut	Tabernacle/ dwelling	The Lord is there	Dwelling in expansion
1 Kgs 8	x						
2 Chr 5–7	x						
1 Chr 17:4–14	x						
2 Chr 7:16	x						
1 Chr 17:4, 10	x		x				
2 Sam 7:5–16	x		xx				
Amos 9:11				x			
Ezek 37:11		x					
Ezek 37:27					x		
Ezek 40–48	x						
Ezek 43:7, 9 et al.					x		
Ezek 38:35						x	
Num 14:21 et al.; Isa 6:3; Isa 11:9; Hab 2:14; Hag 2:9							x

---

50. Kline, *Images of the Spirit*, even considers the divine glory per se to represent a divine dwelling and, therefore, a metaphor, which he pursues through Scripture starting with Gen 1 until Rev 21 (see esp. *Images of the Spirit*, ch. 1); see also Kline, "Creation in the Image," 250–72.

51. Renwick, *Paul, the Temple*, 35–36, elucidates that the case is similar with extra-canonical Jewish literature: e.g., Enoch's visions of a heavenly temple as God's dwelling place (1 Enoch 14:13–24; 1 Enoch 39:12–14) even reveal hints of a connection between divine presence and heavenly praise in that temple.

6.2.4 Temple and other Metaphors of Divine Dwellings in the New Testament

One may be tempted to think that in the New Testament temple terminology referring to the literal temple occurs in the gospels and temple terminology relating to metaphorical temples emerges in the epistles and in Revelation. Now, given Jesus' metaphorical temple logion in the gospels and figurative divine dwellings in Acts, this classification risks an oversimplification. Still quite a few epistles involve temple, dwelling, tent, (eternal) house, God's building, God's field, living stones, and God's presence as temple per se.

All the same, already the gospels use ναός "temple" metaphorically in the Jesus' logion: Jesus, independent from the temple cult,[52] talks about temple referring to his own person and body (Matt 26:61; Mark 14:58; John 2:19). His metaphorical reinterpretation of the literal temple is based on his messianic claim and demonstrates that Jesus perceives himself as God's dwelling place "not made by (human) hands" (Mark 14:58).[53] This reinterpretation is closely linked to the work of the Holy Spirit in the life of Jesus Christ from the very beginning.[54] This work is again modelled in the believers. The Johannine terminology of the Father dwelling in the Son reflects this work of the Spirit in Jesus which models the work of the Spirit in the believers (John 14:10, 17).[55] And so, Jesus identifies first himself and then the believers as the new temple which issues streams of living water (John 7:37–39).[56] Probably, Jesus' temple logion initiated the developing Christian metaphorization of temple terminology.[57]

---

52. Holmén, *Jesus and Jewish Covenant*, 329, maintains that for Jesus the temple and its cult did not serve as covenant markers.

53. Beale, *Temple and the Church's Mission*, 203; Block, "Eden: A Temple," 27–29, and Gäckle, *Allgemeines Priestertum*, 289–90. In connection with Jesus' resurrection, Beale speaks of a replacement of the temple rather than of a metaphorical reinterpretation as Gäckle does. In a different way, Rogers, *After the Spirit*, 75–134, perceives the body of Jesus in the context of his "in-carnation" through the Spirit.

54. Bobrinskoy, "Indwelling of the Spirit," 49–65, who uses early Orthodox theology and its "pneumatic Christology" as examples, asserts that this work of the Spirit connects Christology and pneumatology.

55. See Burns, "John 14:1–27," 307–9.

56. Levison, *Filled with the Spirit*, 372–73, clarifies that the phrase "out of his belly" may refer both to Jesus and the believer/s.

57. Gäckle, *Allgemeines Priestertum*, 310–11. In contrast, Chance, *Jerusalem, the Temple*, 35–45, esp. 35, rejects the idea of any "evidence that Luke transferred to Jesus and/or the church the eschatological functions of the temple."

While in Luke's Gospel the literal temple ἱερόν still plays a prominent role, in the Book of Acts the positive connotation of the temple undergoes a change and the term itself a redefinition. Although Luke's Gospel already uses metaphorical concepts of Spirit dwellings, like Zechariah being filled with the Holy Spirit (Lk 1:67),[58] in Acts ample allusions point to the idea of metaphorical divine dwellings without Luke using the term "temple."[59] Clearly, the Pentecost narrative in Acts 2 alludes to the believers, individually and corporately, as a nonliteral divine dwelling: Acts 2:4 referring to the disciples as being "filled with Holy Spirit," which is repeated in Acts 4:31, implies a dwelling filled with divine Spirit-presence. Following Beale's line of reasoning, Pentecost represents the fulfilment of Jesus' prophecy of Spirit-filled believers, as is announced in John 7:37–39, anticipated in John 20:21–23, and fulfilled in Acts 2:4.[60] Beale supports his argument by referring to Old Testament allusions in Acts 2:1–40[61] which he perceives to be set in direct temple context and proposes: "Acts 2 depicts not merely a theophany, but also the descent of the heavenly end-time temple of God's presence upon his earthly people."[62] Additionally, the Pentecost account contains insinuations enough to allow the inference that Luke was aware of the Sinai background as a divine sanctuary.[63]

Furthermore, in Acts 4:11 with quote from Psalm 118:22, Peter in his speech before the religious authorities denotes Christ as "capstone" or "headstone" of a new metaphorical temple (κεφαλὴν γωνίας or רֹאשׁ פִּנָּה). This theme is taken up in the events around Steven: in his speech in Acts 7:44–49, with hints to Isaiah 57:15 and Isaiah 66:1–2, Steven expounds God's dwelling place in tabernacle and temple.[64] The expression used in

---

58. Lk 1:67 testifies about Zachariah: ἐπλήσθη πνεύματος ἁγίου καὶ ἐπροφήτευσεν "he was filled with Holy Spirit and prophesied," which is also a clear indicator of divine Spirit presence inspiring prophetic praise.

59. Ch. 5, sections 5.2.2 and 5.3.2; see also Walton, "Tale of Two Perspectives," 144–46.

60. Beale, *Temple and the Church's Mission*, 204; e.g., Bennema, "Giving of the Spirit," 86, perceives the giving of the Spirit in John's Gospel as a three stage process.

61. E.g., Exod 19–20, Isa 66, Num 11, 1 Kgs 8, and 2 Chr 7.

62. See first part of Beale's article, "Clearest Evidence," 73–102, esp. 99, and his conclusion in the second part "Corroborating Evidence," 63–90, which he supports by three excursions on OT allusions in Acts 2, the first two of which contain references with direct temple context (cf. Beale, "Corroborating Evidence," 86–90).

63. Beale, *Temple and the Church's Mission*, 204–5, also points to the concept of Sinai as a sanctuary.

64. Beale, *Temple and the Church's Mission*, 216–28.

Acts 7:48 "The Most High does not dwell in (homes) made by (human) hands" (ἐν χειροποιήτοις) suggests a new "God-made" abode, which requires his people's obedience to the Holy Spirit (Acts 7:51).[65]

Correspondingly, Acts 10 and 11 point to the expansion of this divine habitation: as God's people Israel is extended to embrace Gentiles from "the ends of the earth," his house in Jerusalem is enlarged metaphorically to reach to "the ends of the earth."[66] More precisely, its remains are being rebuilt and extended in a metaphorical way. Beale observes a similar link between the expression that God took a "people for his name" from the Gentiles and his promise "I will rebuild the fallen tent of David" (quote from Amos 9:11) in the speech of the apostle James in Acts 15:14, 16.[67] This "temple extension" has been evidenced in the Holy Spirit being poured out on the Gentiles and their being baptized with Holy Spirit (Acts 10:45 and 11:16).

The reference to God not dwelling "in handmade temples" (ἐν ναοῖς χειροποιήτοις) appears again in Paul's speech at Athens in Acts 17:24. This is also why Fletcher-Louis, pointing to Acts 7 and 17, upholds that "The Christian rejection of (literal) temple space as sacred space is a feature of Luke's account of early Christianity . . . and sacred *space* is overtaken by sacred *person(s)*."[68]

Consequently, it is not surprising that the apostle Paul in his epistles explicitly refers in a metaphorical way to the believers and their bodies as God's temple and temple of his Spirit:

1. individually in 1 Corinthians 6:19 "Your body is a temple of the Holy Spirit" (ναὸς ἁγίου πνεύματός)[69] as well as

---

65. Walton, "Tale of Two Perspectives," 138–43, presents a helpful overview on the discussion.

66. See section 5.3.1.

67. Beale, *Temple and the Church's Mission*, 268, also 241, traces this idea of extension even back to Gen 1:28.

68. Fletcher-Louis, "God's Image," 98.

69. Levison, *Filled with the Spirit*, 287–88, identifies the metaphor of believers as living temple also in the Qumran community (1QS V, 5–6). Arrington, "Indwelling," 1–11, esp. 4, argues that 1 Cor 3:16–19 cover individual and corporate aspects, as both need to be kept together; Renwick, *Paul, the Temple*, 42–43, also mentions these two aspects in 1 Cor 6:19. Similarly, Levison, *Filled with the Spirit*, 294–95, perceives Paul's use of the body metaphor in 1 Cor 6:19 in connection with his argument in favor of sexual purity and holiness.

2. corporately in 1 Corinthians 3:16 "You are God's temple" (θεοῦ ναὸς) and 2 Corinthians 6:16[70] "We are the temple of the living God" (ναὸς ζῶντος θεοῦ),[71] and

3. in Ephesians 2:21–22 "The whole dwelling ... grows into a holy temple in the Lord (ἅγιον ναὸν ἐν κυρίῳ) ... a dwelling place for God through the Spirit" (κατοικητήριον θεοῦ ἐν πνεύματι).[72]

In 1 Corinthians 3:9, Paul uses the agricultural metaphor "God's field" (θεοῦ γεώργιον) for the believers which he mixes with the architectural metaphor "God's building" (θεοῦ οἰκοδομή).

In view of the above, it may surprise that Volker Gäckle seems to conclude the temple metaphor plays no major role in Pauline ecclesiology.[73] As a matter of fact, Paul in his letter to the Corinthians does apply the temple metaphor and others to the church in an ethical and pneumatological context. Likewise, Mark Bonnington emphasizes the ethical context over against any other arguing that Paul's temple language as "sacred space" in Corinthians is "essentially ethical rather than ecclesiastical."[74] By doing so Bonnington downplays not only the ecclesiological, but also the pneumatological import of divine presence. Yet, Paul's temple language is not *either* ethical *or* ecclesiological, but *both*. It can be surmised that Paul's picture in Corinthians of the believers as divine dwelling is also reflected in Ephesians 5. The paraenetic text in Eph 5:18–20, which encourages the believers corporately to be filled with God's Spirit in praise instead of being intoxicated with wine, reveals precisely this *ecclesiologcal and ethical-pneumatological* setting, although it does not apply temple terminology.[75] Then, other epistles use building metaphors in connection with the church. For example, 1 Peter 2:4–6 applies the analogy of "living stones" to Jesus (ζῶντα λίθον) and the church

---

70. Greever, "We Are the Temple," 113, asserts that 2 Cor 6:16–18 reveal the "teleological" continuity in the covenants, which involves God's presence: he demonstrates through a chart with a chiastic *inclusio* that "the promises are unpacked in terms of God's presence and relationship with his people" (cf. Greever, "We Are the Temple," 101); by that Greever means covenant relationship.

71. With allusions to Lev 26 and Ezek 37.

72. Gäckle, *Allgemeines Priestertum*, 361–83; Wright, "Worship and the Spirit," 14; Block, "Eden: A Temple," 28; Wick, *Urchristliche Gottesdienste*, 183–93; also ch. 2 of this study, section 2.6.5.

73. Gäckle, *Allgemeines Priestertum*, 374–76.

74. Bonnington, "Is the Old Covenant Renewed," 153.

75. Ch. 5, section 5.6.1.

(ζῶντες λίθοι). Even Volker Gäckle infers: "The church as God's temple is now the eschatological place of God's presence: God is dwelling in this new eschatological temple in the same way as he had dwelt in the Jerusalem temple."[76] This is certainly correct in as far as God's presence is concerned, since God promised that his presence would dwell in his house, a promise which affects not only the literal house, but also the nonliteral dwellings. Nevertheless, as already stated, in the course of salvation history, the mode, extent, and locus of divine presence underwent changes. First, God dwelt among his people in a literal temple. Then, he came to dwell in Jesus Christ incarnate in a metaphorical temple. After that, he came to dwell in the believers in a metaphorical temple through his Holy Spirit.[77] Thus, the literal house as the place of God's abiding presence was substituted by a metaphorical temple.

In addition, the divine abode underwent a change of perspective from earth to Heaven with an eschatological outlook. This eschatological outlook is reflected in 2 Corinthians 5:1 where Paul talks about an "eternal house in the Heavens which is not handmade" (οἰκίαν ἀχειροποίητον αἰώνιον ἐν οὐρανοῖς) contrasting it with the "house of the tent" on earth (οἰκία τοῦ σκήνους). Similarly, God's "exceeding eternal weight of glory" (ὑπερβολὴν αἰώνιον βάρος δόξης) in 2 Corinthians 4:17 opens up an eschatological perspective. David Renwick also understands 2 Corinthians 3:7–11 to imply this eschatological outlook and perceives an intertextual link with Haggai 2:9.[78] In a similar way, Hebrews 8:5 labels Israel's tabernacle (σκηνή) a "copy" of the heavenly "original type" (cf. Heb 10:19–22). Hebrews 9 also relates to these two contrasting tabernacles (σκηνή in Heb 9:2 and 9:11). The Apocalypse develops this eschatological perspective even further:[79] John pictures prophetic visions of a heavenly temple (ναός) which is filled with divine

---

76. Gäckle, *Allgemeines Priestertum*, 374, in the German text: "So ist die Gemeinde als Tempel Gottes nunmehr der eschatologische Ort der Gegenwart Gottes: Gott wohnt inmitten dieses neuen, eschatologischen Tempels in gleicher Weise, wie er es im Jerusalemer Tempel getan hatte."

77. See the discussion in Hamilton, "Old Covenant Believers," 37–54, contra Kaiser, "The Indwelling Presence," 308–15: Hamilton, using John 7, John 14, and John 20 for his argument, holds that OT believers were not indwelt by the Holy Spirit; Kaiser, using the same texts, contests this; actually, there is a transition, which becomes obvious in Luke 1:67 which testifies that Zachariah "was filled with Holy Spirit."

78. Renwick, *Paul, the Temple*, 119–20.

79. E.g., Marshall, "Church and Temple," 203–22, esp. 208–9, explores the idea of a heavenly temple in Hebrews and Revelation.

presence and displays manifestations of God's glory in the context of judgment (Rev 7:15; 11:19; 15:8; and 16:1, 17). The apostle portrays scenes of "post-mortem" praise of the redeemed in this heavenly temple which are embedded in the context of judgment (Rev 14:2–3).[80] As a climax in Revelation 21, John describes visions of a new Heaven and new earth which involve divine presence per se. The restored cosmos is embodied in the Holy City, the New Jerusalem coming down from Heaven (Rev 21:2, 10). The striking characteristic of this city is that the Lord God Almighty and the Lamb are her ναὸς, thus, making any other temple superfluous (Rev 21:22). Hence, the ultimate ναός in the New Testament is God's glory-presence in this city (Rev 21:10–11; Zech 2:5)! The above results are condensed in table 5:

---

80. As to the theme of cosmic eschatological judgment, Beale, *Use of Daniel*, 272–73, perceives a link between Daniel and Revelation.

Chart 5:   Table on temple metaphors et al. in the New Testament

	Body of Jesus	No hand-made dwell.	Mut. indwell. Father/Son	Spirit-filled dwell./temple	Head-, (living) stone/s	Hut /tent etc.	God's field	No temple
Matt 26:61; Mark 14:58; John 2:9	x							
Mark 14:58		x						
John 14:10–17			x					
Acts 2:4 (cf. John 3:37-39; 20:21–23)				x				
Acts 4:11					x			
Acts 4:31				x				
Acts 7:48		x						
Acts 11:16 (cf. 1:5)				x				
Acts 15:16 (cf. Amos 9:11)						x		
Acts 17:24		x						
1 Cor 3:16; 6:19; 2 Cor 6:16;				x				
1 Cor 3:16							x	
2 Cor 5:1		x						
Eph 2:21–22				x				
Eph 5:18				x				
1 Pet 2:4–6					x			
Heb 8:5; 9:1, 11; 10:19						x		
Rev 7:15; 11:19; 15:8; 16:1, 17				x				
Rev 21:22								x

In sum, the difference between divine dwellings in both Testaments is not between material and nonmaterial temples, but between literal and nonliteral ones because nonliteral, i.e., metaphorical dwellings may still be material. Also, the contrast is about man-made and God-made houses because in the end God does not dwell in human-made temples (see Acts 17:24; Heb 9:24).[81] The metaphorical and still material temple as the place of divine presence is epitomized in the person of Jesus Christ incarnate. After Jesus' ascension with his physical presence in Heaven and the outpouring of the Holy Spirit, a new metaphorical and still physical dwelling

---

81. Beale, *Temple and the Church's Mission*, 373–76.

came into being in the believers. This dwelling remains until the ultimate nonliteral dwelling will find its consummation in God's presence in the eschatological Holy City as the new creation of Heaven and earth.

6.2.5 The Divine Indwelling: The Infilling with Divine Presence als Glory and Holy Spirit

Now, concerning the intertextual theme of the divine indwelling in our analyzed texts: just as the intertextual theme of the connection between divine presence and human praise resonates among texts of both Testaments, so does the intertextual theme of the divine indwelling.

The following intertextual echoes can be heard: *just as the first temple is filled with divine glory, God's new dwelling is filled with Holy Spirit. And just as God's glory filling his house inspired his people to praise him, the Holy Spirit filling God's new people inspired their praises. And again, just as his people's praise in return stimulated God to fill his house with his glory, their praise stimulated the Holy Spirit to fill them afresh.*

Here are the corresponding intertextual links: in Acts 2:2–4, the disciples were filled with Holy Spirit, a verbal metaphor which inevitably evokes 1 Kings 8 and 2 Chronicles 5–7. Accordingly, a certain analogy is evident between the initial Spirit-infilling of God's new people in Acts 2 and 10/11, their repeated Spirit-infilling in Acts 4 and Ephesians 5 on the one hand[82] and the glory-infilling of God's new house in 1 Kings 8 and 2 Chronicles 5–7 on the other. In all these cases, the divine infilling/indwelling occurs in the context of praise. There is only one caveat: in Holy War narratives without temple context no divine indwelling occurs. Still, for the rest, the witnesses from both Testaments relating to glory-filled and Spirit-filled divine dwellings in the context of human praise emit echoes which can be heard together in concert, as is summed up in table 6:

---

82. Arrington, "Indwelling," 7–9, distinguishes between the initial indwelling of the Spirit in Acts 2 to identify regeneration and the repeated infilling of the Spirit in Acts 4 to identify empowering (owed to his Pentecostal inheritance?). Yet, both in Acts 2:4 and Acts 4:31 the same terminology "filled with Spirit" is used in the Greek text. In both instances the believers are inhabited by the Holy Spirit and, therefore, represent a divine dwelling; on terminology of indwelling see Arrington, "Indwelling," 1–10.

Chart 6:   Table on analogy of the divine infilling/indwelling

	1 Kgs 8:10, 11	2 Chr 5:13–14; 7:1–2	Acts 2:4	Acts 4:31	Acts 7:55	Acts 11:16	Eph 5:18
Divine glory filling the Lord's house	X	X					
Spirit-infilling/being full of Spirit/baptized with Holy Spirit			X	X	X	X	XX
Praise	XX	XX	X	X			XX

6.2.6 Model of Metaphorical Interpretation of the Divine Indwelling

As to the method of interpretation of the afore mentioned verbal metaphors of divine infilling/indwelling, we suggest to apply the theory of conceptual blending by Gilles Fauconnier and Mark Turner.[83] Their model, which is based on the cognitive-linguistic approach by George Lakoff and Mark Johnson, allows to portray in a simple way complex metaphorical utterances in their intratextual and intertextual conceptual settings.[84]

Lakoff and Johnson consider metaphors as conceptual at their roots and linguistic at their expressions. Similarly to Ricoeur, they criticize formalist theories as microscopic (merely linguistic); in contrast, they deem metaphors to involve a whole world of cognitive conception (macroscopic). Against rhetoric theory and its reducing of metaphors to mere adornment functions, Lakoff and Johnson insist that metaphors involve truth claims, also in every-day life. And so, they developed a theory of cognitive conception, which organizes metaphors in structural, orientational, and ontological categories.

This model represents the basis of the theory of conceptual blending by Fauconnier and Turner, which involves the blending of conceptual spaces: "source space" and "target space" form together a "generic space" and merge into a "blended space" where meaning is generated and which

---

83. Fauconnier and Turner, "The Way We Think"; Fauconnier and Turner, "Rethinking Metaphor," 53–66.

84. Lakoff and Johnson, *Metaphors We Live By*; Lakoff and Johnson, *More than Cool Reason*; their theory evolved into a neural theory of language (cf. Lakoff, "The Neural Theory," 17–38); see also Konsmo, *Pauline Metaphors*, 47–52.

projects meaning back into all the other spaces.[85] Similar theories of conceptual blending and cognitive mapping have already been applied to religious language and concepts.[86] The above method has been applied in the graphics on the metaphorical theme of the divine indwelling identified in the analyzed texts, first, in the Old Testament, second, in the New Testament, and, third, from a biblical theology perspective:

Chart 7: *Theme of the divine indwelling in the OT (1 Kgs 8; 2 Chr 5-7)*

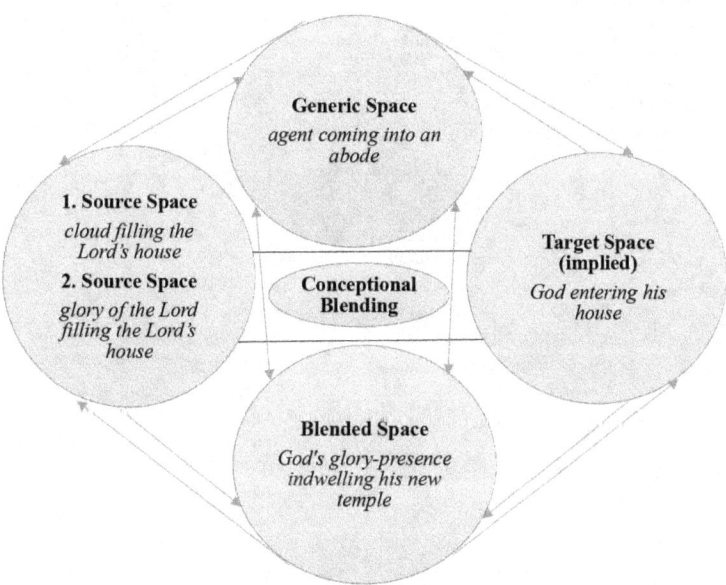

---

85. The terms "source domain" and "target domain" go back to Kövecses, who also organizes metaphors in structural, orientational/spatial, and ontological categories (cf. Konsmo, *Pauline Metaphors*, 50).

86. See Stovell, *Mapping Metaphorical Discourse*.

194 God's Praise and God's Presence

Chart 8:   *Theme of the divine indwelling in the NT (Acts 2)*

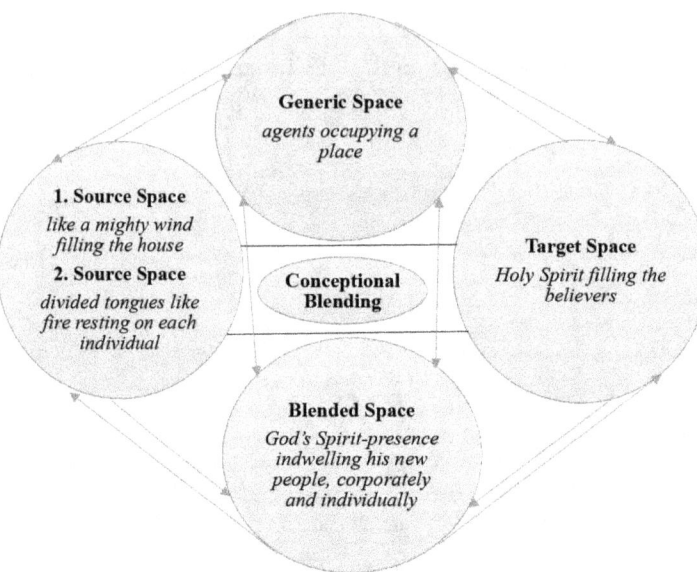

Chart 9:   *Theme of the divine indwelling in BT*

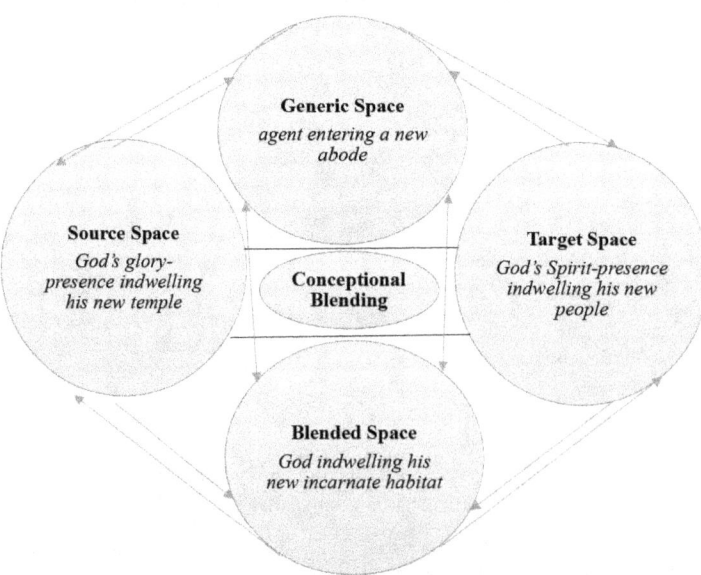

6.2.7 Summary

As has been corroborated, a cosmic temple symbolism sheds light on places of God's presence on earth and on the divine-human relationship. Also, we have seen that metaphorical concepts of divine dwellings are significant for discerning different modes of divine presence including God's indwelling presence. The difference is not about material and nonmaterial, but about literal and nonliteral, i.e., metaphorical divine dwellings, since a metaphorical habitation may still be material in quality. It has been demonstrated that the metaphorical concepts "house" or "temple" are intrinsic to both Testaments, although more frequently in the New. The scriptural witnesses relating to glory-filled and Spirit-filled divine dwellings emit echoes which can be heard together "in concert" in the intertextual theme of the divine indwelling.

As a result, the connection between God's presence and his people's praise often occurs in the context of the theme of the divine indwelling, sometimes with literal and sometimes with nonliteral dwellings filled with divine glory-presence and divine Spirit-presence. Nonetheless, this correlation is also witnessed without any temple context or infilling/indwelling motif, e.g., in Holy War and other conflict narratives in both Testaments. Still, the connection between divine presence and human praise always involves covenant context, as will be probed in the next section on the third intertextual theme, the divine-human covenant relationship.

6.3 The Divine Human Covenant Relationship

6.3.1 Divine Self-Revelation and Human Praise in a Relationship

Once as a fresh student of theology, the present writer made an exciting discovery when reviewing Scriptures: God revealed himself to and initiated communication with humans who then built altars and worshiped him; this involved divine-human relationships which eventually led to covenants:

1. *God talked to Adam and Eve* in the Garden of Eden (Gen 1:28; 3:9–13) and *prepared Noah* for the flood (Gen 6:13–21; 7:1–5; 8:15–22; 9:1–17). He *called Abraham* and the patriarchs leading them into the Promised Land (e.g., Gen 12:1–3). God *revealed himself as Yahweh to Moses* out of the burning bush (Exod 3:4–10). He *hovered over*

Mount Sinai (Exod 19:9, 16; 24:15–18; and 34:5) and *covered and filled the tabernacle with the cloud* of his presence (Exod 40:34–35). Likewise, he was *present in the fire-cloud leading his people* in the wilderness (Exod 40:36–38). Also, he *promised David to build him an eternal house*; then, the Lord was *present in his temple filling it with his glory-cloud* (1 Kgs 8:11; 2 Chr 5:14; 2 Chr 7:1–2). And now he *is dwelling in a metaphorical temple, his people, filling them with his Holy Spirit* (John 10:38; Acts 2:4; 4:31; and Eph 5:18). And so, God has taken initiative in revealing his presence to and communicating with humans and calling out a people for himself, just as he had taken initiative in crafting Creation and creating humankind.

2. As a response, *humans offered sacrifices* (Gen 4:3–4) and started *building altars for God* (Gen 8:20). Accordingly, the patriarchs of God's people and leaders after them erected altars in the land as signs of their worship (Gen 12:7; 26:25; 28:18 etc.). Then, according to the Lord's instructions, the people of Israel Israel built a mobile sanctuary, the *tabernacle* (Exod 36–38), and an immobile sanctuary, the *temple* (1 Kgs 6–7; 2 Chr 3–4), to offer sacrifices praising him. Finally, God himself established a metaphorical temple for his new people *to offer sacrifices of praise* (Acts 2:4; 1 Cor 3:16; and Eph 5:18–20).

3. And so, *God kept revealing himself*, and *his people kept worshiping him* in return. *Divine-human relationships* developed which eventually turned into *covenants*, some of which took the form of legal contracts where God set the terms and which had two partners—God as "senior partner" and his people as "junior partner." There were consequences following observance or non-observance in the form of blessings or curses, like in ANET covenant treaties.[87] A marital perspective of the divine-human relationship envisaged God as "husband" and his people as "wife," which involved terms like in a marriage ceremony.[88]

---

87. Waltke, *Old Testament Theology*, 409–11, points to the contrast between ANET treaties and biblical covenants.

88. Passages such as Ezek 16, Isa 54, and Hos 1–3 portray God's "marital" love; Oeming, "Siehe, deine Zeit," 151–60, esp. 159, considers this marital love as core and centre part of the biblical-theological concept of covenant.

6.3.2 Relationship and Covenant: Terminology and Attempts of Distinction

As shown above, the divine-human interaction led to relationships and covenants. What then is the difference between a relationship and a covenant? It will be argued that covenant is relational interaction, but relational interaction is not always covenant. In other words, every covenant is a relationship, but not every relationship is a covenant.[89]

For example, in Genesis 1:28, God placed the care for Creation into Adam's and Eve's hands blessing them, which attests a relationship arising between Creator and humankind.[90] Some traditions in systematic theology have considered this relationship a covenant, although no characteristic covenant terminology in connection with בְּרִית *berith* is used.[91] Still, a divine commandment in form of the creational mandate is reported. Sacrifice rituals occur later (Gen 4:3-4).

Or, in Genesis 9:1-17, God placed the care for Creation into Noah's hands blessing him and his children, which refers to an already existing relationship between Creator and humankind (Gen 6-8).[92] Likewise, this mutual relationship between God and Noah has been perceived by some systematic theologians as a covenant, although no *berith* terminology is used at this point. Still, Noah's obedience to God's commandments (Gen 7:5) and a sacrifice ritual are reported (Gen 8:20). Genesis 9:1-17 in its post-deluge setting echoes, at first, the Creation mandate God gave to Adam and Eve spelling out more specifically what this involves for Noah and his descendants (9:1-7). And only after that, the text talks about God "setting up" his covenant with them (9:8-17) spelling out what this involves in terms of divine promise and covenant sign. In the second

---

89. Similarly, Hugenberger, *Marriage as a Covenant*, 4, 168; see also Kwakkel, "Berith and Covenants," 2, in his pre-publication version.

90. Berkhof, *Systematic Theology*, 215-17, 287-89, distinguishing between relationship and covenant, holds that in addition to the *natural relationship* in Eden, where every life depended on their Creator, God revealed himself to humankind in *covenant relationships*, e.g., in the form of legal contracts.

91. Barth connects relationship with covenant and covenant with Creation: see Barth's distinctive phrases "creation as the external basis of the covenant" and "the covenant as the internal basis of creation" in CD 3.1, §§41.2, 41.3 (cf. MacDonald, "The Imago Dei," 312).

92. Gen 6:8 says that "Noah walked with God"; Gen 6:13; 7:1; and 8:15 say that "God spoke to him"; Gen 7:5 again report that "Noah obeyed God," which testifies to an already existing relationship before a covenant; cf. Kwakkel, "Berith and Covenants," 2, who also refers to Williamson, *Sealed with an Oath*, 43.

part of the text, seven times the term בְּרִית *berith* is used, three times together with the verb קוּם *qum* to convey that God "set up" or "ratified" his covenant.[93]

The case is similar with Abram. In Genesis 12:1–3, God promised to bless Abram by making him a great nation and a blessing, which witnesses to a divine-human relationship arising, whereas no covenant terminology is stated as yet. Still, Abram's faith and obedience to God's command to leave his home (12:4) and his altar building (12:7) are narrated. This is perhaps why particularly Reformed systematic theologians have traditionally considered this text, which already contains divine promises and human obligations, to testify to a covenant between God and Abram, as Gert Kwakkel elucidates.[94] In contrast, Kwakkel claims that God established a relationship with Abram before he established a covenant with him.[95] Indeed, only Genesis 15:18–21 in its post-Ishmael setting, at first, refers back to the promise God gave to Abram and, then, spells out explicitly what this involves for Abram and his descendants in terms of a *berith* "covenant." In Genesis 15:18, for the first time the typical covenant terminology כָּרַת בְּרִית *karat berith* "to cut a covenant" is used to denote that God has "cut" a *berith* with Abram: just as the animal sacrifices for this covenant were cut (Gen 15:10), which is the ritual the terms relate to, God has "cut" a covenant with Abram, that is, he initiated the covenant.[96]

The Sinai covenant between God and the people of Israel in Exodus 19:5a uses the term *berith* for the people's obedience to God through their "keeping (his) covenant" שָׁמַר בְּרִית; this covenant obedience is connected to God's promise for his people to be his "own treasure" (19:5b). At this point, no sacrifice ritual is recorded, except that the people had to consecrate themselves for God, which means they had to be clean and holy inwardly and outwardly. This covenant is confirmed in Exodus 24 and connected with the ritual of sacrifice and the sprinkling of blood.[97] The animals were cut, and so was the covenant, that is, established and ratified. And so, the phrase כָּרַת בְּרִית *karat berith* occurs in Exodus 24:8 in connection with the "Book of the Covenant" containing the Lord's words and rules (24:7). After Israel's idolatry with the golden calf, the covenant

---

93. See, e.g., Waltke on the Noahic covenant, *Old Testament Theology*, 284–90.

94. Kwakkel, "Berith and Covenants," 12.

95. Kwakkel, "Berith and Covenants," 11–12.

96. On the initiatory meaning of the phrase *karat berith* in connection with Abraham see Dumbrell, *Covenant and Creation*, 14.

97. See Exod 24:5–8.

between God and Israel, and this time with Moses as well, is renewed or rather restored in Exodus 34 in terms of *karat berith*, but without sacrifices being explicitly mentioned.[98] This covenant restoration occurs in the context of God's commandments (34:1) and God's revelation to Moses (34:5–7), which led to Moses' prostrate praise (34:7) and his intercession on behalf of Israel (34:8). The three stages of covenant making witness a process and development.[99] Deuteronomy 28 echoes the Sinai covenant in the context of God's "commandments" (seven times מִצְוָה) and "words of the law" (twice תּוֹרָה), and together with God's blessings in case of his people's obedience[100] and his curses in case of their disobedience.[101] Yet, the terms *karat berith* do not occur there[102] nor any sacrifice ritual.

Then, 2 Samuel 7 and 1 Chronicles 17 refer to the messianic Davidic covenant in terms of a dynasty promise without the reference to *karat berith*, but with the commandment for David to walk with God, and with consequences in the form of blessings or curses.[103] All the same, the phrase *karat berith* is used again in 2 Chronicles 21:7 to recall this messianic Davidic covenant and in Psalm 89:3 in connection with a divine oath affirming the dynasty promise.

Again, the veterotestamental promises of a new covenant in Jeremiah 31 and Ezekiel 37 are expressed in terms of *karat berith*.[104] A similar promise is referred to in Ezekiel 11:19–20, but without *berith* terminology. This new covenant is believed to have come to its fulfilment in Acts 2.

In addition to that, there is an issue of language: the Hebrew term *berith* opens up a broad semantic horizon:[105] it may signify a divine promise and a mutual obligation in terms of a compact and treaty between two partners, whether interhuman or divine-human. The Greek term *diathēkē*,

---

98. See Exod 34:10, 27.

99. Interestingly, Kwakkel, "Berith and Covenants," 6–8, also identifies a process of *berith*-making at a human-human level between Jonathan and David.

100. See Deut 28:2–14.

101. See Deut 28:15–68; Kwakkel would disagree that Dtn 28 and 29 relate to the Sinai covenant because Dtn 29:1 would talk of another covenant at Moab besides the one at Horeb/Sinai. However, the development of covenant making at Sinai may well justify the assumption that Moab represents just another stage in this process.

102. Only in Dtn 29:1.

103. See 2 Sam 7:10–16; 1 Chr 17:10–14; cf. Goldingay, *Old Testament Theology*, 1:372.

104. Three times in Jer 31:31–33; once in Ezek 37:26.

105. Kwakkel, "Berith and Covenants," 18–23.

which has been used by the LXX for the Hebrew term *berith*, originally denoted in the secular setting an agreement and a disposition in terms of a last will.[106] The Latin term *pactum*, which has been used by the Vulgate for *berith*, reflects rather the meaning of compact.[107] Then, the German term *Bund* and the French term *alliance* tend to emphasize the relationship between the partners and their union rather than the treaty itself. Differently, the English term covenant tends to cover a broader horizon just as the Hebrew *berith*, while the terms may not be congruent.

As a result, the above example texts of covenant ratification reveal two characteristics: first, a divine-human relationship may have existed before a divine-human covenant was established and, second, a covenant can be identified even without the typical terminology *berith*, *qum berith*, or *karat berith* being used, but with the reference to a divine promise/oath and commandments, as well as human commitments and/or sacrifice/rituals.

6.3.3 Different Modes of Covenant: Conditional or Unconditional, Limited or Eternal

In connection with the different covenants, scholars have debated whether some of them are unilateral and unconditional, e.g., the Creation covenants between God and Adam and Eve/Noah,[108] and others bilateral and conditional, e.g., the Sinai covenant.[109] The first ones have been understood to contain divine promises only and the second ones to involve human commitments as well. Nevertheless, when God established the creational covenant with Adam and Eve at Eden, this meant not only a unilateral divine promise, but also a responsible commitment on the human side by way of the cultural mandate (Gen 1:28). The case was similar with the other creational covenant between God and Noah

---

106. Frey, "Die alte und die neue diathēkē," 266, points out that the translators rendered the Hebrew בְּרִית in the MT by the Greek *diathēkē* in the LXX, which originally was a technical term for a unilateral last will.

107. Gräbe, *Der neue Bund*, 15–17, mentions that the Vulgate distinguishes between *pactum* in the OT and *testamentum* in the NT, which led to distinguishing between *Bund* (covenant) and *Testament* (testament, last will) in the old Bible translations.

108. On covenant and creation see Blocher, "Old Covenant, New Covenant," 255–56; or Sutton, *That You May Prosper*, 126–27; also Dumbrell, *Covenant and Creation*.

109. E.g., Dumbrell, *Covenant and Creation*, 201; on a distinction between conditional and unconditional covenants see Goldingay, *Old Testament Theology*, 1:371–72; McComiskey, *Covenants of Promise*, 193–211, calls the conditional covenants administrative, which would still hold promises.

which implied not only God's promise of blessing for Noah's family and the earth after the flood, but also the cultural mandate (Gen 9:1–3) and the commandment to refrain from consuming blood (Gen 9:4). Then, God initiated a bilateral *berith* with Abraham which not only involved the gracious promise of blessing and land on God's side (Gen 15:18), but also on the human side a general commitment to walk with God (Gen 17:1) and circumcision as a specific covenant sign (Gen 17:10–11).[110] Clearly, the law covenant which the Lord established with Moses and Israel at Sinai represented a bilateral, conditional covenant which required of God's people to keep specific divine commandments (Exod 20–23, Deut 5).[111] Again, the messianic covenant with David and his house involved not only an eternal divine promise, but also the human commitment of a walk with God, as in the covenant with Abram, and consequences in form of blessings or curses as in the covenant with Moses (2 Sam 7:10–16; 1 Chr 17:10–14).[112] For those reasons, the differentiation between unilateral/nonconditional and bilateral/conditional covenants appears to be problematic.

The other distinction between limited and eternal covenants seems to be more helpful, as the Davidic covenant was termed an eternal covenant (2 Sam 7:16; 1 Chr 17:12, 14) in contrast to the Sinai covenant, which turned out to be limited in nature, not least because of its restriction to the people of Israel. Then, the new *berith* or *diathēkē*, anticipated by the prophets between God and believers from all nations including Israel and established in Jesus Christ through the Spirit, involves eternal divine promises, but still requires human commitment.[113] This new covenant is of an unlimited, eschatological, and eternal nature, but still not entirely unconditional (e.g., Heb 9:11–14; 13:20).

Consequently, these various covenants may encompass similarity and continuity and, yet, dissimilarity and discontinuity. At times, scholars have emphasized the aspect of continuity, while at other times they stressed discontinuity, as Henri Blocher makes clear:[114] the "law cov-

---

110. See Goldingay, *Old Testament Theology*, 1:371.

111. Berkhof, *Systematic Theology*, 293–301.

112. Goldingay, *Old Testament Theology*, 1:372.

113. In connection with that, Reformed theology developed the doctrine of a a *covenant of grace* in Jesus Christ, which humans were enabled to keep, in contrast to a *covenant of works* like the Edenic and Mosaic covenants, which they were not able to keep (cf. Berkhof, *Systematic Theology*, 211–18, 265–83).

114. Blocher, "Old Covenant, New Covenant," 240–52; see debate Bonnington

enant" would involve discontinuity—because limited in nature—and the "grace covenant" would involve continuity—because eternal. Accordingly, attempts have been made to bridge the ditch between "law-and-grace" positions.[115] For example, T. E. McComiskey perceived covenant in terms of promise, the latter serving as a common link which runs through all covenants.[116] Then, Andrew McGowan developed a "headship theology" with Adam and Christ as representative "heads."[117]

Suffice it to mention these examples of the past and present scholarly debate on covenant. Still, issues of relationality and relationship will be addressed in connection with covenant in a subsequent section.[118] The relevant point for our investigation is: in each case, the human-divine relationship is embedded in some sort of covenant setting between God and his people which arises out of the relationship, no matter when this covenant is considered to begin. Bearing these differences in mind, it may be legitimate to use the term "covenant relationship."

As a result, relationship is not equivalent to covenant, but may exist before and lead to it. The establishing of covenants can be expressed in different ways: first, through a typical terminology in connection with *karat berith* and, second, through signals, such as divine promises and commandments, blessings and curses, as well as human commitments and rituals. These terms and signals will be referred to as "covenant markers."

In view of the above, divine revelation, human worship, and divine-human covenant relationship may form a recurring pattern: divine self-revelation is frequently followed by the response of human worship, and both are associated with covenant relationships. Therefore, the next section will explore to what extent covenant settings in general and covenant markers in particular emerge in the texts on divine presence and human praise which have been examined so far.

contra Dunn (cf. Bonnington, "Is the Old Covenant Renewed," 57–66).

115. This issue has divided scholarship, e.g., Kline et al. contra Blocher, McGowan et al., the latter of whom hold that God's gracious presence was there with Adam before the Fall (cited by Green, *Covenant and Commandment*, 147–51). Still, whether Adam was already indwelt by the Holy Spirit before the Fall, as Smeaton presumes (cited by McGowan, "In Defense of 'Headship Theology,'" 191), seems to be rather hypothetical.

116. McComiskey, *Covenants of Promise*, 91–93.

117. McGowan, "In Defense of 'Headship Theology,'" 178–99, wishes to replace the term "covenant theology" with "headship theology"; however, this term involves a certain ambiguity because it has also been used in connection with the concept of a man being considered the head of his wife (1 Cor 11:3–12).

118. See section 6.5.2.

6.3.4 Covenant Setting in the Passages Analyzed

At this point, the familiar passages will be explored for evidence of elements which simply reflect an overall covenant setting either in the text or in the cotext, and elements which represent specific covenant markers. The setting and/or the markers may relate to existing covenants or a new covenant as the fulfilment of existing covenant promises.

As corroborated, 1 Kings 8–9 and 2 Chronicles 5–7 narrate how the new temple was consecrated as a sanctuary where God's people offered sacrifices and praise to him and which he filled with his presence as promised. Scholars have maintained that, therefore, the temple and its sacrificial cult could also be considered "covenant path markers" and associated with patriarchal, Sinaitic, and Davidic covenants.[119] In any case, through the human-divine interaction of the partners in the ceremony of temple dedication a general *covenant context* is evidenced, and the following elements could be considered particular *covenant markers*: *animal sacrifices* (1 Kgs 8:5; 2 Chr 5:6) not only display a form of worship, but also reverberate the establishing or renewing of a covenant because of the blood involved.[120] Then, the *ark of the covenant* being brought into the Holy of Holies (1 Kgs 8:6–9; 2 Chr 5:7–10) has been explained by scholars in connection with the Davidic covenant as a sign of Yahweh being "enthroned in the midst of his people."[121] The *tablets with the Ten Commandments* in the ark evoke the covenant at Mount Sinai.[122] Orchestral and vocal praise on a grand scale is indicative of *covenant offerings* (2 Chr 5:12–13). King Solomon's prayers with priestly-pastoral supplication on behalf of the people represent an *appeal to the divine covenant partner and his promises* (1 Kgs 8:22–61; 2 Chr 6). The *Lord's promise of his presence* in this place hints at the Davidic covenant.[123] The king's prayer is succeeded by worship addressed to God through *burnt offerings, fellowship offerings* (1 Kgs 8:62–64; 2 Chr 7:4–5), and *praise offerings* (2 Chr 7:6) displaying a rich variety of *covenental sacrifice rituals*. The

---

119. Holmén, *Jesus and Jewish Covenant*, 275–76.

120. See also Gen 15:17–18 and Heb 9:10–26: Heb 9:10 explains that in the Sinai covenant the blood of animals was brought into the tabernacle, while Heb 9:15, 24–26 reveal that in the new covenant Jesus entered the heavenly sanctuary with his own blood.

121. Williamson, *Sealed with an Oath*, 122–23, points to Robertson, Dumbrell et al.

122. Goldingay, *Old Testament Theology*, 1:369, 385–86.

123. Williamson, *Sealed with an Oath*, 132–33, refers to the divine covenantal promise to David and his dynasty.

manifestations of God's presence in glory and fire signal the *approval of the covenant offerings*.[124] This provokes the *prostrate praise* of all the Israelites as a response extolling their God and his *chesed, the Lord's "faithful love*," a term which is specifically used in covenant context (2 Chr 7:1-3). A *divine admonition and warning* to keep the covenant was added as part of the *covenant formula* (1 Kgs 9:4-9):[125] this formula contains *affirmations and blessings* as well as *warnings and curses* (Deut 28-30) in which Yahweh declares that he is Israel's God and they are his people.[126] Similarly, 2 Chronicles 7:14 alludes to *covenant renewal* after violation.[127] As a result, the above components evidence both covenant settings in general and covenant markers in particular.

In Joshua 6, the process leading to the downfall of the walls and the city of Jericho involves the following factors which are indicative of covenant context:

1. the background in 5:14 with the "prince of the army of the Lord" appearing on scene and Joshua leaving the command in this battle to the Lord implies the *Holy War motif*;

2. the *ark of the covenant* leading the march around the city in preparation for the battle (6:8, 9, 12) embodies the Lord's presence and hints at the *divine war motif*;[128]

3. the *number seven* symbolizes *divine involvement*: the *seven priests* blowing the *seven ram's horns* (6:4, 9, 13, 20)[129] and the *seven march*

---

124. Similarly, Lev 9 prescribes various covenant offerings for the purpose of purification of priest and people, which was followed by God's presence appearing in glory and fire. Then, Lev 10:2 reveals that fire is mentioned in judgment context, which could be interpreted as a negative covenant marker.

125. On covenant formula in Deut and covenant renewal in Kings and Chron, esp. in 1 Kgs 8:33-40, see Baltzer, *Bundesformular*, 40-47, 59-69, esp. 68; concerning the covenant formula, Rendtorff, *Covenant Formula*, 57-92, elucidates the different patterns and shapes in which this formula and others occur and where covenant or its renewal are concerned without even the term בְּרִית being used.

126. Keil and Delitzsch, *1 and 2 Kings*, 3:139.

127. Sutton, *That You May Prosper*, 31.

128. On the role of the ark in the wars of the Lord, see van der Lingen *Les guerres de Yahvé*, 163-67.

129. The ram's horns being blown may also mean a call to assembling for war; besides, Sutton, *That You May Prosper*, 64, points to the judgmental character of the trumpets: the Greek term σάλπιγξ in the LXX translation of the Hebrew term שׁוֹפָר in the MT corresponds to σάλπιγξ used, e.g., in Rev 8:6-18, a coincidence which, however, represents only a slight hint at judgment; then, Sutton, *That You May Prosper*,

circuits for *seven days* in silence, except for the last one accompanied by the battle cry of God's people;[130]

4. the *warning* in 6:18 against taking things banned for destruction[131] and the *blessing* in 6:25 on Rahab and her families;[132] and

5. the supernatural manifestations which evidence divine presence in action and lead to the military conquest signal the *Holy War motif* (6:5, 20).[133]

Many of the above elements point to the Holy War motif and, thus, represent covenant setting in general.[134] The warning and blessing denote covenant markers.

Similarly, in 2 Chronicles 20, the narrative in two parts about the people of Judah being threatened by their enemies demonstrate the divine war motif and, thus, imply covenant setting together with subtle covenant markers: verses 3–13 tell of the prayer and fasting of Jehoshaphat and the people of Judah reminding the Lord of his *faithfulness to his covenant and people*. Verses 14–17 narrate the response, a *prophetic promise* that the *battle is the Lord's*. The ensuing threefold *anticipatory praise* extols God and his covenantal *chesed "steadfast love"* (vv.18–22a). The praise is succeeded by a *military divine intervention* which prevents Judah's defeat in this battle (v.22b).[135] These elements point to the *divine war motif* in the

---

263–64, draws a parallel between the curses in Deut 28:15–68, Jos 6, and Rev 8–14, all of which result in judgment; hence, this may represent a negative covenant marker.

130. Sutton, *That You May Prosper*, 67, perceives the march around the city as a "symbolic circumcision," which also could be a covenant marker; even more, he identifies the divine war motif in covenant context according to Deut 7:16.

131. Earl, "Joshua and the Crusades," 57, states that the ban signals Yahweh's ownership and, thus, points to the divine origin of the victory.

132. Again, the allusion to the blessings and curses in Deut 28–30 reflect the covenant formula in which Yahweh declares that he is Israel's God and that they are his people (cf. Keil and Delitzsch, *1 and 2 Kings*, 3:139), which in this case would even include a foreign prostitute.

133. Differently, Hobbs, *Time for War*, 205, claims that the concept of Holy War is of Greek origin and that Scripture speaks rather of the "wars of Yahweh" (1 Sam 25:28), which would refer to "an early form of warfare done in the name of Yahweh"; yet, this may be just some sophisticated differentiation.

134. Chang, "Priestly Covenants in 1QM and 1 QSb," 147–62, links the Holy War motif in the War Scroll of Qumran with priestly covenant motifs, which are also implied in Joshua 6; see section 4.4.

135. In connection with 2 Chr 20, von Rad, *Holy War*, 131–32, asserts that the ancient Holy War tradition has been spiritualized without that the earlier tradition

context of God's judgment on his people's enemies who are also his own enemies, an identification based on the Lord's covenant with his people.[136]

In 1 Samuel 16, the account on the conflict between king Saul and his servant David includes subtle hints to covenant setting, but no covenant markers. Verse 23 reveals that David must have made music to God, since the evil spirit sent by the Lord departed from Saul. This deliverance could be interpreted as *divine intervention in spiritual conflict*. Referring to 1 Samuel 16:13, Paul Williamson explains the prophetic anointing on David as the *prophetic empowering of the one, who speaks and acts on God's behalf*, which would insinuate covenant setting in the broader sense.[137] Besides, the narrative around 1 Samuel 16 about David and Saul exposes the fact that Saul had broken the covenant with God, while David kept it (1 Sam 15:22–23, 28).

Again, the account in 2 Kings 3 hints at an existing covenant. Verses 9–12 tell that the prophet of the Lord was asked to seek God's counsel for Israel, supported by Judah, to solve a twofold problem. While the minstrel was playing, Elisha received divine revelation promising water and victory for Israel and Judah (vv.15–19). Again, the *divine anointing on the prophet* implies a broader covenant context. The fulfilment of the prophetic promise through *divine intervention* in both matters insinuates the *divine war motif* and, thus, evidences covenant context (vv.20–25). Besides, the reference to *sacrifice* in v.20 could count as a covenant marker.

In Psalm 22, a psalm of lament by David, the reference to *praise* in v.3 is embedded *in a setting of lament*, which is introduced in verses 1–2 by a *threefold use of covenant language*:[138] "My God, my God, why have you forsaken me? Oh, my God, I cry by day, but you do not answer, and by night, but I find no rest." The first part of this prayer, which is taken up by Jesus in his exclamation on the cross (e.g., Matt 26:46), epitomizes covenant relationship in a situation of utmost physical, emotional, and spiritual agony. The second part in v.3 appeals to a holy covenant God who is enthroned in the praises of his people Israel; he is faithful to

---

ceased to exist; during this process of spiritualization, the import of liturgical praise increased, which brought about divine intervention and victory.

136. Vogel, *Heil des Bundes*, 265–83; also Sutton, *That You May Prosper*, 114–15; then, Lind, *Yahweh Is a Warrior*, 27, referring to Smend, questions scholars' practice of seeing the covenant motif in contrast to the Holy War motif, which is a legitimate criticism.

137. Williamson, *Sealed with an Oath*, 164.

138. Berkhof, *Systematic Theology*, 267.

deliver those who trust in him (v.4). The expression of Yahweh being "enthroned in the midst of his people" may point to the Davidic covenant, as Williamson suggests.[139] Overall, these elements represent subtle clues of covenant setting.

In Acts 2, the Pentecost narrative starts with the obedience of Jesus' disciples:[140] according to the instructions of their master to wait for the promised gift, they were gathered together about to celebrate Israel's *covenant feast*. The *infilling of the disciples with Holy Spirit* (v.4) or *outpouring of God's Spirit* (vv.17–18) represents the *fulfilment of covenant promises* made to Israel and, thus, a new covenant marker.[141] Williamson rightly points out that, although the term διαθήκη "covenant" is used only twice in Acts (3:25; 7:8), the concept of covenant is clearly expressed through the fulfilment of these promises.[142] Williamson asserts that the *Abrahamic covenant* is alluded to. All the same, the various prophetic allusions to covenant promises being fulfilled in Acts 2 refer to the *messianic Davidic covenant* as well. Besides, the covenantal promise of the bestowal of the Spirit is connected with the *judgment motif of the Day of the Lord* in Acts 2:20, which could be seen as a negative covenant marker.[143] The disciples' *praise* extols Israel's covenant God lauding his mighty deeds (v.11). Thus, these elements reveal covenant background plus a new covenant marker.

The narratives of Acts 10 and 11 both display the extension of God's people Israel for Gentiles to be included into the new covenant. This *covenant extension* was prepared through Peter's vision and his obedience in following it (10:10–16; 11:5–10), and confirmed *through the outpouring of the same Holy Spirit on Gentiles* just as on God's people Israel (10:45–46; 11:16–17). The Holy Spirit was interpreted as a sign of God grafting Gentiles into this new extended people, which was sealed through water baptism as a *covenantal initiation rite* (10:48). Hence, both *Spirit-baptism* and *water-baptism* signify new covenant markers.[144]

The situation in Acts 4 displays a spiritual and physical conflict, as Peter and John had been censured and imprisoned for proclaiming the Good News of Jesus. That this situation of conflict reverberates the

139. Williamson, *Sealed with an Oath*, 122–23.
140. See ch. 5, section 5.2.
141. See Ezek 37:26–28; Jer 31:33; Joel 2:28–29.
142. Williamson, *Sealed with an Oath*, 185–86; for the relationship between promise and covenant see McComiskey, *Covenants of Promise*, 59–93.
143. Williamson, *Sealed with an Oath*, 42.
144. See ch. 5, section 5.3.

divine war motif is emphasized through the quote from Psalm 2 in Acts 4:26. The citation is embedded in the prayer of the new Christian community, as they offered *praise to their Creator God* imploring him to reveal his sovereignty over adverse political and religious leaders. Likewise, they *addressed their Saviour God* entreating him to grant miracles *through his "holy servant Jesus"* (4:23–30). These prayers allude to the Creation covenant and the new covenant, both in the context of the *Holy War motif*.

Similarly, the narrative in Acts 16 exposes a spiritual and physical conflict. In the face of increasing persecution, the apostles were imprisoned for acting out the gospel through exorcism. *Prison praise expressing covenant faith* occurred on the basis of an existing covenant relationship (16:25–26). The increasing persecution and imprisonment succeeded by deliverance through doors opening up in more ways than one resonate the *divine war motif*. Additionally, this way, newcomers were added to God's covenant people, a fact which was sealed through *water baptism, a covenantal initiation rite* (16:33). These elements reveal, first, the *Holy War motif*, second, *covenant setting*, and, third, *new covenant markers*.

Finally, the entire letter to the Ephesians witnesses to *salvation and the new covenant life* in Jesus Christ and, thus to covenant setting. Furthermore, Timothy Gombis claims there is a rhetoric of *divine warfare* in Ephesians, epitomized in Ephesians 6:[145] the divine war has been won through the death and resurrection of Christ, which led to a radical reinterpretation of the divine war tradition: "The powers' triumph over Christ on the cross was their own defeat, and Christ's defeat won him victory," and the church as the new Spirit-filled people/temple shares in the subversive way of this victory through a self-sacrificial love.[146] Thus, the *divine war theme is reinterpreted* in terms of *love instead of war* (covenantal discontinuity), but with the armor of God against the powers of the dark (covenantal continuity) (see Eph 6:10–18). Seen in such light, the appeal in Ephesians 5:18–20 to the believers to let themselves be constantly refilled with Holy Spirit would have their Spirit-inspired praise appear as a "spiritual missile" and part of their divine armor. This would then, at least, recall the Qumran writings if not put Ephesisans in line with the the Holy War narratives in Josua 6, 2 Chronicles 20, and

---

145. Gombis, "Rhetoric of Divine Warfare," 87–107; see also Gombis, "Triumph of God," 157–60.

146. Gombis, "Rhetoric of Divine Warfare," 93.

the conflict narratives in Acts 4 and 16 which all reflect covenant background.[147] Likewise, the appeal to Spirit-inspired praise and thanksgiving to the Father through the Son (Eph 5:19-20) is indicative of the believers' *covenant with the triune God*. Therefore, the above elements would point to a test of God's people spiritual integrity rather than their own capacity. Still, one should not overrate the divine war motif in Ephesians 5. Even without a rhetoric of divine warfare, there is enough evidence of covenant context.

In sum, as has been demonstrated, all the passages and their cotext on God's praise and God's presence involve covenant context and/or covenant markers. The indicative elements of covenant setting refer to existing covenants or a new covenant; in some cases, they imply the Holy War motif. The indicative elements of old and new covenant markers refer to divine promises and commandments, divine blessings and curses, as well as human obligations, sacrifice rituals, praise offerings, and initiation rites like water baptism and Spirit-baptism.

6.3.5 A Word on Holiness

The above results disclosed that the divine-human covenant and its compliance or violation are connected with holiness. All the covenants, whether old or new, entail holiness in terms of God's people "being set apart," i.e., consecrated to God. Without going into the details of a concept of holiness we will limit ourselves to a minor note on the aspect of holiness in connection with covenant and temple. It can safely be stated: there is no covenant between God and his people without holiness.

As validated before, the condition of holiness is spelled out in the covenant markers relating to divine blessings and curses (2 Chron 6). It is also implied in the Lord's promise to dwell in his temple—on condition of the holiness of priests and people (e.g., 2 Chr 5:11; 2 Chr 6:14-40). The requirement of holiness is spelled out in Leviticus 9:6-24 where the glory of the Lord appeared after the priests had duly been cleansed through the offerings before they were able to serve in the temple. Or, in Leviticus 10:1-3 where fire from the Lord devoured those who had offered unholy temple sacrifices. Hence, holiness is pictured powerfully as the *conditio*

---

147. This reminds of the Qumran community's perspective of praise in divine war, as Falk and Vogel demonstrated: cf Falk, "Prayer, Liturgy, and War," 285-89, section "Worship as Warfare"; Vogel, *Heil des Bundes*, 268-78, on hymnic praise in war in 1QM; see also ch. 4, section 4.4, and ch. 5, sections 5.4 and 5.5.

sine qua non for priests and people, so that God could demonstrate his glory in the temple and judgment could be avoided, as Leviticus 10:9 resumes. God says: "Be holy, for I am holy," as is expressed in Leviticus 19:2; 20:26; 21:8; and echoed in 1 Peter 1:15–16.

Correspondingly, this veterotestamental command for God's people to be holy is implied in the neotestamental calls for repentance and sanctification: the call of John the Baptist for repentance (Matt 3, Mark 1, and Luke 3), Jesus' teachings as in the gospels, or Peter's Pentecost sermon calling for repentance (Acts 2), not to speak of the Paulines and other epistles when it comes to sancification in respect to the temple metaphor (Eph 2:21).

In this connection, Joshua Greever elucidates that God's presence in his temple is tied up with covenant, and this again with the holiness of his people, using 2 Corinthians 6:16–18 with a quote from Leviticus 26:12 as an example:[148] "Put briefly, temple and covenant go hand in hand ... If God is to dwell among his people, they must live accordingly."[149] Hence, God's presence in his dwelling is based on a holy covenant relationship.

Concerning the divine part in this covenant, God's presence in his temple and in the praises of his people is based on his covenantal חֶסֶד and אֱמֶת towards them. Both terms can appear together almost as synonyms to describe God's faithfulness in general[150] and his faithfulness to his covenant people in particular.[151] Concerning the human part, this steadfast love of God represents an incentive for God's people to love him and keep the covenant in return. If God's people allow themselves to be set apart for him, then their worship and praise naturally reflect their consecration: holiness spelled out as a life of love dedicated to God and each other, which is true worship.[152] Accordingly, divine presence and human praise are bound to a holy covenant relationship.

In contrast to that, unholy worship and praise are an abomination in God's eyes (Amos 5:21–25).[153] Moreover, the covenantal holiness of his people affects their relationship not only with God, but also with their

---

148. Greever, "We Are the Temple," 97–118.

149. Greever, "We Are the Temple," 101–3.

150. E.g., Gen 24:27; Exod 34:6; Ps 25:10.

151. E.g., 1 Kgs 8:23; 2 Chr 6:14; Ps 136; see Jenni and Westermann, *Theologisches Handwörterbuch*, 1:602.

152. On the holiness of God's people see, e.g., Wells, *God's Holy People*, 241–46.

153. Also section 2.7.1 on holiness in worship.

fellow humans, a point we will revisit later on.[154] Holy worship and praise cannot address God and, at the same time, ignore one's neighbour, or God's Creation.[155] Thus, covenant and communion with God involve covenant and communion among his people and beyond. This is what the Orthodox scholar Ioannis Zizioulas recommends in his concept of *koinōnía*, that is, communion for the church.[156]

As has been confirmed so far, the response of holy covenant praise in a holy covenant life inspires God to continue revealing his holy covenant presence in his temple and people. This way, God's presence and his people's praise are interwoven in a holy covenant relationship as witnessed in the texts explored above and condensed in the following table 10:

---

154. Section 6.5.2 on relationality and *imago Dei*; also section 6.5.3.

155. See Aleaz, "Some Distinctive Features," 178–91, on worship in the context of a theology of creation as an expression of Eastern Christian spirituality.

156. The article by Zizioulas, "Church as Communion," 1–15, is based on a lecture given by him before the WCC in 1993; see also Zizioulas, *Being as Communion*.

Chart 10: Table on theme of the divine-human covenant relationship

Covenant Setting/ Markers	1 Kgs 8, 9	2 Chr 5–7	Josh 6	2 Chr 20	1 Sam 16	2 Kgs 3	Ps 22	Acts 2, 10	Acts 4, 16	Eph 5
Ark of the covenant	x	x	x							
Divine manifestations:										
divine glory filling temple		x								
supernatural phenomena:										
fire	x	x						x		
shaking			x						x	
deliverance				x	x	x			x	
Spirit-infilling								x	x	x
Covenant offerings:										
sacrifices	x	xx								
praise	xx	xx	x	xx	(x)	(x)	x	x	x	x
Covenant formula:										
blessings/ promises	x	X	x	x				x	x	x
curses/ warnings/ judgment	x	X	x	x	(x)	x		(x)	(x)	
Holy War/ conflict motif:										
march			x	x						
blowing of trumpets			x							
battle cry			x							
anticipatory prophetic praise				x	x	x	x		x	
divine intervention/ victory				x	x	x	x		x	
extension of covenant people:										
Spirit baptism								x		
water baptism								x	x	

6.3.6 Summary

As has been corroborated, God's self-revelation, the praise of his people, and divine-human covenants may form a recurrent paradigm: divine self-revelation and presence are often followed by the response of human praise and occur in the setting of covenant relationships.

Relationship is not equivalent to covenant, but may lead to it. Similarly, relational interaction does not not ocur in a covenant, but a covenant always involves relational interaction. The covenants of the First and Second Testaments reveal two characteristics: first, a divine-human relationship may exist before a divine-human covenant is established and, second, a covenant can be referred to even without the typical terminology *berith*, *qum berith*, or *karat berith*, but with the mention of a divine promise/oath and commandments, as well as human commitments and/or offerings/rituals. There are different modes of covenant that may encompass similarity and continuity and, yet, dissimilarity and discontinuity.

As a result, all the passages examined on God's praise and God's presence, and their cotext in the Hebrew and the Greek Bible have evidenced the intertextual theme of the divine-human covenant relationship. The texts involve, first, general covenant settings, which refer to existing covenants or a new covenant, and some of them indicate the divine war motif. Second, they encompass specific covenant markers, old and new, like blessings and curses, sacrifice rituals or praise offerings, and new initiation rites, like Spirit baptism and water baptism.

In sum, there is no covenant without holiness: God's holy covenant presence and his people's holy covenant praise are interwoven in a holy covenant relationship. All the same, there are other responses to God's self-revelation than praise.

6.4 Contraindications and Queries about Worship

During the course of history, God's people have also responded to his self-revelation through idolatry and the hardening of their hearts with the consequence of judgment. Evidently, these "contraindications" exclude a connection between divine presence and human praise. In addition, we may be familiar with queries about the difference between worship and praise, or about Trinitarian worship. It matters whether or not praise is embedded in our worship life, just as it matters whether or not praise is embedded in a holy covenant relationship. Likewise, it matters whether or not the Holy Spirit is included in our praises, as we will review later on.[157]

---

157. See section 6.4.3.

6.4.1 Idolatry and Hardness of Heart

Greg Beale states an interesting observation in his biblical theology of idolatry where he describes the phenomenon of emulation: we imitate behavioural patterns which we see in our environment.[158] Beale attributes this phenomenon to the fact that God created humankind as "imaging beings who reflect his glory."[159] And so, he relentlessly emphasizes: "What people revere they resemble, either for ruin or restoration."[160] As a result, when worshipers worship God, they increasingly reflect his image.[161] In contrast, when idolaters worship an idol, they increasingly reflect and resemble the idol they deify. As a consequence, the reflection of God's image and glory (2 Cor 3:8, 11; 2 Cor 4:6) becomes perverted through idolatry.[162] Idolatry can also involve being overly committed to self, to a certain sacred or secular tradition, or giving the place which belongs to God alone to anything or anyone else. Interestingly enough, Beale defines idolatry as worshiping an object in the assumption that the presence of the deity or its spirit is in the object.[163] Following this line of argument, there is a certain analogy between idol worship and its assumed spirit-presence on the one hand and God worship and his real Spirit-presence on the other. And so, this phenomenon of emulation through identification and mirroring impinges on our worship relationship, whether as God worship or as idolatry.

In connection with that, Edward Meadors perceives idolatry as one reason for the hardening of the human heart.[164] That idolatrous stubbornness and God hardening a person's heart may interact can be seen from the example of the Egyptian pharaoh (Exod 4–9). Then, the golden calf episode exhibits wayward idolatry among Israel as well (Exod 32). That rebelliousness and idol worship was a repetitive pattern in Israel, which led to a vicious cycle, becomes obvious in the Book of Judges: Israel, oppressed by their enemies, cried out to the Lord, and the Lord

---

158. Beale, *We Become What We Worship*, 16–17.
159. Beale, *We Become What We Worship*, 16.
160. Beale, *We Become What We Worship*, 16, 22.
161. See section 6.5.2 on the concept of *imago Dei*.
162. In connection with that, Beale, *We Become What We Worship*, 186–200, identifies subtle textual echoes in Acts 7 and 28 coming from Isa 40–60.
163. Beale, *We Become What We Worship*, 311; for conceptions of idol worship see Block, *Glory of God*, 29–35; or Grenz, "Jesus as the Imago Dei," 621–23.
164. Meadors, *Idolatry*, 3, 19; see also Fowl, *Idolatry*.

compassionately gave them a judge to save them until they returned to their corrupt ways (e.g., Judg 2:16–23). Likewise, the Law, Prophets, and Writings witness to the frequent obstinacy of God's people.[165] Human rebellion plus worship results in a perversion of worship. This theme is addressed in texts like Isaiah 1:10–17; Jeremiah 7:21–26; or Ezekiel 20:25–26. That God despises the praise of his people when coupled with permanent disobedience and injustice is particularly evident in Amos 5:21–25. Eventually, the idolatry and waywardness of God's people led to divine judgment with God's presence leaving the temple and his people being expelled from their land into Babylonian Exile (Ezek 21). As Beale reminds us, it was idolatry that made the glory of the Lord depart from the temple (Ezek 10:18) suggesting it may not have returned before the times of Jesus.[166] This idea would support the metaphorical reinterpretation of Jesus' body as the new temple, although Beale does not bring into play this concept. It also discloses a link which connects idolatry and the Lord's glory-presence, or his absence in judgment and temple.[167]

Sadly, the above negative qualities in God's people with their dire consequences are not limited to the First Testament, but extend into the Second Testament as well (Rom 1:18–23; Heb 2:2). Finally, the theme of eschatological Spirit-presence is connected with the theme of eschatological judgment:[168] the Book of Revelation displays ample examples of eschatological judgment on humankind. This judgment is announced and fulfilled in the context of enormous, theophanic manifestations alongside with praise offered by heavenly beings in God's heavenly temple. A notable example is found in Revelation 5 and 6 where heavenly praise precedes the lamb's opening of the book with the seven seals of judgment.

In sum, contraindications may occur in the form of divine absence or presence in judgment on God's side because of idolatry, rebelliousness, and a perversion of worship on his people's side. As a result, the above contraindications encompass a correlation between human idolatry and divine absence in contrast to a connection between human praise and divine presence.

---

165. E.g., Deut 31:27; 2 Chr 7:19–22; also Isa 1 or Amos 2.
166. Beale, *We Become What We Worship*, 185.
167. On God's absence in our worship see also ch. 2, section 2.8.
168. Beale, *Temple and the Church's Mission*, 212–15, Hamilton, *God's Glory*.

6.4.2 Worship or Praise?

Obviously, we have used the term "praise" more frequently than the term "worship" being aware that uncertainties about the difference between worship and praise risk to stifle both. Therefore, the issue is addressed to some extent at this point. Chapter 2 already shed light on the characteristics of praise, its pertinent terminology, and the meaning of "worship" in connection with a "worship service" and beyond.[169] To put it in a nutshell: *in our context, worship is perceived more generally as covering the broad spectrum of people's adoration addressed to God flowing from their hearts into their lives. And praise is perceived more specifically as covering the distinct expressions of this worship.* Admittedly, the boundaries are fluid, as the beautiful quote by James Torrance conveys:

> God made men and women in his own image . . . *to express* on behalf of all creatures *the praises of God*, so that through human lips the Heavens might declare the glory of God. When we, who know we are God's creatures, *worship* God together, we gather up the *worship* of all creation.[170]

This quote makes clear, first, that the terms "worship" and "praise" may be used almost synonymously and, second, that they are not limited to the setting of a "worship service."

Another issue is that the boundaries between the forms and content of praise can be fluid, as forms of praise are determined by their content. Then, the question is: To which extent do the forms of our praise as the expression of our worship convey Gospel content? And are these forms able to "make the real presence of Christ transparent"? This is the question raised by James Torrance.[171] As already mentioned, the absence of Scripture in some contemporary worship services has been deplored.[172]

Besides, scholars, among them Tony Costa, have remarked that it is difficult to find a clear and formal definition for worship in the biblical texts, e.g., in the Pauline epistles, since the biblical authors describe

---

169. See ch. 2, esp. sections 2.4.2, 2.4.3, and 2.6.2.

170. Torrance, *Worship*, 1; the italics are by the present writer.

171. Torrance, *Worship*, 3.

172. See Anderson, "Organic Liturgy," 81–97, esp. 81–82, on Bible-absent worship/praise; see also ch. 2, sections 2.3.1 and 2.8.2.

worship through a wide range of terms rather than define what is meant by worship.[173]

6.4.3 Trinitarian Worship?

Another uncertainty concerns Trinitarian worship and praise: Do we offer our praises to the Father only, or also to the Son, or even to the Holy Spirit?

Praise offered to God as Father was not entirely uncommon in Judaism, as Jews were to some extent familiar with picturing Yahweh as the father of his people Israel (e.g., in Mal 2:10).

Praise mediated and assisted by the Holy Spirit as in Ephesians 5:18–20, however, was something new. Already Jesus himself talks in John 4:23–24 about the role of the Holy Spirit who mediates the worship of the worshipers to the Father *in Spirit and truth* (ἐν πνεύματι καὶ ἀληθείᾳ).[174] Consequently, Bernadeta Jojko affirms that it is the specific contribution of John's "pneumatic" Gospel to help us comprehend the relationships among the Father, Jesus, and the Holy Spirit.[175]

Moreover, invoking Jesus as Lord and Messiah, as the Christian believers did (e.g., in 1 Cor 1:2), is different from the worship of the Father mediated through the Son and the Spirit. Ascribing to the Son the same adoration as to the Father was definitely new in Judaism.[176]

Then again, offering praise to the Holy Spirit represents an even bigger challenge. It seems that there is no biblical reference which explicitly testifies to praise addressed to the person of the Holy Spirit. This may be partly due to the indirect way Scripture deals with the theme of the Trinity and partly to the inner-Trinitarian relationship gradually revealed in the course of salvation history. Clearly, there are texts implying praise which involves the three persons of the Trinity, e.g., Ephesians 5:18–20, but none on praise which explicitly addresses the person of the Holy Spirit. Coming back to John 4:23–24, Jesus asserts that the true worship of the Father is offered *in*, that is, *through* the Spirit. According to Don Carson, Jesus' argument develops as follows: because God is Spirit (and not flesh), "true" worship, in contrast to "false" worship which is

---

173. Costa, *Worship and the Risen Jesus*, 252.
174. Carson, "Gospel According to John," 224–26.
175. Jojko, *Worshipping the Father*, 220.
176. On Trinitarian pneumatology and the worship of Jesus see Turner, "'Trinitarian' Pneumatology," 167–86; on Trinitarian worship see Torrance, *Worship*, 8, 18–20.

attached to a particular place, is offered *through* the Spirit (and not *to* the Spirit).[177] Similarly, Fred Sanders quotes Cole whom he understands to warn against overemphasizing the prayer *to* the Holy Spirit, thus, bringing the Trinitarian stance of the gospel out of balance.[178] All the same, Graham Cole concedes that Christians may pray to the Holy Spirit, but that without explicit biblical reference there is only permission and no obligation for Christians to address praise to the divine Spirit. At least, we find examples of invoking the Holy Spirit in Church history. Hence, we will recur to Church history to review the divine nature of the Holy Spirit as the basis of our praise addressed to the Holy Spirit.[179]

6.4.4 Summary

"Contraindications" in Scripture have revealed dynamisms which exclude the connection between divine presence and human praise. God's absence or his presence in eschatological judgment is the consequence of his people's idolatry and rebelliousness. Then again, these indications have demonstrated that God's presence, although embedded in the context of holy covenant relationships together with his people's praise, does not depend on human preconditions like praise.[180]

As to Trinitarian worship, the biblical witnesses point to the involvement of Father, Son, and Holy Spirit in praise, but not to praise explicitly addressed to the Holy Spirit. Yet, the subsequent section will reveal that the Church Fathers paved the way for the worship of the third person of the Godhead by upholding the deity of the Holy Spirit, as is reflected in the Creeds and in liturgy.

6.5 Interdisciplinary Transitions to Systematic Theology

The biblical-theological results obtained so far will now be considered against their systematic-theological background. We have seen that these results involve three intertextual themes in terms of analogies: first, the connection between divine presence and human praise,

---

177. Carson, *Gospel According to John*, 224–26.
178. Sanders, *Triune God*, 225; Cole, *Engaging*, 55–72, esp. 71–72.
179. Cole, *He Who Gives Life*, 59–91, esp. 73–78.
180. Torrance, *Worship*, 24–25, reminds us that worship and communion, whether with God or with other humans, are gifts of grace.

Results from a Biblical Theology Perspective 219

second, the divine indwelling, and, third, the divine-human covenant relationship. Because our praise involves the third person of the Trinity, and because the divine-human covenant relationship touches on issues of personhood, relationality, and the *imago Dei*, these topics will be explored in the subsequent section. The reflections will close on a minor philosophical excursus.

6.5.1 Praise Addressed to the Divine Spirit

In the fourth century, the Cappadocian Fathers defended the Spirit's deity. Without going into the details of a developing Trinitarian terminology,[181] suffice it to say that Basil the Great of Caesarea (330–379 CE), based on Ephrem and the Syrian tradition, spelled out the difference between *ousía* "essence" and *hypóstasis* "person" in relation to the Trinity.[182] He also affirmed the full and equal divinity or divine "essence" of the Holy Spirit. Refining this approach further, Gregory of Nazianzus (329–90 CE) described the Holy Spirit to be *homoóusios* "of the same nature" as Father and Son.

Then, Gregory of Nyssa (335/340–394 CE) deduced from the identical divine nature of the three persons of the Godhead and their perichoresis as implied in Scripture that the Holy Spirit receives equal adoration.[183] The term "perichoresis" dates back to John of Damascus in the sixth century CE and relates to the mutual indwelling of Father, Son, and Holy Spirit. Alister McGrath describes the concept of perichoresis quite fittingly:

> It allows the individuality of the persons to be maintained, while insisting that each person shares in the life of the other two. An image often used to depict this idea is that of a "community of

---

181. See recent publications on a developing Trinitarian terminology and theology by Bates, *Birth of the Trinity*, and Sanders, *Triune God*: Bates and Sanders represent relational approaches to the Trinity; Yong, *Discerning the Spirit(s)*, seeks to bridge patristic and contemporary approaches.

182. E.g., Bobrinskoy, "Indwelling of the Spirit," 54.

183. For the mutual Trinitarian indwelling see, e.g., John 6:52–57; 10:38; 14:10–11; on problems as to perichoresis see, e.g., Otto, "Use and Abuse," 366–84, and Crisp, "Problems with Perichoresis," 119–40: Otto addresses use and misuse of perichoresis; Crisp in his philosophical-theological approach tackles problems with perichoresis, e.g., the lack of distinguishing between nature-perichoresis referring to the two natures of Christ, and person-perichoresis referring to the persons of the Trinity, or divine-human perichoresis.

being" in which each person, while maintaining its distinctive identity, penetrates the others and is penetrated by them.[184]

This strikes a chord with the classical Orthodox perception of perichoresis which envisions a love dance between the three persons of the Trinity. Similarly, in line with Athanasius of Alexandria, Gregory of Nyssa spoke of a "revolving circle of glory" among Father, Son, and Spirit calling to mind John 8:54.[185] These insights contribute to a rich pool to draw from for our worship and praise.

As a consequence of defending the Spirit's deity, the Church Fathers, each in his own way, contributed to an increasing dogmatic clarity on the address of *all* three divine persons in worship. Their writings were intended to oppose concepts of inner-Trinitarian hierarchical subordination held by the Macedonians which contradicted the deity and, thus, the worship of the Holy Spirit, as Robert Letham indicates.[186] One major result of the Church Fathers' work, the Niceno-Constantinopolitan Creed, bears particularly the hallmark of Basil the Great and affirms "the Holy Spirit, the Lord and life-giver, who proceeds from the Father (and the Son),[187] who is worshipped and glorified together with the Father and the Son."[188] Graham Cole, quoting Turner, mentions an even earlier example in church history of praise addressed to the Holy Spirit which dates from the second century CE.[189]

In a similar way, Augustine of Hippo (354–430 CE) was influenced by the Cappadocian Fathers. At the same time, he was accused of having been persuaded by Neoplatonism and, thus, by modalism, i.e., the belief

---

184. McGrath, *Christian Theology*, 325, (reference owed to Theopedia, 2019).

185. Letham, *Holy Trinity*, 156.

186. Letham, *Holy Trinity*, 147–49.

187. The Western *Filioque* clause was added later at this point and refers to the procession of the Spirit from the Father *and the Son*. Since Cyril of Alexandria, who maintains the formula of the Spirit proceeding *from the Father in the Son*, Western scholars have made attempts to solve the *Filioque* problem: Moltmann prefers the formula of the Spirit proceeding *from the Father of the Son*, Pannenberg discards the *Filioque* formula because of the risk of subordination, whereas Bray defends it (cf. Letham, *Holy Trinity*, 215–19).

188. The first council at Nicea took place in 325 CE, and the second council at Constantinople in 381 CE; the quote on the Spirit stems from the latter: "τὸ Πνεῦμα τὸ Ἅγιον, τὸ Κύριον καὶ Ζωοποιόν, τὸ ἐκ τοῦ Πατρὸς ἐκπορευόμενον, τὸ σὺν Πατρὶ καὶ Υἱῷ συμπροσκυνούμενον καὶ συνδοξαζόμενον" (cf. Early Church Texts, 2019).

189. Cole, *Engaging*, 56, referring to Turner, "'Trinitarian' Pneumatology," 168, mentions the *Martyrdom and Ascension of Isaiah* (9:33–36).

that God revealed himself as one person in three modes, contrary to the Trinitarian doctrine.[190] Nevertheless, Trinitarian dogmatic imprints reflecting the Nicean influence can be found not only in Augustine's major work *De Trinitate*, but also in *De Civitate Dei* and *Confessiones* as well as in various tractates and letters.[191] Furthermore, Augustine's prayer addressed to the Holy Spirit witnesses to his own attitude, as he adored and implored the Holy Spirit to breathe and act in him to make him holy:

> Breathe in me, O Holy Spirit, that my thoughts may all be holy. Act in me, O Holy Spirit, that my work, too, may be holy. Draw my heart, O Holy Spirit, that I love but what is holy. Strengthen me, O Holy Spirit, to defend all that is holy. Guard me, then O Holy Spirit, that I always may be holy.[192]

Hence, a modalism which emphasizes the one divine essence over against the three divine persons seems to have affected the reception of Augustine rather than the man himself. Still, this danger of modalism, which dampened the part attributed to the Holy Spirit in worship, has been quite real in the post-Augustinian era of church history down to renowned theologians like Karl Barth.[193] The Alexandrian Church Fathers Athanasius (298–373 CE) and Cyril (385/380–444 CE) have been considered a valuable remedy against this danger, as their writings present a balanced view on the perichoresis of Father, Son, and Spirit.[194]

By the same token, the ancient Trinitarian doxology of the *Gloria Patri* (Thessalonica, 380 CE), the so-called minor doxology which is still in use in contemporary liturgy in Eastern and Western churches, attributes equal glory to the Holy Spirit: "Glory to the Father, and to the Son, and to the Holy Ghost! As it was in the beginning, is now, and ever shall be, world without end."[195] This example represents a balanced approach

---

190. Bray and Gunton, contra Studer, Barnes, and Williams, assumed a greater Neoplatonic influence and, therefore, accused Augustine of modalism; see Bray, "Engaging Unbelief," 184–85; or Gunton, "Ad litteram," 787–89 (cf. Letham, *Holy Trinity*, 184–200).

191. Letham, *Holy Trinity*, 184–85.

192. Augustine, *Prayer to the Holy Spirit*.

193. Letham, *Holy Trinity*, 212–14.

194. Here, Letham, *Holy Trinity*, 215–19, also refers to the 1991 Agreement between Orthodox and Reformed Churches, and to the Orthodox scholars Staniloae and Bobrinskoy, the latter supporting Basil's formula *from the Father through the Son to the Spirit* (cf. Bobrinskoy, "Indwelling," 55–56).

195. See Sanders, "Turning the Mind to Doxology"; also Sanders, *Triune God*, on

to explicit Trinitarian praise! And throughout church history most scholars have been persuaded that Trinitarian worship entails the three persons of the Godhead.[196] This means when one divine person receives praise, the others are implicitly included. Still, if we are convinced that God is Father, Son, and Spirit, would it not be legitimate to offer our praise to the Holy Spirit as well who is present in our praises? This question has been beautifully answered by by Clark Pinnock in the attempt to keep praise and divine Spirit-presence together:

> The Spirit is elusive, but profound and worthy of adoration. If Father points to ultimate reality and Son supplies the clue to the divine mystery, Spirit epitomizes the nearness of the power and presence of God.[197]

In spite of that, church history has also been shaped by different epochs with different emphases. It seems that, after an emphasis on salvation, which merged Christ and the Spirit in an almost monistic way,[198] contemporary pneumatology is marked by an emphasis on Creation, which merges cosmos and cross in another monistic way.[199] Consequently, the divine Spirit-presence in the world is referred to "indiscriminately," as Ben Engelbrecht labels it.[200] As a result, such tendencies do not always encourage a distinct and balanced Trinitarian worship, especially as concerns the Holy Spirit.

In sum, the Church Fathers shed light on the divinity and the worship/praise of the Holy Spirit, as well as on the perichoretic indwelling and relationship within the triune Godhead. Their understanding is reflected in the creeds and doxological prayers. In a similar way, our understanding of the triune God including the Holy Spirit shapes our worship and our relationships. Hence, we will now explore whether and how the Trinitarian perichoretic relationship is reflected in divine-human

---

Trinitarian theology as doxology.

196. Torrance, *Worship, Community*, 25–27.

197. Pinnock, *Flame of Love*, 9.

198. Engelbrecht, "Indwelling," 19–33, esp. 32–33, refers to Moltmann and Berkhof as examples of such binitarian pneumatology.

199. Maybe this oversimplifies a certain trend, and there is certainly room for more research in this area, e.g., the ST study group of the TF Conference at Cambridge, UK, in July 2015 on the topic "Holy Spirit", or the FEET Conference to take place at Prague, Czechia, in August 2020 on the same topic.

200. Engelbrecht, "Indwelling," 32.

relationships, which could be a model for interhuman relationships and for male-female "perichoretic unity," as James Torrance suggests.[201]

6.5.2 Personhood, Perichoresis, and *Imago Dei*

It is agreed among biblical scholarship that the God of Scripture is distinct from the world and the universe he created. For example, in contrast to extrabiblical concepts of monism and pantheism, the philosopher and theologian Martin Buber talks of a God who is characterized by a "personalistic dualism."[202] In other words, God is portrayed in the Scriptures as Creator and, thus, as a subject who interacts with his Creation.[203] For this reason as well, God is a personal and relational being. Accordingly, the Reformed theologian Louis Berkhof asserted that God as a speaking and acting subject conveys, first of all, knowledge to humankind by revealing himself to and initiating communication with them.[204] God revealing himself means that he "mediates" his presence to humans in the course of salvation history through the persons of the Father, Son, and Holy Spirit, so that they can experience God as a present reality in their lives.[205] Otherwise, they would not be aware of God and could not relate to him. As established earlier, the distinction between Father, Son, and Spirit is of a "personal" and not of an "essential" kind, since the otherness of each of them refers to their persons and relations and not to their essence. Therefore, God is personal and relational in more ways than one.

Admittedly, there is a problem with terminology, as our theological terminology of "person" and "personhood," which dates from the third and fourth centuries CE, was not known to the biblical authors.[206] The Latin term *persona* "person" translates the Greek terms *hypóstasis* "person" and *prosōpon* "face" which are relational expressions used by the

---

201. Torrance, *Worship, Community*, 27.

202. De Vries, *Kåabôd of YHWH*, 63.

203. Subject is here understood in contrast to an object which can be manipulated; on God interacting with Creation see, e.g., Gen 1:3–26, 28; and John 1:1–3; on God as a personal and relational being see, e.g., Gen 1:26–28; Exod 3:14; and John 1:14.

204. Berkhof, *Systematic Theology*, 34.

205. Dalferth, "Representing God's Presence," 240–44, stresses that God's presence which is mediated, revealed, and known still differs in quality and quantity from who God is because he is always greater than what we can conceive of him (see esp. section on "God's mediate immediacy," 240–41).

206. See section 6.5.1 of this chapter.

Cappadocian Fathers.[207] Besides, in the process of a developing Trinitarian terminology, the terms *ousía* and *hypóstasis* were still used synonymously, as Ioannis Zizioulas elucidates the understanding of personhood in antiquity.[208] In fact, the Scriptures employ a relational terminology to portray the triune God, and this without using the dogmatic term "Trinity." More recently, Matthew Bates uses the image of a Trinitarian "birth process" to portray the development of this dogma.[209] Following Bates, with the unfolding of salvation history a Trinitarian credo emerged which is associated with divine economy established in the historical Jesus and anticipated in dyadic (Father and Son) and triadic statements (Father, Son, and Holy Spirit).[210] These statements are already intimated, e.g., in John 14:10 and 2 Corinthians 13:14. This way, Bates recognizes a bridge which connects the New Testament and Nicea.

The crucial thing is that our image of the triune God defines our image of humankind and vice versa, as James Torrance expounds: "From the history of Christian thought, we can see that our doctrine of God reflects our understanding of humanity and, conversely, our understanding of the human being reflects our view of God."[211] Consequently, the relational personhood of the triune God is again connected with the relational personhood of humans and with the *imago Dei*, a theological concept referring to humankind's divine likeness.

The *imago Dei* has been the topic of extensive discussions among scholarship.[212] Thomas F. Torrance, for example, perceives the interpersonal and relational structure of humans as reflected in their social and sexual relationships to image the Trinity.[213] In contrast, David Fergusson warns against equating human personhood and divine personhood.[214]

---

207. Zizioulas, *Being as Communion*, 87–88; Bates, *Birth of the Trinity*, 16.

208. Zizioulas, *Being as Communion*, 27–49.

209. This understanding is reflected in Bates' title *Birth of the Trinity*.

210. Bates, *Birth of the Trinity*, 14–15, 191–93.

211. Torrance, *Worship, Community*, 26.

212. At this point, Turner, "Approaching 'Personhood,'" 215, refers to Zizioulas, Volf, and Grenz; concerning definitions of personhood, Turner, referring to Gunton, also points to McFadyen, *Call to Personhood*, 317.

213. Torrance, *Christian Doctrine of God,* mentions males and females in terms of their "co-humanity": by that he relates to their "complementary otherness" and "ontological togetherness" which would reflect the divine interpersonal and relational nature (cited by Flett, "Priests of Creation," 168, 171–72).

214. Fergusson, "Humans Created," 444.

Results from a Biblical Theology Perspective 225

What is more, theology in the course of history has overloaded the concept of *imago Dei* by projecting meaning into it which Scripture does not contain, or attributed more weight to one meaning over against the others.²¹⁵ Accordingly, James B. Torrance makes clear that Western concepts of rationalism or individualism, which use the term "individual" for "person," have been projected into the idea of *imago Dei*.²¹⁶ Without engaging in detail with the debate on the *imago Dei*, suffice it to focus on one of its aspects, namely relationality, which affects all three intertextual themes of our biblical-theological results, i.e., the connection between divine presence and human praise, the divine indwelling, and the divine-human covenant relationship.²¹⁷

Although not limited to it, the concept of *imago Dei* has largely been understood in connection with Genesis 1:26–28, one of the key texts in the discussion. Hence, two main issues in Genesis 1:26 will be outlined: first, the interpretation of the divine plural in the verbal construction "let us make" and, second, the translation of the two Hebrew terms צֶלֶם "image" and דְּמוּת "likeness."

Concerning the first issue, Victor Hamilton draws attention to the change of the verbal construction from a jussive singular "let there be" in Genesis 1:3–24 to a cohortative plural "let us make" in Genesis 1:26.²¹⁸ This change intends to introduce an important information on what was about to happen on the sixth day: the making of humankind as the climax of Creation. God spoke then as he had spoken into being the rest of Creation before.²¹⁹ The verbal construction is best explained as a volitive plural of self-deliberation with God speaking "here we go" or "let us make," since a plural of majesty would occur with nouns only and not with verbs.²²⁰ This explanation would correct the plural of majesty option²²¹ and, thus, deflate the Trinitarian interpretation of some Church

---

215. On texts illuminating the idea of *imago Dei* see, e.g., Gen 1:26–27; Rom 8:29; 1 Cor 11:7; 2 Cor 4:4; Eph 4:24; and Eph 5:1.

216. Torrance, *Worship, Community*, 26.

217. See sections 6.1, 6.2 and 6.3.

218. Hamilton, *Genesis*, 1:134.

219. Klingbeil, "He Spoke," 43, claims that language is also part of the *imago Dei* in humankind reflected in their capacity to name the animals (Gen 2:19b, 20a).

220. Joüon, *Grammaire* §114e, §136e; Hamilton, *Genesis*, 1:133, and Wenham, *Genesis 1—15*, 1:28, quote Joüon, *Grammaire*, 416, in support of a plural of self-deliberation; cf. also Lettinga and von Siebenthal, *Grammatik*, 314–18.

221. Keil and Delitzsch, *Pentateuch*, 1:62.

Fathers and of later scholarship.[222] It may also weaken the divine court interpretation.[223]

With regard to the second issue, problems arose from a variety of translations of the Hebrew terms צֶלֶם "image" and דְּמוּת "likeness." Since the times of the Greek and Latin Church Fathers, distinction has been made between צֶלֶם as *eikōn* or *imago* on the one hand and דְּמוּת as *homoíōsis* or *similitudo* on the other. This is why scholars came to believe that "image" could represent physical elements of the resemblance between humans and God and "likeness" could portray cognitive-ethical elements.[224] Yet, as concerns a "physical resemblance," there is no physical image, since God is Spirit (John 4:24). Thus, *imago* was perceived to anticipate the incarnation of Christ. According to the late medieval rhyme "In the Old the New lies concealed, in the New the Old is revealed," Adam would anticipate the coming of Christ and Christ would represent the second Adam.[225] The problem, however, with an exclusively Christocentric, incarnational view is that Genesis 1:26 relates to human existence in the image of God as a given before the Fall and long before the incarnation of Christ. This image cannot be claimed to have been entirely corrupted in postlapsarian humanity.[226] As concerns a cognitive-ethical resemblance, the Church Fathers Augustine and Aquinas considered "likeness" to refer to cognitive-rational properties of the human mind, while the Reformer Calvin perceived "likeness" in terms of cognitive-spiritual capacities of the human soul; both abilities were deemed to have suffered more or less from the Fall.[227] The problem with a cognitive view

---

222. Clines, "Image of God," Hasel, "Recent Translations."

223. Middleton, *Liberating Image*, 55–56; Waltke, *Old Testament Theology*, 214; Kline, "Investiture with the Image," 38–62, esp. 43–44; for a summary of the different positions see Hamilton, *Genesis*, 1:133–38.

224. Keil and Delitzsch, *Pentateuch*, 1:63–64. The physical view is held by anthropomorphites like Swedenborg (cf. Eckardt, "Another Look," 70).

225. This opinion has already been expressed by the Church Fathers Irenaeus and Tertullian, as well as Basil of Caesarea and Gregory of Nyssa (cf. Eckardt, "Another Look," 73–74); see also Grenz, "Jesus as the Imago Dei," 617–28, and Carter, "Imago Dei as the Mind," 753.

226. More recently, scholars differentiate between a narrower meaning of human righteousness, which has been completely lost in the Fall, and a wider meaning, which has not been completely corrupted (cf. Eckardt, "Another Look," 67–68).

227. Augustine, proposing an analogy, considered the divine Trinity to be reflected in the human mind in terms of knowledge, wisdom, and love, but understood this reflection to have suffered from corruption through the Fall; likewise, the Reformers considered the human image to have been more (Luther) or less (Calvin) corrupted

of *similitudo*, whether intellectual or ethical, is that it emphasizes mind and soul/spirit over against the body. Such imbalance is not supported by Hebrew notions of divine likeness, which safeguard the integrity of humans in a holistic way without surmising a "physical resemblance" between God and humans. David Fergusson criticizes the above "default setting of Western theology" since Augustine and Descartes which has led to gender-biased assumptions and other social prejudices.[228] Meanwhile there is agreement among scholarship that this theory needs to be abandoned.[229] Consequently, it has been suggested that both terms in Genesis 1:26 should be regarded as more or less equivalent expressions in a synonymous parallelism which emphasizes one and the same thing: humankind was created in the *very likeness* of God.[230]

Then, Genesis 1:27, without mentioning דְּמוּת "likeness," repeats and highlights צֶלֶם "image" twice in a chiastic parallelism without spelling out explicitly what this resemblance involves: "God created Adam in his *image*, in his *image* he created *him*." Then, the verse takes up the structure of the second line of the parallelism replacing צֶלֶם "image" with "male and female" and "him" with "them": "*Male and female he created them*." If the parallelism, which emphasizes image, were to emphasize male and female as well, this would support the idea that God is embodied as male and female.[231] The question is whether this is what the texts means to communicate or whether it rather says: *God created humankind in his own image, male and female, i.e., as individual and relational beings*. Karl Barth has been understood to maintain that the male-female differentiation represents divine likeness.[232] Yet, as Nathan MacDonald pointed out, particularly Old Testament scholars tend to reject the "equation of the image with the male-female differentiation."[233] The problem with such

---

after the Fall, but with humans still being able to relate to God (cf. Fergusson, "Humans Created," 439–53).

228. Fergusson, "Humans Created," 443.

229. MacDonald, "Imago Dei," 304.

230. Keil and Delitzsch, *Pentateuch*, 1:63.

231. The text often referred to in connection with that is Isa 66:13 saying that God comforts like a mother, which expresses God's maternal qualities in addition to his paternal ones.

232. MacDonald, "Imago Dei," 304–16, refers to Barth's exegesis of Gen 1:26–28, which has been criticized by Westermann et al. as exegetical negligence, but which MacDonald defends as coherent within Barth's own hermeneutics.

233. MacDonald, "Imago Dei," 321; also Kline, "Investiture," 54.

equation is that, as a consequence, persons with gender identity disorder or intersex conditions would not be able to reflect divine likeness to the same extent as others. Quite the reverse, it seems that Barth himself emphasized the aspect of complementary relationality rather than that of sexual differentiation.[234]

Possibly, Genesis 1:28 sheds some light on the issue by revealing a *representative-functional analogy*: through the twofold cultural mandate כָּבַשׁ "to subdue" the earth and רָדָה "to rule" over Creation like a king, humanity has been made vice-regents with the Creator God.[235] This cultural mandate in Genesis 1:28 is supported through the mandate in Genesis 2:15 to cultivate and keep Creation. For that reason, the *cultural mandate does not mean carte blanche for the abuse of Creation, but it means caring for it like a shepherd, which represents the image for kings in the First Testament*. Or, as Gerald Klingbeil, referring to Middleton, puts it: "Humanity was to be royal-priestly mediators of God's presence and power on earth."[236] And so, scholars have increasingly recognized this functional-representative analogy, but they have not been in one accord whether it represents divine likeness or its consequences.

In any case, *the idea of divine likeness according to Genesis 1:26–28 affects not only humankind's representative functions, but also their relationship to Creation and to the Creator of all. Hence, the concept of imago Dei involves both representative-functional and relational analogies*, which, in contrast to some scholarly opinions, are not mutually exclusive.[237] *Analogy is here best understood as a resemblance between God and humans* and not as an ontological identity. The relational analogy is labelled by Karl Barth as *analogia relationis*[238] or expressed by Ioannis Zizioulas in his

---

234. Barth, *Kirchliche Dogmatik*, 3.1:206–10.

235. Eckardt, "Another Look," 69, referring to Erickson; also Middleton, *Liberating Image*, 50–51.

236. Klingbeil, "He Spoke," 46; for Middleton, *Liberating Image*, 81–88, the functional aspect of divine likeness affects all humankind and also involves a cosmic-priestly feature, since he perceives Creation as a cosmic temple.

237. MacDonald, "Imago Dei," 304–5, mentions Barr, Bird et al. contra Barth, Gunton et al.

238. Cited by MacDonald, "Imago Dei," 303–27, who reshapes Barth's relational approach in terms of an analogy of election: just as God elected and related to Israel, he wishes to relate to his extended people. In contrast to that, Fergusson, "Humans Created," 450, asserts that "God establishes a set of relations with embodied humans that are marked by freedom, interaction, responsiveness, dependence, and love"; he prefers this model to the merely relational model that he deems to be too specific and

motto of "Being as Communion."[239] Both scholars explore relationships at human-divine and interhuman levels.

Attempts have been made to connect the representative-functional and relational aspects of the *imago Dei* and reconcile them with the findings of contemporary sciences.[240] Certainly, there are pitfalls to be avoided, such as a Christocentric approach to the *imago Dei* in Genesis 1, which risks resulting in an anthropological restraint, or an anthropocentric approach, which risks resulting in a Christological restraint.[241] Still, we can infer that the *imago Dei* according to Genesis 1 is a given for *all* humankind, in whatever way this divine likeness is perceived to have been moderated through the Fall and whether humans are committed to a human-divine covenant relationship or not. David Fergusson makes this plain: "Human beings, whether prelapsarian or postlapsarian, inside or outside the church, are made in the image and likeness of God."[242]

In addition to that, there are other texts in Scripture that shed light on the concept of divine likeness. Taking into account Jesus' quote from Ps 82:6 in John 10:34 "You are gods," one may be inclined to think of a certain existential analogy which does not mean ontological identy. In a similar way, Karl Barth refers in connection with the divine image to human identity on the whole and not to some human faculties or functions only.[243] Then, Stanley Grenz, referring to Ridderbos, points out that there

---

anthropologically restrained; however, both concepts complement each other, as is demonstrated by Pinnock in his theology of the Holy Spirit, *Flame of Love*, 149–84: he invites the reader "to view Spirit as the bond of love in the triune relationality" (*Flame of Love*, 247). Turner, "Approaching 'Personhood,'" 229, perceives a model of "dynamic-relational" personhood, human and divine, in Ephesians. Similarly, Rabens identifies a dynamic relational approach in the Pauline letters, *Holy Spirit and Ethics*; Grenz, "Jesus as the Imago Dei," 621, refers to Wolff among others for a relational approach to *imago Dei* in the OT; other German scholars, e.g., Ebeling, have also favored relational approaches, but have been overly concerned to avoid "emotionalism" [*Schwärmerei*].

239. See section 6.3.4.

240. Fergusson, "Humans Created," 440, interacts with theistic and evolutionary theories, as well as modern sciences like neuropsychology suggesting the concept of *imago Dei* is best interpreted as "designating a complex identity that is established by a providential ordering of human life."

241. In connection with that, Grenz, "Jesus as the Imago Dei," 624–25, complains that Erickson and Grudem focus on anthropological aspects of the *imago Dei* while leaving aside Christological aspects.

242. Fergusson, "Humans Created," 447.

243. MacDonald, "Imago Dei," 314.

are links that connect Genesis 1:26–28 with Romans 8:29; 2 Corinthians 4:6; Colossians 1:15; and Hebrews 1:3.[244] These New Testament texts relate to Christ incarnate as the glorious fulfilment of the *imago Dei*.[245] Then again, 2 Corinthians 3:8, 18 raise the Spirit's ministry as one of a greater glory that leads to transforming humans into divine likeness when they behold and reflect God's glory. Such glorious transformation by mirroring requires divine-human interaction and, therefore, is relational in nature.

In view of the above, *divine likeness means for humankind to be bearers of God's glory for the purpose of representing him and of embodying his relational presence.*[246] Ultimately, this is made possible in Christ. The idea of relationality is taken up again in the short excursion to the domain of philosophy, which focusses on one classic example.

6.5.3 Minor Philosophical Excursus

As has become evident, relationality at vertical and horizontal levels represents an essential feature of the biblical model of divine likeness in humankind. This thinking was to some extent still reflected in premodern philosophy, but in modern philosophy the idea of *imago Dei* has gradually lost its significance on account of philosophers like Feuerbach and scientists like Darwin who both discarded this idea as anthropomorphism.[247] Then again, postmodern philosophy seems to open up again to metaphysics, which may also create new openings for the concept of *imago Dei*.

Still, one eminent representative of a model of relationality[248] in the twentieth century is Martin Buber (1878–1965), a Jewish religious philosopher and theologian. His treatise *Ich und Du*[249] represents a pioneer work which has wielded a far-reaching influence. It was labelled a

---

244. Grenz, "Jesus as the Imago Dei," 618–19.

245. On the incarnation of Christ and *imago Dei* in cosmic scope see also Moritz, "Deep Incarnation," 436–43.

246. See Grenz, "Jesus as the Imago Dei," 621–22; Beale, *We Become What We Worship*, 216.

247. On some anthropological ideas of Feuerbach and Nietzsche see Buber, *I and Thou*, 179–91.

248. In this context, relationality is referred to simply as the condition of being in relationship/s.

249. Buber's *Ich und Du* (1923) was translated as *I and Thou* (1937).

"philosophical-religious poem" influenced by Jewish mystical writings rather than discursive philosophy, as his translator R. G. Smith pronounces in his introduction.[250] Buber's treatise, however, needs to be seen in existential rather than mystical terms.[251] Although profoundly spiritual, Buber did not fall for an "ecstatic spiritual sensibility," but held up an "existential trust" that interhuman relationships cannot be considered in separation from the relationship with God.[252] And Buber was not the only one to rock the pillars of Hegel's house and Schleiermacher's mansion, as he was preceded by others like Kierkegaard.[253]

In connection with that, Kenneth Kramer fittingly sums up that Buber acknowledged the "deeply reciprocal bond between genuine interhuman dialogue and the divine-human relationship."[254] This is why Buber has been called both a "religious existentialist" and a "philosophical anthropologist" who exercised major influence on theologians and philosophers alike, among them Barth and Brunner, Marcel and Heim, Schweitzer and Niebuhr, Gogarten and Tillich.[255]

Reading Buber one gets the impression he believes that words addressed to the other speak a relation into existence. This idea recalls God speaking Creation into existence. Buber himself points to the incarnation with the Word becoming flesh.[256] His concept of words is very comprehensive incorporating locutionary, illocutionary, and perlocutionary acts:[257] simply put, in linguistics and philosophy, the locutionary act refers to the speech-act itself, the illocutionary act to the meaning of this speech-act, and the perlocutionary act refers to the effect of this

---

250. Buber, *I and Thou*, v–vi.

251. Buber knew enough of non-Christian mysticism and, although he stood on the foundations of Christian mysticism, seemed to think in terms of mystery rather than mysticism; certainly, he cannot be accused of an ecstatic, self-centered spiritualism which he may have encountered in his youth (cf. Kramer, "Tasting God," 225–26); see also Buber, *I and Thou*, 85–86.

252. Kramer, "Tasting God," 225.

253. Buber, *I and Thou*, xi.

254. See article by Kramer, "Tasting God," 224–45, esp, 224, in which he particularly refers to Buber's opus *I and Thou*.

255. Kramer, "Tasting God," 226; both Richard Niebuhr and Reinhold Niebuhr; presumably, Barth's idea of the encounter with God as the "wholly Other" has been influenced by Buber's notion of "dialogue with the other."

256. Buber, *I and Thou*, 85.

257. Buber, *I and Thou*, 3–5.

speech-act.[258] This comprehensive relating to the other through such speech-acts engages fellow humans and Creation, as well as God himself.[259]

Buber's own endeavor in bridging the love for God and one's neighbour is reflected in this idea of nurturing horizontal and vertical relationships. In his own marital life, he pursued a "dialogue of love" which involves turning to, addressing, listening, and responding to the other.[260] Correspondingly, Buber desires *talking to God* rather than *talking of God*.[261] This conversation concentrates not on intellectual explanation, but on the relational presence of the other, whether divine or human, which becomes tangible in a "sacramental dialogue." The gentleman thinker would humbly call himself neither a theologian nor a philosopher, but one who "points to something in reality." Buber perceives this "something in reality" in terms of a twofold "sacramental dialogue" between the I and Thou which he identifies as a "life-claiming experience of the other" and, hence, as a sacrament.[262] This sacramental-relational view may have been influenced by Hasidic tradition Buber was obviously familiar with.

As a result, Buber, affirming that "In the beginning there is relation,"[263] spells out:

> The Thou meets me through grace—it is not found by seeking. But my speaking of the primary word to it is an act of my being, is indeed the act of my being. The Thou meets me, but I step into direct relation with it ... I become through my relation to the Thou; as I become I, I say Thou.[264]

Similarly, Buber conceives of Jesus and his "I Am" Sayings in relation with his Father as "I and Thou."[265] Nevertheless, we would do injustice to Buber by squeezing his thinking into the formula "I relate, therefore I am" as an altered version of the Cartesian motto. If at all, he would probably have chosen the motto "I relate to the Thou, therefore I am."

Our modest dialogue with Buber reminds us of the inner-Trinitarian indwelling as a model for divine-human and interhuman covenant

---

258. See Cotterell and Turner, *Linguistics*, 91.
259. Buber, *I and Thou*, 6–8.
260. Kramer, "Tasting God," 231–33, 240.
261. Kramer, "Tasting God," 236.
262. Kramer, "Tasting God," 226, 229.
263. Buber, *I and Thou*, 18.
264. Buber, *I and Thou*, 11, 76.
265. Buber, *I and Thou*, 66–68.

relationships in that it entails a holy, whole-hearted dedication of one's self and an all-embracing interaction between the partners.

6.5.4 Summary

To sum up, we have explored divine personhood, and this especially regarding the Holy Spirit. The Church Fathers, the creeds, and liturgy shed light on the personhood of God, the deity of the Holy Spirit, and the relationship within the Trinity. The triune God as implied in Scripture is characterized by "three in one," that is, "one divine essence in three divine persons." This confirms the equal divinity of the Holy Spirit who is equally involved in our worship. Also, this verifies that God has revealed himself as a personal and relational being with a mutual inner-Trinitarian relationship. The inner-Trinitarian mutual indwelling called perichoresis represents a model for the divine indwelling which, again, provides a paradigm for relationships at all levels. Thus, the concept of perichoresis elucidates our understanding of personhood and relationality.

We have seen that divine and human personhood can be best perceived by means of analogy in terms of a resemblance between God and humans. In this respect, the idea of *imago Dei* or divine likeness has been elucidated: God in a deliberate resolution had chosen to create humankind in his very likeness. This divine likeness holds representative-functional and relational analogies which affect the relationships of all of humankind at all levels, whether with their Creator or his Creation including their fellow humans. In brief, divine likeness means for humankind to be bearers of God's glory for the purpose of representing him and of embodying his relational presence. Ultimately, this is made possible in Christ. The aspect of relational analogy is well grasped by Martin Buber in his religious-philosophical treatise on a "sacramental dialogue" between the "I and Thou" which spells out strikingly that divine-human and interhuman relationships by nature are dialogical and reciprocal, as well as wholly and holy.

To conclude, particularly the relational analogy affects the biblical-theological results of this investigation, whether the connection between God's presence and his people's praise, the divine indwelling, or, of course, the divine-human covenant relationship.

6.6 Summary

The biblical-theological results in this chapter allowed us to identify the following intertextual themes in terms of analogies in the passages analyzed: first, the connection between divine presence and human praise, second, the divine indwelling and, third, the human-divine covenant relationship.

As has been corroborated, first, the connection between presence and praise reverberates among passages in both Testaments: divine presence as divine glory or divine Spirit inspiring human praise, and/or human praise initiating manifestations of divine presence; still, this connection is not reciprocal in every instance, nor does it depend on temple context. We have seen, second, that the divine indwelling affects literal and nonliteral dwellings filled with a specific mode of divine presence, whether literal dwelling places filled with the Lord's glory or metaphorical dwellings filled with the Holy Spirit. And, third, the inquiries have substantiated that divine self-revelation and presence are often followed by the response of human praise and occur in the setting of divine-human covenant relationships, thus, forming a paradigm. Relationships may lead to covenants, but they are not identical. The theme of the divine-human covenant relationship has been identified in all the passages analyzed, whether through a general covenant setting or specific covenant markers; both express that holiness and covenant belong together, since God's faithful love and holy presence on the one side and his people's holy life of worship on the other are embedded in a holy divine-human covenant relationship.

Obviously, there are contraindications in Scripture, like human idolatry and rebellion, which lead to divine judgment in connection with divine absence. From this can also be inferred that divine presence in all its manifestations does not depend on human preconditions such as praise as an expression of worship. Still, as has been elucidated, our praise depends on our perception of the triune God including the divine nature of the Holy Spirit.

The Church Fathers, creeds, and liturgy have affirmed God as a personal and relational being as "three in one," and the deity of the Holy Spirit as the equal recipient of our praise. Also, they have shed light on perichoresis, the mutual inner-Trinitarian indwelling as implied in Scripture, which represents a model for the divine indwelling and for interhuman relationships as well. This model can enlighten our understanding of personhood and relationality which are at the heart of the *imago Dei* as in Genesis 1. This idea of divine likeness relates to God's deliberate decision to have created humankind in his very likeness. It spells out the resemblance between humankind and God in terms of representative-functional and relational analogies. The relational analogy is aptly exemplified in Martin Buber's religious-philosophical treatise on the "sacramental dialogue" between the "I and Thou". And particularly this relational analogy affects the interaction of divine presence and human praise, the divine indwelling, and the divine-human covenant relationship.

7.0

Conclusion and Outlook

I am not troubled by the things in the Bible which I do not understand, but I am troubled by those things which I do understand and which I find very difficult to measure up to.

—MARK TWAIN

THE MAIN QUESTION RAISED in this book and expanded in its introductory chapter has been: Is there a connection between God's presence and God's people's praise? This question has been answered in the affirmative.

To start with the answer, in the second chapter we explored to what extent scholarly contributions to a biblical theology of worship kept together the two elements of God's praise and God's presence. Some studies which approached the topic of worship from a biblical theology perspective represent a valuable foundation for the development of a biblical theology of worship, albeit most of them did not focus on a liaison between God's presence and his people's praise as their primary goal.

Hudson offered a thoughtful evaluation of Pentecostal influence on Christian worship. Steven raised our awareness of how contemporary pop culture is able to influence Christian worship, as he helped us to distinguish between biblical and cultural issues. Greenslade and his idea of a "God-sponsored hedonism" implied an association between presence and praise in that both elements converge in the double pleasure that God's presence brings to his people and their praises bring to God. Marshall in his understanding of the temple as the place of God's presence and his people's praise insinuated a subtle link between both, which is supported through his conclusion that worship is relational and responsive. Peterson in his biblical theology of worship perceived worship to start with a divine initiative and involve a divine-human relationship, which implies a vague bond between presence and praise. Wick touched lightly on such link through his view of a "cultless" Christian worship which excludes worship sacrifices to make God's presence appear. Block in his critique of certain phenomena in contemporary worship risked eclipsing God's Spirit-presence and its vital role in human praise. In contrast to that, Davis focused on God's absence in worship suggesting a "pneumatic praise" with a change of perspective as a remedy for recovering God's presence. Faix and Künkler with their analysis of the "generation praise" helped us gain an understanding of the young Christian generation's focus on worship and relationships at all levels.

As has been corroborated, cultural and denominational aspects in Christian worship, if not identified and differentiated as such, can be mistaken for biblical ones and, as a consequence, risk leading to false concepts of God's presence or its misuse in praise. This peril can be avoided by going back to careful exegesis and hermeneutics as the basis for interpreting biblical texts.

Accordingly, the third chapter responded in the affirmative to the question whether biblical theology as a distinct discipline with a canonical and intertextual model as a method is suitable to interpret passages from both Testaments involving the elements of God's praise and God's presence.

A historical review summarized the major tendencies: the critical source analysis of the nineteenth century with a history of religion approach was followed by a concern for theological synthesis in the twentieth century, which effected a quest for the unity of both Testaments. This is the "turf" on which biblical theology grew and developed. Some of the contemporary canonical debate, again, tackles the issue of theological unity of the biblical books.

Against this background, representative methods in biblical theology, such as the canonical approach of Brevard Childs alongside the contrasting view of James Barr, highlighted the core issues of the discussion. This debate revealed conflicting interpretative interests depending on how one perceives the nature of the text. We have seen that, despite its desire for comprehensiveness, which may represent both its strength and weakness, the canonical approach of Childs not only values the unity of Scripture, but also gives room for its diversity by listening separately to the voice of each biblical book. It allows both tracing the theme of God's praise and God's presence through individual biblical texts and envisaging a synoptic perspective on the trajectories detected on this journey. As a result, the main asset of such canonical approach lies in its regard for the nature of the biblical texts in terms of their canonical entirety and, consequently, their scriptural authority. In contrast to that, models like the one offered by Barr do not presuppose a canonical unity. For that reason, they did not prove to be useful tools for biblical theology in connection with the purpose of our inquiry.

Similarly, intertextual models which are not based on a final textual form on account of hypotheses of literary dependence did not turn out to be suitable (Brodie). Intertextual models which work with a final textual form allowing intertextual echoes to be heard within this discourse (Litwak) proved to be more beneficial for our purposes.

Finally, a view on the contemporary hermeneutical debate made clear that no method should be considered on its own, whether we deal with the principlizing method of Kaiser, the redemptive-historical approach of Doriani, the drama-of-redemption hypothesis of Vanhoozer, or the redemptive-movement model of Webb. Webb's model appeared the most useful of all for both exegesis and application, since it works with scriptural trajectories which permit the development of meaning and application.

This discussion has been relevant insofar as the results of this investigation need to be applied to the contemporary worship scene sketched in the first chapter. If the flaws of an "anthropocentric praise" are to be avoided, an appropriate application of the results of biblical-theological exegesis is imperative. Certainly, this leaves much room for further work to be done.

The question still remains open whether in the foreseeable future, biblical theology will be acknowledged as an independent theological discipline in Germany and elsewhere, or whether a canonical approach will be accepted as a method in such discipline. Obviously, this subject matter bears significance beyond the present investigation. In any case, biblical theology and a final-form canonical approach with an intertextual model turned out valuable to explore the theme of a bond between God's praise and God's presence.

Correspondingly, in the fourth chapter, narrative texts from the Hebrew Bible, the Old Testament, were investigated. The structural and exegetical analyses of 1 Kings 8 proved that divine glory is portrayed as prompting human praise and bringing priestly ministry to an end. The corresponding analyses of 2 Chronicles 5–7 added a reciprocal dimension: human praise inspired divine glory-presence, which, in return, may have prompted human praise again. Both narratives spelled out the irony: the Lord's glory-presence made his priests powerless and his people praise. Covenant background conveyed through a detailed description of temple worship and its pertinent pointers has been demonstrated. And so, we have inferred that, whether in 1 Kings 8 or in 2 Chronicles 5–7, praise cannot be considered *the one and only* precondition for divine presence, for this would neglect the imperative of covenant fidelity. Then, narratives mostly without temple setting, but with battle context revealed a consecutive correlation between God's people's praise and supernatural manifestations of divine presence in action, e.g., in Joshua 6 and 2 Chronicles 20. These accounts suggested not only that human praise provoked divine presence, but they also conveyed covenant background through the Holy War motif. On a slightly different note, the narratives with conflict context in 1 Samuel 16 and 2 Kings 3 corroborated that worshipful music may have entailed spiritual "side effects," whether in terms of making an evil spirit leave or releasing divine counsel through prophecy and its subsequent fulfilment. We have seen that, indeed, Ps 22:3 with God dwelling in or being enthroned upon his people's praises testifies to an obvious correlation between God's people's praise and God's presence, again in covenant context. All the same, except for this instance, we have found hardly any hints in Psalms which would evidence a link between divine presence and human praise. The case is similar with Ezekiel which largely portrays the absence of God's glory-presence in judgment.

The fifth chapter explored texts from the Greek Bible, the New Testament, taken from Acts and Ephesians—passages which depict the initial and repetitive infilling of God's new people with his Spirit in the context of their praise. Acts 2 provides a hermeneutical key for other Spirit narratives in Acts making clear that divine Spirit-presence literally "inspired" human praise, since the initial Spirit-infilling prompted glossolalia/xenolalia. This connection is narrated as being embedded in a new human-divine covenant relationship through Jesus Christ which comprises human repentance, divine salvation, and prophetic empowerment. These three elements can be discerned as "three in one," but are not to be divorced from each other. Acts 10 confirmed that divine Spirit presence prompted human praise, since the Gentiles' glossolalia praise was considered a manifest sign of the Holy Spirit poured out. Besides, this initial Spirit bestowal was also indicative of God's house being enlarged. Then, Acts 4 revealed a reciprocal dimension: human praise instigated divine presence in various manifestations, since the reverential exaltation of God is reported to have provoked the seismic activity and re-filling with the Holy Spirit. Likewise, Acts 16 proposed that hymnic praise "unleashed" an earthquake with "liberating" effects in more ways than one. Faith expressed through praise in suffering expected divine intervention, which allowed to infer a divine origin of these manifestations and verified covenant setting. Then, Ephesians 5:18–20 invites a constant Spirit-infilling of the believers in association with their praise. This Spirit-filled worship involves mutual hymnic edification and praise songs, both Spirit-inspired, which are offered whole-heartedly and with gratitude to the Father through Jesus Christ. Therefore, the connection between human praise and divine Spirit-presence implies reciprocity and testifies to covenant relationships at innerhuman and divine-human levels. In brief: Spirit-infilling in the milieu of covenant praise.

As a result of the textual analyses of Acts and Ephesians, we were able to infer that, again, there is a connection between divine presence in the form of an initial Spirit-infilling and human praise with the former prompting the latter. Vice versa, there is also a connection between human praise and Spirit-refilling, and/or theophanic manifestations with the former instigating the latter. Both directions are portrayed within covenant setting.

In the sixth chapter, this journey of exploring texts from both Testaments led us to a biblical theology perspective with three intertextual themes: *the connection between divine presence and human praise, the divine indwelling, and the divine-human covenant relationship.* These themes revealed issues of personhood and relationality, which were explored within their systematic theological setting and perceived against a philosophical background.

First, it has been established: the theme of the *connection between presence and praise* reverberates among narratives with the setting of a literal temple (1 Kgs 8 and 2 Chr 5–7), narratives mostly without any temple setting (Josh 6 and 2 Chr 20, 1 Sam 16 and 2 Kgs 3), and texts with the setting of a metaphorical temple (Acts 2 and 10/11, Acts 4 and 16, as well as Eph 5). We have seen that, therefore, this connection does not depend on the temple context.

Second, it has been corroborated: the theme of the *divine indwelling* reverberates among narratives with the setting of a literal temple (1 Kgs

8 and 2 Chr 5–7) and texts with the setting of a metaphorical temple (Acts 2 and 10, Acts 4, and Eph 5). These biblical witnesses relating to glory-filled and Spirit-filled divine dwellings emit echoes which can be heard together in concert in the intertextual theme of the divine indwelling. And so, the divine indwelling affects literal and metaphorical divine dwellings alike, both of which can still be material in quality. This has been evidenced through the application of recent models of metaphorical interpretation to the metaphor of the divine indwelling.

Third, it has been demonstrated: the theme of the *divine-human covenant relationship* reverberates among all the passages analyzed which show a literal temple context (1 Kgs 8 and 2 Chr 5–7), mostly no temple setting (Josh 6 and 2 Chr 20, 1 Sam 16, and 2 Kgs 3), and a metaphorical temple context (Acts 2 and 10, Acts 4 and 16, plus Eph 5). This theme can be identified either through a general covenant setting or particular covenant markers both relating to an existing or new covenant relationship. Relationship is not identical with covenant, but may lead to it. Covenant context and covenant markers imply holiness, since this covenant relationship is characterized by God's holy presence and faithful love on the one side, and his people's holy praise and worship life as a response on the other.

As a result, it has been verified that God's presence, his people's praise and a divine-human covenant relationship may form a recurrent paradigm.

Nevertheless, a look into Scripture also revealed contraindications, such as human idolatry and rebellion, which lead to divine judgment and divine absence. Then again, we have seen that divine presence in all its manifestations does not depend on human preconditions, like worship and its expressions of praise. Quite the reverse, our praise depends on our perception of the triune God and of the divine nature of the Holy Spirit.

In an "interdisciplinary crossover," we have ascertained that the Church Fathers, creeds, and liturgy shed light on the triune God as a personal and relational divine being in terms of "three in one." All three sources have affirmed the equal divinity and equal worship of the Holy Spirit. Likewise, they elucidated perichoresis, the inner-Trinitarian indwelling as implied in Scripture which represents a model for the divine indwelling and also for divine-human relationships. That paradigm has also enlightened our perspective on human personhood and relationality, which are at the heart of the *imago Dei* motif. This concept spells out humanity's likeness in God's image in terms of representative, functional, and relational analogies. The relational analogy is reflected in religious-philosophical writings such as Martin Buber's "sacramental dialogue" between the "I and Thou." And particularly the relational analogy affects the biblical-theological results of our study, i.e., the intertextual themes of the connection between God's presence and his people's praise, the divine indwelling, and the divine-human covenant relationship.

At the same time, the investigation disclosed that more work remains to be done. There is room for further exploring the interaction between divine presence and human praise in its pneumatological as well as inter-disciplinary settings. There is also room for studying the shades of the divine indwelling in the period of transition between both Testaments or probing contemporary contributions on divine Spirit-presence in Creation and salvation. Then, of course, the results of this biblical-theological appraisal need to be applied in the ecclesial-liturgical settings of pastoral theology to be fruitful for contemporary worship. This, however, was not the goal of this book. Certainly, the above intertextual themes identified need to be perceived in a larger theological setting to avoid their dominating the line of reasoning.

Last, but not least, the issue is not about accepting or rejecting a historical-critical method. The actual issue is about bridging the "ugly ditch" between "what it meant" and "what it means," that is, between a historical perspective and a theological perspective. Biblical theology as a discipline and a canonical approach with an intertextual model as method offer a real route in leading the way forward to bridge that gap. Especially in the German setting, an intertextual methodology could serve as a connecting link and stepping stone on this bridge. This may prepare the way for a restoration of our praise and a return of God's presence.

The great devotional poet George Herbert (1593–1633) crafted a poem titled "Man," but it is also about building a dwelling place for God:

My God, I heard this day,
That none doth build a stately habitation,
But he that means to dwell therein.
What house more stately hath there been,
Or can be, than is Man? to whose creation
All things are in decay . . .

Since then, my God, thou hast
So brave a palace built; O dwell in it,
That it may dwell with Thee at last!
Till then afford us so much wit;
That, as the world serves us, we may serve thee,
And both Thy servants be.[1]

---

1. Herbert, *One Hundred Poems*, 72–73 (first and last verse).

Bibliography

Aleaz, K. P. "Some Distinctive Features of Eastern Christian Spirituality." *IJT* 42, 2 (2000) 178–91.

Alexander, T. Desmond. *From Eden to the New Jerusalem: An Introduction to Biblical Theology*. Grand Rapids: Kregel, 2009.

Alexander, T. Desmond, and Simon Gathercole, eds. *Heaven on Earth: The Temple in Biblical Theology*. Carlisle: Paternoster, 2004.

Allen, Leslie C. *1–2 Chronicles*. CCOT 10, edited by Lloyd J. Ogilvie, Waco, TX: Word, 1987.

———. *Psalms 101–150*. WBC 21, edited by David A. Hubbard et al., Milton Keynes, UK: Word Books, 1983.

Anderson, Warren J. "Organic Liturgy as the Cure for Bible-Absent Worship in the Contemporary Church." *Reformation & Revival* 15, 2 (2006) 81–97.

Arcadi, James M. "God Is where God Acts: Reconceiving Divine Omnipresence." https://philpapers.org/rec/ARCGIW. doi: 36, 4 (2017) 631–39.

Arrington, French L. "The Indwelling, Baptism, and Infilling with the Holy Spirit: A Differentiation of Terms." *Pneuma* 3, 2 (1981) 1–10.

Ash, Carisa A., and Glenn R. Kreider. Review of *God's Wider Presence: Reconsidering General Revelation*, by Robert Johnston. *BSac* 172, 686 (2015) 239–40.

Atkinson, William P. *Baptism in the Spirit: Luke-Acts and the Dunn Debate*. Eugene, OR: Pickwick, 2011.

Augustine of Hippo. *Augustine Confessions I: Books 1–8*, edited by Carolyn J.-B. Hammond. LCL 26. Cambridge, MA: Harvard University Press, 2014.

———. *Augustine Confessions II: Books 9–13*, edited by Carolyn J.-B. Hammond. LCL 26. Cambridge, MA: Harvard University Press, 2016.

———. *The City of God (De civitate Dei): Books 1–10. The Works of Saint Augustine*. Hyde Park, NY: New City, 2012.

———. *De Trinitate: Libri 15. Volume 2*. CCCM. Turnhout: Brepols, 1968.

———. *Prayer to the Holy Spirit*. http://www.loyolapress.com/Our-Catholic-Faith/Prayer/Traditional-Catholic-Prayers/Saints-Prayers/Holy-Spirit-Prayer-of-Saint-Augustine.

Austin, T. "The Glory of God." *Reformation & Revival* 4, 2 (1995) 41–57.

Averbeck, Richard E. "Breath, Wind, Spirit and the Holy Spirit in the Old Testament." In *Presence, Power and Promise: The Role of the Spirit of God in the Old Testament*, edited by David G. Firth and Paul D. Wegner, 25–37. Downers Grove, IL: IVP Academic, 2011.

Baigent, John. "Worship: Essence and Form in Scripture and Today." *Christian Brethren Review* 39 (1988) 9–28.

Baldwin, J.G. *1 and 2 Samuel: An Introduction and Commentary.* Leicester: Inter-Varsity, 1988.

Balla, Peter. "Challenges to Biblical Theology." In *New Dictionary of Biblical Theology*, edited by T. Desmond Alexander and Brian S. Rosner, 20–27. Leicester: Inter-Varsity, 2000.

Ballhorn, Egbert, and Georg Steins, eds. *Der Bibelkanon in der Bibelauslegung: Methodenreflexionen und Beispielexegesen.* Stuttgart: Kohlhammer, 2007.

Baltes, Guido. "Rituelle Reinheit in Apostelgeschichte 10." Paper presented at the Annual Meeting of the NT Arbeitskreis für evangelikale Theologie. Marburg, Germany, 29 February 2016.

Baltzer, Klaus. *Das Bundesformular.* Wissenschaftliche Monographien zum Alten und Neuen Testament. Neukirchen-Vluyn: Neukirchener Verlag, 1960.

Barker, Margaret. *On Earth as It Is in Heaven: Temple Symbolism in the New Testament.* Edinburgh: T & T Clark, 1995.

Barr, James. *The Concept of Biblical Theology: An Old Testament Perspective.* London: SCM, 1999.

———. *Holy Scripture: Canon, Authority, Criticism.* Oxford: Clarendon, 1983.

Barrett, C. K. *A Critical and Exegetical Commentary on the Acts of the Apostles. Volume 1: Preliminary Introduction and Commentary on Acts 1–14.* ICC, edited by J. A. Emerton et al. Edinburgh: T & T Clark, 1994.

Barth, Karl. *Church Dogmatics.* Translated by Geoffrey W. Bromiley. 1936–1975. London: T & T Clark, 2008.

———. *Die Kirchliche Dogmatik Band 3: Die Lehre von der Schöpfung 1. Teil.* Zürich: Theologischer Verlag, 1967.

Barth, Markus. *Ephesians 4–6: A New Translation with Introduction and Commentary.* AB. Garden City, NY: Doubleday, 1974.

Bates, Matthew W. *The Birth of the Trinity: Jesus, God, and Spirit in New Testament and Early Christian Interpretations of the Old Testament.* Oxford: Oxford University Press, 2015.

Bauer, Walter. *Griechisch-Deutsches Wörterbuch zu den Schriften des Neuen Testaments und der frühchristlichen Literatur.* 6th rev. ed., edited by Kurt Aland and Barbara Aland, Berlin: de Gruyter, 1988.

Baugh, S. M. *Ephesians.* Bellingham, WA: Lexham, 2016.

Baum, Armin. *Lukas als Historiker der letzten Jesusreise.* Wuppertal: Brockhaus, 1993.

Baumert, Norbert. "'Charism' and 'Spirit-Baptism': Presentation of an Analysis." *JPT* 12, 2 (2004) 147–79.

Beale, Greg K. "The Descent of the Eschatological Temple in the Form of the Spirit at Pentecost. Part 1: The Clearest Evidence." *TynBul* 56, 1 (2005a) 73–102.

———. "The Descent of the Eschatological Temple in the Form of the Spirit at Pentecost. Part 2: Corroborating Evidence." *TynBul* 56, 2 (2005b) 63–90.

———. "The Final Vision of the Apocalypse and its Implications for a Biblical Theology of the Temple." In *Heaven on Earth*, edited by T. Desmond Alexander and Simon Gathercole, 191–209. Carlisle: Paternoster, 2004a.

———. *The Temple and the Church's Mission: A Biblical Theology of the Dwelling Place of God.* New Studies in Biblical Theology. Leicester: Apollos, 2004b.

———. *The Use of Daniel in Jewish Apocalyptic Literature and in the Revelation of St John*. Lanham, MD: University Press of America, 1984.

———. *We Become What We Worship: A Biblical Theology of Idolatry*. Downers Grove, IL: InterVarsity, 2008.

Beall, Todd S., and William A. Banks. *Old Testament Parsing Guide. Genesis–Esther*. Chicago: Moody, 1986.

Beckwith, Roger T. "The Canon of Scripture." In *New Dictionary of Biblical Theology*, edited by T. Desmond Alexander and Brian S. Rosner, 27–34. Leicester: InterVarsity, 2000.

Begbie, Jeremy S. "The Spirituality of Renewal Music—A Preliminary Exploration." *Anvil* 8, 3 (1991) 227–39.

Bennema, Cornelis. "The Giving of the Spirit in John 19–20: Another Round." In *The Spirit and Christ in the New Testament and Christian Theology: Essays in Honor of Max Turner*, edited by I. Howard Marshall et al., 86–104. Grand Rapids: Eerdmans, 2012.

Berkhof, Louis. *Systematic Theology*. 1938. Repr. 4th rev. and enl. ed. Grand Rapids: Eerdmans, 1991.

Biblia Hebraica, edited by Rudolf Kittel, 3rd ed. Stuttgart: Württembergische Bibelanstalt, 1937.

Biblia Hebraica Stuttgartensia, edited by Rudolf Kittel et al., 3rd rev. ed. Stuttgart: Deutsche Bibelgesellschaft, 1981.

Bird, Michael F. "The Unity of Luke-Acts in Recent Discussion." In *Rethinking the Unity and Reception of Luke and Acts*, edited by Andrew F. Gregory and C. Kavin Rowe, 3–16. Columbia, SC: University of South Carolina Press, 2010.

Blass, Friedrich, and Albert Debrunner. *A Greek Grammar of the New Testament and Other Early Christian Literature*. Transl. and rev. by Robert W. Funk. Chicago: University of Chicago Press, 1961.

Blocher, Henri. "Old Covenant, New Covenant." In *Always Reforming: Explorations in Systematic Theology*, edited by Andrew H. T. McGowan, 240–70. Leicester: Apollos; 2006.

Block, Daniel I. *The Book of Ezekiel: Chapters 25–48*. NICOT. Grand Rapids: Eerdmans; 1998.

———. "Eden: A Temple? A Reassessment of the Biblical Evidence." In *From Creation to New Creation: Biblical Theology and Exegesis*, edited by Daniel M. Gurtner and Benjamin L. Gladd, 3–29. Peabody, MA: Hendrickson, 2013.

———. *For the Glory of God*. Grand Rapids: Baker Academic, 2014.

———. Review of *For the Glory of God. Recovering a Biblical Theology of Worship*, by Benjamin Foreman. *EJT* 25, 1 (2014) 97–99.

Bobrinskoy, Boris. "The Indwelling of the Spirit in Christ: 'Pneumatic Christology' in the Cappadocian Fathers." *SVTQ* 28, 1 (1984) 49–65.

Bock, Darrell L. *Acts*. BECNT. Grand Rapids: Baker Academic, 2007.

———. *A Theology of Luke and Acts: Biblical Theology of the New Testament*, edited by Andreas J. Köstenberger. Grand Rapids: Zondervan, 2012.

Bonnington, Mark. "Is the Old Covenant Renewed in the New? A Response to James D. G Dunn." In *Covenant Theology: Contemporary Approaches*, edited by Mark J. Cartledge and David Mills, 57–84. Carlisle: Paternoster, 2001.

———. "New Temples in Corinth: Paul's Use of Temple Imagery in the Ethics of the Corinthian Correspondence." In *Heaven on Earth*, edited by T. Desmond Alexander and Simon Gathercole, 151–59. Carlisle: Paternoster, 2004.

Braun, Gabriele G. "The Concept of a Baptism in the Holy Spirit in the Book of Acts." MTh diss., Regent College, 1994.

———. "The Connection between God's Praise and God's Presence." PhD diss., North-West University, 2017.

———. "Die Erfüllung mit dem Heiligen Geist nach Epheser 5, 18–20—wie geschieht das"? MDiv equiv. diss., Giessen School of Theology, 1992.

Brawley, Robert L. *Centering on God: Method and Message in Luke–Acts*. Louisville: Westminster John Knox, 1990.

Bray, Gerald L. *Biblical Interpretation: Past and Present*. Downers Grove, IL: InterVarsity, 1996.

———. "Engaging Unbelief: A Captivating Strategy from Augustine and Aquinas." *The Churchman* 115, 2 (2001) 184–85.

Brett, Mark G. *Biblical Criticism in Crisis: The Impact of the Canonical Approach on Old Testament Studies*. Cambridge: Cambridge University Press, 1991.

Bright, John. *The Kingdom of God: The Biblical Concept and its Meaning for the Church*. Nashville, TN: Abingdon, 1953.

Brodie, Thomas L. *The Birthing of the New Testament: The Intertextual Development of the New Testament Writings*. NTM 1. Sheffield: Sheffield Phoenix, 2004.

Bruce, F. F. *The Acts of the Apostles: The Greek Text with Introduction and Commentary*. Leicester: Apollos, 1990.

Brueggemann, Walter. *Divine Presence amid Violence: Contextualizing the Book of Joshua*. Eugene, OR: Cascade Books, 2009.

———. *Ichabod Toward Home: The Journey of God's Glory*. Grand Rapids: Eerdmans, 2002.

———. *Worship in Ancient Israel: An Essential Guide*. Nashville: Abingdon, 2005.

———. *1 and 2 Kings*. SHBC 8. Macon, GA: Smyth & Helwys, 2000.

Brueggemann, Walter, and Patrick D. Miller. *Old Testament Theology: Essays on Structure, Theme, and Text*. Minneapolis, MN: Fortress, 1992.

Buber, Martin. *I and Thou*. Translated by Ronald Gregor Smith. Edinburgh: T & T Clark, 1937.

Buhl, Frants, ed. *Wilhem Gesenius' Hebräisches und Aramäisches Handwörterbuch über das Alte Testament*. 1915. Repr. 17th ed. Berlin: Springer, 1962.

Burns, J. Lanier. "John 14:1–27: The Comfort of God's Presence." *BSac* 172, 687 (2015) 299–315.

Callow, John. *A Semantic Structure Analysis of Colossians*. Dallas, TX: Summer Institute of Linguistics, 1983.

Carson, Donald A. *The Gospel According to John*. Leicester: Inter-Varsity, 1991.

———. *Showing the Spirit: A Theological Exposition of 1 Corinthians 12–14*. Grand Rapids: Baker Academic, 1996.

Carter, Christopher. "The Imago Dei as the Mind of Jesus Christ." *Zygon* 49, 3 (2014) 752–60.

Chance, Bradley J. *Jerusalem, the Temple, and the New Age in Luke-Acts*. Macon, GA: Mercer University Press, 1988.

Chang, Dongshin Don. "Priestly Covenants in 1QM and 1 QSb." In *The War Scroll, Violence, War and Peace in the Dead Sea Scrolls and Related Literature: Essays in*

Honour of Martin G. Abegg on the Occasion of his 65th Birthday. Studies on the Texts of the Desert of Judah 115, edited by Kipp Davis et al., 147–62. Leiden: Brill, 2016.

Childs, Brevard S. *Biblical Theology: A Proposal.* Minneapolis, MN: Fortress, 2002.

———. *Biblical Theology in Crisis.* Philadelphia: Westminster, 1970.

———. *Biblical Theology of the Old and New Testaments: Theological Reflection on the Christian Bible.* London: SCM, 1992.

———. "The Canon in Recent Biblical Studies: Reflection on an Era." In *Canon and Biblical Interpretation.* SHS 7, edited by Craig Bartholomew et al., 33–57. Grand Rapids: Zondervan, 2006.

———. *Exodus: A Commentary.* OTL. London: SCM, 1974.

———. *Introduction to the Old Testament as Scripture.* London: SCM, 1979.

———. *The Struggle to Understand Isaiah as Christian Scripture.* Grand Rapids: Eerdmans, 2004.

Clines, D. J. A. "The Image of God in Man." *TynBul* 19 (1968) 53–103.

Cole, Graham A. *Engaging with the Holy Spirit: Six Crucial Questions.* Nottingham: Apollos, 2007a.

———. *He Who Gives Life.* Wheaton, IL: Crossway, 2007b.

Combs, William W. "Spirit-Filling in Ephesians 5:18." *DBSJ* 19 (2014) 23–52.

Costa, Tony. *Worship and the Risen Jesus in the Pauline Letters.* StBibLit 157. New York: Lang, 2013.

Cotterell, Peter, and Max Turner. *Linguistics and Biblical Interpretation.* Downers Grove, Il: InterVarsity, 1989.

Craigie, Peter. *Psalms 1–50.* WBC 19, edited by David A. Hubbard et al., Waco, TX: Word Books, 1983.

Crisp, Oliver D. "Problems with Perichoresis." *TynBul* 56, 1 (2005) 119–40.

Culy, Martin M., and Mikeal C. Parsons. *Acts. A Handbook on the Greek Text.* Waco, TX: Baylor University Press, 2003.

Dalferth, Ingolf U. "Representing God's Presence." *IJST* 3, 3 (2001) 237–56.

Davis, John Jefferson. *Worship and the Reality of God.* Downers Grove, IL: IVP Academic, 2010.

Delitzsch, Franz. *Die Psalmen.* 1894. Repr. 5th ed. Giessen: Brunnen, 1984.

De Vries, Pieter. *The Kâabôd of YHWH in the Old Testament: With Particular Reference to the Book of Ezekiel.* SSN 65. Leiden: Brill, 2016.

De Vries, Simon J. *The Achievements of Biblical Religion: A Prolegomenon to Old Testament Theology.* Lanham, MD: University Press of America, 1983.

———. *1 Kings.* WBC, 12. Waco, TX: Word Books, 1985.

Dillard, Raymond B. *2 Chronicles.* WBC 15. Waco, TX: Word Books, 1987.

Doriani, Daniel M. "A Redemptive-Historical Model." In *Four Views on Moving beyond the Bible to Theology,* edited by Stanley N. Gundry and Gary T. Meadors, 75–120. Grand Rapids: Zondervan, 2009.

Dozeman, Thomas B. *Joshua 1–12: A New Translation with Introduction and Commentary.* The Anchor Yale Bible 6 B. New Haven: Yale University Press, 2015.

Dreytza, Manfred. *Der theologische Gebrauch von RUAḤ im Alten Testament: Eine wort- und satzsemantische Studie.* Giessen: Brunnen, 1990.

Driver, Daniel R. "Childs and the Canon or Rule of Faith." In *The Bible as Christian Scripture: The Work of Brevard S. Childs.* SBLBSNA 25, edited by Christopher R. Seitz and Kent H. Richards, 243–78. Atlanta, GA: SBL, 2013.

Dumbrell, William J. *Covenant and Creation: An Old Testament Covenant Theology*. Milton Keynes: Paternoster, 2013.

Dunn, James D. G. *Baptism in the Holy Spirit: A Re-Examination of the New Testament Teaching on the Gift of the Spirit in Relation to Pentecostalism today*. Philadelphia: Westminster, 1970.

———. *Jesus and the Spirit*. London: SCM, 1975.

Earl, Douglas. "Joshua and the Crusades," In *Holy War in the Bible: Christian Morality and an Old Testament Problem*, edited by Heath A. Thomas et al., 19-43. Downers Grove, IL: IVP Academic, 2013.

Early Church Texts. *The Nicene Creed—Agreed at the Council of Constantinople in 381*. http://www.earlyChurchTexts.com/public/nicene_creed.htm.

Eckardt, Burnell F. "Another Look at the Imago Dei: Fulfilled in the Incarnate One." *CTQ* 79, 1-2 (2015) 67-78.

Egger, Wilhelm, and Peter Wick. *Methodenlehre zum Neuen Testament: Biblische Texte selbständig auslegen*. 6th rev. enl ed. Freiburg im Breisgau: Herder, 2011.

Engelbrecht, Ben. "The Indwelling of the Holy Spirit." *JTSA* 30 (1980) 36-45.

Ervin, Howard M. *Conversion-Initiation and the Baptism in the Holy Spirit : A Critique of James D. G. Dunn, Baptism in the Holy Spirit*. Peabody, MA: Hendrickson, 1970.

ESV. The Holy Bible, English Standard Version. 2001. Crossway Good News Publishers, 2016.

Faix, Tobias, and Tobias Künkler. *Generation Lobpreis und die Zukunft der Kirche*. Neukirchen-Vluyn: Neukirchener Verlag, 2018.

Falk, Daniel K. "Prayer, Liturgy and War." In *The War Scroll, Violence, War and Peace in the Dead Sea Scrolls and Related Literature*, edited by Kipp Davis et al., 275-94. Leiden: Brill, 2015.

Farrar, Frederic William. *The First Book of Kings*. London: Hodder & Stoughton, 1893-1894.

Fauconnier, Gilles, and Mark Turner. "Rethinking Metaphor." In *The Cambridge Handbook of Metaphor and Thought*, edited by Raymond W. Gibbs, 53-66. Cambridge: Cambridge University Press, 2008.

———. *The Way We Think: Conceptual Blending and the Mind's Hidden Complexities*. New York: Basic Books, 2002.

Fee, Gordon D. *God's Empowering Presence: The Holy Spirit in the Letters of Paul*. Peabody, MA: Hendrickson, 1994.

———. *Gospel and Spirit: Issues in New Testament Hermeneutics*. Peabody, MA: Hendrickson, 1991.

———. *Paul, the Spirit, and the People of God*. Peabody, MA: Hendrickson, 1996.

Fergusson, David A. "Humans Created according to the *Imago Dei*: An Alternative Proposal." *Zygon* 48, 2 (2013) 439-53.

Finnern, Sönke. *Narratologie und biblische Exegese: Eine integrative Methode der Erzählanalyse und ihr Ertrag am Beispiel von Matthäus 28*. WUNT 2/282. Tübingen: Mohr Siebeck, 2010.

Fletcher-Louis, Crispin H. T. "God's Image, his Cosmic Temple and the High Priest: Towards an Historical and Theological Account of the Incarnation." In *Heaven on Earth*, edited by T. Desmond Alexander and Simon Gathercole, 81-99. Carlisle: Paternoster, 2004.

Flett, Eric G. "Priests of Creation, Mediators of Order: The Human Person as a Cultural Being in Thomas F. Torrance's Theological Anthropology." *SJT* 58, 2 (2005) 161-83.

Fowl, Stephen E. *Ephesians: A Commentary*. NTL. Louisville: Westminster John Knox, 2012.

———. *Idolatry*. Waco, TX: Baylor University Press, 2019.

Frei, Hans W. *The Eclipse of Biblical Narrative: A Study in Eighteenth and Nineteenth Century Hermeneutics*. New Haven: Yale University Press, 1974.

Fretheim, Terence E. *The Suffering of God: An Old Testament Perspective*. OBT 14. Philadelphia: Fortress, 1984.

Frey, Jörg. "Die alte und die neue diathēkē nach dem Hebräerbrief." In *Bund und Tora: Zur theologischen Begriffsgeschichte in alttestamentlicher, frühjüdischer und urchristlicher Tradition*, edited by Friedrich Avemarie and Hermann Lichtenberger, 263–310. Tübingen: Mohr Siebeck, 1996.

Frye, Northrop. *The Great Code: The Bible and Literature*. London: Routledge & Kegan Paul, 1982.

Gäckle, Volker. *Allgemeines Priestertum: Zur Metaphorisierung des Priestertitels im Frühjudentum und Neuen Testament*. WUNT 1/331. Tübingen: Mohr Siebeck, 2014.

Gese, Hartmut. *Alttestamentliche Studien*. Tübingen: Mohr Siebeck, 1991.

Goldingay, John. *Old Testament Theology Volume 1: Israel's Gospel*. Downers Grove, IL: InterVarsity, 2003.

———. *Psalms Volume 1: Psalms 1–41*. Grand Rapids: Baker Academic, 2006.

Gombis, Timothy G. "Being the Fullness of God in Christ by the Spirit: Ephesians 5:18 in its Epistolary Setting." *TynBul* 53, 2 (2002) 259–71.

———. "The Rhetoric of Divine Warfare in Ephesians." In *Holy War in the Bible: Christian Morality and an Old Testament Problem*, edited by Heath A. Thomas et al., 87–107. Downers Grove, IL: IVP Academic, 2013.

———. "The Triumph of God in Christ: Divine Warfare in the Argument of Ephesians." *TynBul* 56, 2 (2005) 157–60.

Gosnell, Peter W. "Ephesians 5:18–20 and Mealtime Propriety." *TynBul* 44, 2 (1993) 363–71.

Gräbe, Petrus J. *Der neue Bund in der frühchristlichen Literatur unter Berücksichtigung der alttestamentlich-jüdischen Voraussetzungen*. FB 96. Würzburg: Echter, 2001.

Green, Bradley G. *Covenant and Commandment: Works, Obedience, and Faithfulness in the Christian Life*. NSBT. Downers Grove, IL: IVP Academic, 2014.

Greenslade, Philip. *Worship in the Best of both Worlds*. Milton Keynes: Paternoster, 2009.

Greever, Joshua M. "'We Are the Temple of the Living God' (2 Corinthians 6:14—7:1): The New Covenant as the Fulfillment of God's Promise of Presence." *SBJT* 19, 3 (2015) 97–118.

Grenz, Stanley J. "Jesus as the Imago Dei: Image-of-God Christology and the Non-linear Linearity of Theology." *JETS* 47, 4 (2004) 617–28.

———. *The Social God and the Relational Self: A Trinitarian Theology of the Imago Dei*. Louisville: Westminster John Knox, 2007.

Gundry, Stanley N., and Gary T. Meadors, eds. *Four Views on Moving beyond the Bible to Theology*. Grand Rapids: Zondervan, 2009.

Gunton, Colin E. "Ad litteram: How Augustine, Calvin and Barth Read the Plain Sense of Genesis 1–3." *JTS* 51, 2 (2000) 787–89.

Hafemann, Scott J. "Biblical Theology: Retrospect and Prospect." In *Biblical Theology: Retrospect and Prospect*, edited by Scott J. Hafemann, 15–21. Downers Grove, IL: InterVarsity, 2002.

———. "The Covenant Relationship." In *Central Themes in Biblical Theology: Mapping Unity in Diversity*, edited by Scott J. Hafemann and Paul R. House, 21–65. Nottingham: Apollos, 2007.

Hahn, Scott. *The Kingdom of God as Liturgical Empire: A Theological Commentary on 1–2 Chronicles*. Grand Rapids: Baker Academic, 2012.

Hamilton, James M. J. *God's. Glory in Salvation through Judgment: A Biblical Theology*. Wheaton, IL: Crossway Books, 2010.

———. *God's Indwelling Presence: The Holy Spirit in the Old & New Testaments*. NAC Studies in Bible & Theology, edited by E. Ray Clendenen. Nashville: B & H Academic, 2006.

———. "Old Covenant Believers and the Indwelling Spirit: A Survey of the Spectrum of Opinion." *TJ* 24, 1 (2003) 37–54.

Hamilton, Victor P. *The Book of Genesis: Chapters 1–17*. NICOT 1. Grand Rapids: Eerdmans, 1990.

Harstad, Adolph L. *Joshua*. Saint Louis: Concordia, 2004.

Hasel, Gerhard F. "Recent Translations of Genesis 1:1, a Critical Look." *BT* 22, 4 (1971) 154–67.

Haubeck, Wilfried, and Heinrich von Siebenthal. *Neuer sprachlicher Schlüssel zum griechischen Neuen Testament: Matthäus bis Apostelgeschichte*. Giessen: Brunnen, 1997.

Haya-Prats, Gonzalo. *Empowered Believers: The Holy Spirit in the Book of Acts*. Eugene, OR: Wipf & Stock, 2011.

Hays, Richard B. *Echoes of Scripture in the Letters of Paul*. New Haven: Yale University Press, 1989.

Heil, John Paul. *Luke-Acts: Foundations for Christian Worship*. Eugene, OR: Cascade, 2018.

———. Review of *Luke-Acts: Foundations for Christian Worship*, by Boris Paschke. *RBL* 2 (2019). http://www.Book reviews.org/subscribe.asp.

Helberg, Jaap L. *The Lord Reigns: Revelation History of the Old Testament*. Translated by J. J. F. Krüger. CPD-publications 22. Potchefstroom: North-West University, 2011.

Herbert, George. *One Hundred Poems*. Cambridge: Cambridge University Press, 2016.

Hildebrandt, Wilfred. *An Old Testament Theology of the Spirit of God*. 1993. Republished. Eugene, OR: Wipf & Stock, 2019.

Hobbs, T. Raymond. *A Time for War: A Study of Warfare in the Old Testament*. OTS. Wilmington, DE: Glazier, 1989.

Hollis, Wendall. "Become Full in the Spirit: A Linguistic, Contextual, and Theological Study of 'πληροῦσθε ἐν πνεύματι.'" PhD diss., Trinity International University, 2001.

Holmén, Tom. *Jesus and Jewish Covenant Thinking*. BibInt 55. Leiden: Brill, 2001.

Hudson, D. Neil. "Worship: Singing a New Song in a Strange Land." In *Pentecostal Perspectives*, edited by Keith Warrington, 177–203. Carlisle: Paternoster, 1998.

Hugenberger, Gordon P. *Marriage as a Covenant: A Study of Biblical Law and Ethics Governing Marriage Developed from the Perspective of Malachi*. VTSup 52B. Leiden: Brill, 1994.

Hundley, Michael B. *Gods in Dwellings: Temples and Divine Presence in the Ancient Near East*. WAWSup 3. Atlanta: Society of Biblical Literature 2013.

———. *Keeping Heaven on Earth: Safeguarding the Divine Presence in the Priestly Tabernacle*. FAT 2/50. Tübingen: Mohr Siebeck, 2011.

Hur, Ju. *A Dynamic Reading of the Holy Spirit in Luke-Acts*. Sheffield: Sheffield Academic, 2001.

Hurowitz, Victor. *I Have Built you an Exalted House: Temple-Building in the Bible in the Light of Mesopotamian and Northwest Semitic Writings*. JSOTSup/ASOR 115. Sheffield: JSOT Press, 1992.

Janowksi, Bernd. *Gottes Gegenwart in Israel: Beiträge zur Theologie des Alten Testaments*. Neukirchen-Vluyn: Neukirchener Verlag, 1993.

Japhet, Sara. *1 and 2 Chronicles: A Commentary*. Louisville: Westminster John Knox, 1993.

Jenni, Ernst., und Claus Westermann. *Theologisches Handwörterbuch zum Alten Testament*, edited by Ernst Jenni, with assistance from Claus Westermann. 2 vols. Munich: Kaiser, 1984.

Jervell, Jacob. *Die Apostelgeschichte*. Göttingen: Vandenhoeck & Ruprecht, 1998.

Johnston, Robert K. *God's Wider Presence: Reconsidering General Revelation*. Grand Rapids: Baker Academic, 2014.

Jojko, Bernadeta. *Worshipping the Father in Spirit and Truth: An Exegetico-Theological Study of Jn 4:20–26 in the Light of the Relationships among the Father, the Son and the Holy Spirit*. Tesi Gregoriana. Serie Teologia 193. Rome: Gregorian University Press, 2012.

Joüon, Paul. *Grammaire de l'Hébreu Biblique*. 1923. Repr. Rome: Pontifical Biblical Institute, 1987.

Kärkkäinen, Veli-Matti. *Pneumatology: The Holy Spirit in Ecumenical, International and Contextual Perspective*. Rev. ed. Grand Rapids: Baker Academic, 2018.

Kaiser, Walter C. "The Indwelling Presence of the Holy Spirit in the Old Testament." *EvQ* 82, 4 (2010) 308–15.

———. "A Principlizing Model." In *Four Views on Moving beyond the Bible to Theology*, edited by Stanley N. Gundry and Gary T. Meadors, 19–50. Grand Rapids: Zondervan, 2009.

Kaiser, Walter C., and Moises Silva. *An Introduction to Biblical Hermeneutics: The Search for Meaning*. Grand Rapids: Zondervan, 1994.

Kalimi, Isaac. *Zur Geschichtsschreibung des Chronisten: Literarisch-historiographische Abweichungen der Chronik von ihren Paralleltexten in den Samuel- und Königsbüchern*. Berlin: de Gruyter, 2016.

Keener, Craig S. *Acts: An Exegetical Commentary. Volume 1: Introduction and 1:1—2:47*. Grand Rapids: Baker Academic, 2012.

———. *Acts: An Exegetical Commentary. Volume 2: 3:1—14:28*. Grand Rapids: Baker Academic, 2013.

———. *Acts: An Exegetical Commentary. Volume 3: 15:1—23:35*. Grand Rapids: Baker Academic, 2014.

———. *The Spirit in the Gospels and Acts: Divine Purity and Power*. Peabody, MA: Hendrickson, 1997.

Keil, Carl Friedrich, and Franz Delitzsch. *Joshua, Judges, Ruth, 1 and 2 Samuel*. Volume 2 of *Commentary on the Old Testament*. Translated by James Martin. 1887. Repr. Peabody, MA: Hendrickson, 1989.

———. *The Pentateuch*. Volume 1 of *Commentary on the Old Testament*. Translated by James Martin. 1887. Repr. Peabody, MA: Hendrickson, 1989.
———. *Psalms*. Volume 5 of *Commentary on the Old Testament*. Translated by Francis Bolton. 1887. Repr. Peabody, MA: Hendrickson, 1989.
———. *1 and 2 Kings, 1 and 2 Chronicles, Ezra, Nehemiah, Esther*. Volume 3 of *Commentary on the Old Testament*. Translated by James Martin. 1887. Repr. Peabody, MA: Hendrickson, 1989.
Kelsey, David H. *Eccentric Existence: A Theological Anthropology*. Louisville: Westminster John Knox, 2009.
Keulen, Percy S. F. van. Two Versions of the Solomon Narrative: An Inquiry into the Relationship between MT 1 Kgs. 2–11 and LXX 3 Reg. 2–11. VTSup 104. Leiden: Brill, 2005.
Kilchör, Benjamin. *Wiederhergestellter Gottesdienst: Eine Deutung der zweiten Tempelvision Ezechiels (Ez 40–48) am Beispiel der Aufgaben der Priester und Leviten*. Herders Biblische Studien 95. Freiburg im Breisgau: Herder 2020.
Kittel, Gerhard, and Gerhard Friedrich, eds. *Theological Dictionary of the New Testament*. Translated by Geoffrey W. Bromiley. 10 vols. Grand Rapids: Eerdmans, 1964–1976.
———. *Theologisches Wörterbuch zum Neuen Testament*. Vol. 6. 1933–1979. Repr. Stuttgart: Kohlhammer, 1990.
Klein, Ralph W. *1 Chronicles: A Commentary*. Minneapolis: Fortress, 2006.
Kline, Meredith G. "Creation in the Image of the Glory Spirit." *WTJ* 39 (1977a) 250–72.
———. *Images of the Spirit*. Grand Rapids: Baker House, 1980.
———. "Investiture with the Image of God." *WTJ* 40 (1977b) 38–62.
Klingbeil, Gerald A. "'He Spoke and it Was': Human Language, Divine Creation, and the Imago Dei." *HBT* 36, 1 (2014) 42–59.
Köhlmoos, Melanie. "Kanon und Methode. Zu einer Zwischenbilanz der 'kanonischen Auslegung': Der Bibelkanon in der Bibelauslegung." *TRu* 74 (2009) 135–46.
Köstenberger, Andreas J. "Diversity and Unity in the New Testament." In *Biblical Theology: Retrospect and Prospect*, edited by Scott J. Hafemann, 144–58. Leicester: Inter-Varsity, 2002.
———. "The Present and Future of Biblical Theology." *Them* 37, 3 (2012) 445–64.
Konsmo, Erik. *The Pauline Metaphors of the Holy Spirit: The Intangible Spirit's Tangible Presence in the Life of the Christian*. StBibLit 130. New York: Lang, 2010.
Kramer, Kenneth P. "Tasting God: Martin Buber's Sweet Sacrament of Dialogue." *Horizons* 37, 2 (2010) 224–45.
Kremer, Jacob. "Pneuma." *EDNT* 3:117–23, edited by Horst Balz and Gerhard Schneider, Grand Rapids: Eerdmans, 1993.
Kwakkel, Gert. "Berith and Covenants in the Old Testament: A Contribution to a Fruitful Cooperation of Exegesis and Systematic Theology." In *Covenant(s): Biblical, Historical and Systematical Perspectives*. prelim., edited by Hans Burger et al., Leiden: Brill, forthcoming.
Lakoff. George. "The Neural Theory of Metaphor." In *The Cambridge Handbook of Metaphor and Thought*, edited by Raymond W. Gibbs, 17–38. Cambridge: Cambridge University Press, 2008.
Lakoff, George, and Mark Johnson. *Metaphors We Live By*. Chicago: University of Chicago Press, 1980.

Lakoff, George, and Mark Turner. *More Than Cool Reason*. Chicago: Chicago University Press, 1989.
Lambdin, Thomas, and Heinrich von Siebenthal. *Lehrbuch Bibel-Hebräisch*. 2nd ed. Theologische Verlagsgemeinschaft. Giessen: Brunnen, 1993.
Lampe, Geoffrey William H. *God as Spirit: The Bampton Lectures, 1976*. Oxford: Clarendon, 1977.
Larkin, William J. *Ephesians: A Handbook on the Greek Text*. BHGNT. Waco, TX: Baylor University Press, 2009.
Lederle, Henry I. *Treasures Old and New: Interpretations of 'Spirit-Baptism' in the Charismatic Renewal Movement*. Peabody, MA: Hendrickson, 1988.
Letham, Robert. *The Holy Trinity: In Scripture, History, Theology and Worship*. Phillipsburg, NJ: Presbyterian & Reformed, 2004.
Lettinga. Jan P., and Heinrich von Siebenthal. *Grammatik des Biblischen Hebräisch*. Giessen: Brunnen, 2016.
Levinsohn, Stephen H. *Textual Connections in Acts*. SBLMS 31. Atlanta: Scholars, 1987.
Levison, John R. *Filled with the Spirit*. Grand Rapids: Eerdmans, 2009.
Lincoln, Andrew T. *Ephesians*. WBC. Dallas, TX: Word, 1990.
Lind, Millard C. *Yahweh Is a Warrior: The Theology of Warfare in Israel*. Scottdale, PA: Herald, 1980.
Lingen, Anton, van der. *Les guerres de Yahvé: l'implication de YHWH dans les guerres d'Israël selon les livres historique de l'Ancien Testament*. LD 139. Paris: Cerf, 1990.
Linnemann, Eta. *Gibt es ein synoptisches Problem?* 1991. Repr. 3rd ed. Nürnberg: VTR, 1998.
Litwak, Kenneth D. *Echoes of Scripture in Luke-Acts: Telling the History of God's People Intertextually*. JSNTSup 282. New York: T & T Clark, 2005.
Louw, Johannes P., and Eugene A. Nida. *Greek-English Lexicon of the New Testament Based on Semantic Domains*. Vol. 1. 1988. Repr. 3rd ed. New York. United Bible Societies, 1989.
Macchia, Frank D. *Baptized in the Spirit: A Global Pentecostal Theology*. Grand Rapids: Zondervan, 2006.
MacDonald, Nathan. "The Imago Dei and Election: Reading Genesis 1:26-28 and Old Testament Scholarship with Karl Barth." *IJST* 10, 3 (2008) 303-27.
Maier, Gerhard. *Biblische Hermeneutik*. Wuppertal: Brockhaus, 1990.
———. *Das Ende der Historisch-Kritischen Methode*. 3rd ed. ABC Team. Wuppertal: Brockhaus, 1975.
Mallen, Peter. *The Reading and Transformation of Isaiah in Luke-Acts*. LNTS 367. London: T & T Clark, 2008.
Marshall, I. Howard. "Church and Temple in the New Testament." *TynBul* 40, 2 (1989b) 203-22.
———. "Evangelical New Testament Interpretation within the Contemporary Scene." *EJT* 20, 1 (2011) 4-14.
———. "How Far Did the Early Christians Worship God?" *Churchman* 99, 3 (1985) 216-29.
———. *Luke: Historian and Theologian*. Grand Rapids: Zondervan, 1989a.
———. "Worshipping Biblically." *SBET* 20, 2 (2002) 146-61.
McCollough, David J. *Ritual Water, Ritual Spirit: An Analysis of the Timing, Mechanism, and Manifestation of Spirit-Reception in Luke-Acts*. PBM. Milton Keynes: Paternoster, 2017.

McComiskey, Thomas Edward. *The Covenants of Promise: A Theology of the Old Testament Covenants*. Grand Rapids: Baker Books, 1985.

McDonald, Lee Martin. *The Biblical Canon: Its Origin, Transmission and Authority*. 3rd ed. Peabody, MA: Hendrickson, 2007.

McFadyen, Alistair I. *The Call to Personhood: A Christian Theory of the Individual in Social Relationships*. Cambridge: Cambridge University Press, 1990.

McGowan, Andrew T. B. "In Defense of 'Headship Theology.'" In *The God of Covenant: Biblical, Theological and Contemporary Perspectives*, edited by Jamie A. Grant and Alistair I. Wilson, 178–99. Leicester: Apollos, 2005.

McGrath, Alister E. *Christian Theology: An Introduction*. 3rd ed. Oxford: Blackwell, 2001.

McNamara, B. M. D. "A Theology of Wisdom as the Imago Dei: A Response to when God Talks Back." *EvQ* 87, 2 (2015) 151–68.

McQueen, Larry R. *Joel and the Spirit: The Cry of a Prophetic Hermeneutic*. Sheffield: Sheffield Academic, 1995.

Mead, James K. *Biblical Theology: Issues, Methods, and Themes*. Louisville: Westminster John Knox, 2007

Meadors, Edward P. *Idolatry and the Hardening of the Heart: A Study in Biblical Theology*. New York: T & T Clark, 2006.

Menzies, Robert P. *Empowered for Witness: The Spirit in Luke-Acts*. Sheffield: Sheffield Academic, 1994.

Metzger, Bruce M. *A Textual Commentary on the Greek New Testament: A Companion Volume to the United Bible Societies' Greek New Testament*. 3rd corr. ed., edited by Kurt Aland et al., Stuttgart: Deutsche Bibelgesellschaft, 1975.

Middleton, J. Richard. *The Liberating Image: The Imago Dei in Genesis 1*. Grand Rapids: Brazos, 2005.

Montgomery, James A. *A Critical and Exegetical Commentary on the Books of Kings*. ICC. New York: Scribner, 1951.

Moritz, Joshua. "Deep Incarnation and the Imago Dei: The Cosmic Scope of the Incarnation in Light of the Messiah as the Renewed Adam." *Theology and Science* 11, 4 (2013) 436–43.

Nestle, Eberhard, and Erwin Nestle, eds. *Novum Testamentum Graece*. Stuttgart: Deutsche Bibelgesellschaft, 2012.

Noble, Paul R. *The Canonical Approach: A Critical Reconstruction of the Hermeneutics of Brevard S. Childs*. BibInt. Leiden: Brill, 1995.

Noth, Martin. *Könige 1: Teilband 1–16*. Neukirchen-Vluyn: Neukirchener Verlag, 1968.

Oeming, Manfred. "'Siehe, deine Zeit war gekommen, die Zeit der Liebe' (Ez 16, 8). Die 'Psychologie der Liebe' als sachlicher Kern der Bundestheologie im Alten Testament." In *Für immer verbündet: Studien zur Bundestheologie der Bibel*, edited by Christoph Dohmen and Christian Frevel, 151–60. SBS 211. Stuttgart: Katholisches Bibelwerk, 2007.

Olson, Dennis T. "Seeking 'the Inexpressible Texture of thy Word': A Practical Guide to Brevard Childs' Canonical Approach to Theological Exegesis." *PTR* 14, 1, 38 (2008) 53–68.

Otto, Randall E. "The Use and Abuse of Perichoresis in Recent Theology." Abstract. *SJT* 54, 3 (2001) 366–84.

Owens, John Joseph. *Analytical Key to the Old Testament. Volume 2*. Grand Rapids: Baker Academic, 1992.

Parsons, Mikael C, and Richard I. Pervo. *Rethinking the Unity of Luke and Acts.* Minneapolis: Augsburg Fortress, 1993.

Petersen, David L. "Brevard Childs and Form Criticism." In *The Bible as Christian Scripture: The Work of Brevard S. Childs,* edited by Christopher R. Seitz and Kent H. Richards, 9–20. SBLBSNA 25. Atlanta: Society of Biblical Literature, 2013.

Peterson, David G. *The Acts of the Apostles.* Grand Rapids: Eerdmans, 2009.

———. *Engaging with God: A Biblical Theology of Worship.* Downers Grove, IL: InterVarsity, 1992.

———. "The Motif of Fulfilment and the Purpose of Luke-Acts." In *The Book of Acts in its Ancient Literary Setting.* Vol. 1 of *The Book of Acts in its First Century Setting,* edited by Bruce W. Winter and Andrew D. Clarke, 83–104. Grand Rapids: Eerdmans, 1993.

Philo, of Alexandria. *De ebrietate. De sobrietate: Philo of Alexandria. Works. French, Greek and Latin.* 11–12. Translated by Jean Gorez with introduction and comments. Paris: Cerf, 1962.

Pierce, Timothy M. *Enthroned on our Praise: An Old Testament Theology of Worship.* Nashville: B & H Academic, 2008.

Pinnock, Clark H. *Flame of Love.* Downers Grove, IL: InterVarsity, 1996.

Polhill, John B. *Acts.* New American Commentary. Nashville: Broadman & Holman, 1992.

Powell, Mark Allan. *What are they Saying about Acts.* New York: Paulist, 1991.

Rabens, Volker. *The Holy Spirit and Ethics in Paul: Transformation and Empowering for Religious-Ethical Life.* 2nd rev. ed. Minneapolis, IL: Fortress, 2014.

Rad, Gerhard von. *Holy War in Ancient Israel.* Trans. and edited by Marva J. Dawn and John Howard Yoder. 1958. Grand Rapids: Eerdmans, 1991.

Rapske, Brian. "Opposition to the Plan of God and Persecution." In *Witness to the Gospel: The Theology of Acts,* edited by I. Howard Marshall and David G. Peterson, 235–56. Grand Rapids: Eerdmans, 1998.

Rechberger, Uwe. *Von der Klage Zum Lob: Studien zum 'Stimmungsumschwung' in den Psalmen.* Neukirchen-Vluyn: Neukirchener Verlag, 2012.

Rendtorff, Rolf. *The Covenant Formula: An Exegetical and Theological Investigation.* OTS. Edinburgh: T & T Clark, 1998.

Renwick, David A. *Paul, the Temple, and the Presence of God.* BJS 224. Atlanta: Scholars, 1991.

Ricoeur, Paul. *Interpretation Theory: Discourse and the Surplus of Meaning.* Fort Worth: Texas Christian University Press, 1976.

Robinson, Dominic. *Understanding the Imago Dei: The Thought of Barth, von Balthasar and Moltmann.* Farnham, Surrey, UK: Ashgate, 2011.

Robinson, Joseph. *The First Book of Kings.* London: Cambridge University Press, 1972.

Robson, James R. *Word and Spirit in Ezekiel.* LHBOTS 447. New York: T & T Clark, 2006.

Rochester, Kathleen M. *Israel's Lament and the Discernment of Divine Revelation: A Narrative Study.* Saarbrücken: Lambert Academic, 2012.

Rogers, Cleon L., Jr. "The Dionysian Background of Ephesians 5:18." *BSac* 136, 543 (1979) 249–57.

Rogers, Eugene F., Jr. *After the Spirit: A Constructive Pneumatology from Resources outside the Modern West.* Grand Rapids: Eerdmans, 2005.

Rosner, Brian S. "Biblical Theology." In *New Dictionary of Biblical Theology*, edited by T. Desmond Alexander and Brian S. Rosner, 3–11. Leicester: Inter-Varsity, 2000.

Rudnig, Thilo Alexander. "König ohne Tempel: 2 Samuel 7 in Tradition und Redaktion." *VT* 61, 3 (2011) 426–46.

Runge, Steven E., and Stephen H. Levinsohn. *Discourse Studies & Biblical Interpretation: A Festschrift in Honor of Stephen H. Levinsohn*. Bellingham, WA: Logos Research Systems, 2012.

Salter, Martin C. *The Power of Pentecost: An Examination of Acts 2:17–22*. Eugene, OR: Resource Publications, 2012.

Sanders, Fred. *The Triune God*. Grand Rapids: Zondervan, 2016.

———. "Turning the Mind to Doxology: An Excerpt from The Triune God," *ZA Blog*, 2 December 2016, http://zondervanacademic.com/blog/turning-the-mind-to-doxology-an-excerpt-from-the-triune-god-by-fred-sanders.

Sanders, James A. *Canon and Community: A Guide to Canonical Criticism*. Guides to Biblical Scholarship.1984. Repr. Philadelphia: Fortress, 2000.

Schnabel, Eckhard J. *Acts*. ZECNT. Grand Rapids: Zondervan, 2012.

Schnackenburg, Rudolf. *Der Brief an die Epheser*. Band 10. Zurich: Benziger, 1982.

Schneider, Wolfgang. *Grammatik des Biblischen Hebräisch. Ein Lehrbuch*. 8th ed. Munich: Claudius Verlag, 1993.

Schultz, Richard. "Brevard S. Childs' Contribution to Old Testament Interpretation: An Evangelical Appreciation and Assessment." *PTR* 14, 1, 38 (2008) 69–93.

Schwöbel, Christoph, and Colin Gunton, eds. *Persons, Divine and Human: King's College Essays in Theological Anthropology*. Edinburgh: T & T Clark, 1991.

Scobie, Charles H. H. "History of Biblical Theology." In *New Dictionary of Biblical Theology*, edited by T. Desmond Alexander and Brian S. Rosner, 11–20. Leicester: Inter-Varsity, 2000.

———. "The Structure of Biblical Theology." *TynBul* 42, 2 (1991) 163–94.

———. *The Ways of our God: An Approach to Biblical Theology*. Grand Rapids: Eerdmans, 2003.

Seitz, Christopher R. "The Canonical Approach and Theological Interpretation." In *Canon and Biblical Interpretation*, edited by Craig C. Bartholomew et al., 58–110. Scripture and Hermeneutics Series 7. Milton Keynes: Paternoster, 2006.

———. *The Character of Christian Scripture: The Significance of a Two-Testament Bible*. Grand Rapids: Baker Academic, 2011.

Seitz, Christopher R., and Kent H. Richards. *The Bible as Christian Scripture: The Work of Brevard S. Childs*. SBL Biblical Scholarship in North America 25. Atlanta: Society of Biblical Literature, 2013.

Selman, Martin J. *1 Chronicles: A Commentary*. Leicester: Inter-Varsity, 1994.

———. *2 Chronicles: A Commentary*. Leicester: Inter-Varsity, 1994.

Shelton, James B. *Mighty in Word and Deed: The Role of the Holy Spirit in Luke-Acts*. Peabody, MA: Hendrickson. 1991.

Shepherd, William H., Jr. *The Narrative Function of the Holy Spirit as a Character in Luke-Acts*. SBLDS 147. Atlanta: Scholars, 1994.

Siebenthal, Heinrich von. *Ancient Greek Grammar for the Study of the New Testament*. Rev. and enl. ed. of *Griechische Grammatik zum Neuen Testament* by Ernst Hoffman and Heinrich von Siebenthal. 2011. Oxford: Lang, 2019.

Society of Biblical Literature Handbook of Style. 2nd ed. Atlanta: SBL, 2014.

Spatafora, Andrea. *From the 'Temple of God' to God as the Temple: A Biblical and Theological Study of the Temple in the Book of Revelation*. Tesi Gregoriana. Serie Teologia 27. Rome: Gregorian University Press, 1997.
Spawn, K. L. "Sacred Song and God's Presence in 2 Chronicles 5, the Renewal Community of Judah and beyond." *JPT* 16, 2 (2008) 51–68.
Spencer, F. Scott. *Acts*. Sheffield: Sheffield Academic, 1997.
Steins, Georg. *Die 'Bindung Isaaks' im Kanon (Gen 22): Grundlagen und Programm einer kanonisch-intertextuellen Lektüre*. HBS 20. Freiburg im Breisgau: Herder, 1998.
———. *Kanonisch-Intertextuelle Studien zum Alten Testament*. SBAB 48. Stuttgart: Katholisches Bibelwerk, 2009.
Steven, James H. S. *Worship in the Spirit: Charismatic Worship in the Church of England*. Carlisle: Paternoster, 2002.
Stovell, Beth M. *Mapping Metaphorical Discourse in the Fourth Gospel*. Leiden: Brill, 2012.
Stronstad, Roger. *The Charismatic Theology of St Luke*. Peabody, MA: Hendrickson, 1984.
———. *The Prophethood of all Believers: A Study in Luke's Charismatic Theology*. Sheffield: Sheffield Academic, 1999.
Stuhlmacher, Peter, ed. *How to Do Biblical Theology*. PTMS 38. Allison Park, PA: Pickwick, 1995.
Sumpter, Philip. "Brevard Childs as Critical and Faithful Exegete." *PTR* 14, 38, 1 (2008) 95–116.
Sutton, Ray. *That You May Prosper: Dominion by Covenant*. Tyler, TX: Institute for Christian Economics, 1987.
Sweeney, Marvin A. *1 and 2 Kings: A Commentary*. Louisville: Westminster John Knox, 2007.
Theopedia. "Perichoresis." http://www.theopedia.com/Perichoresis.
Thiselton, Anthony C. *The Holy Spirit: In Biblical Teaching, through the Centuries, and Today*. London: SPCK, 2013.
Torrance, James B. *Worship, Community, and the Triune God of Grace*. Carlisle: Paternoster, 1996.
Torrance, Thomas F. *The Christian Doctrine of God: One Being Three Persons*. Edinburgh: T. & T Clark, 1995.
Turner, Max. "Approaching 'Personhood' in the New Testament, with Special Reference to Ephesians." *EvQ* 77, 3 (2005) 211–33.
———. *Power from on High: The Spirit in Israel's Restoration and Witness in Luke-Acts*. Sheffield: Sheffield Academic, 1996.
———. "The Spirit in Luke-Acts: A Support or a Challenge to Classical Pentecostal Paradigms"? *VE* 27 (1997) 75–101.
———. "'Trinitarian' Pneumatology in the New Testament? Towards an Explanation of the Worship of Jesus." *AsTJ* 57/58, 2/1 (2002–2003) 167–86.
Vanhoozer, Kevin J. "A Drama-of-Redemption Model." In *Four Views on Moving beyond the Bible to Theology*, edited by Stanley N. Gundry and Gary T. Meadors, 151–99. Grand Rapids: Zondervan, 2009.
———. *Is there a Meaning in this Text? The Bible, the Model, and the Morality of Literary Knowledge*. Leicester: Apollos, 1998.

Van Rooy, Herrie F. "Ezekiel, Prophet of the Glory of the Lord." In *The Lion Has Roared: Theological Themes in the Prophetic Literature of the Old Testament*, edited by H. G. L. Peels and S. D. Snyman, 127–48. Eugene, OR: Pickwick, 2012.

Verheyden, Jozef. "The Unity of Luke-Acts." *HvTSt* 55, 4 (1999) 964–79.

———. "The Unity of Luke-Acts: What are we up to?" In *The Unity of Luke-Acts*, edited by Jozef Verheyden, 3–56. Leuven: Leuven University Press, 1999.

Vogel, Manuel. *Das Heil des Bundes: Bundestheologie im Frühjudentum und im frühen Christentum*. TANZ. Tübingen: Francke, 1996.

Volf, Miroslav. *After our Likeness: The Church as the Image of the Trinity*. Sacra Doctrina. Grand Rapids: Eerdmans, 1998.

Vollenweider, Samuel. "Göttliche Einwohnung: Die Schechina-Motivik in der paulinischen Theologie." In *Das Geheimnis der Gegenwart Gottes—Zur Schechina-Vorstellung in Judentum und Christentum*, edited by Bernd Janowski et al., 203–17. Tübingen: Mohr Siebeck, 2014.

Wall, Robert W. "Israel and the Gentile Mission in Acts and Paul: A Canonical Approach." In *Witness to the Gospel: The Theology of Acts*, edited by I. Howard Marshall and David L. Peterson, 437–57. Grand Rapids: Eerdmans, 1998.

Walsh, Jerome T. *Style and Structure in Biblical Hebrew Narrative*. Collegeville, MN: Liturgical, 2001.

———. *1 Kings*. Collegeville, MN: Liturgical, 1996.

Waltke, Bruce K., and Charles Yu. *An Old Testament Theology: An Exegetical, Canonical, and Thematic Approach*. Grand Rapids: Zondervan, 2007.

Walton, Steve. "A Tale of Two Perspectives? The Place of the Temple in Acts." In *Heaven on Earth*, edited by T. Desmond Alexander and Simon Gathercole, 135–49. Carlisle: Paternoster, 2004.

Ward, Pete. *Selling Worship: How what We Sing Has Changed the Church*. Carlisle: Paternoster, 2005.

Warrington, Keith. *Pentecostal Theology*. London: T & T Clark, 2008.

Watson, Francis. "Gospel and Scripture: Rethinking Canonical Unity." *TynBul* 52, 2 (2001) 161–82.

———. *Open Text: New Directions for Biblical Studies?* London: SCM, 1993.

———. *Text and Truth: Redefining Biblical Theology*. Grand Rapids: Eerdmans, 2009.

Webb, William J. "A Redemptive-Movement Model." In *Four Views on Moving beyond the Bible to Theology*, edited by Stanley N. Gundry and Gary T. Meadors, 215–48. Grand Rapids: Zondervan, 2009.

———. *Slaves, Women and Homosexuals: Exploring the Hermeneutics of Cultural Analysis*. Carlisle: Paternoster, 2001.

Weingreen, Jacob. *A Practical Grammar for Classical Hebrew*. 2nd ed. Oxford: Oxford University Press, 1959.

Welker, Michael. *Gottes Geist: Theologie des Heiligen Geistes*. Neukirchen-Vluyn: Neukirchener Verlag, 1992.

Wells, Jo Bailey. *God's Holy People: A Theme in Biblical Theology*. JSOTSup 305. Sheffield: Sheffield Academic, 2000.

Wenham, Gordon J. *Genesis 1–15*. WBC 1. Waco, TX: Word, 1987.

Wenk, Matthias. *Community-Forming Power: The Socio-Ethical Role of the Spirit in Luke-Acts*. Sheffield: Sheffield Academic, 2000.

Westermann, Claus. *Lob und Klage in den Psalmen*. 6th ed. Göttingen: Vandenhoeck & Ruprecht, 1983.

Wenzel, Heiko. "Wie viel Erzählung(en) braucht Geschichtsschreibung in der Chronik?" Paper presented at the Annual Meeting of the OT/NT Arbeitskreis für evangelikale Theologie. Marburg, Germany, 2 March 2020.

Wick, Peter. *Die Urchristlichen Gottesdienste: Entstehung und Entwicklung im Rahmen der frühjüdischen Tempel-, Synagogen- und Hausfrömmigkeit.* Stuttgart: Kohlhammer, 2002.

Willi, Thomas. *Die Chronik als Auslegung: Untersuchungen zur literarischen Gestaltung der historischen Überlieferung Israels.* Göttingen: Vandenhoeck & Ruprecht, 1997.

Williamson, Hugh G. M. *1 and 2 Chronicles.* Grand Rapids: Eerdmans, 1982.

Williamson, Paul R. *Sealed with an Oath: Covenant in God's Unfolding Purpose.* Downers Grove, IL: InterVarsity, 2007.

Wright, N. T. "Worship and the Spirit in the New Testament." In *The Spirit in Worship—Worship in the Spirit*, edited by Teresa Berger, and Bryan D. Spinks, 3–24. Collegeville, MN: Liturgical, 2009.

Yong, Amos. *Discerning the Spirit(s): A Pentecostal-Charismatic Contribution to Christian Theology of Religions.* Sheffield: Sheffield Academic, 2000.

Zerwick, Maximilian. *Biblical Greek.* Adapted from the 4th Latin ed. by Joseph Smith. 1963. Repr. Rome: Pontifical Biblical Institute, 1990.

Zerwick, Maximilian, and Mary D. Grosvenor. *A Grammatical Analysis of the Greek New Testament.* 3rd rev. ed. Rome: Pontifical Biblical Institute, 1988.

Zizioulas, Ioannis. *Being as Communion: Studies in Personhood and the Church.* Crestwood: St Vladimir's Seminary Press, 1985.

———. "The Church as Communion." *SVTQ* (1993) 1–15.

Author Index

Aleaz, K. P., 211
Alexander, T. Desmond, 53, 179
Allen, Leslie, 93, 100, 104, 109, 110, 118
Anderson, Warren J., 216
Arcadi, James M., 177
Arrington, French L., 186, 191
Ash, Carisa A., 177
Atkinson, William P., 129, 132
Augustine of Hippo, 220-21, 226-27
Austin, T., 87, 178
Averbeck, Richard E., 128

Baigent, John, 22
Baldwin, Joyce G., 112-13
Balla, Peter, 56-57
Ballhorn, Egbert, 4, 68
Baltes, Guido, 139
Baltzer, Klaus, 204
Banks, William A., 87
Barker, Margaret, 179-80
Barr, James, 4, 52, 57, 63-67, 70, 79-80, 228, 237-38
Barrett, C. K., 124, 127-28, 146, 151-53, 157
Barth, Karl, 197, 221, 227-29, 231
Barth, Markus, 159, 160
Bates, Matthew W., 219, 224
Bauer, Walter, 126, 128
Baugh, S. M., 161-64, 167
Baum, Armin, 123
Baumert, Norbert, 132
Beale, Greg K., 53, 141, 179-82, 184-86, 189-90, 214-15, 230
Beall, Todd S., 87
Beckwith, Roger T., 58

Begbie, Jeremy S., 14
Bennema, Cornelis, 185
Berkhof, Louis, 197, 201, 206, 222-23
Bird, Michael F., 123, 228
Blocher, Henri, 200-202
Block, Daniel I., 3, 9, 37-42, 49-50, 119, 163, 165, 167, 180-82, 184, 187, 214, 237
Bobrinskoy, Boris, 184, 219, 221
Bock, Darrell L., 123, 127, 130, 135-36, 139, 145
Bonnington, Mark, 187, 201
Braun, Gabriele G., 130-31, 160, 163
Brawley, Robert L., 136
Bray, Gerald L., 70, 220-21
Brett, Mark G., 69-70
Bright, John, 93
Brodie, Thomas L., 4, 71-73, 80, 238
Bruce, F. F., 126, 133, 137, 139, 145, 151-52
Brueggemann, Walter, 16, 74-75, 87, 90, 109
Buber, Martin, 223, 230-33, 235, 242
Buhl, Frants, 116
Burns, J. Lanier, 184

Callow, John, 163-64
Carson, Donald A., 134-35, 217-18
Carter, Christopher, 226
Chance, Bradley J., 184
Chang, Dongshin Don, 205
Childs, Brevard S., 4, 52, 54, 57-63, 65-70, 72, 79-80, 171, 181, 237
Clines, D. J. A., 226
Cole, Graham A., 162, 218, 220

Costa, Tony, 22, 216–17
Cotterell, Peter, 128–29, 232
Craigie, Peter, 116, 131, 137, 141, 152, 157
Crisp, Oliver D., 219
Culy, Martin M., 127, 130, 145–46, 150–52, 156

Dalferth, Ingolf U., 223
Davis, John Jefferson, 3, 9, 42–46, 50, 237
De Vries, Simon J., 82–83, 223
Delitzsch, Franz, 83, 87, 93, 97, 99, 101–3, 108, 112, 114, 116–17, 204–5, 225–27
Dillard, Raymond B., 91, 95, 97, 101, 110
Doriani, Daniel M., 5, 75–77, 80, 238
Dozeman, Thomas B., 109
Dreytza, Manfred, 128
Driver, Daniel R., 58, 62–63, 67, 70
Dumbrell, William J., 198, 200, 203
Dunn, James D. G., 127, 132, 134, 164, 201

Earl, Douglas, 205
Eckardt, Burnell F., 226, 228
Egger, Wilhelm, 52, 68
Engelbrecht, Ben, 222
Ervin, Howard M., 132

Faix, Tobias, 3, 9, 47–48, 50, 237
Falk, Daniel K., 112, 209
Farrar, Frederic William, 85, 87, 90
Fauconnier, Gilles, 192
Fee, Gordon D., 164
Fergusson, David A., 224, 226–29
Finnern, Sönke, 71
Fletcher-Louis, Crispin H. T., 180, 186
Flett, Eric G., 224
Foreman, 163
Fowl, Stephen E., 158, 161, 163, 214
Frei, Hans W., 56, 58, 71
Fretheim, Terence E., 81, 87, 89
Frey, Jörg E., 200
Frye, Northrop, 56, 71

Gäckle, Volker, 33, 119, 130, 141–42, 184, 187–88
Gathercole, Simon J., 179
Gese, Harmut, 55, 69, 116
Goldingay, John, 116, 199–201, 203
Gombis, Timothy G., 159, 161–62, 165–67, 208
Gosnell, Peter W., 162
Gräbe, Petrus J., 54
Green, Bradley G., 202
Greenslade, Philip, 9, 15–19, 49, 236
Greever, Joshua M., 187, 210
Grenz, Stanley J., 214, 224, 226, 228–30
Grosvenor, Mary, 126, 130
Gundry, Stanley N., 5, 75
Gunton, Colin E., 221, 224, 228

Hafemann, Scott J., 53, 56–57
Hahn, Scott, 91
Hamilton, James M. J., 129, 134, 178, 188, 215
Hamilton, Victor P., 225–26
Harstad, Adolph L., 108
Hasel, Gerhard F., 226
Haubeck, Wilfried, 126, 130, 166
Haya-Prats, Gonzalo, 130, 142
Hays, Richard B., 73
Heil, John Paul, 30, 36, 112, 206, 209
Helberg, Jaap L., 93
Herbert, George, 242–43
Hildebrandt, Wilfred, 128
Hobbs, T. Raymond, 205
Hollis, Wendall, 161
Hudson, D. Neil, 3, 9–11, 48, 236
Hugenberger, Gordon P., 197
Hundley, Michael B., 86–88, 180
Hur, Ju, 124, 132–33
Hurowitz, Victor, 83, 86, 88, 90, 103

Janowski, Bernd, 89, 134, 177, 182
Japhet, Sara, 91, 92, 99, 101–6, 109, 110
Jenni, Ernst, 210
Jervell, Jacob, 139
Johnson, Mark, 192
Johnston, Robert K., 177
Jojko, Bernadeta, 217
Joüon, Paul, 225

Author Index

Kaiser, Walter, 5, 75–77, 80, 134, 178, 188, 238
Kaminsky, 119
Kärkkäinen, Veli-Matti, 133
Keener, Craig S., 126, 128, 131, 136–37, 141–42, 145–46, 151–52, 157
Keil, Carl Friedrich, 83, 87, 91, 93, 97, 99, 101–3, 108, 112, 114, 116–17, 204–5, 225–27
Kilchör, Benjamin, 119
Kittel, Gerhard, 131
Klein, Ralph W., 91–92
Kline, Meredith G., 87, 183, 202, 226–27
Klingbeil, Gerald A., 225, 228
Köhlmoos, Melanie, 4, 68, 69
Konsmo, Erik, 192–93
Köstenberger, Andreas J., 53
Kramer, Kenneth P., 231–32
Kreider, Glenn R., 177
Kremer, Jacob, 131
Künkler, Tobias, 3, 9, 47–48, 50, 237
Kwakkel, Gert, 197–99

Lakoff, George, 192
Lambdin, Thomas, 86, 99
Lampe, Geoffrey W. H., 178
Larkin, William J., 161–63, 165
Lederle, Henry I., 131–33
Letham, Robert, 178, 220–21
Lettinga, Jan P., 225
Levinsohn, Stephen H., 73
Levison, John R., 119, 130, 135, 180, 184, 186
Lincoln, Andrew T., 158–61, 163–65
Lind, Millard C., 206
Lingen, Anton van der, 204
Linnemann, Eta, 55
Litwak, Kenneth D., 4, 71–74, 80, 238
Louw, Johannes P., 130

Macchia, Frank D., 132
MacDonald, Nathan, 197, 227–29
Maier, Gerhard, 55
Mallen, Peter, 73
Marshall, Howard I., 3, 9, 19–26, 30, 49, 74–79, 101, 123, 137, 188, 236
McCollough, David J., 73, 123, 133, 135, 145

McComiskey, Thomas Edward, 200, 202, 207
McFadyen, Alistair I., 224
McGowan, Andrew T. B., 202
McGrath, Alister E., 219–20
McNamara, B. M. D., 12
McQueen, Larry R., 136
Mead, James K., 52–54
Meadors, Edward P., 214
Meadors, Gary T., 5, 75
Menzies, Robert P., 132–33
Metzger, Bruce M., 126, 151–52
Middleton, J. Richard, 226, 228
Miller, Patrick D., 75
Montgomery, James A., 84
Moritz, Joshua, 162, 179, 230

Nida, Eugene A., 130
Noble, Paul R., 59, 70
Noth, Martin, 83

Oeming, Manfred, 55, 67, 196
Olson, Dennis T., 63
Otto, Randall E., 219
Owens, John Joseph, 87, 102

Parsons, Mikeal C., 123, 127, 130, 145–46, 150–52, 156
Pervo, Richard I., 123
Petersen, David L., 62
Peterson, David G., 3, 9, 19–20, 24–28, 30, 40, 49, 124, 130, 135, 142, 152, 237
Philo of Alexandria, 161
Pierce, Timothy M., 118
Pinnock, Clark H., 222, 228
Polhill, John B., 137, 139, 145–46, 157
Powell, Mark Allan, 123

Rabens, Volker, 131, 228
Rad, Gerhard von, 54, 110, 119, 205
Rapske, Brian, 153
Rechberger, Uwe, 116
Rendtorff, Rolf, 62, 67, 204
Renwick, David A., 179, 182–83, 186, 188
Richards, Kent H., 58
Ricoeur, Paul, 16, 128–29, 192

Robinson, Joseph, 84, 86–89
Rochester, Kathleen M., 89
Rogers, Cleon L., Jr., 162
Rogers, Eugene F., Jr., 178, 184
Rosner, Brian S., 52–53
Rudnig, Thilo Alexander, 181
Runge, Steven E., 73

Salter, Martin C., 129, 136
Sanders, Fred, 218–19, 221
Sanders, James A., 56–57, 59
Schnabel, Eckhard J., 157
Schnackenburg, Rudolf, 159, 163
Schneider, Wolfgang, 86, 99, 102, 104, 113
Schultz, Richard, 62
Scobie, Charles H., 53–55
Seitz, Christopher R., 58–59, 63, 70
Selman, Martin J., 92, 100, 102, 173
Shelton, James B., 132
Shepherd, William H., Jr., 123–24
Siebenthal, Heinrich von, 86, 99, 126, 130, 166, 225
Silva, Moises, 75
Spatafora, Andrea, 182
Spawn, K. L., 95, 100
Spencer, F. Scott, 155
Steins, Georg, 4, 68, 70, 72
Steven, James H. S., 3, 9, 12–15, 35, 49, 115, 138, 153, 185, 236
Stovell, Beth M., 193
Stronstad, Roger, 132
Stuhlmacher, Peter, 55, 69
Sumpter, Philip, 59, 62
Sutton, Ray, 200, 204–6
Sweeney, Marvin A., 90

Thiselton, Anthony C., 128, 132–33, 135

Torrance, James B., 178, 216–18, 222–25
Torrance, Thomas F., 224
Turner, Mark, 192
Turner, Max, 16, 127–30, 132, 133, 136–37, 217, 220, 224, 228, 232

van Keulen, Percy S. F., 86
Van Rooy, Herrie F., 118–19
Vanhoozer, Kevin J., 5, 75, 77–78, 80, 238
Verheyden, Jozef, 123
Vogel, Manuel, 112, 206, 209
Volf, Miroslav, 224
Vollenweider, Samuel, 177

Wall, Robert W., 135
Walsh, Jerome T., 83, 85, 88, 90
Waltke, Bruce K., 196, 198, 226
Walton, Steve, 141, 185–86
Watson, Francis, 74, 171
Webb, William J., 5, 75, 78–80, 238
Weingreen. Jacob, 104
Wells, Jo Bailey, 210
Wenham, Gordon J., 225
Wenk, Matthias, 132
Wenzel, Heiko, 91, 107
Westermann, Claus, 115–17, 210, 227
Wick, Peter, 3, 9, 21, 24–25, 28–41, 49, 52, 68, 101, 167, 187, 237
Williamson, Hugh G. M., 92, 97, 100, 103, 110
Williamson, Paul R., 114, 197, 203, 206–7
Wright, N. T., 28–29, 187

Zerwick, Maximilian, 126, 130
Zizioulas, Ioannis, 45, 132, 211, 224, 228

General Index

Analogy, 7, 23, 104, 164, 176, 178–79, 182, 187, 191–92, 214, 226, 228–29, 233, 235, 241–42

Biblical theology, 1–9, 24–25, 27–28, 37, 45, 48–57, 60–71, 74, 79– 80, 95, 134, 138, 141, 163, 170–71, 179, 193, 214, 236–38, 240, 242

Canon, 1, 4, 29, 46, 50–52, 56–60, 62–72, 74, 77, 79–80, 158, 237–38, 242
Charismatic worship, 9, 12, 14–15, 76–77
Charismatics, 14, 132–33
Communication, divine-human, 2, 5, 7, 18, 24, 41, 93, 142–43, 151, 179–80, 197, 230
Covenant, 2, 6–7, 18, 26–28, 31, 38–40, 43, 49, 54, 72, 82–98, 100–105, 107–9, 111–12, 115–21, 126–27, 131, 133–34, 136, 138, 143, 149–50, 152, 157–60, 167–72, 174–79, 184, 187–88, 195–213, 218–19, 225, 229, 231–35, 237, 239–42
Covenant markers, 184, 202–9, 212–13, 234, 241
Covenant setting, 6, 100, 109, 111, 115, 120, 202–9, 212–13, 234, 240–41
Creation, 17–18, 31, 39, 44, 59, 87, 177–83, 191, 196–98, 200, 208, 211, 216, 222–25, 228, 231–33, 242–43

Doxology, 2–3, 23, 31–32, 43, 45–46, 50, 221–22

Empowerment, 114, 135–36, 138, 144, 168, 239

Glory, xiv, 2, 5–7, 17–18, 27, 37–41, 43, 46, 50, 81–82, 84–90, 94, 96–107, 118–20, 122, 130, 134, 138, 141, 153, 162–63, 165, 167–68, 172–78, 181–83, 188–89, 191–92, 195–96, 204, 209–10, 214–16, 220–21, 230, 233–34, 238–39, 241
Glossolalia, xiv, 35, 125, 134–35, 137–38, 140, 143–45, 147, 153, 164–65, 168–69, 173, 239

Hermeneutics, 5, 51–52, 61–62, 66–67, 71, 74–76, 78–80, 91, 168, 227, 237–39
Historical criticism, 53–56, 60–62, 70–72, 79, 132, 242
Holiness, 32, 39, 43, 106, 128, 186, 209–10, 213, 234
Holy of Holies, 84, 88, 94, 180, 203
Holy Spirit, xiv, 2, 6–7, 14, 23–24, 26, 34–36, 39, 41–42, 45, 50, 59, 62, 113, 121–55, 158–59, 161, 163–64, 167, 169, 172–74, 178, 184–86, 188, 190–91, 194, 196, 202, 207–8, 213, 217–24, 228, 233–34, 239–41

Holy War, xv, 109–12, 115, 152, 157, 175, 191, 195, 204–6, 208–9, 212, 239
House of God, 99, 138, 142, 181, 183, 192–93

Idolatry, 7, 31, 38, 162, 172, 198, 213–15, 218, 234, 241
Imago Dei, 7, 172, 179, 197, 211, 214, 219, 223–30, 233–34, 241
Incarnation, 7, 26, 39, 60, 178–79, 188, 190, 194, 226, 230–31
Indwelling, divine, 2, 6–7, 27, 34, 121–22, 129, 134, 137–38, 141, 159, 162, 164, 166, 172, 175–79, 182, 184, 186, 188, 191–96, 202, 219, 221–22, 225, 232–35, 239–42
Intertextuality, 1, 2, 4–7, 50–52, 68–74, 79–80, 87, 117, 170–77, 181, 188, 191–92, 195, 213, 218, 225, 234, 237–38, 240–42

Judgment, 6, 78, 109, 118–21, 128, 134, 136, 174, 189, 204, 206–7, 210, 213, 215, 218, 234, 239, 241

Levites, xiv, 32, 84, 95–100, 113
Liturgy, 3, 8–9, 12–17, 38, 40, 42, 46–47, 49, 56, 91, 107, 112, 151, 205, 209, 216, 218, 221, 233–34, 241–42

Manifestation, divine, 2, 6, 26, 32, 82, 98, 102–3, 105–7, 109, 111–12, 115, 120, 122–26, 128, 142, 144, 146–47, 150, 152–58, 169–76, 189, 204–5, 212, 215, 234, 239–41
Metaphor, 23–24, 27, 33–34, 36–37, 49, 60, 87, 101, 125, 128–31, 134, 137–38, 140–42, 144–45, 147, 169, 172, 175–96, 210, 215, 234, 241
Music in worship, 9, 13–14, 40, 42, 46, 94, 99, 112–14, 121, 167, 175, 206, 239

Pentecost, Day of, 124–27, 129, 134, 136–37, 145–46, 185, 207, 210
Pentecostals, 3, 9–11, 13, 42, 46, 48, 100, 132–33, 137, 191, 236
Perichoresis, 7, 172, 178–79, 219–23, 233–34, 241
Personhood, 7, 172, 219, 223–24, 228, 233–34, 240–41
Pop culture, 1–2, 8–9, 12–15, 49, 236
Prophecy, 10, 17–19, 32, 49, 72, 91–92, 99, 109–15, 119, 121, 130, 133–36, 144, 147, 164, 168, 175–76, 182, 185, 188, 201, 205–7, 215, 239

Salvation, 20, 22–23, 27, 31, 39, 54, 72, 76, 110–11, 121, 123, 127, 133, 136, 138, 141, 158–59, 168, 175, 177–79, 188, 208, 217, 222–24, 239, 242
Self-revelation, divine, 7, 26–27, 31–32, 38, 60, 64, 76, 79, 93, 99–100, 102, 114–15, 127, 141, 152, 156, 171, 177, 195–97, 199, 202, 206, 211–13, 221, 223, 228, 233–34
Songs, spiritual, 26, 35, 38, 100, 116–17, 160, 162–64, 168–69, 174, 240
Spirit-baptism, 122, 125, 127, 129, 131–33, 136–37, 140–45, 147, 159, 169, 186, 207, 209, 212
Spirit-infilling, xv, 28–29, 34, 36, 125, 130, 132–34, 137–39, 147–48, 152–53, 158–59, 161, 166–70, 173–76, 191–92, 212, 239–40
Spirit-refilling, 2, 6, 36, 123, 132, 147–50, 152, 158, 160, 167–70, 174, 208, 240

Temple, xiv, 2–3, 5–7, 17, 23–24, 27–30, 32–37, 39, 41, 45, 49, 81–97, 100–107, 109–10, 113, 118–20, 122, 124, 130, 134, 138, 141–42, 147–48, 159, 167–69, 172, 174–91, 195–96, 203, 208–11, 215, 228, 234, 236, 239–41
Trinity, 7, 14–15, 27, 39, 43, 46, 49, 137–38, 165, 172, 178, 213, 217–26, 232–34, 241

Worship, instrumental, 6, 32, 60, 82, 94, 96, 99–100, 107, 111–14, 172–73
Worship, theology of, 2–4, 9, 24, 29, 45, 48, 236

Xenolalia, 134–35, 137–38, 239

Scripture Index

GENESIS

1	18, 31, 134, 178, 183, 186, 195, 196–198, 200, 201, 203, 223, 234, 225–30
1:26–29	18, 186, 195, 197, 200, 223, 225–30
2	61, 128, 180, 181, 228
2:7	128
2:15	228
2:19	225
3:8	179
4:3–4	196–7
6:8–21	195, 197
7:1–5	197
8:15–22	196–7
9:1–17	197, 201
11:1–9	134
12:1–7	195–6, 198
12:8	31
15:10–21	198, 201, 203
17:1–11	201
22	61, 72
24:27	210
26:25	196
28:18	196

EXODUS

3	38, 43, 90, 195–6, 199, 210, 214, 223
3:14	223
3:4–10	195
3:5	43
4–9	214
14:14	111
19–24	38, 45, 185
19	38–39, 45, 74, 87, 101, 108, 128, 174, 185, 196, 198
19:5	198
19:9	101, 196
19:16	87, 108
19:18–20	128, 174
20–23	201
20:18	104
24:5–8	198
24:16	104
26	181
29:10	90
29:45	182
32	214
33:7	90
34:1–10	199, 210
36–38	196
40	17, 104, 196
40:34–38	101, 104, 196

LEVITICUS

7:12	37
9:23–24	87, 103
9:6	204
10:1–3	204, 209

LEVITICUS (CONT.)

10:6–24	209–210
11	39, 139
16:2	86
19:2	39, 210
23:9–16	126
23:24	108
25:9–10	108
26	90, 182, 187
26:11	182
26:12	34, 210

NUMBERS

7:89	90
9:15–23	87
10:1–10	108
11	133, 145, 185
11:25	133
14:21	182–83
17:7	90
28:26	126
35:34	182

DEUTERONOMY

1–34	73
5	104, 201
7:16	205
20:5	83
28–30	90, 199, 204–5
31:15	101
31:27	215

JOSHUA

5:13–15	108
6	2, 5, 82, 107–8, 110–11, 115, 120, 175–6, 204–5, 208, 212, 239, 241
6:2	5, 82, 108
6:4	108
6:13	110
6:17	110
6:20	5, 82, 108

JUDGES

2:16–23	215
7:19–22	109

1 SAMUEL

4:4	116
10:5	113
18	112
15	87, 206
16	2, 107, 114–15, 120, 175–76, 206, 212, 239, 241
16:23	6, 82, 112–13
18:10	112
19:9	112
25:28	205

2 SAMUEL

6	84
7	88, 93, 181, 183, 199, 201

1 KINGS

3:4–5	83
6–9	85, 196
6	181–82, 196
6:12–13	83, 182
7:9	83
8–9	84, 105–6, 176, 212, 203
8	2, 5, 17, 32, 73, 81–90, 93, 95, 100, 102–6, 108–9, 116–17, 119–20, 128, 130, 138, 162, 168, 172–74, 181, 183, 185, 191, 193, 196, 203–4, 210, 238–41
8:1–11	86
8:1	84, 86, 89, 90, 100, 103, 105, 106, 174
8:1–3	32, 84, 203, 210

8:4	90
8:5	xiii, 105, 203
8:6–9	82, 84, 117, 203
8:10–13	86, 89, 90, 100, 103, 106, 108, 116, 174, 192, 196
8:22–61	203
8:23	210
8:27	32
8:29	89
8:31–53	105, 109, 204
8:62–64	203
8:65–66	84
9:1–9	83, 90, 204
11:9–13	83
11:41	82
14:19	82
16:20	82
19:11	128
20:13	115

2 KINGS

2	82, 114, 241
3	2, 6, 82, 107, 113–15, 120, 175–76, 206, 212, 239, 241
3:7–9	114
3:11	113
3:15–16	6, 82, 114

1 CHRONICLES

1:1–4	91
6:1–32	92
9	32
10	92
15	100
17:1–15	92–93, 181, 183, 199, 201
23–27	92, 99
25:1	99, 114

2 CHRONICLES

	91–107
2:5	89
3	34, 92, 181, 196
5–7	xiv, 5, 73, 81, 90–98, 103–7, 117, 119–20, 138, 162, 168, 172–76, 181, 183, 191, 193, 203, 212, 239
5:1–10	87, 94–106, 110, 117, 196, 203, 209
5:11–14	xiv, 87, 94–95, 98–106, 110, 117, 174, 192, 196, 203, 209
6	89, 94–95, 101, 105–6, 109, 203, 209–10
6:1–2	89, 94
6:11–13	95, 105
6:14–40	109, 209
6:40–42	105
7	93, 102–6, 120, 128, 173–74, 181, 204
7:1–3	xiv, 89, 92, 94, 95, 102, 104–6, 173–74, 192, 196, 204, 215
7:4–6	94, 100, 203
7:7–10	94
7:11–22	89, 92, 95, 104, 181, 183, 204
9	92, 105
11:6–10	92
20	xv, 2, 5, 82, 92, 107, 109–12, 115, 117, 120, 175–76, 205, 208, 212, 239
21:7	199
24:6	90
27:7	92
29:31	37
36:20–23	92

EZRA

1:1–4	92

NEHEMIAH

	92

PSALMS

1	87
2	6, 82, 87, 115–18, 121, 151–52, 175, 206, 208
11	87
15	39
17	136, 138
22	xiii, 6, 82, 115–18, 121, 175–76, 212, 239
25	210
32	34
43	182
45	104
49	37
50	117, 128
69	32
75	34
80	116
82	229
89	199
95	38
99	116
107	100, 117
110	136, 138
118	185
132	89, 180
136	6, 100, 104–5, 110, 117, 210
139	44
145–150	6, 82, 118
148	117

PROVERBS

23:31	162

ISAIAH

1	87, 107, 182, 215
1:10–17	87, 215
4:4	136
6:1–4	101, 128, 182–83
11:9	107, 182–83
32:15	127
37:16	116
40–60	214
44:3–4	129
53:3–5	61
54	182, 196
57:15	182, 185
61:1	123
66	32, 128, 180, 185, 227

JEREMIAH

3:16–18	182
7:4–5	87
7:21–26	215
23:24	162
31	127, 199, 207

EZEKIEL

1:4	128
3:23	120
9:3	118
10	6, 82, 118–19, 215
11	118–19, 199
16	196
20:25–26	215
21	215
36	123
37	118, 182–83, 187, 199, 207
38:35	183
39:29	127
40–48	119, 182–83
43:1–12	119, 180, 182–83
44:4	119, 162
46:3	120
47	119, 180, 183
48:35	182

HOSEA

1–3	196

JOEL

1	136
2	123, 127, 129, 135–36, 138, 207
3:17	182

AMOS

2	215
5:21–25	87, 210, 215
9:11	182–83, 186, 190

MICAH

6:6–8	87

HABAKKUK

2:14	107, 182–83
3:3	182

HAGGAI

2:1–9	107, 182–83, 188

ZECHARIAH

1:16	182
2:5	189
2:10–13	182
8:3	182

MALACHI

2:10	217
3	41

MATTHEW

2:2	22
3	129, 210
5	39
15:9	21
21	61
26:46	206
26:61	184, 190
27:46	116

MARK

1	129, 184, 210
7:7	21
7:19	140
14:58	184, 190
15:34	116

LUKE

1–2	73
1:15	135
1:46	146
1:67	185, 188
3	129, 131, 136, 152, 210
4:18–19	123
9	74
12:11–12	153
22:19	45
24:44–52	22, 123–25, 127, 137

JOHN

1:1–3	223
1:14	223
1:33	129
2:19	184, 190
3	39, 128, 190
4:23–26	22, 161, 175, 217, 226
6:52–57	219
7:37–39	184–85, 188
8:54	220
10:34	229
10:38	178, 196
12:20	22
12:45	137
14:9–11	184, 188, 190, 224
15:4	178
17:23	178
20:21–23	185, 188, 190

ACTS

1	36
1:4–8	125, 127, 129, 131, 136, 145
1:12–14	124–25
2	2, 20, 22, 35–36, 73, 122–131, 134–40, 144–47, 152–53, 162, 168–69, 172–74, 176, 185, 191, 194, 196, 199, 207, 210, 212, 239, 241
2:1–4	xiv, 124–130, 134–38, 144–46, 152, 162, 173, 185, 190–92, 196, 207
2:4–11	134, 137
2:13	162
2:15–21	127, 129, 135, 138, 145
2:20	207
2:22–39	130, 136, 138, 152
2:46–47	137
3	35
4	xv, 2, 6, 20, 36, 123, 138, 147, 149–50, 153–54, 157, 169, 172, 174–76, 185, 191, 207–9, 212, 240–41
4:1–13	150, 185, 190
4:23–31	6, 150, 153, 174, 185, 190–92, 208
5:11	142
6	153
7	22, 35, 90, 115, 138, 153, 185–86, 214
7:43–55	22, 35, 90, 185–86, 190, 192
8	22, 36, 129, 139
9	36, 129, 139
10	122, 138–42, 144–47, 153, 169, 173–74, 176, 186, 207, 212, 239
10:28	140
10:44–48	xiv, 144–45, 147, 169, 174, 186
11	142, 144, 146–47, 190, 192
12–20	147
12	147, 153–57
13:2	154
13:52	129
15	142, 186, 190
16	xv, 2, 123, 147, 153–58, 169, 174–76, 208, 212, 240
17:24	186, 190
18:13	21
19:6	147
19:17	146
24:11–14	22
28	73

ROMANS

1:18–23	215
2:12–24	39
8:29	225, 230
9:4	22
12:1–3	30, 33
12:5	24

1 CORINTHIANS

1:2	217
3:9	187
3:16–19	23, 34, 142, 186, 187, 190, 196
6:19	34, 186, 190
10:16–17	45
11:3–12	202, 225
11:17–34	23, 39, 45
12–14	20
12:12–31	24, 129
14	10, 23, 35, 164

2 CORINTHIANS

3:7–11	188, 214, 230
4:4	225

4:6	214, 230	**1 TIMOTHY**	
4:17	188		
5:1	188, 190	2:13	78
5:17	43		
6:16–18	34, 187, 190, 210	**2 TIMOTHY**	
6:19	142		
13:14	224	1:3	22

EPHESIANS

HEBREWS

1	158, 159	1:3	230
1:1–3	38, 158	2:2	215
1:11–12	xiii	3:3	22
1:23	162	8	180, 188, 190
2:19–22	27, 34, 142, 187, 190, 210	9:1–2	22, 188, 190, 201, 203
3	159	9:10–26	190, 201, 203
4	23, 43, 159, 225	10:19–31	39, 188, 190
5	2, 6, 34–35, 40, 123, 135, 147, 157–70, 172, 174–76, 187, 191, 196, 208–9, 212, 217, 225, 240–1	11:17–19	61
		12:18–29	45
		13:15	22, 37
5:1	225	**1 PETER**	
5:18–22	6, 34, 35, 40, 135, 157–70, 174, 187, 190, 192, 196, 208–9, 217, 240	1:15–16	39, 210
		2:4–6	22–24, 187, 190
		2:9	xiii
6:10–18	208		

PHILIPPIANS

1 JOHN

2:17	22	1:3	24

COLOSSIANS

REVELATION

1:15	230	1:5–6	38
2:6	164	3:1–6	39
3:12–20	35, 40, 161, 163–64	4:10	22
		5	215
		6	215

1 THESSALONIANS

5:7–8	161	7:15	22, 181, 189–90
		8–14	204
		8:6–18	204
		11:19	174, 190
		14:2–3	189
		15	101, 174, 190

REVELATION (CONT.)

16:17–18	174, 190	21	37, 180–83, 189
19–21	37	21:2	37, 189
		21:10–11	189
		21:22–23	37, 182, 189–90
		22	183

www.ingramcontent.com/pod-product-compliance
Lightning Source LLC
Chambersburg PA
CBHW070234230426
43664CB00014B/2300